Genocide on Trial

Genocide on Trial

War Crimes Trials and the Formation of Holocaust History and Memory

DONALD BLOXHAM

OXFORD

UNIVERSITY PRESS

*This book has been printed digitally and produced in a standard specification
in order to ensure its continuing availability*

OXFORD
UNIVERSITY PRESS

Great Clarendon Street, Oxford OX2 6DP

Oxford University Press is a department of the University of Oxford.
It furthers the University's objective of excellence in research, scholarship,
and education by publishing worldwide in

Oxford New York

Auckland Cape Town Dar es Salaam Hong Kong Karachi
Kuala Lumpur Madrid Melbourne Mexico City Nairobi
New Delhi Shanghai Taipei Toronto
With offices in
Argentina Austria Brazil Chile Czech Republic France Greece
Guatemala Hungary Italy Japan South Korea Poland Portugal
Singapore Switzerland Thailand Turkey Ukraine Vietnam

Oxford is a registered trade mark of Oxford University Press
in the UK and in certain other countries

Published in the United States
by Oxford University Press Inc., New York

Oxford is a registered trade mark of Oxford University Press
in the UK and in certain other countries

Published in the United States
by Oxford University Press Inc., New York

ISBN 0-19-925904-6

For TONY *and for* COLIN

Preface

Knowing what we now do of Nazi atrocity in the Second World War, the heated debates of that era on the legitimacy of trying the perpetrators can appear rather unreal. Yet in the years around 1945 a variety of moral and political justifications were required to prevent, on the one hand, mass and summary executions of Germans and their accomplices and, on the other, the passage of the majority of the iniquitous back, unnoticed, into ordinary civilian life. The idea of legal re-dress for state crimes was novel and contentious, and there was no certainty as to whom to try, or the precise crimes with which to charge them. The arguments employed in favour of trials in 1945 can be divided into two general categories: punishment/deterrent and education. The first of these is at the heart of most of the critiques of the postwar punishment programmes, which centre upon the legal bases and legacies of the various 'war crimes trials' and often feature the ex-tensive re-creation of the events of the courtroom. The second is more complex. It encompasses the didactic aims of illustrating to the conquered peoples the benefits of due legal process, whilst simultaneously creating a historical record for the edification of victors, vanquished, and posterity alike. That second func-tion is the concern of this book.

By opting for legal action, the Allied nations succeeded in establishing a record of Nazi criminality and aggression. Unwittingly, however, in the conduct of the trials they also laid bare much about their own attitudes to what had tran-spired in Europe. There is an important connection between these two areas, and one which has not been brought out in the historiography of either the trials or Nazi atrocity; that connection concerns how the practices of those who con-ducted the trial affected the portrayal of the acts of the tried through the medium of the courtroom.

The trials were not disinterested conduits of that which they were instituted to consider. They were not blank pages onto which the history of the Nazi years was inscribed in an 'objective' fashion. At the most basic level, considerations such as the rules of courtroom procedure, the role of judicial precedent, and the difference between legal and historical evidence meant that trials had the poten-tial to re-shape their subject matter. Overtly political influences were another matter again, and must be considered in relation to each polity that played a part in the trials.

In order to explain the development of representations of Nazi crime through the trial medium, it is necessary to understand the approaches that the Allied and formerly occupied nations employed in dealing with suspected 'war criminals'. In other words, we need to see precisely what the prosecuting powers were attempting to achieve by trial, and how they went about achieving it. This analysis of trial policy—or rather policies—requires exploration in the realms of international legal, political, and social history.

Furthermore, just as the representations of atrocity that the trials created were only abstracts when standing alone, outside the context in which they were formed, it is of limited value to examine them without considering the impact they made on the understanding of their subject. Therefore, to assess the ways in which trial representations informed perceptions of Axis criminality both contemporaneously and subsequently, this book will encompass apprehensions of the subject from the end of the war until the present day. In sum then, what follows is a form of deconstruction, showing how understandings of a particular past or set of pasts have been mediated by factors that were not themselves of that past.

How to go about the task in hand? First, it is necessary to specify the particular Nazi crimes on which we will concentrate. Secondly, it is equally important to identify the trials—the prisms through which the crimes were viewed—to be studied. Thirdly, it remains to establish the criteria by which the value of those trials as informative media is to be assessed.

On the criminal side, the focus will be upon the destruction of European Jewry in what is now called 'the Holocaust'. If justification is required for this choice, it may be found in the proposition of the German philosopher Edmund Husserl that comprehension of any phenomenon requires comprehension of its essential features. Since this book is written from the viewpoint that the racial murders committed by the Third Reich were expressions of the essential quality of the regime, understanding those crimes was and is fundamental to understanding Nazism. And of all the genocidal schemes embarked upon between 1939 and 1945, the murder of the Jews stands out as the most total, the most determinedly pursued, and hence that which has most to tell us about the *essence* of Nazism.

However, the Holocaust is an ill-defined area of investigation for two related reasons that may be termed 'historical' and 'epistemological'. In the first category, we should consider the Nazi killing programmes as a whole. These were so complex and interrelated that examination of the murder of the Jews on its own is actually rather ahistorical, as the work of Götz Aly, Suzanne Heim, and Christian Gerlach, amongst others, has illustrated. The Jews were murdered where and when they were not just because of Nazi antisemitism, but because that antisemitism was allied with other racisms—pre-eminently anti-Slavism—and with anti-Bolshevism and perhaps amoral utilitarianism in a context of extreme wartime radicalization and barbarization. The chronological and conceptual parameters of the 'Holocaust' are unclear; in short, and this brings us to the second (epistemological) problem identified above—the Holocaust is a construct.

Adopting this position does not imply any doubt that approximately 6 million Jews died at the hands of the Nazis and their accomplices during World War Two, but simply asserts that the infinitely complex constituent parts of that murder process may not be neatly packaged under the popular epithet. The prosecutors at the war crimes trials did not encounter the murder of the Jews in the same way as would today's reader of an introductory history of 'the Holocaust'. To begin with, unlike the author of that hypothetical introductory text, most of these post-war actors did not emphasize the murder of the Jews amongst Nazi crimes; indeed, for reasons that will be explained throughout this book, the opposite was the case. Conversely, in their own diverse ways, intentionally and inadvertently, and both by omission and commission, these prosecutors contributed to the creation of some of the most influential paradigms of Nazi criminality. This book attempts to invoke the world of the period immediately after the Second World War when trials were an intrinsic part of making sense of a monstrous and immensely complex past.

Exactly what it meant to 'make sense' of the Hitler era was not a constant. Even in the courtroom the means and purposes of examining the past varied in accordance with the different political agendas of the period. The most obvious coercion of the past for the purposes of the present occurred in the political culture of the post-war Soviet bloc. The reduction in one trial of Sachsenhausen concentration camp guards to 'tools of monopoly capitalism' is indicative, as is the constant reference to the crimes of a generic 'fascism'—as a crisis stage of capitalism—rather than the historically and geographically specific 'Nazism'. Meanwhile, the official Soviet line refused to recognize that Jews and other ethnic groups had suffered as groups, preferring to describe the dead in terms of national citizenship, and particularly preferring anti-fascist resisters as victims of choice. This exaggeration of martyrdom at the expense of a more accurate representation of the thrust of Nazi murderousness was also replicated by the Soviet client regime in eastern Germany.

Yet such skewed representations of the past were arguably only of a different degree, not a different order, to processes set in motion further westward. The postwar 'Vichy syndrome', with its overblown emphasis on the French resistance and de-emphasis on collaboration, particularly in the fate of the Jews, is worthy of comparative consideration. As this book will show, the 'liberal democracies' were also authors of subtle re-writings of the Nazi extermination projects. This brings us to the next axis of the study.

On the legal side, the matter of which trials are to be examined, it is important to state at the outset that this monograph does not claim to include a comprehensive history of the postwar prosecutions. Little will be read of the trials conducted under Soviet influence, because the aforementioned, overbearing influence of Marxism-Leninism on the creation of the historical record is already well known. There is no mention of the trials of Axis defendants in the Far East. Nor is much written of the 'denazification' process, which was as much an attempt to prevent former Nazis occupying positions of influence in post-war Germany as a means of punishing them. The focus is upon the European trial programmes of Britain and the USA, which are examined in parallel in the interests of comparative study of two closely linked occupation regimes.

Again, though, these programmes will not be considered *in toto*. The criterion for consideration is the relevance of each trial in the 're-educational' sense; a relevance that was, generally speaking, related to the prominence of the criminal.

Owing to the rapid westward exodus of the German forces before the Soviet advance in the latter stages of the war, the British and Americans had come into possession of a disproportionately large number of leading Nazis. And as two of the chief Allies, going on to occupy two of the four zones into which the defeated Germany was divided, both bore a considerable moral and historical duty to shed light on the darkest deeds of their unwilling hosts. They had now acquired responsibility for inscribing the past not just on behalf of their own compatriots, but for most of the population of western Germany; thus this study is also a contribution to the early history of what has become known in German historiography as that region's process of 'coming to terms with the past'.

The American and British trial programmes were undoubtedly those that chiefly preoccupied the western Germans, though the trials enacted by the other western occupying power, France, actually involved more criminals than either. In discharging their duties, the USA and Britain pursued trial schemes that were very different in scope, but nevertheless were the only genuinely international programmes of any then running in western Europe. The two countries fielded respectively the largest and second-largest army of investigators in this sphere, and deployed them more widely than any other: in Germany, Austria, and Italy. Moreover, it was a unique feature of their policies that Britain and the USA each concerned itself to a large degree between 1945 and 1949 with trials of those in whom it had no direct national interest.

It remains to ask how the efficacy of the trials in their educational and historical capacity is to be judged. As victors, the edification of the USA and Britain through the trials will be considered for comparative purposes alongside the study of western Germany, the perpetrating and defeated nation. On the creation of a record for posterity, the object of consideration will be the influence of the trials on the western European and American historiography of the Holocaust.

Examination of the historiographical legacy of the post-war trials will often be a matter of considerable detail, with close reference to the evidence and argumentation of select works in the ever-growing field of Holocaust scholarship. However, in assessing the course of popular representations and perceptions, we shall not enter into an examination of minutiae. Rather, we shall consider the apprehension of two distinctive features of Nazi criminality: its 'depth' and its 'breadth' respectively.

The Nazi camp system is used to represent the 'depths' Nazism reached and the role of the Wehrmacht to illustrate the 'breadth' of German depravity. Despite the murder of the mentally and physically 'handicapped' in Germany and eastern Europe, and that of between 200,000 and 500,000 of Europe's Roma and Sinti, and of nearly 2 million non-Jewish Poles, and over 3 million Soviet prisoners-of-war, as well as an untold number of Soviet and other civilians, and despite the fate of millions of Jews outside the gas chambers, the extermination camps remain as the emblematic manifestation of discriminatory mass killing—genocide—in history. And, as the largest organization directly involved in Nazi mass murder that was not itself a product of Nazism, but was rather a pre-eminent German institution, the actions of the Wehrmacht may be seen to represent the participation of Germany as a whole in the crimes of Hitler and Himmler. The legal treatment of the crimes of the camp system and of German soldiery may be seen as an index of the success or otherwise of the trials in their 're-educational' capacity.

Overall, this book is a study of a dynamic relationship between sections of society that each play a role in the formation of 'collective memory' or consciousness of the past. The three-way division of the book reflects different strands of that relationship. The first section charts and analyses the implementation of punishment policies. In other words, it considers the reactions of the Allied political and administrative establishments, and the ways in which these shaped confrontation with the past through the medium of trial. The second section develops the chain of consciousness as the past was re-presented through the prism of the courtroom to the publics of the post-war world. Accordingly, that section examines the function of the legal profession, within and in juxtaposition to that of the media, politicians, social elites and other opinion-formers in each country. The final section examines the connections between courtroom and posterity, between the practices of the lawyers and those of the professional inscribers of the past: historians.

It might seem peculiar today, with the 'Shoah business' in rude health, to focus upon representations of the Holocaust provided more than half a century ago. However, the crucible of the post-war years still has a twofold relevance. First, with the exception of a small number of dedicated archival historians who are continuing to develop their understanding of the murder of the Jews, broader perceptions of that crime, including those of some contemporary Holocaust scholars, remain over-informed by what might be termed a 'Nuremberg historiography'. Secondly, for decades the murder of the Jews impinged hardly at all upon the consciousness of the post-war world. A part of the explanation for that is the peculiar way the story was used in the punishment and re-education programmes of the Allies.

Since this book is a revised version of my doctoral thesis, first mention must go to the British Academy as it then was for funding four years of postgraduate study, including an extended visit to the USA. Additional American research was funded by the Southampton University School of Research and Graduate Studies and by the Royal Historical Society. Receipt of the Richard Newitt Prize from Southampton University facilitated a brief period in The Hague. My former employers, the Holocaust Educational Trust, were generous enough to allow me a short paid period away from work to make the final alterations to this manuscript.

I would also like to express my gratitude to the following institutions and their staff: the Bodleian Library, Oxford; Churchill College Archives, Cambridge; the House of Lords Records Office; the Imperial War Museum; Lambeth Palace Library; the Liddell Hart Centre for Military Archives, King's College, London; the National Library of Wales; the Public Records Office, Kew; the Shropshire County Records Office, Shrewsbury; the University of Birmingham Archive; the University of Sussex Archive; the Modern Records Centre, the University of Warwick; the Wiener Library, London; the John F. Kennedy Library, Boston, Mass.; the Library of Congress; the National Archives and Records Administration, College Park, Md.; the Syracuse University Archive; the United States Holocaust Memorial Museum Archives, Washington, DC; and the Thomas J. Dodd Centre at the University of Connecticut. Particular thanks are owed to Arthur Eyffinger from the library of the International Court of Justice at The Hague; to Ulrike Talay of the archive of the Institut für Zeitgeschichte, Munich; to Jenny Ruthven of the Special Collections Department of the Hartley Library at the University of Southampton; and to Chris Woolgar and the other archivists in the Hartley Library for all their hard work and forbearance.

Morris Anspacher, Peter Calvocoressi, Theodor Fenstermacher, and Benjamin Ferencz have benefited the book by their personal recollections of the Nuremberg trials. The last two were kind enough to allow me to trouble them at a conference in November 1996 on the subsequent Nuremberg trials. Jonathan Bush was a sounding board for some of my thoughts and, with the generous acquiescence of his family, provided gratefully received hospitality and accommodation on a draining research visit to Washington. Bill Hoglund was equally charitable at the University of Connecticut at Storrs.

Mark Levene and Michael Biddiss read early drafts of some of my work, and provided constructive criticism and much-needed encouragement. Jeremy Noakes and Alan Bance were assiduous as my doctoral examiners, and their observations were most helpful in the process of revising the Ph.D. for publication. Andrew Charlesworth, meanwhile, has added another dimension to my grasp of the Shoah on two memorable field trips to Poland and Lithuania. Nick Kingwell, David Brown, Larry Day, John Oldfield, John McGavin, David Laven, Cedric Parry, the members of the Cavaliers Cricket Club, Joanne Reilly, and Deborah Spruce have befriended and supported me in various ways, and I owe them all much. John Little, a friend who passed away in 1999, would have been very happy to see this project come to fruition. I treasure his memory. Meanwhile, my parents, and my brother, Andrew, have contributed vastly by their support. In this connection, special mention goes to Alice Haythornthwaite, who for a long time tolerated all the stresses accompanying a relationship with a Ph.D. student.

Thanks also go to Ruth Parr, the history commissioning editor at Oxford University Press, for her enthusiasm for the project and her tolerance of my many unsolicited alterations, and to Genevieve Lester for her pertinent observations on those changes. David Cesarani also gave useful advice in the latter stages of the project. My chief debt, however, is to two friends under whom I have had the privilege of studying history. Colin Richmond must take the responsibility for much of my intellectual development, beginning with his third-year special subject course on the Holocaust at the University of Keele. He maintained a close interest in this project and frequently stimulated me with his profound and diverse insights. He was kind enough to read over the final drafts of the manuscript. Tony Kushner, director of the Parkes Centre for the Study of Jewish–Non-Jewish Relations, was my doctoral supervisor. Despite his own onerous workload, he always found time to advise and to comfort. He and his wife Mag have regularly accommodated me at their home, and bolstered me in the difficult times with good humour and counsel. This book, and the Ph.D. that preceded it, would never have been completed without him.

D. B.

Acknowledgements

The author would like to thank the following for permission to reproduce unpublished material: the Trustees of the Mass-Observation Archive, University of Sussex Library; the Trustees of the Liddell Hart Centre for Military Archives, King's College, London.

Illustrations (except those indicated on page 892) © Soun Vannithone.

Contents

Part II: Post-War Representations and Perceptions

Part III: The Trials and Posterity

Acronyms and Abbreviations

BAOR	British Army of Occupation of the Rhine
BRD	Bundesrepublik Deutschland (Federal Republic of Germany)
BUA	Birmingham University Archive
BWCE	British War Crimes Executive
CCG	Control Commission for Germany
CCG(BE)	Control Commission for Germany (British Element)
CCL10	Control Council Law Number 10
CDU	Christian Democratic Union, BRD
C.-in-C.	Commander-in-Chief
COGA	Control Office for Germany and Austria
FO	Foreign Office
FH	*Frankfurter Hefte*
FR	*Frankfurter Rundschau*
Gestapo	Geheime Staatspolizei (German State Secret Police)
HiCOG	(US) High Commission in Germany
HSSPF	Höhere Schutzstaffeln- und Polizeiführer (Higher SS and Police Leader)
IfZ	Institut für Zeitgeschichte, Munich
IG Farben	Interessengemeinschaft Farben Aktiengesellschaft (The 'Community of Interests' of the Farben joint stock company)
IKL	Inspektion der Konzentrationslager (Inspectorate of Concentration Camps)
IMT	International Military Tribunal
IMT	Published proceedings of the International Military Tribunal
JAG	Judge Advocate General
JCS	Joint Chiefs of Staff
LCO	Lord Chancellor's Office
LHCMA	Liddell Hart Centre for Military Archives
M-OA	Mass-Observation Archive
NARA	National Archives and Records Administration, College Park, MA
NMT	Nuremberg Military Tribunal, Subsequent Nuremberg Proceedings
NYT	*New York Times*
OCCPAC	Office of the Chief-of-Counsel for the Prosecution of Axis Criminality
OCCWC	Office of the Chief-of-Counsel for War Crimes, Subsequent Nuremberg Proceedings
OKW	Oberkommando der Wehrmacht (High Command of the German Armed Forces)
OMGUS	Office of Military Government, United States zone of Germany
OSS	Office of Strategic Services
PRO	Public Record Office, Kew, UK

RG	Record Group (of NARA)
RSHA	Reichssicherheitshauptamt (Reich Security Head Office)
RuSHA	Rasse- und Siedlungshauptamt (SS Race and Settlement Head Office)
SA	Sturmabteilungen (Nazi 'Stormtroopers')
SD	Sicherheitsdienst (Security Service of the SS)
SHAEF	Supreme Headquarters, Allied Expeditionary Force
SPD	German Socialist Party, BRD
SS	Schutzstaffeln
SUA	Southampton University Archive
TWC	*Trials of War Criminals*: published extracts of the proceedings of the (subsequent) Nuremberg Military Tribunals
UNWCC	United Nations War Crimes Commission
USHMM	United States Holocaust Memorial Museum
VfZ	*Vierteljahreshefte für Zeitgeschichte*
Waffen-SS	Armed SS, the military wing of the organisation
WCG(NWE)	War Crimes Group (North West Europe)
WJC	World Jewish Congress
WO	War Office
WRB	War Refugee Board
WVHA	Wirtschafts-Verwaltungshautptamt (Business Administration Head Office of the SS)
ZAL	Zwangsarbeitslager für Juden (Forced Labour Camp for Jews)

Introduction

1. AIMS AND METHODOLOGY

Michael Marrus, one of the foremost historiographers of the Holocaust, recently wrote that 'the Trial of the Major War Criminals at Nuremberg in 1945–46 . . . presented the first comprehensive definition and documentation to a non-Jewish audience of the persecution and massacre of European Jewry during World War II'. 'After Nuremberg', Marrus concluded, 'the murder of European Jewry could be authoritatively pointed to as an established fact of great historical importance.'[1] Though he concedes that what we now call 'the Holocaust' was not the centre of attention at the trial, that 'information about it could easily be drowned in the greater flood of crimes and accusations', that for many reasons the murder of the Jews was not a popular topic of conversation in the immediate post-war world, and that the trial itself 'added a few distortions' to the picture, 'Nuremberg' remains, for Marrus, 'a turning point'.[2]

In different ways Jürgen Wilke and Jeffrey Herf have added to these conclusions. The former has argued with reference to the press coverage of the trials in West German newspapers that the Nuremberg proceedings made a meaningful impression on the public's understanding of Nazi genocide and its confrontation with the past. The latter, in an otherwise convincing work, *Divided Memory: The Nazi Past in the Two Germanies*, published in 1997, also identified a 'Nuremberg interregnum' period of temporary West German consciousness of the crimes of Nazism.[3]

The 'trial of the major war criminals'—Hermann Göring *et al.*—did of course have a number of significances. As a multinational attempt to prosecute the leaders of a criminal regime for acts of state, thus extending the rule of international law beyond its existing practical jurisdiction, 'Nuremberg' was a watershed. And if the trials did not sound the death-knell of legal positivism, Nuremberg certainly fired a warning shot across its bows. The influences of the trials can be traced directly and indirectly to the formation of latter-day international criminal courts, the United Nations Charter of Human Rights and the Genocide Convention, and the 'Nuremberg code' of medical and scientific ethics. Diverse

---

[1] Michael R. Marrus, 'The Holocaust at Nuremberg', *Yad Vashem Studies*, 26 (1998), 5–41, at 5, 41.

[2] Ibid. 6.

[3] Jürgen Wilke *et al.*, *Holocaust und NS-Prozesse* (Cologne: Böhlau, 1995); Jürgen Wilke, 'Ein früher Beginn der "Vergangenheitsbewältigung": Der Nürnberger Prozess und wie darüber berichtet wurde', *Frankfurter Allgemeine Zeitung* (15 Nov. 1995); Jeffrey Herf, *Divided Memory: The Nazi Past in the Two Germanies* (Cambridge, Mass.: Harvard University Press, 1997), 206–8; see also Adalbert Rückerl, *NS-Verbrechen vor Gericht: Versuch einer Vergangenheitsbewältigung* (Heidelberg: C. F. Müller, 1982), 111–12.

human rights campaigners have adopted the Nuremberg precedent in their campaigns against allegedly criminal state regimes or their representatives. Finally, the documentation gathered at Nuremberg undoubtedly expedited the compilation of histories of Nazism, and helped to conceptualize 'the Holocaust' for a relatively small number of intellectuals in the direct aftermath of the war. However, as this book seeks to show, long-term philosophical developments in the law in no way equate to a short- or even medium-term collective consciousness of, or confrontation with, genocide. A sharp, analogous distinction should also be made between the establishment of the broad principles of the murder of the Jews for posterity and more immediate, specific shifts in conceptions of that crime. In other words, what might be termed 'judicial memory'[4]—which the Nuremberg trials served passably well—did not equate with 'collective memory'.[5]

This book stands in large part counter to the positions adopted by Marrus, Wilke, and Herf. With reference to the case study of the murder of the European Jews—the definitive crime of Nazism—and the 'war of annihilation' between Germany and the USSR that precipitated the genocide, it will attempt to show that the war crimes trials did little to clarify conceptualizations of Nazi criminality in the public sphere anywhere. Sometimes they actually muddied the waters by drawing attention away from the victims of Nazi genocide and onto much more ambiguous symbols of suffering. Indeed, the trials had the peculiar effect of helping to elide the fate of the victims.

Not only were legal proceedings of dubious didactic value contemporaneously, however; their legacy to posterity is also qualified. The collection and cataloguing of documentation was a uniquely valuable service to students of Nazism, but the overall analyses of the murder of the Jews by the Allied courts were nowhere near as helpful. Indeed, beyond the basic outlines of the murder programme, which were actually evident during wartime for those concerned to look, the jurists got it wrong more often than they got it right. The prosecutorial investigations and judicial pronouncements on the Holocaust were indelibly marked by interpretative distortions that stemmed both from preconception and from the legal process itself, and these, it is argued, had repercussions for later historical writing.

---

[4] In a way that has not been attempted for the Allied trials of the Nazis, Martin Broszat has pointed to the relevance of trials of Nazis in Germany within the polymorphous (*vielgestaltigen*) process of 'mastering the past' (*Vergangenheitsbewältigung*). See his 'Siegerjustiz oder strafrechtliche Selbstreinigung: Aspekte der Vergangenheitsbewältigung der deutschen Justiz während der Besatzungszeit', *VfZ*, 29 (1981), 477–544, esp. 480–1. Regardless of their educative role, trials of former perpetrators have an important function for the society trying them. See Rückerl, *NS-Verbrechen vor Gericht*; Dick De Mildt, *In the Name of the People: Perpetrators of Genocide in the Reflection of Their Post-War Prosecution in West Germany* (The Hague: Martinus Nijhoff, 1996).

[5] See Peter Novick's discussion of the origin of the idea of 'collective memory' in *The Holocaust in American Life* (New York: Houghton Mifflin, 1999), 5–7. In terms of the examinations that follow, Mary Fulbrook's term 'shared discourses' is probably more appropriate. See her *German National Identity after the Holocaust* (Cambridge: Polity Press, 1999), 143–7.

Thus it is not enough simply to do as Marrus does and reproduce the evidence that was presented at Nuremberg to illustrate what 'knowledge' the trials made available in 1945–6. The cognitive frameworks in which that evidence was placed by its recipients were vital in the post-war world, as they would be to the future historian. For every piece of the mosaic that was presented at Nuremberg and elsewhere, another was missing, another concealed, and another co-opted to support an untenable position. Moreover, particularly on a popular level, the style in which the evidence was presented—the concrete foundation on which the Allied re-educational 'lessons' were to be based—was every bit as important as the simple instance of that presentation. Given that legal reckoning was a part of a broader Allied scheme, it is essential also to address the historical contexts in which the 'facts' of Nazism were presented. Accordingly, the trials are examined here within Allied occupation policy and the political environments of the post-war period.

The study reveals a series of tensions in the formation of different forms of memory via the trial process. Some of these are inherent to the trial mechanism itself,[6] some specific to the period in question, and some to the representational problems posed by the Holocaust. Yet the relationship between the trials and what may broadly be termed 'memory' can only be theorized so far. In the final analysis, this is a historical study and demands reference to individual trials and strands of representation in their specificity. Understanding the relationship of different trials to each other and to prosecutors, defendants, and the law is no small matter, for the legal machinery wheeled into place in Europe was immensely complicated, and the general epithet 'war crimes trials' has perhaps obscured the great variety of those proceedings.

2. THE TRIAL TABLEAU

There is only an incomplete record of the trials enacted after the Second World War. The number of proceedings runs to several thousands, the number of individual convictions to tens of thousands. Courts were established throughout the continent by nations that had been occupied by, allied to, and in conflict with Nazi Germany and Italy. The quality of the justice dispatched varied greatly, as did the profile of the defendants and the nature of the trials themselves.

A large number of trials were directed throughout Europe against those defined, often arbitrarily, as 'traitors' or 'collaborators'. In the political purges imposed upon the perpetrating nations themselves such proceedings found their equivalent in the 'denazification' and equivalent proceedings. These are to be distinguished, though not always clearly, from criminal trials enacted in the various countries to prosecute manifestly illegal acts committed both by domestic and foreign nationals in pursuit of Axis aims. Proceedings in the latter class have come to be known generically as 'war crimes trials', and it is these with which we

---

[6] Mark Osiel, *Mass Atrocity, Collective Memory, and the Law* (New Brunswick, NJ: Transaction, 1997).

are concerned here. Within the complex of war crimes trials a distinction should also be made between the cases concerning, respectively, so-called 'major' and 'minor' war criminals. This awkward terminology denoted the stature of the criminal rather than the seriousness of the crime, and requires some explanation.

The best known of all war crimes trials is that, already touched upon, of 'the major war criminals' before the International Military Tribunal (IMT) at Nuremberg. 'The' Nuremberg trial, as it is popularly and erroneously known, was a creation of the agreement of the prosecuting and judging nations, the USA, the UK, France, and the USSR, and was the one instance of full inter-Allied co-operation in the punishment of Nazi criminals. It also featured the introduction of criminal charges unprecedented in international law, notably that of 'crimes against peace'. It has spawned a considerable historiography both broadly supportive and critical, and has cast the myriad other trials of the period into the shade. As the most significant manifestation of what came to be known critically as 'victor's justice', and as the proposed foundation for the imposition of a legal framework on the conduct of international affairs, for a time the IMT trial excited the passions of the concerned nations and the interest of many a jurist and would-be expert on the years preceding 1945.[7]

Though the springs of public interest had long since dried by the end of the IMT trial, it was succeeded by an even more substantial undertaking. The American military authorities in Germany, into whose zone of occupation Nuremberg fell, forged ahead at that place until well into 1949 with a series of proceedings against what were known as 'major war criminals of the second rank'. Owing to the location of the courtrooms and to their definite relationship with the trial of Göring *et al.*, these came to be known as the 'subsequent Nuremberg proceedings', or Nachfolgeprozessen. They were legitimated by an occupation statute known as Control Council Law no. 10 (CCL10). Twelve in all, the subsequent trials included 185 defendants prominent in a range of spheres of German life: the SS, the Nazi party, the German bureaucracy, the military, industry and finance, and the professions.

In providing both an organized documentary base and a corpus of oral testimony, the thirteen 'Nuremberg trials' in their different guises established

---

[7] Treatments of the formation and events of the IMT trial are legion. See e.g. Bradley Smith's *The Road to Nuremberg* (London: Andre Deutsch, 1982); id., *Reaching Judgment at Nuremberg* (New York: Basic Books, 1977); Telford Taylor, *The Anatomy of the Nuremberg Trials* (London: Bloomsbury, 1993); Ann Tusa and John Tusa, *The Nuremberg Trial* (London: Atheneum, 1983); Arieh J. Kochavi, *Prelude to Nuremberg* (Chapel Hill, NC: University of North Carolina Press, 1998); George Ginsburgs and V. N. Kudriavtsev (eds.), *The Nuremberg Trial and International Law* (Dordrecht: Martinus Nijhoff, 1990); Robert E. Conot, *Justice at Nuremberg* (New York: Harper and Row, 1983); Joe Heydecker and Johannes Leeb, *Der Nürnberger Prozess: Bilanz der Tausend Jahre* (Cologne: Kiepenheuer and Witsch, 1959); Whitney Harris, *Tyranny on Trial: The Evidence at Nuremberg* (Dallas, Tex: Southern Methodist University Press, 1954); Peter Calvocoressi, *Nuremberg: The Facts, the Law and the Consequences* (London: Chatto and Windus, 1948); Airey Neave, *Nuremberg: A Personal Record of the Trial of the Major War Criminals* (London: Hodder and Stoughton, 1978); Victor Bernstein, *Final Judgement: The Story of Nuremberg* (New York: Boni and Gaer, 1947).

themselves as a paramount historical source for the period with which they were concerned. They were derived conceptually from the idea of trying individuals and groupings involved in the formation and initiation of criminal policies that, because of the breadth of their application, had 'no particular geographical location'—this was the criterion according to which the criminals were termed 'major'. The concern with examining the channels of authority and the very nature of the Nazi regime set the Nuremberg series apart from the welter of 'war crimes' investigations (again, using the generic term) conducted elsewhere in Europe, and indeed was not really imitated until the prosecution of Adolf Eichmann in 1961, which David Ben-Gurion was to term the 'Nuremberg of the Jewish people'.[8]

If the subsequent Nuremberg proceedings contributed notably to the historical record rather than to contemporary awareness, they found a counterpart in the glut of prosecutions instituted independently by different national authorities around Europe for crimes committed against their subjects or on their territory. Germany was divided between the major Allies, who, as the sovereign powers, conducted their own zonal trial programmes, which are to be distinguished from the Nuremberg trials and served during the occupation period as an approximation to national proceedings for Germany. (Since France and the Soviet Union had been subject to German domination or influence, both of those powers also enacted trials of war criminals and collaborators in their own territory.) This distinction also goes for the American occupiers, who did not consider the subsequent Nuremberg proceedings to be zonal affairs *per se*, given the international basis of CCL10 and the significance of the cases, and who indeed instituted a separate series of trials of lower-ranking personnel before military tribunals. The suspects in the German zonal trials and the national tribunals of the other European countries could usually be associated with specific geographical locations, and were consequently of considerable interest to the prosecuting powers, but frequently of less immediate value to students of the full sweep of Nazi criminality. Neither did these trials generally feature the broad charges used at Nuremberg.

There were exceptions to these general rules. The French, for example, exploited the full breadth of CCL10 as the Americans did in the subsequent Nuremberg proceedings, in the prosecution before a multinational bench of the German industrialist Hermann Röchling for crimes against peace.[9] (Otherwise, the French zonal tribunals, based primarily at Rastatt, and also operating under CCL10 focused on more tangible, localized crimes, notably of the personnel of various concentration camps and prisons.)[10] More importantly, the fact that a

---

[8] Annette Wieviorka, 'La construction de la mémoire du génocide en France', *Le Monde Juif*, no. 149 (1993), 23–37, esp. 30.

[9] Yveline Pendaries, *Les procès de Rastatt (1946–1954): Le jugement des crimes de guerre en zone française d'occupation en Allemagne* (Berne: Lang, 1995), 49–55. The verdict was later overturned. The French tried more than 2,000 lesser criminals for crimes against humanity and war crimes.

[10] Ibid. 146–7.

defendant was tried by a national tribunal because his or her crime had a 'particular geographical location' did not mean that the crime or the criminal did not have international significance. Thus, for instance, a Polish national tribunal adjudicated in the case of Rudolf Höss, former commandant of Auschwitz-Birkenau, and a British zonal trial featured Field Marshal Erich von Manstein, one of the most vaunted of all the German military commanders.

The trials featuring in this volume are selected for their significance in the representation of Nazi anti-Jewish crimes from some of the aforementioned instances and schemes: the Göring case, the subsequent Nuremberg proceedings, and the American and British zonal series.[11] How each trial and series assumed the shape that it did is a matter of primary concern, for shape very much defined content, and there were real differences of opinion over the form and purpose of such proceedings.

3. THE EARLY FORMATION OF PUNISHMENT POLICY

Periodic official and semi-official declarations of retributive intent were made by representatives of each of the 'big three' powers, beginning in October 1941 with Roosevelt's and Churchill's pronouncement that 'the punishment of [Nazi] crimes should now be counted among the major aims of the war'.[12] The Soviets put a little steel into their words with a trial of collaborators at Krasnodar and one involving German prisoners at Kharkov in the second half of 1943.[13] However, well into the course of 1945, the near-victorious Allies had reached no agreement as to the overall treatment that should be meted out to Axis war criminals. There was no clear sign of international commitment to the principles outlined at the Moscow Conference of Foreign Ministers in November 1943, whence Britain, the USA, and the USSR had declared that

at the time of the granting of any armistice to any government which may be set up in Germany, those German officers and men and members of the Nazi party who have been responsible for or who have taken part in . . . atrocities, massacres and executions, will be sent back to the countries in which their abominable deeds were done in order that they may be judged and punished according to the laws of those liberated countries and of the Free Governments which will be erected therein. [However] the above declaration is

---

[11] The IMT records are published as *Trial of the Major War Criminals before the International Military Tribunal*, 42 vols. (Nuremberg: IMT, 1947); hereafter '*IMT*'. The proceedings of the subsequent Nuremberg Tribunals consulted for this book are housed in the University of Southampton Archives, and denominated 'NMT'. Additionally, substantial extracts from each of the trials has been published as: Nuremberg Military Tribunals, *Trials of War Criminals before the Nuremberg Military Tribunals under Control Council Law No. 10*, 15 vols. (Washington, DC.: USGPO, 1953), hereafter '*TWC*'. Material cited from American 'zonal' trials will be denoted by the microfilm number of the record in the National Archives and Records Administration, College Park, MD, hereafter 'NARA'. The comparable British sources have been studied either at the Public Record Office, Kew, hereafter 'PRO', or the Liddell Hart Centre for Military Archives, hereafter 'LHCMA'.

[12] Cited in Tusa and Tusa, *The Nuremberg Trial*, 21.

[13] Kochavi, *Prelude to Nuremberg*, 64–7.

without prejudice to the case of major criminals whose offences have no particular geographical location and who will be punished by a joint declaration of the Governments of the Allies.[14]

There was an international consensus that something be done to punish someone in the German hierarchy, though opinions varied as to who exactly to hold responsible, and for what. Much Anglo–American vengefulness was predicated upon the fact that those peoples had been plunged once again into world war within a few decades of the previous conflict. Periodic revelations of 'war crimes' stirred the western publics, and the discovery of the remnants of a number of German concentration camps along with their decimated inmate populations in the spring of 1945, scandalized both nations. The 'Hunnish' and 'Prussian' qualities of imperialism, militarism, and aggression were shown in their true light, it was held, and they warranted punishment and demanded reform.[15] The Cold War had yet to descend upon Europe, and the foreign policy volte-face of the near future, with its moves towards 'reintegration' and leniency for Germany, would at that time have seemed light years away outside Whitehall and Capitol Hill.

The USSR had been longer and more acutely aware of what it was to be cast as an ideological enemy of Nazism. Besides experiencing the unparalleled barbarity of Operation Barbarossa, the German invasion of its territories, the Soviets overran the combined extermination and concentration facilities of Auschwitz-Birkenau and Majdanek months before the name of Belsen and Dachau meant anything to the British and American people. These establishments in Poland were different from and worse than the camps uncovered in the west, featuring the machinery of industrialized mass murder: huge gas chambers and crematoria served with supplies of human material from the nations of Europe by an ever-ready railway system.

Many of the 'junior' partners in the Allied coalition, countries which had also experienced life under Nazism, undertook their own trial programmes in accordance with the Moscow declaration. Indeed, representatives of most of the member countries of the United Nations War Crimes Commission (UNWCC), the first multinational body established to consider the issue of punishment, had been actively using that organization as a vehicle for the investigative works of their own national commissions since its establishment in 1943.[16]

---

[14] Ibid. 23–4.

[15] On the views of Churchill and de Gaulle on 'Prussianism', see Tony Judt, 'The Past is Another Country: Myth and Memory in Postwar Europe', in Istvan Deak, Jan T. Gross, and Tony Judt (eds.), *The Politics of Retribution in Europe: World War II and Its Aftermath* (Princeton, NJ: Princeton University Press, 2000), 293–323, esp. 296, 318. On the general 're-educational' intentions of the trial, see Frank Buscher, *The US War Crimes Trial Program in Germany, 1946–1955* (Westport, Conn.: Greenwood Press, 1989); Robert Sigel, *Im Interesse der Gerechtigkeit: Die Dachauer Kriegsverbrecherprozesse 1945–48* (Frankfurt am Main: Campus Verlag, 1992), 61.

[16] See United Nations War Crimes Commission (ed.), *History of the United Nations War Crimes Commission and the Development of the Laws of War* (London: HMSO, 1948); Kochavi, *Prelude to Nuremberg*.

By November 1944 the British government, which was by no means a whole-hearted supporter of the UNWCC, also decided to prosecute under its own auspices certain German crimes committed against Allied nationals.[17] The legislation under which the British zonal trials were conducted was known as the 'Royal Warrant'. The cases were prosecuted by the Judge Advocate General's department of the army (JAG), which was answerable to the War Office, though the general policy of the British trial programme was the responsibility of the Foreign Office. The first trial conducted under the Royal Warrant began on 17 September 1945. It was dubbed the 'Belsen' trial, after the name of the camp where all the defendants had served.

Importantly, the promulgation of the Royal Warrant was preceded by a series of inter- and intra-ministerial debates about the legality of trials, with particular emphasis on the questions of jurisdiction over crimes committed in Axis or Axis-occupied territory, and against nationals of Axis states. The document emerged in its final form closely constrained by these concerns, and was in no way compatible with the sort of trial that occurred at Nuremberg of those individuals whose crimes had 'no particular geographical location'.[18]

The American army made a similar investment in the prosecution of 'conventional war crimes'[19] with a programme of investigation and trial spanning the period June 1944 to July 1948. This programme, and much of the initiative for punishment in US circles generally, was spurred by news of the massacre of American troops by a Waffen-SS division at Malmédy in December 1944. Despite an initial lack of manpower, its scope expanded with the growing awareness of the extent of Nazi criminality in Europe.[20]

These proceedings came to be known as the 'Dachau series', as many of the trials were conducted on the site of the former concentration camp. They encompassed cases against former concentration camp guards, murderers of downed American pilots (in the so-called Fliegerprozesse) and a third miscellaneous grouping including the Malmédy murderers and the personnel of the 'euthanasia' institution, Hadamar. Like the British trials, the Dachau trials were conducted under the authority of the Judge Advocate and Deputy Judge Advocate, but unlike the British case, policy-making power resided with the American forces in the European theatre, and then with the occupation regime, rather than in Washington.[21]

The institution of the IMT, as distinct from these zonal developments, derived from inter-departmental debate in the US government. The concept of

---

[17] Priscilla Dale Jones, 'British Policy towards German Crimes against German Jews, 1939–1945', *Leo Baeck Institute Year Book*, 36 (1991), 339–66.

[18] For analysis of the way the Royal Warrant limited the scope of trials, see below, Chapter 2, and also Frederick Honig, 'Kriegsverbrecher vor englischen Militärgerichten', *Schweizerische Zeitschrift für Strafrecht*, 62 (1947), 20–33.

[19] Institut für Zeitgeschichte (hereafter 'IfZ'), FG 16, preface.

[20] IfZ, FG 16, pp. 1–4.

[21] Ibid. See below, Chapter 1.12, on the importance of this distinction.

what emerged as the trial of the major war criminals had to be sold to the other powers. It was not inevitable that the select senior Germans, and the organizations deemed complicit in their wrongdoing, would reach a courtroom, and it was certainly no foregone conclusion that they would face the type of charges which they eventually met.

In the initial negotiations about the nature of the peace the British expressed a preference for summary execution of a large group of arbitrarily defined Nazi leaders, over and above those lesser perpetrators who would be given the benefit of trial. The guilt of the former was simply too obvious for a trial which, it was held, was problematic legally in terms of legal precedent. The courtroom might also provide a platform for revanchist Nazi propaganda.[22] An even more extreme position was taken by an American lobby centred around the Department of the Treasury and its secretary, Henry Morgenthau Jun. No manner of legal proceeding was envisaged in his plan for Germany.

The Treasury Department was more sensitive to the reality of the war in Europe, as it had close contacts with the War Refugee Board. The latter body had been established in 1944 in a belated American recognition of the seriousness of the plight of the Jews, and was thus a vital conduit for information about the Holocaust and pressure on behalf of its victims. Morgenthau's anti-German vitriol was manifest in his demands for the emasculation of that country by the outright execution of its leaders and by systematic de-industrialization and pastoralization, in order that it never again have the capacity to wage war.[23]

The Soviets favoured a trial of some description of a group of leading Nazis, perhaps for propaganda purposes similar to those served by their previous 'purge' trials. In any case, this idea was the closest approximation to another American proposal forwarded as a counter to the 'Morgenthau plan'. The rival Department of War under Henry Stimson was desperate to coax President Roosevelt away from his enthusiasm for the Treasury's idea, fearing that not only was de-industrialization impractical and immoral, it might well sow the seeds of discontent for a third World War. Conversely, the course of extending 'due process' to prominent Nazis was morally unimpeachable and it would also expose the evils of that regime, thereby, it was hoped, preventing their repetition.[24]

Self-evidently, the trial option won the day. It achieved hegemony in the final quarter of 1944, aided by the propaganda value the Morgenthau plan yielded to Josef Goebbels in the latter's struggle to make the Germans fight to the last. By April 1945 some form of legal action against prominent war criminals was all but certain, particularly when the death of Roosevelt resulted in the succession to the presidency of Truman, an avid supporter of the trial idea.[25]

---

[22] Tusa and Tusa, *The Nuremberg Trial*, 25–8, 61–4; Smith, *The Road to Nuremberg*, 45–6.
[23] Tusa and Tusa, *The Nuremberg Trial*, 50–1; Smith, *The Road to Nuremberg*, 25–9.
[24] For extensive details of these interdepartmental rivalries, see Smith, *The Road to Nuremberg*, ch. 1; Tusa and Tusa, *The Nuremberg Trial*, 51–3.
[25] Smith, *The Road to Nuremberg*, 54–5.

The multinational flavour of the prosecution of the major war criminals was assured by first Soviet, and then French, acquiescence in the principle of far-reaching legal proceedings. The British were the last to come on board, never really discarding their fears about the propriety and wisdom of this type of trial. They ultimately only surrendered in the face of the more-or-less united front of their confederates,[26] and would happily retreat to the more limited form of legal procedure beyond the IMT trial.

The formal agreement to trial was signed by representatives of the four Allied powers in London in August 1945. It affirmed the intention to deploy the IMT 'for the trial of war criminals whose offences have no particular geographical location, whether they be accused individually or in their capacity as members of organizations or groups or in both categories'. Attached to the agreement was a document which came to be known as the Charter of the IMT, setting out the rules of procedure for the court, and enumerating the charges on which it would adjudicate.[27]

The necessary factor in the victory of the War Department in Washington and then in London was the formulation of a prosecution plan of sufficient scope to encompass, first, the breadth and depth of the penetration of Nazi criminality into Germany and, secondly, the corpus of acts which distinguished Nazi atrocities from anything previously accounted for in international law. In recognition of the extremity and peculiarity of Nazi criminality, the IMT was called upon by the charter to adjudicate on actions that did not correspond to traditional notions of breaches of the 'laws of war': for instance, persecutions dating from before the outbreak of war and against Axis nationals; crimes committed during wartime but outside war situations; and ultimately the very act of aggressive war itself. The multi-faceted, international importance of this prosecution effort thrusts the IMT trial to the centre of any analysis of the legal accounting for Nazism. The IMT trial is the key point of departure for this book, for within it, and the lesser proceedings that surrounded and followed it, lay the seeds of the misrepresentations that were to characterize portrayals of Nazi criminality in the post-war era and in some cases up to the present day.

4. THE HOLOCAUST ON TRIAL: AN OVERVIEW

The first section of this book is its empirical core, establishing with reference to diplomatic and legal records the fault lines of the various trial processes, and thus providing a basis for the subsequent discussion of the images of genocide that emerged from the courtrooms and the occupation milieux. The first chapter is a study of the prosecution of prominent war criminals within the context of the broader trial policy of the British and Americans. It brings out the distinctly American flavour of the IMT concept, particularly the controversial strategy

---

[26] Tusa and Tusa, *The Nuremberg Trial*, 66–7.
[27] *IMT*, i, 8–10.

employed to ensnare the diverse individuals and organizations brought to trial and simultaneously to scrutinize the history of Nazism. The chapter proceeds to examine the interrelationship of trial strategy and broader political aims and influences, and the way in which these combined to shape the subsequent Nuremberg programme. Alongside this analysis, it considers the course of the British Royal Warrant trial series and how that defined itself in regard to further prosecutions of 'major' and other important war criminals.

The development of the Cold War is afforded a prominent place within this analysis, in discussion first of the abortive proposal for a second international trial of 'major war criminals' and then of the phasing-out of criminal proceedings altogether. As the 1940s drew to a close, the imperative of reconciliation with Germany in the face of the perceived Soviet threat required the termination of trials. In these and later pages we examine the way that policy realignments in turn impacted, in an entirely negative way, on the educative objectives of the trial initiative.

While Chapter 1 describes the general contours of the trials, Chapter 2 examines the specific question of the treatment of anti-Jewish crimes within that framework. It suggests continuities between the latter and the attitude of the liberal democracies to the Jewish plight in wartime. Thus, in crude terms, on both sides of the German surrender responses were characterized either by a failure to recognize the fate of the European Jews or a reluctance to act upon any such recognition. For our purposes, only limited allowance was made for the catastrophe in the formulation of legal charges, and no priority assigned to the prosecution of its perpetrators. Sometimes, in fact, anti-Jewish crimes were deliberately downplayed by the trial planners. They were certainly almost absent from the wider complementary re-educational material presented by the occupation authorities, material that concentrated largely on crimes committed within Germany.

Moving into the second section, Chapter 3 shows the effect of this 'relativization' of the Jewish case in the Allied courts. It focuses upon the representation of the Nazi camps in the earliest and most widely publicized war crimes trials. It looks in detail at the way that prosecution agendas influenced the presentation of evidence on this complex system of persecution, and how that history was consequently simplified and homogenized, with the murder of the Jews downplayed. As the camp was the pre-eminent symbol of Nazi atrocity, such misrepresentations played a key role in forming misconceptions of the extent and intent of the crimes of the war years.

Chapter 4 differs slightly in its aim. It seeks to show why the trials did not alter pre-existing conceptions of German criminality. It argues that trials were conceptually flawed as didactic tools, and that their shortcomings were magnified by the political discourses of the post-war years. Between 1945 and 1953, Allied policy shifted rapidly from enforcing the idea of collective German guilt to differentiation between Germans, then, somewhat more gradually, to appeasement of

German indignation at the earlier punishment of war criminals. In the main, this was the result of simple political pragmatism, but there were also interesting commonalities between the Germans and the Allies at both the political and public levels as to who warranted trial and who did not. That freedom of expression was given to these partisan interests, unhindered by recourse to the actuality of gross German criminality, was accommodated by an Allied educational initiative whose only consistency was that from day one it focused on 'Germanism' and ignored the concrete effects of Nazi policy.

This analysis focuses particularly on the trials, and debates around those trials, of regular German soldiers. With the passage of time after the end of the war, such debates accommodated and were accommodated by broader international discourses about Germany's position *vis-à-vis* the USSR, the 'west' versus the 'east', civilization versus barbarism and the Christian order versus totalitarianism. They contributed eventually to significant distortions in each country of the nature of the German invasion of the Soviet Union in 1941, and more generally to sweeping diminishments of the breadth of German guilt, as the supposed innocence of the German soldier was transposed to the whole of the German population.

The final section and chapter concern the record of Nazism and its specific crimes that the trials created for posterity. The point of departure is again the evidence in which the judges and prosecutors were prepared to trust and that which they were not. We see that the preconceptions of the Allied lawyers took no account of many criminal groupings whilst inflating the role of others. Thus, for instance, some of the lesser-known police organizations that murdered Jews and others in eastern Europe received lenient treatment despite some evidence at Nuremberg as to their activities. These absences, and some of the exaggerations that are their counterparts, have found remarkably accurate reflection in the historiography of Nazi genocide.

On an interpretative level, the subjective elements of prosecution and judgement contributed towards the depiction of the Holocaust as a by-product of a monolithic German-Nazi conspiracy for European domination through war. This concept fed directly into the thinking of the subsection of Holocaust historiography known as the 'intentionalist' school, and thus into many of the blind alleys into which Holocaust scholarship has wandered. Examining this connection is not simply a matter of making the conceptual link between the idea of a long-standing conspiracy for war with that of a purported plan, long held by Hitler, for the extermination of the Jews. It concerns the elision of inter-Nazi conflicts over the exact course of the treatment of subject peoples; it is also an issue of the reduction of the complex of agencies involved in decision-making and 'executive action' and the distortion of important episodes to fit the grand narrative, to tie up the loose ends. Finally, it touches upon the removal of the question of individual motivation to murder by subordinating it totally to meta-historical forces.

In short, with reference to both the judicial and historical examination of criminal groupings and actions, Chapter 5 suggests a linkage between the earliest investigation of Nazi genocidal policy and most of the major historiographical debates about that subject in the succeeding half-century. These are brought together in the largest, and concluding, case study, which concerns the complicated and oft-misunderstood subject of the Nazi exploitation of Jewish slave labour.

Part I: The Legal Prism

CHAPTER ONE

Shaping the Trials: The Politics of Trial Policy, 1945–1949

One of the primary purposes of the trial of the major war criminals is to document and dramatize for contemporary consumption and for history the means and methods employed by the leading Nazis in their plan to dominate the world and to wage an aggressive war.

(Gordon Dean to Robert Jackson, 11 August 1945)[1]

The words of this American prosecutor are instructive, revealing the intent to make the trial of the major war criminals a history lesson writ large. Indeed, few criminal proceedings in history with any serious claim to being bona fide have been so explicitly accorded didactic functions. The relationship between the judicial and the extra-judicial underpins this book. The present chapter, though, is more directly concerned with the second half of Gordon Dean's communiqué.

Proving the Nazi 'plan to dominate the world and to wage an aggressive war' was the leitmotiv of the American prosecution throughout the Göring trial and the subsequent Nuremberg proceedings. It was the most important influence on the way in which 'major' war criminals were prosecuted between 1945 and 1949. In examining the course of that prosecutorial mission and others that were pursued beside it, this chapter provides the context and much of the empirical grounding for the conclusions of the rest of the study.

1.1 THE THEORY BEHIND THE IMT PROSECUTION

The indictment presented to the IMT contained four counts,[2] of which the defendants each faced his own permutation. (The organizations were simply to be judged upon whether or not they were 'criminal'.) The first count concerned participation in 'the formulation or execution of a common plan or conspiracy to commit, or which involved the commission of, crimes against peace, war crimes and crimes against humanity'. The second charged complicity in 'the planning, preparation, initiation and waging of wars of aggression, which were also wars in violation of international treaties, agreements and assurances'. The third involved 'war crimes' committed between 1 September 1939 and 8 May 1945 'in

---

[1] Library of Congress, papers of Robert H. Jackson, hereafter 'Jackson papers', container 107, Gordon Dean to Jackson, 11 Aug. 1945.

[2] The IMT Charter contained three generic charges, as reproduced below in Appendix A; the first of these charges was subdivided in the IMT indictment.

Germany and in all those countries and territories occupied by the German armed forces . . . and in Austria, Czechoslovakia and Italy, and on the High Seas'. The final count addressed 'crimes against humanity' enacted 'during a period of years preceding 8th May, 1945, in Germany and in all those countries and territories occupied by the German armed forces since 1st September, 1939, and in Austria and Czechoslovakia and in Italy and on the High Seas'.[3]

The Americans allocated to themselves responsibility for proving the first charge; the British had the second; and the Soviets and the French divided the third and fourth between them, according to whether the crimes had been committed in western or eastern Europe. The substance and development of these four counts are of great importance in understanding the shape that American and British trials took. The last two are rather more straightforward and will be examined first.

In general terms, there was a core of events concerning which legal authorities agreed charges could be brought against suspected war criminals. These constituted the class of acts for which there was some precedent for legal accountability, namely 'violations of the laws and customs of war' (war crimes *stricto sensu*, as legal terminology has it). More specifically, they embraced crimes committed against members of opposing armed forces, and of the civilian population of occupied territories. These categories failed to encompass acts from before the outbreak of war, or deeds against the citizens of Axis countries and their confederates.[4] The prime example of the interrelation of the latter two groupings was the pre-war treatment of German Jews, though they also incorporated much of the oppression of the Nazis' political and ideological opponents, homosexuals, and the Roma and Sinti peoples, and the murder of those considered mentally and physically defective.

The initiative to expand the traditional interpretation of war crimes began in 1942 with pressure from Jewish organizations for the governments of the western Allies to make some sort of policy commitment in the light of revelations about the systematic massacres in eastern Europe.[5] The mood of the time was certainly conducive to general Allied declarations of intent, for the various governments-in-exile were making their voices heard on behalf of their compatriots.[6]

Though there was comparatively little specific sympathy for Jews, the Polish representatives played on their suffering out of a misguided, stereotyping faith in Jewish influence in the west.[7] Substantial pressure was exerted on the British Government to expand its definition of 'war crimes', but the fear of creating ad hoc and *ex post facto* law was overriding and, aside from the IMT trial, the British

---

[3] *IMT*, i, 29–68.

[4] Dale Jones, 'British Policy', 339; IfZ, FG 16, pp. 62–3, for the situation in the Dachau programme.

[5] Smith, *The Road to Nuremberg*, 35, 43; Dale Jones, 'British Policy', 347–9.

[6] Dale Jones, 'British Policy', 346.

[7] David Engel, *In the Shadow of Auschwitz: The Polish Government-in-Exile and the Jews, 1939–1942* (Chapel Hill, NC: University of North Carolina Press, 1987), 183.

never concerned their military courts with anything other than war crimes *stricto sensu*. The Jewish call was nevertheless taken up at the end of 1943 by members of the nascent UNWCC, particularly the American representative Herbert Pell and the Czech Bohuslav Ecer,[8] but it received its greatest impetus from the War Refugee Board. Despite the rejection of the Morgenthau plan, his message of the unprecedented scope of Nazi criminality had a considerable impact. It was the intention of all of the American proponents of trial, from Presidents Roosevelt and Truman downwards, to expand the concept of 'war crimes', and this was realized in the formulation of 'crimes against humanity'.[9]

It is telling that, this contribution notwithstanding, the Americans wished to preside over the implementation of the conspiracy count. This was the very concept that had been used by the US War Department to foil the Morgenthau plan. It was the brainchild of one Colonel Murray C. Bernays, and was employed to connect all of the unusual brutalities of Nazism with one central idea: the plan for continental and world domination.[10] One necessary manifestation of the quest, it was held, was the repression and murder of real and conceptual opponents of the regime. However, the inexorable logic of this reduction to a single principle was that aggressive warfare became the most significant act, because it facilitated and encouraged further atrocities. War, apparently, was the ultimate and all-inclusive crime; and to explain that act required recourse to the conspiracy.[11]

The way this concept related to the defendants and organizations before the IMT is best illustrated in the words of Robert H. Jackson. A Supreme Court Justice, Jackson was appointed to lead the American prosecution in April 1945, and his determination to establish a prominent role for international law in the conduct of world affairs has been widely noted.[12] He later described the prosecution's task as

to try in two phases the question of war guilt [*sic*]. The first phase would be to establish the existence of a general conspiracy to which the Nazi party, the Gestapo and other organisations were parties. The object of the conspiracy was to obtain by illegal means, by violation of treaties, and by wholesale brutality control of Europe and the world. When this plan should be proved, the second phase would be entered upon which would consist of the identification of individuals who were parties to this general conspiracy.[13]

---

[8] Kochavi, *Prelude to Nuremberg*; Southampton University Archives, MSS 238/2/20, minutes of meeting held in New Cavendish St., London, 22 Sept. 1944.

[9] Smith, *The Road to Nuremberg*, 258, for the emphasis in American political circles.

[10] Bernays had originally devised the plan to take account of the extent of Nazi atrocity, including pre-war crimes, but the emphasis was shifted to that on aggressive war. See Chapter 2, below; Shlomo Aronson, 'Preparations for the Nuremberg Trial: The OSS, Charles Dwork, and the Holocaust', *Holocaust and Genocide Studies*, 12 (1998), 257–81, esp. 261–4.

[11] Tusa and Tusa, *The Nuremberg Trial*, 73; on the Bernays plan: Smith, *The Road to Nuremberg*, passim.

[12] e.g. Tusa and Tusa, *The Nuremberg Trial*, 68–9.

[13] Jackson papers, container 191, 'Justice Jackson's story', fos. 1046–7. The aims of the first part of this plan were only partially realized, and those of the second, in American eyes, hardly at all, as we shall see.

This was what the historian Bradley Smith has termed the conspiracy–criminal organization plan. The idea was that evidence against individuals could be held against organizations and vice versa. A finding of criminality against an organization would then expedite mass prosecutions, as guilt would hold for every member of that organization, and the burden of proving innocence would lie with the defendant.

Ultimately, the IMT qualified both elements of the prosecution plan heavily, circumscribing the scope of the alleged conspiracy and ruling that it had to be proved that any individual member of a criminal organization had joined voluntarily and with an awareness of its criminality.[14] The theoretical American approach was not universally welcomed amongst the prosecutors either. As one French legal expert put it, 'the difference between us is that you Americans want to prove that a war of aggression is illegal. We just want to prove the Nazis were bandits.'[15] That was certainly true of the Soviet delegation also. (Though the Soviets, like, to a lesser extent, the Americans, were worried about the potential of a focus upon the idea of 'crimes against humanity' to set a precedent for interference in the domestic activities of a sovereign power.)[16]

Part of the Soviet and French reaction stemmed from their direct experience of the realities of occupation, part was legalistic. The concept of conspiracy had been predominantly implemented in American courts in anti-trust and organized crime cases, and it was unknown, at least in this form, in continental law. The conspiracy charge also caused a certain resentment, as it became clear that Jackson intended to use much evidence pertaining directly to the war crimes and crimes against humanity charges in order to 'prove' the master conspiracy.[17] Vitally, Jackson was to be given the stage at the beginning of the trial, establishing the tone of the proceedings. This was not just to be the dominant count in his mind, it was to be imposed on the whole of the prosecution, and there was little that anyone could do, given that American investigators had also secured most of the relevant documentation.

The conspiracy device was employed at Nuremberg in one sense as a practical way to reach diverse defendants. There was of course also an element of idealism in the desire to regulate international affairs with recourse to the ideas of natural justice. In another sense, however, the approach was of philosophical importance to the US chief of counsel for the prosecution of Axis criminality (OCCPAC). Hannah Arendt identified the impotence of the law in providing adequate

---

[14] The IMT declared that the conspiracy could not be traced back to the early days of Nazi power, and instead had to be judged only in close chronological proximity to the war. Equally, the conspiracy could only apply to preparation for aggressive war and not to the planning of war crimes and crimes against humanity. See Tusa and Tusa, *The Nuremberg Trial*, ch. 17; below, Chapter 2. On the organization judgement: Taylor, *Anatomy*, ch. 20.

[15] 'Justice Jackson's story', fo. 1140.

[16] Lawrence Douglas, 'Film as Witness: Screening *Nazi Concentration Camps* before the Nuremberg Tribunal', *Yale Law Journal*, 105 (1995), 449–81, esp. 461.

[17] Smith, *Reaching Judgment at Nuremberg*, 82–90.

punishment for the massive crimes of the Nazis. Indeed, it might be argued that the Holocaust itself was in part an outcome of, and therefore a shattering indictment of, the moral and legal systems that were now required to sit in judgement upon its perpetrators. The particular emphasis on the conspiracy to perpetrate aggressive war, though controversial, avoided this philosophical conundrum, while questioning the then-dominant, positivist, state-led theory of law by attempting to establish individual responsibility for 'acts of state'.[18] In combination, and given the American possession of what a British observer estimated as 'at least 70 percent of the principal criminals',[19] these factors ensured that the 'conspiracy–criminal organisation plan' remained the greatest influence on the way in which major war criminals were prosecuted after World War II. It also impacted upon who reached trial.

I.2 THE IMT DEFENDANTS: INDIVIDUALS AND ORGANIZATIONS

The American prosecutor Telford Taylor once described Hitler's rule as predicated upon 'the unholy trinity of Nazism, militarism and economic imperialism'.[20] These three elements were the chief components of the conspiracy, it was held, and pursuit of the three together was a mainstay of the subsequent Nuremberg trials programme and of the Göring trial. In the Göring trial, the emphasis was upon combining 'representatives' of those tendencies with the presence of 'household' names.[21] Naturally, there was a large cross-over between these categories.

'Representative' of Nazism as a political movement were, it was decided, the Reich Cabinet (Reichsregierung) and the Leadership Corps of the Nazi party. The SS (Schutzstaffeln), and particularly the infamous Gestapo, were obvious choices encompassing the paramilitary-police manifestations of the phenomenon. (Alongside the latter, the Sicherheitsdienst, or SD was indicted, because the two had related functions within the SS Reich Security Head Office, the RSHA.) Moreover, indictment of the SA, the Sturmabteilungen, the praetorian guard of the Nazi party before 1934, was consistent both with a general western awareness of the pre-war Nazi hierarchy and with tracing the conspiracy back to the earliest days. In accordance with the IMT's view of the conspiracy charge, the SA, alone of these organizations, was ruled not to be criminal.

The majority of the individual defendants fitted the profile of 'notorious individuals' who were also representative of the overtly political groupings: Göring himself, Rudolf Hess, Joachim von Ribbentrop, Robert Ley, Ernst

---

[18] Douglas, 'Film as Witness', 457–63.

[19] Memorandum on trials of major war criminals by Patrick Dean, 14 Aug. 1945, printed in *Documents on British Policy Overseas, Ser 1, v. Germany and Western Europe, 11 Aug.–31 Dec. 1945*, ed. Her Majesty's Stationery Office (London: HMSO, 1990), 34–43, point 4.

[20] Cited in Frederick Elwyn Jones, *In My Time: An Autobiography* (London: Futura, 1983), 129.

[21] Dean memorandum, 14 Aug. 1945, printed in *Documents on British Policy Overseas, 11 Aug.–31 Dec. 1945*, 34–43, point 14.

Kaltenbrunner, Alfred Rosenberg, Hans Frank, Wilhelm Frick, Julius Streicher, Baldur von Schirach, Fritz Sauckel, Martin Bormann, Artur Seyss-Inquart, Albert Speer, Constantin von Neurath, and Hans Fritszche.[22] Franz von Papen was also included because of his role in Hitler's assumption of power. What, though, was meant by 'militarism' and 'economic imperialism', and how were these to be quantified in a courtroom?

Sectors of American public opinion had long seen the German Armed forces as criminal, and 'Prussian militarism' was viewed as a constant factor in recent German history, and one which had facilitated the Nazi campaigns of aggression.[23] The ideas propounded by OCCPAC that the conspiracy to pursue aggressive war, and the act of embarking upon it, were in themselves crimes required a condemnation in law not only of the perpetrating agency (the armed forces) but also of the industrialists and financiers who had contributed to rearmament. Moreover, it was realized that both the Wehrmacht and German industry had contributed in considerable part to the massive human disasters—the 'crimes against humanity'—which the Americans held to have been an intrinsic part of the conspiracy, and which anyway stood by themselves as criminal acts by all decent standards.

In accordance with American wishes, alongside accusing notables of the Wehrmacht, the indictment contended that the General Staff and High Command of the German armed forces was a criminal organization. Economic policy-makers were also included, foremost amongst whom for our purposes was Hjalmar Schacht (though Speer, Sauckel, Ley, and Walther Funk were also important in this connection). Schacht had been a prominent influence in Hitler's rise to power, and, as President of the Reichsbank, Minister of Economics, and General Plenipotentiary for the War Economy, was seen as the genius behind the Nazi economic miracle—simultaneously adding respectability to the movement and attracting further financial supporters—and a major player in Germany's rearmament.

In addition to the official agencies of the Third Reich, Jackson wished to indict at least one private businessman who had contributed to the Nazi potential for war. The selection of a 'representative' industrialist seemed straightforward; in the eyes of the victors, the outstanding malefactor in the armaments industry was the Krupp family of Essen. It was somewhat simplistically held that

since the dawn of modern Europe the mysterious, powerful Krupp dynasty had flourished on war and rumors of war . . . Its steel forges had disgorged armor, bayonets, field guns, shells, battleship armor and flotillas of submarines, always at immense profit to the House of Krupp . . . For a century [the German governments and the Krupp family]

---

[22] It was only really as a sop to the Soviets, who had captured very few prominent Nazis, that Hans Fritzsche, like Admiral Erich Raeder, was included in the trial. Tusa and Tusa, *The Nuremberg Trial*, 92–3. Ley committed suicide prior to trial and Bormann was tried *in absentia*.

[23] Ibid. 435.

were inseparable partners . . . And never has the parallel become more striking than in the appalling spring of 1945, when it appeared to have become deadly.[24]

So a Krupp was added to the indictment, alongside representatives of the military which had been the grateful recipient of his products. Yet force of circumstance was to combine with unfavourable judgements to blunt the Allies' ambition with regard to the prosecution of industrialists and the military. Though General Alfred Jodl, Field Marshall Wilhelm Keitel, and Admirals Raeder and Dönitz were convicted by the IMT (Keitel and Jodl on all four counts, Raeder on the first three, and Dönitz on counts two and three), the General Staff and High Command was declared not to be a criminal organization. It was not considered a sufficiently coherent body to be an organization 'within the meaning . . . of the Charter'.[25] As the British had predicted, the mass of undeniably incriminating evidence thrown at the German military had simply not proved the involvement *as a group* of the General Staff and High Command, nor its character outside the imagination of OCCPAC.[26]

The campaign against the Krupps was interrupted at a rather earlier stage than the judgement. No Krupp appeared before the IMT owing to an unfortunate misunderstanding between the prosecuting teams. The confusion leading to this omission stemmed from the existence of two candidates for the role. Gustav Krupp had been in charge of the firm until 1942, when illness and old age compelled him to surrender the reins to his son Alfried, who retained control until the surrender. Though less fit for trial, Jackson wished to see Gustav arraigned, since his role in the pre- and early war periods made him a more suitable subject for their innovations: the charges of criminal conspiracy and of crimes against peace. It was considered that he had figured significantly in the illegal rearmament of Germany in the wake of Versailles, and had organized contributions from industry for the Nazi party after 1933.[27] Alfried appeared more culpable under the other two counts for the firm's exploitation of slave labour in the second half of the war.

The American view predictably prevailed, and Krupp senior was duly indicted.[28] Gustav's dementia overtook him, however, and medical opinion ruled

---

[24] William Manchester, *The Arms of Krupp, 1587–1968* (New York: Bantam, 1970), 2; Eugene Davidson, *The Trial of the Germans: An Account of the 22 Defendants before the International Military Tribunal at Nuremberg* (New York: Macmillan, 1966), 26.

[25] *IMT*, i, 276.

[26] The Great General Staff, the so-called 'brain of the army', had been abolished at Versailles and, despite something of a revival in the guise of the Truppenamt in the 1920s, had suffered a sharp decline as Hitler assumed personal control of the armed forces. By the time of the Nuremberg trial, it was scarcely recognizable, and even the Americans agreed that they were dealing with a 'group of top officers' involved in military planning, 130 in number of whom 114 were still alive, rather than with an organized entity. For British arguments to this effect, see University of Connecticut Archives, papers of Thomas J. Dodd, hereafter 'Dodd papers', box 320, file 'Prisoner lists, 1945 August–1946 January', undated note by Peter Calvocoressi.

[27] Neave, *Nuremberg*, 30–2, 212.

[28] Taylor, *Anatomy*, 90–4; Neave, *Nuremberg*, 29–32.

him unfit for trial, as did the IMT. Further, the Tribunal rejected the request that either Gustav be tried *in absentia* or Alfried arraigned instead. The first part of the request was rejected because Gustav's condition, rather than his absence (through flight, as was the case with Martin Bormann) precluded his involvement. The second part was rejected in accordance with 'the British view that this was not a game of football in which a reserve could be fielded without much delay',[29] even though straightforward substitution was not Jackson's intention.

1.3 THE PROSPECT OF A SECOND INTERNATIONAL TRIAL

The Krupp issue did not fade away after these decisions. Rather, it gave added impetus to demands made by the French and the Soviets for a second trial of 'major' criminals not included in the indictment. The idea of a further trial or trials had first been mooted at the London Conference of June to July 1945, but with the onset of the Krupp episode it achieved an immediate significance. The economic part of the case was at least as important to the French and Soviets as to Jackson, for both of the continental nations had experienced considerable and often extreme exploitation and spoliation of their natural and human resources under German occupation.

The French, it was judged, wished to try industrialists not only for their own actions but in order to 'strengthen the hand' of the French authorities in dealing with collaborationist French industrialists.[30] Indeed, the French appeared to have pushed hard even into 1947 for a second trial of such people. The Soviets harboured the simplistic Marxist view that Hitler was an instrument of the German bankers and industrialists, and without them could not have risen to power.[31] Conversely, the British Foreign Office and sections of the American prosecution were worried both about the prominence and complexity of the economic case in Jackson's scheme. The former in particular feared that the case against Schacht was weak enough to result in an embarrassing acquittal, to say nothing of the poor prospects for proving the knowing participation in a grand aggressive conspiracy of a private industrialist like Krupp.[32]

However, the net result of French agitation over the issue was that the British Chief Prosecutor, Hartley Shawcross, in an attempt to ensure the timely initiation of the trial, assured his French counterpart, François de Menthon, that the British would participate in a second international trial against a group of industrialists including Alfried Krupp.[33] Article 14 of the IMT Charter established

---

[29] Cooper, *The Nuremberg Trial*, 37.

[30] PRO, WO 311/39, Maxwell-Fyfe to BWCE, 25 Jan. 1946.

[31] Neave, *Nuremberg*, 209; *IMT*, vi, *passim*; David W. Ellwood, *Rebuilding Europe: Western Europe, America and Postwar Reconstruction* (London: Longman, 1992), 52–3.

[32] Taylor, *Anatomy*, 80–92.

[33] PRO, PREM 8/391, Orme Sargeant to Attlee, 31 July 1946; Tusa and Tusa, *Nuremberg*, 138, concludes that 'for the British the desire for a prompt start always overcame any other consideration'.

that any two of the chief prosecutors could designate candidates for future trial by the Tribunal. Accordingly, on the day the trial began, the delegations published a joint declaration to the effect that they were 'engaged upon an examination of the cases of other leading German industrialists with a view to their joinder with Alfried Krupp in an indictment to be presented at a subsequent trial'.[34]

For a number of reasons both political and practical this second international case never materialized. That non-event illustrates the shift in principles underlying Allied trial policy. If the IMT and the first zonal trials were almost solely products of the reaction to Nazism, to be promoted even in the presence of the doubtful moral authority of the Soviets, and, of course, in complete disregard of German sensibilities, the realities of the post-war world were now influencing the trial agenda. The overriding development in world affairs during the years in question was the onset of what would come to be known as the 'Cold War', and this left its indelible mark on Allied German policy, of which the treatment of war criminals was an integral part.

1.4 THE POLITICAL CONTEXT OF THE OCCUPATION OF GERMANY

Historiographical consensus suggests that British foreign-political thinking as a whole was ahead of its American counterpart, in perceiving before the end of the war the threat that Soviet expansionism was held to pose to Europe.[35] Likewise, Whitehall was first to see that Germany would have to be resurrected in some form, as the mainstay of a central European power bloc designed to check the advance of Communism. By mid-1946 this impulse had grown stronger than fear of a revival of German nationalism.[36] Hence trials of Germany's former leaders came to be seen as detrimental to Britain's interests.

Yet though these views found a sympathetic audience with the new Foreign Secretary Ernest Bevin, they were not universally popular within Attlee's Cabinet; and they were diametrically opposed to the feelings of the British public in the immediate aftermath of a war in which the Soviets had fought heroically against a demonized enemy. Nor were they consonant with all of the principles of the Potsdam agreement, as enshrined in the 'four "d"s' of demilitarization, decartelization, denazification, and democratization. Thus at first it was incumbent upon Bevin to maintain publicly the façade that co-operation with the Soviets over the future of Germany was still a viable option, emphasizing British Germanophobia and expressing the wish merely to reform the Potsdam terms (and criticizing the Soviets for their failure to comply with them), while all

[34] Elwyn Jones, *In My Time*, 125.
[35] Anne Deighton, *The Impossible Peace: Britain, the Division of Germany and the Origins of the Cold War* (Oxford: Oxford University Press, 1990), 25.
[36] Ibid. 78, 115, 224.

the time his department was trying to enmesh the Americans in an anti–Soviet coalition propping up at least a part of Germany; this practice developed into his so-called 'Western' policy.[37]

Bevin's task was, however, made easier at home because the primacy of the Foreign Office was never seriously threatened. Attlee made it clear that he considered that the conduct of foreign affairs stood above party politics, and was therefore not necessarily subject to Britain's prevailing socialist agenda, in as much as that doctrine provided a foreign policy line in any case. The Control Office for Germany and Austria (COGA), the 'ministry' for German affairs which oversaw the government of the British zone, was progressively marginalized by the larger department, and its effective subordination was formalized in July 1946.[38] Moreover, though the War Office had official jurisdiction over trials under the Royal Warrant, and supplied the administrative and legal personnel, when the subject matter of these cases was politically sensitive, the Foreign Office had the final say, as we shall see.

The situation in Washington was far less clear-cut. The more conciliatory line pursued by Roosevelt towards the Soviets was continued in the early months of the Truman administration, and at the end of 1945 co-operation in Europe with the USSR seemed likely. Though relations deteriorated during the first quarter of 1946 as Soviet actions in Iran and the stirrings of the proponents of the 'Riga axiom' (the doctrine of 'containment' of the USSR) began to colour foreign-political thinking, the future of Germany was still not central to the United States' European policy.[39]

Roosevelt had neither established, nor allowed to materialize, a definite German policy, and this vacuum was only slowly filled as Truman's support for toughness with the Soviets was translated into tangible policy influenced by Foreign Service diplomats and sections of the Departments of State and War.[40] A succession of weak and ill-informed Secretaries of State, combined with the unwillingness and inability of that department to take an active role in the occupation of Germany, and the traditional lack of influence within Congress of a department with no home constituency, had meant that previously the genuine experts on Soviet intentions had been marginalized.[41]

The real seat of power in German affairs rested with the man on the ground charged with implementing American policy. General Lucius Clay, Deputy Military Governor from 1945 to 1947—though *de facto* the supreme occupation authority—and Military Governor from 1947 until 1949, was given a virtually free hand in running the American zone, in stark contrast to his British opposite

---

[37] Deighton, *The Impossible Peace*, 78, 113, 128.
[38] Ibid. 128–34.
[39] Ibid. 78–9.
[40] Edward N. Peterson, *The American Occupation of Germany* (Detroit: Wayne State University Press, 1977), 20–3.
[41] Ibid. 23–6.

numbers.[42] Indeed, Clay's successor, John McCloy, called the governorship the closest approximation to a 'Roman proconsulship' that was possible in the twentieth century.[43] The deference shown Clay by his War Department superiors enabled him to interpret the chief occupation statute, the harsh and retributive JCS 1067, as he saw fit.[44] After assessing the German situation, his views broadly coincided with those of the so-called foreign policy 'realists'; namely, that Germany, or at least part of it, had to be resurrected economically both to remove a burden upon the Allies and to establish a bulwark against Soviet Communism.

The Potsdam Agreement alleviated JCS 1067 somewhat, and in addition Clay was able to exploit legal loopholes in that document to allow the recommencing of significant production in Germany, the halting of the dismantling of German industrial plant and of reparations payments, and the economic fusion of the British and American zones.[45] Beside these measures, however, Clay remained committed to the US war crimes trial programme; the realities of European politics did not deflect him from taking the 'denazification' part of his original brief very seriously, though he was astute enough to realize the limitations of that policy.[46]

In July 1947, however, the more lenient directive JCS 1779 replaced JCS 1067 and formalized the ongoing recovery, stipulating the desirability of a 'stable and productive Germany'. It further instructed Clay to 'make every effort to facilitate and bring to early completion the war crimes program'. The move was symptomatic of the larger shift in American European policy as the 'realists' under Truman exerted their influence.[47] A speech in Stuttgart in September 1946 by Secretary of State James Byrnes following the Paris Peace Conference suggested a change of objective on behalf of himself and the administration; but proof positive of an American commitment to Europe, founded upon a continued presence in Germany, was provided only between March and June 1947.

During that time, the 'Truman Doctrine' predicted a tougher line with the Soviets, and American support for 'free peoples who [were] resisting attempted subjugation by armed minorities or by outside pressures'. A conference of

[42] Ibid. 56; Deighton, *The Impossible Peace*, 67–8; Robert Morgan, *The United States and West Germany, 1945–73: A Study in Alliance Politics* (London: Oxford University Press, 1974), 14.

[43] Cited in Thomas Alan Schwartz, *America's Germany: John J. McCloy and the Federal Republic of Germany* (Cambridge, Mass.: Harvard University Press, 1991), 42.

[44] JCS 1067 stipulated that Germany was not to be treated as a liberated country but as an occupied one, and in its tone bore some of the imprint of the Morgenthau plan.

[45] John Backer, 'From Morgenthau Plan to Marshall Plan', in Robert Wolfe (ed.), *Americans as Proconsuls: United States Military Government in Germany and Japan, 1944–1952* (Carbondale, Ill.: Southern Illinois University Press, 1984), 155–65, esp. 155–8; Morgan, *The United States and West Germany*, 14, 17–21.

[46] Backer, 'From Morgenthau Plan to Marshall Plan', 159; Telford Taylor, *Final Report to the Secretary of the Army on the Nuernberg War Crimes Trials under Control Council Law No. 10* (Washington, DC: USGPO, 1949), 33–4.

[47] Morgan, *The United States and West Germany*, 14, 21.

foreign ministers in Moscow also apparently confirmed the lack of progress that was to be made in Soviet–American co-operation in Europe; and the 'Marshall Plan' promised a substantial contribution by the US to (western) European economic recovery.[48]

These wedges were hammered deeper into Europe at the London conference of foreign ministers at the end of the year, as the incompatibility of western and perceived Soviet intentions for Germany—a rift which resulted in the break-up of the four-power Control Council in March 1948 and the consequent division of that country—achieved overwhelming importance. The cumulative weight of such developments left a visible imprint on British trial policy and, while less immediately relevant for the American programmes, high political influences were evident in both cases in the negotiations around the possible second IMT trial.

1.5 'THE TRIAL THAT NEVER WAS':[49] THE ABORTED SECOND TRIAL OF MAJOR WAR CRIMINALS

The Shawcross–de Menthon statement on a future indictment of Alfred Krupp by no means guaranteed another international trial. Though the London Agreement made provision for a series of trials before the IMT, any power could terminate that agreement given one month's notice. The Americans had never committed themselves to a further international trial, and a consensus emerged between Jackson, the War Department, and the Office of Military Government for Germany (OMGUS) by the end of 1945 that this form of proceeding was undesirable, and that further trials against major war criminals were best conducted by the individual occupying powers.[50]

American options remained open owing to an amendment to the executive order that had established Jackson's position as holder of the office of Chief of Counsel. Issued on 16 January 1946, order 9679 authorized the pursuit of 'leaders of the European Axis powers and their accessories' *either* before another international tribunal or United States military or occupational tribunals. Jackson was directed to select a deputy to arrange these trials in whichever type of court 'developments [might] dictate', and provision was made for the succession to his office in the event of his retirement. The new office was to be known as OCCWC—the Office of the Chief of Counsel for War Crimes.

Importantly, the new Chief of Counsel was to be appointed within the machinery of OMGUS, thus making the office a part of the occupational authority, and answerable directly to that entity, rather than to the national governments as was the case with the chief prosecutors before the IMT. The proceedings of the OCCWC were governed by the amended executive order and by the four-power occupation statute CCL10, which was derived from, and similar but not

48 Deighton, *The Impossible Peace*, 140, 162–7.   49 Elwyn Jones, *In My Time*, 128.
50 NARA, RG 260, OMGUS, Adjutant-General's decimal files, 1945–8, box 2, Smith to Jackson, 5 Dec. 1945; McNarney to Chief of Staff, Washington, 5 Dec. 1945.

identical to, the London Charter establishing the IMT. It provided for separate zonal trials, while expressing the desire for uniformity between zones.[51]

Colonel Telford Taylor was the man chosen both by Jackson as his deputy to plan for further prosecutions and by the War Department as the next CCWC.[52] In the months leading up to the IMT trial, Taylor had become increasingly dissatisfied with the rather arbitrary selection of defendants, and had reached the now obvious conclusion that it was impossible to deal with all the major perpetrators in one sitting, and so a number of trials would have to be held. This line of thought coincided with sentiments expressed in a revised Joint Chiefs of Staff directive of July 1945. JCS 1023/10 defined 'war crimes' in a similar fashion to the Charter of the IMT, and ordered the pursuit by the American occupation forces of 'members of organizations' implicated in such acts.[53] It was a precursor of CCL10. The Judge Advocate General's Department of the US Army framed the Nuremberg organization as that best suited to the purpose of carrying out such trials, and consequently approached OMGUS and Jackson to enquire whether he or any of his staff might be prepared to participate.[54]

Importantly, and despite the burgeoning American opposition, Taylor was careful not to discount the possibility of a second international trial. He was mindful of the potential of the Krupp issue to upset any plans laid prematurely, since it was clear that the French and the Russian delegations remained in principle in favour of another international trial.[55] France would in fact continue to push for that end into 1947.

Hartley Shawcross considered with resignation that his promise had bound Britain to the French. Indeed, the British War Crimes Executive (BWCE), the approximate counterpart to OCCPAC, had been making speculative preparations for a second trial for some time. Shawcross emphasized, however, that any venture should be closely circumscribed and co-ordinated by direct Anglo-American co-operation.[56] Other interested parties on the British side were not so resigned. The Treasury Solicitor's Office feared the potential cost of a second

---

[51] Jackson to the President, 4 Dec. 1945; executive order 9679, amending order 9547, printed in Taylor, *Final Report*, 262–3, 267, appendices F, G, respectively. Emphasis added.

[52] Office, Chief of Counsel, general memorandum no. 15, 29 Mar. 1946; Jackson to the President, 4 Dec. 1945; Taylor, 'Nuremberg Trials: War Crimes and International Law'. All printed in Taylor, *Final Report*, 262–3, 268, 155, appendices H, F, B, respectively.

[53] OCCWC would not have to proceed against the mass of people implicated by membership of 'criminal organizations'. It would only be concerned with the 'few hundred, or at the outside . . . few thousand major and sub-major war criminals'. The 'Law for Liberation from National Socialism and Militarism', published on 5 Mar. 1946 by the Länderrat—the joint Provincial Council in the US zone—provided for the prosecution of the majority of lesser defenders, which was the real meat of the denazification process, before German courts, or Spruchkammern. See IfZ, FG 16, p. 24; Taylor, *Anatomy*, 274–86.

[54] Taylor, *Anatomy*, 96, 272–3.

[55] Memo for President from Jackson, 13 May 1946, cited in Taylor, *Final Report*, 276–9, appendix J.

[56] Jackson papers, container 98, office files, US Chief of Counsel, chief prosecutors' meeting 5 Apr. 1946; Shawcross to Jackson, 25 July 1946, cited in Taylor, *Final Report*, 283–4, appendix J. See also PRO, FO 371/57583, Shawcross to Newton, 28 Feb. 1946; for early BWCE preparations, see PRO, WO 311/39, Maxwell-Fyfe to BWCE, 25 Jan. 1946.

trial.[57] The Foreign Office was even more reticent, wary of a second lengthy trial which they feared would be anti-climactic and would detract from the real achievements of the first. While not wishing to be seen to be letting off the industrialists, it felt that the IMT trial was a sufficient measure of their commitment to the cause of the trials. In this, the Foreign Office was in tune with popular British sentiment.[58]

Orme Sargeant, Permanent Under-Secretary in the ministry, suggested also that an international trial of German industrialists could degenerate into 'a wrangle between the capitalist and communist ideologies'. 'The Russians might exploit the proceedings to discuss irrelevancies such as . . . our attitude to German rearmament', he considered;[59] and though this view was not shared by Patrick Dean, the Foreign Office representative on the BWCE,[60] it was in accord with the general thrust of British foreign policy at the time. Moreover, Sargeant is credited as being one of the officials with the most influence over European strategy, a strident voice warning of the dangers of repeating history by appeasing the Soviets.[61] He had the ear of Bevin, and the church of which he was a founding member towered over the small and impermanent BWCE.

As we shall see, there is no evidence that the Foreign Office intended to exercise their prerogative of trying the industrialists in British zonal proceedings; indeed, quite the opposite. The main priority now was to avoid a trial if they could do so 'honourably'.[62] 'Honourably', because they still felt committed by the enthusiasm of their allies and, relatedly, by Shawcross's pledge; they certainly did not wish to be seen as responsible for terminating the London Agreement.[63] Caught on the horns of a dilemma, one option was the tried-and-tested policy of 'wait and see'. The British would allow their Allies 'to make the running . . . and not hasten too fast to keep up with them'. This strategy was confirmed when, towards the end of April, the Foreign Office received early intelligence that US opposition to another international trial was stiffening.[64]

On practical grounds alone, Jackson was wary of further involvement in lengthy proceedings that he considered would cover much of the same ground as the current trial. Moreover, he was opposed to hosting a second trial at Nuremberg because of the cost and the responsibilities implied; a sentiment very much shared by OMGUS, the War Department, and the State Department.[65] Other

[57] Tusa, *The Nuremberg Trial*, 373.   [58] See below, Chapter 4.

[59] Elwyn Jones, *In My Time*, 126; PRO, PREM 8/391, Sargeant to Attlee, 31 July 1946.

[60] PRO, FO 371/57584, Dean to Shawcross, 16 May 1946.

[61] Deighton, *The Impossible Peace*, 25–8, 78.

[62] PRO, LCO 2/2989, Coldstream to Napier, 20 July 1946; PRO, FO 371/57583, memo (signature illegible), 8 Jan. 1946; Newton to Shawcross, 26 Mar. 1946.

[63] PRO, FO 371/57583, Scott-Fox to German Dept. FO, 7 Jan. 1946; PRO, PREM 8/391, Sargeant to Prime Minister, 31 July 1946.

[64] PRO, FO 371/57583, minute (signature illegible) 8 Jan. 1946; Scott-Fox minute, 24 Apr. 1946.

[65] Jackson papers, container 98, office files, US Chief of Counsel, chief prosecutors' meeting 16 Apr. 1946; container 110, office files, US Chief of Counsel, subsequent trials 1, Jackson to Maxwell-Fyfe, Rudenko, and de Ribes, 17 Apr. 1946; Jackson to McNarney, Jackson to McNarney for Clay, 18 Apr. 1946;

objections also featured. Jackson feared that attacking industrialists would 'tend to discourage industrial co-operation with our Government in maintaining its defenses in the future while not at all weakening the Soviet position, since they [did] not rely upon private enterprise'. His papers are replete with barbed references to the Soviets at Nuremberg, and it is not surprising that he was among the first to be concerned about the image of a trial of industrialists by Americans working in tandem with 'the Soviet Communists and the French Leftists'. Furthermore, he worried that the principle of the rotation of the presidency of the Tribunal might mean the elevation to that position of a Soviet or French judge, and the consequent imposition onto the proceedings of a legal code which was alien to the American people, and thus might foster doubts as to the fairness of the trial.[66] These objections were also echoed by the State and War Departments.

A further international trial would be an unnecessary and potentially damaging additional engagement, these agencies perceived. The quadripartite programme should give the US the best of both worlds: it implied international jurisdiction but also total control by the respective occupying nations of the four zones. Thus continuity and the appearance of inter-Allied unity could be maintained in the prosecution of such individuals, without the costs and complications of another IMT proceeding.[67] Concerned about the 'overall international situation', they feared that a second fully international trial, particularly one focusing on industrialists as seemed inevitable, would serve to 'emphasize ideological differences between the prosecuting nations', even to the extent of facilitating Communist attacks on the methods of government of the US.[68] The many links between the pre-war German and American economies could, it was felt, be a focal point of an attempt by the Soviets to embarrass the US.[69]

The private consensus reached in British and American diplomatic circles was not consonant with the attitudes of the Russian and French delegations, nor with Telford Taylor's view that unilateral American action would do harm to the principles of the London Agreement and would incur political repercussions involving the affronted continental nations.[70] Nevertheless, when in mid-August

NARA, RG 260, records maintained for Military Governor, 1945–9, box 22, Clay to AGWAR, Aug. 1946; NARA, RG 153, entry 1018, Nürnberg administrative files, 1944–9, box 1, Petersen to Taylor, 17 June 1946; Fahy to Secretary of State (State Dept.), 24 July 1946.

[66] Memo for President from Jackson, 13 May 1946, cited in Taylor, *Final Report*, 276–9, appendix J.

[67] NARA, RG 107, Assistant Secretary of War, correspondence of Howard Petersen, 1945–7, box 2, file ASW 000.5, 'War crimes, criminals', Fahy to Secretary of State, 24 July 1946; memorandum for the Assistant Secretary of War from Gunn, 5 Aug. 1946.

[68] NARA, RG 153, Nürnberg administrative files, 1944–9, box 1, Fahy to Secretary of State, 24 July 1946; NARA, RG 260, records maintained for Military Governor, entry 3, box 22, Clay to AGWAR, Aug. 1946; PRO, FO 371/57584, Dean to Shawcross, 16 May 1946.

[69] NARA, RG 107, Assistant Secretary of War, correspondence of Howard Petersen, 1945–7, box 2, file ASW 000.5, 'War crimes, criminals', memo for the Secretary of War from Rusk, 6 Aug. 1946.

[70] NARA, RG 153, Nürnberg administrative files, 1944–9, box 1, memo from Taylor to Secretary of War, 29 July 1946. For State and War Dept. concerns, see NARA, RG 107, Assistant Secretary of War, correspondence of Howard Petersen, 1945–7, box 2, file ASW 000.5, 'War crimes, criminals', Petersen to Taylor, 17 June 1946; memo for the Secretary of War from Rusk, 6 Aug. 1946.

news filtered through to London that Taylor had been instructed to cease negotiations about the second trial pending further instructions,[71] the Foreign Office
now seized the initiative for the first time in the trial deliberations. Bevin raised
the trial issue with Byrnes at a conference in Paris. He reiterated the moral im-
pediments to open British opposition to further proceedings but suggested that,
were the Americans to take the lead against it, British support would be forthcoming.[72] He was at pains to stress that His Majesty's Government was not opposed to the trial of industrialists *per se*, but wished to see them tried in zonal
proceedings.

American convergence was predictable: Byrnes declared that not only were he
and his department at odds with the present plan, but the President and large
portions of the American judiciary concurred. He reputedly confided that there
was also vocal opposition from American business leaders to an international
trial of industrialists.[73] In the second half of September, Jackson asked the State
Department to notify the other powers of the official US opposition to the trial;
and in the next month he submitted his final report to Truman formalizing his
position. In the meantime the Foreign Office received a request from the Americans for the extradition from British custody of six industrialists, including Alfried Krupp, and three other suspects, for trial in the subsequent Nuremberg
programme.[74]

1.6 UNEQUAL PROGRESSIONS: THE COURSES OF BRITISH AND AMERICAN
     TRIAL POLICY FROM 1946

The granting of the American extradition request—after a brief period, during
which the IMT's acquittal of Schacht confirmed British fears about the wisdom
of trying industrialists—signified the victory of the zonal trials option.[75] The
USA consequently issued notes in January 1947 to its erstwhile confederates to
the effect that further proceedings before the IMT were 'not required'. 'German
war criminals', it was held, could be tried 'more expeditiously . . . in national or
occupation courts.' Moreover, the first two trials to be conducted under CCL10
were by that time in full swing; and, as it was quite reasonably pointed out, that
law defined crimes very similarly to the IMT Charter.[76]

---

[71] NARA, RG 260, OMGUS, Adjutant-General's decimal files, 1945–8, box 2, AGWAR to OMGUS
(Clay), 16 Aug. 1946.
[72] National Library of Wales, papers of Lord Elwyn Jones, hereafter Elwyn Jones papers, C14, Elwyn
Jones to Warren, 9 Aug. 1946; Scott-Fox to Reed, 15 Aug. 1946; Taylor, *Final Report*, 25–6.
[73] PRO, LCO 2/2989, Scott-Fox to Reed, 18 Aug. 1946; Elwyn Jones papers, C14, Elwyn Jones to
Shawcross, 22 Aug. 1946.
[74] PRO, FO 937/143, secret memo from Permanent Secretary FO, 16 Sept. 1946; PRO, LCO 2/2989,
Garner to Hartley Shawcross, 2 Oct. 1946; telegram from Control Commission for Germany, Berlin, to
COGA, 21 Sept. 1946.
[75] PRO, FO 937/143, FO minute, 17 Oct. 1946; PRO, LCO 2/2989, Sargeant to Lord Chancellor, 23
Oct. 1946; PRO, FO 371/57583, minute by Beaumont, 13 Apr. 1946.
[76] Taylor, *Final Report*, 27, appendix K, 285, substance of note addressed to London, Moscow, and
Paris embassies, 22 Jan. 1947.

If it was now clear that the way ahead involved reliance on national initiatives alone, it was also to become apparent that concomitantly there was little in the way of concerted pressure on the individual countries to pursue trial programmes. This was perhaps the major weakness of the quadripartite system compared with further full international co-operation. Taylor had been informed by the British JAG in July 1946 that the latter intended to pursue a programme of trials in the British zone which was to be 'roughly parallel' to that in the American zone, and prisoner exchange was to facilitate a 'division of business' in this regard.[77] However, though the subsequent Nuremberg proceedings under CCL10 were supposedly an expression of international law, the British were swift to dissociate themselves from responsibility for these trials.[78] They themselves declined to try under CCL10, predictably choosing to work exclusively through the War Office within the limited parameters of the Royal Warrant. Meanwhile, by Cabinet decision of November 1946, the Government was looking to begin winding down the whole process of war crimes trials.[79]

The surrender of prisoners was not an expression of the desire to begin a reciprocal process of exchange of suspected 'major' war criminals in a harmonious trial programme.[80] As had been observed within the Foreign Office several months previously, if Britain's allies chose to indict industrialists, this did not necessarily bind the British to do likewise. Their only obligation was to transfer on request suspects whom they did not intend to try themselves.[81] Thus the letter of CCL10 triumphed over the spirit, and Alfried Krupp was tried at Nuremberg, despite the fact that the nerve-centre of his operations—the Ruhr—lay in the British zone of occupation.

The transfer of the first batch of suspects to the US authorities proved to be the thin end of the wedge, as the British proceeded to offload the responsibilities of trying many prominent individuals. This phenomenon contributed in no small way to the form of the US trial programme. Aside from Alfried Krupp, and the majority of his co-defendants who featured in the tenth subsequent Nuremberg trial, the British contributed Otto Ohlendorf,[82] Oswald Pohl,[83] and Erhard Milch, respectively the chief defendants in Trials Nine and Four, and the only defendant in case 2. Defendants, and evidence concerning them, were transferred from British custody for trial in the first of the subsequent proceedings, the Doctor's trial.[84] Likewise a case in preparation against members of Amtsgruppe D ('office-group' D: the Inspectorate of Concentration Camps) of the

[77] John F. Kennedy Library, Boston, MA, papers of Drexel Sprecher, hereafter 'Sprecher papers', box 57, file 'Administrative matters', memorandum for all section heads from Taylor, 23 July 1946.
[78] Robert K. Woetzel, *The Nuremberg Trials in International Law* (London: Stevens, 1960), 219–26.
[79] PRO, PREM 8/391, CM (46) 94th conclusions, 4 Nov. 1946.
[80] Ibid. minute 2, 4 Nov. 1946.
[81] PRO, FO 371/57583, Newton to Shawcross, 26 Mar. 1946; PRO, LCO 2/2989, Sargeant to Lord Chancellor, 23 Oct. 1946.
[82] PRO, WO 309/1455 contains a series of extradition requests, including one for Ohlendorf.
[83] Taylor, *Final Report*, 77–8.
[84] Paul Weindling, 'The Anatomy of the Nuremberg Medical Trial,' presented at 'Nuremberg

SS Business and Administration Head Office was handed over to the Americans for incorporation in the Pohl trial.[85] In fact, the majority of the twelve trials sported defendants surrendered by the British,[86] signifying an imbalance in commitment.

There was no organization even approximately parallel to the OCCWC in existence within the British occupation set-up, and certainly no initiatives emanating from the Foreign Office; this left further prosecution of war criminals within the sole purview of the JAG. It should be borne in mind that the only weapon *vis-à-vis* the mass criminality of Nazi Germany was the limited Royal Warrant. This statute precluded the trial of anyone who could not be linked with the direct commission of atrocities, and thereby many of the administrators of Nazi policies who were targeted at Nuremberg.

At the other end of the criminal spectrum the British authorities, like the Americans, adopted a realistic stance and put most of the members of the criminal organizations through the ordinary denazification courts, which could impose maximum sentences of ten years.[87] Thousands who were judged 'comparatively innocuous' were released without trial. Particularly 'hard core' suspects went through quasi-civil courts constituted under British judges by the British Element of the Allied Control Council for Germany (CCG[BE]).[88] Many crimes by Germans against other Germans, including Jews, and stateless persons, were tried by German courts themselves.

The cases tried under the Royal Warrant were, like the analogous Dachau programme, concerned solely with substantive crimes, though membership of a criminal organization could also be charged against many of the defendants in either series.[89] Other than the 'Belsen' trials, the British conducted trials of the staff of the Neuengamme concentration camp and its sub-camps, and against the personnel of the Ravensbrück women's camp. A series of lesser-known camps, collectively designated the Emsland group,[90] were also the subject of trials conducted by the CCG(BE). The Ravensbrück case was unusual in that the camp was situated beyond the British zone, in Soviet-occupied territory; several suspects were ultimately handed over to the Soviets for trial. (The investigative effort concerned medical experiments that had been conducted at the camp, and

Medical Trial Symposium', Linacre College, Oxford, 14 Mar. 1997; id. 'From International to Zonal Trials: The Origins of the Nuremberg Medical Trial', *Holocaust and Genocide Studies* (forthcoming).

[85] PRO, WO 311/435, A. G. Somerhough to War Crimes Investigation Unit, HQ, BAOR, 25 Oct. 1946.

[86] The names of extradited defendants who appeared in Cases 3, 5, 9, and 10 may be found in the Sprecher papers, box 57, file 'Administrative matters.'

[87] PRO, FO 371/64713, c8815/7675/180, FO brief for Secretary of State, 2 June 1947.

[88] PRO, FO 371/64712, draft report of Lord Chancellor on war crimes trials, comments on draft report by Dean *et al.*, 5 June 1947.

[89] British courts did not, however, generally choose to impose sentences on the 'mere fact' that defendants held high rank in criminal organizations. PRO, WO 309/1674, quarterly report of legal section WCG(NWE) Oct.–Dec. 1947.

[90] A brief description of the Emsland camps may be found in Eugen Kogon, *Der SS-Staat: Das System der Deutschen Konzentrationslager* (Frankfurt am Main: Europäische Verlagsanstalt, 1961), 39–40.

the prosecution was a rare effort to complement actions of OCCWC in the overlapping Nuremberg 'Doctor's Trial'.)[91] The other major categories of trial under the Royal Warrant were against the personnel of several Gestapo prisons and Arbeitserziehungslager (the murderous 'work education camps' to which forced foreign labourers deemed to be 'slacking' were sent) and against the murderers or maltreaters of British soldiers and airmen.[92]

The limited trial programme would court little diplomatic controversy and would be comparatively cheap, dealing more and more with localized offences and lower-ranking defendants. With the passage of time the trials were also increasingly limited to prosecuting atrocities against British servicemen. Most of the little interest—apart from antipathy—regarding the trials shown by the British public was on matters relating directly to Britain, and, understandably, the Government felt a particular duty to investigate these. Priscilla Dale Jones illustrates that the pursuit until the end of 1948 of the murderers of fifty British airmen at Stalag Luft III (a POW camp in Silesia) in March 1944 was vital in the prolongation of the British trial programme. Immortalized subsequently in the Hollywood film *The Great Escape*, the Stalag Luft murders held the interest of the British public like no other case, and consumed a great part of the time and budget of the war crimes investigation unit.[93]

The emphasis on such crimes was one manifestation of the consistent tightening of the parameters of the Royal Warrant programme. At the very beginning of that programme responsibility was jettisoned by the War Office for cases pertaining to concentration camps that were not in the British zone, apart from parts of the Ravensbrück case. Further, in attempting to process more trials, and to give the impression of greater activity—as in the matter of confusing numbers of cases and individuals tried—suggestions were made about trying easier, more trivial cases. Likewise, owing to criticism of the length of time the 'Belsen' trial had taken, it was proposed to divide large cases into smaller ones that could be disposed of more speedily, though the whole would then in fact take longer.[94]

The idea of prioritizing trivial crimes was rejected, and it seems that, by the lights of the British prosecutors at least, emphasis remained on the more serious ones.[95] The principle of division of cases was, however, applied, as for instance in the prosecution of the subsidiary 'Belsen' trials and the Neuengamme case.[96] These deliberations were closely related to the issue of ending the trial

[91] Weindling, 'From International to Zonal Trials', 7.

[92] See e.g. PRO, WO 309/1674, quarterly reports of legal section WCG(NWE), July–Sept. 1947, Oct.–Dec. 1947. On the Arbeitserziehungslager: Ulrich Herbert, *Hitler's Foreign Workers: Enforced Foreign Labour in Germany under the Third Reich* (Cambridge: Cambridge University Press, 1997), 338–40.

[93] PRO, FO 371/64723, c15911/7675/180, Barratt to O'Grady, 9 Dec. 1947; Priscilla Dale Jones, 'Nazi Atrocities against Allied Airmen: Stalag Luft III and the End of British War Crimes Trials', *Historical Journal*, 41 (1998), 543–65.

[94] PRO, WO 309/1, cable, WO to HQ 21 Army Group, BAOR, 19 June 1945; WO 309/1, Chilton to WO, 16 Dec. 1945; C.-in-C. Rhine Army to Under-Secretary of State WO and JAG, 3 Nov. 1945.

[95] PRO, FO 371/64718, c13471/7675/180, note on policy by Shapcott, 15 Oct. 1947.

[96] PRO, WO 309/1, C.-in-C. of BAOR to Under-Secretary of State WO and JAG, 3 Nov. 1945.

programme *in toto*, a question that was debated from almost as soon as trials began, in autumn 1945.[97] The investigators and prosecutors were worked to impossible deadlines to expedite the conclusion of what, with the passage of time, was nevertheless becoming an increasingly controversial aspect of Allied occupation policy both in Germany and Britain.[98]

By Cabinet decision of November 1946, the British Government was looking to wind down the whole process of war crimes trials.[99] Working through new cases and the backlog of old ones was a lengthy process, and it was only in April 1948 that a time limit was set on the trial programme. All proceedings were to be completed by 1 September 1948. Beyond that date extradition requests would only be granted subject to the provision of prima-facie evidence of murder as defined under German law.[100]

Predictably, Cold War pressures topped the political agenda. In addition—and the two factors are certainly not unrelated—the resources at the disposal of the investigating and prosecuting units were meagre. They were experiencing severe manpower and financial shortages. The general British austerity drive of the post-war years was particularly acute in the occupation budget. Moreover, staff shortages resulting from demobilization were experienced almost as soon as trial preparations began in 1945.[101] Manpower limitations also resulted in difficulties in locating both the accused and relevant witnesses.[102] Finally, speedy progress was further hindered by technical problems relating to the unusual nature of war crimes trial procedure.[103]

In any case, ending the trials became a policy aim. As such, it was pursued administratively according to the same principles as any other executive action. There are notable instances of opposition from British legal personnel in Germany, but the structural-political emphasis was clearly on the side of closure. The populations of the civilian internment camps that contained suspected war criminals were radically reduced by extradition and also by the wholesale release of suspects who were not requested by any nation—810 in the last quarter of 1947, for instance.[104] Some cases were handed over by the war crimes staff to the Control Commission tribunals, some ultimately to German courts. Many

[97] Dale Jones, 'Nazi Atrocities against Allied Airmen', 548.

[98] PRO, WO 309/1, fo. 28, minute of 30 Oct. 1945; WO 309/1642, Deputy Military Governor's Office, CCG(BE) to regional commissioners, n.d., on British and German desire to end the whole process of trials generally.

[99] PRO, PREM 8/391, CM (46) 94th conclusions, 4 Nov. 1946.

[100] Establishing such a prima-facie case was by no means straightforward. For the peculiarities of German law in this connection, see e.g., Broszat, 'Siegerjustiz oder strafrechtliche Selbstreinigung', 480–1. For the potential abuses of this system, see below, Chapter 5.

[101] PRO, WO 309/1, cable, WO to HQ 21 Army Group, BAOR, 19 June 1945.

[102] Ibid. fo. 42, BAOR to WO, May 1946.

[103] Ibid. fo. 27, minute of 12 Nov. 1945 (signature illegible).

[104] PRO, WO 309/1674, quarterly report of legal section WCG(NWE), Oct.–Dec. 1947. For the inadequate screening processes of the British occupiers, see Tom Bower, *Blind Eye to Murder: Britain, America and the Purging of Nazi Germany—A Pledge Betrayed* (London: Andre Deutsch, 1981); Weindling, 'From International to Zonal Trials', 2.

criminals would then run free or face lenient judgement, but at all times the British legal machinery in Germany could point to the fact that it was stretched to deal with those suspects under investigation.

The situation was markedly different in the American zone. With an unfavourable conclusion to part of the military case before the IMT, and a false start in the pursuit of the industrialists, much remained to be done by the OCCWC, which was still enamoured of the idea of prosecuting a criminal conspiracy to wage criminal war. OCCWC devoted three of the twelve trials in the subsequent Nuremberg series to culpable industrialists; two others had large economic connections.[105] Further, two of the trials concentrated on the crimes of the Wehrmacht. The onset of both of these sets of cases brought with it the proposition of further British involvement in joint proceedings, both as a means of sharing the economic burden of trial and increasing the moral weight of the prosecution. Each time the British response was resoundingly in the negative.

1.7 THE DEVELOPMENT OF THE OCCWC

In retrospect at least, the divergence between the intentions of the British and the Americans for the continued prosecution of major war criminals was discernible long before the latter part of 1946. The development of Taylor's role has been described; and in the time before his official designation as Jackson's deputy a 'Subsequent Proceedings Division' was already in existence within OCCPAC. To this body were seconded staff no longer required in the IMT case, enabling rudimentary preparations for further proceedings, in whatever form they might take, to be made from the beginning of 1946. This personnel was supplemented by a recruitment drive in the US by Taylor, and by the end of October 1946, when the OCCWC effectively replaced OCCPAC, the division was 400 strong. (At the height of its powers a year later the OCCWC had 1,774 staff.)[106]

Taylor claims that by April 1946—scarcely a month after Foreign Office officials had advocated a policy of 'slowing down' as much as possible the activities of the Subsequent Proceedings Division—the broad outlines of the future Nuremberg programme had been drawn.[107] Such expedition was vital in securing the objectives of the American trial programme, for if the trials were to serve a re-educative end, laying bare the Nazi past while exhibiting the virtues of fair trial

---

[105] The Krupp, Flick, and Farben trials fall into the first category, the Milch and Ministries cases into the second.

[106] NARA, RG 260, OCCWC administrative division records, 1946–9, box 2, file 'Personnel general', memo for Jackson from Taylor, 30 Jan. 1946; Taylor, *Final Report*, 10–14, 43–4; Dodd papers, box 319, file 'General memoranda 1945 Oct.–1946 Apr.', general memorandum no. 3, 'Subsequent proceedings division', 12 Jan. 1946.

[107] Elwyn Jones papers, C11, Dean to Newton, 15 Mar. 1946, advising a 'go very slow' policy; and undated correspondence (which the content and context suggest is from later in Mar.) between Phillimore and Dean advocating the view of 'slowing down' American action. See also Taylor, *Final Report*, 15.

within a democratic system, justice had to be seen to be done quickly. Delays and drawn-out trials inevitably meant the gradual loss of interest of the German— not to mention the American and British—population, and a concomitant growth in cynicism about the whole process.[108] Thus in September 1946 OMGUS's stated aim was the completion of the subsequent proceedings by the end of 1947.[109] This was compatible with a speculative schedule suggested by Taylor of prosecuting 266 individuals in thirty-six trials.[110]

Preparations in the Subsequent Proceedings Division were such that by the end of the brief interlude between the conclusion of the IMT case and the resurgence of French pressure for a second international trial, the Americans were able to present their former Allies with the aforementioned *fait accompli*. They had filed an indictment against one group of suspects the day after the formal establishment of the OCCWC, begun proceedings in the first two trials under CCL10 before the year was out, and were confident enough to describe other cases in the pipeline as 'very well developed'. The intention was to have six military courts functioning concurrently, and, in March 1947, Taylor submitted modified though still ambitious plans for a programme of between fifteen and eighteen trials.[111]

1.8 THE OCCWC AND THE FOREIGN OFFICE (I): THE INDUSTRIALISTS

The shape of the Subsequent Proceedings Division was subject to frequent change. As investigations on the locations of criminality progressed and the numbers of prospective defendants increased, the original six groups were merged and altered or further subdivided. This pattern of fluctuation was sustained in the organization of the OCCWC throughout its existence. An impression of this flux and of the multiplication of American responsibilities can be gleaned through an overview of one of the pillars of the subsequent trial programme: the prosecution of industrialists and financiers.[112]

In mid-May, the staff of the subsequent proceedings division was divided into six groups assigned to investigation of different areas of criminality within the Third Reich. Two of them were concerned with industry and finance. One of these was charged with the preparation of the evidence against Alfried Krupp and the top officials of IG Farben; the men whom the Americans would suggest

---

[108] Buscher, *The US War Crimes Program*, 2; Taylor, *Final Report*, 76; *The Papers of General Lucius D. Clay: Germany, 1945–1949*, ed. Jean Edward Smith, 2 vols. (Bloomington, Indianapolis: University of Indiana Press, 1974), i, 261–2 Clay for Echols, 4 Sept. 1946.

[109] *Clay Papers*, ed. Smith, i, 261–2, Clay to War Department, 23 Aug. 1946.

[110] Bower, *Blind Eye to Murder*, 391.

[111] Taylor, *Final Report*, 15–21, 80–1; NARA, RG 153, entry 1018, Nürnberg administrative files, 1944–9, box 1, 'Draft precis', 16 Aug. 1946; Sprecher papers, box 51, file 'Trial preparation', Sprecher to Ervin, 31 Dec. 1946. The first indictment to be filed was in the Medical trial: that case and the proceedings against Field Marshal Erhard Milch were in progress before the end of 1946. The 'well-developed' cases were those which would form the bases of the Farben, Flick, and Krupp trials.

[112] The prosecution of sections of the SS is examined in Chapter 5, below.

two months later to be part of the select band of defendants to appear in a second international trial. (Taylor had allocated the preliminary responsibilities to his staff because of the amount of work already done on the Krupps in anticipation before the trial of Göring *et al.*, and because of the general US interest in the chemical producers as a result of their associations with the likes of Standard Oil of New Jersey.)[113] With the dissolution of the IMT, the evidence thus gathered could be marshalled quickly and easily into the presentation of an all-American case under CCL10.

Other individual industrialists fell under the purview of the second Subsequent Proceedings Division economic group, including Friedrich Flick, suspected of exploiting slave labour, of the spoliation of property in France and the Soviet Union, and the 'aryanization' of Jewish industrial plant.[114] The lines of battle were more clearly defined during 1946, as more evidence and suspects were located or transferred and the prospect of another international trial dimmed. By the end of that year, now as part of the OCCWC, trial teams emerged from the task forces. The Krupp-Farben group was divided and the contingent parts enlarged into Trial Teams III and I, respectively, and the other group came to focus specifically on Flick and his associates, as Team II, while retaining responsibilities for other economic concerns.[115]

When Taylor submitted his speculative programme in March 1947, the indictment had been filed in the Flick case, the smallest and least complicated of the economic trials. The number of defendants to be incorporated in the forthcoming Farben and Krupp trials—and hence their total scope—had yet to be decided; and there was a proposed trial of officials of the Dresdner Bank. In addition, two other trials touched upon relevant issues: a military-economic case already in progress against Field Marshall Erhard Milch, including evidence of slave labour, and a projected case against a series of government officials and related industrial concerns, including members of the Hermann Göring works.[116]

Two months later the situation was further clarified. An indictment had been served against twenty-four IG Farben officials and estimates were posted of the number of defendants in the Krupp, Dresdner Bank, and government officials-industrialists cases. At this time, the number of individuals either convicted (Milch, with a life sentence), on trial, or predicted to be indicted with substantial financial or industrial connections was between fifty-nine and seventy-one, out

---

[113] NARA, RG 260, administrative division records, 1946–9, box 2, file 'Subsequent proceedings division', organizational memo no. 1, 17 May 1946; RG 107, Assistant Secretary of War, correspondence of Howard Petersen, 1945–7, box 2, file ASW 000.5, 'War crimes, criminals', Taylor to Petersen, 22 May 1946. For details on Farben's international links, see e.g. Joseph Borkin, *The Crime and Punishment of I. G. Farben* (New York: Free Press, 1978).

[114] Sprecher papers, box 57, file 'Administrative matters', inter-office memo, 27 June 1946.

[115] Sprecher papers, box 51, Sprecher to Ervin, 31 Dec. 1946.

[116] NARA, RG 153, Nürnberg administrative files, 1944–9, box 13, Taylor to Chief of Staff, OMGUS, 14 Mar. 1947.

of a total of approximately 220 projected defendants of all kinds. The total number of cases to be tried was now tentatively established as sixteen.[117]

Conversely, on 18 January 1947, the BWCE was dissolved.[118] Within a month of that date, members of the UNWCC had criticized the British government for its 'disappointingly slow progress' in the matter of trials.[119] The lack of British enthusiasm had not gone unnoticed by the overworked Americans either; nor had the absence of interest displayed by His Majesty's Government in the ongoing trials at Nuremberg. This undermining of quadripartite solidarity, it was feared, would magnify Allied divisions over the future of Germany, and invite German criticism of inequality of treatment between the zones.[120] Telford Taylor observed as much in a tersely worded letter to the former BWCE member Elwyn Jones. To reinvigorate the British, Taylor suggested a contribution, alongside the French and Russians, to the prosecution in the forthcoming trial at Nuremberg of Alfried Krupp and associates before an American bench.[121]

There is some confusion about the exact reasoning behind the almost inevitable rebuttal of Taylor's proposition. The Foreign Office maintained that it simply did not wish to embroil Britain in another lengthy trial; Taylor himself claimed that the opposition reflected dubiousness about an enforced collaboration with the French and Soviets, even though the alliance would be under the direction of the OCCWC. From what we know of British policy at this time, either of these reasons alone would have been sufficient to discount British participation, and it is likely that both played their part. (It is also reasonable to project that the interested US government departments were chary of French, and particularly Soviet, involvement.) In any case, wilful amnesia seems to have been the basis for the Foreign Office rationale that 'the Americans [could] have no possible complaint on this score since it was perfectly open to them to propose that the industrialists should be tried on an international basis had they wished to do so'.[122]

In a move acknowledged within Foreign Office circles as a palliative to OMGUS, an official British 'observer', Gordon Hilton, was sent to Nuremberg in April on a three-month renewable tenure. Hartley Shawcross expressed his reservations about the value of sending a mere observer and about the motivation behind the decision to do so, and these doubts were proven to be well founded when, within two weeks of his departure, Hilton declared that he would rather

---

[117] NARA, RG 260, administrative division records, 1946–9, box 2, file 'Program—war crimes trials', Taylor to Chief of Staff, OMGUS, 20 May 1947.

[118] Sprecher papers, box 54, file 'Foreign delegations', memo dated Nuremberg, 13 May 1948, p. 7.

[119] J. H. Hoffman, 'German Field Marshals as War Criminals? A British Embarrassment', *Journal of Contemporary History*, 23 (1988), 17–36, esp. 18–19.

[120] NARA, RG 107, Assistant Secretary of War, correspondence of Howard Petersen, 1945–7, box 2, file ASW 000.5, 'War crimes, criminals', memo for McCarthy from Gunn, 26 July 1946; NARA, RG 153, entry 1018, Nürnberg administrative files, 1944–9, box 1, OCCWC to War Crimes Branch, 13 Oct. 1947.

[121] PRO, FO 371/66564, Elwyn Jones to Bevin, 24 Jan. 1947.

[122] PRO, LCO 2/2989, Henniker to Addis, 6 Feb. 1947.

be sent home on unpaid leave than remain in Nuremberg.[123] He eventually left Germany after witnessing the three trials of industrialists, and his hand-written reports of the issues he deemed noteworthy are indicative of the concerns of the Foreign Office. His elucidation of the Farben trial, for instance, was predominantly concerned with the extent and nature of the collaboration of British industrial concerns with the giant chemical combine in the pre-war years. It cast into sharp relief the revelations of the courtroom, which witnessed much documentary and verbal testimony on the wider human concerns of the trial—the murderous exploitation of slave labour and the involvement of IG Farben with the Nazi preparations for war.[124]

Hilton was dubious about the utility of his own position, and equivocal about the trials themselves. He also expressed his concern about the 'background of transatlantic politics which an observer sitting in Nuremberg cannot easily interpret'. His solution: that 'the dollar stringency affords an opportune reason for withdrawing the British observer'.[125] (There was mileage in this excuse, as Britain was then undergoing a financial crisis of some magnitude.)

Thus British involvement was half-hearted, and demonstrably so. The grand total of those attached to the British Nuremberg delegation after the formation of the OCCWC was seven, compared with seventy-two French personnel, and eight representatives each from Czechoslovakia, the Netherlands, and Greece.[126] Nevertheless, the issue of some sort of commitment by the UK to the ongoing Nuremberg adventure did not depart with Hilton. The context was the second half of 1947, when OCCWC was involved in preparations for what would turn out to be the twelfth and last of the subsequent proceedings. This case was officially entitled the 'Trial of Wilhelm von Leeb and thirteen others' and concerned high-ranking officers in the Wehrmacht. Its advent interrupted the winding-down of the British Royal Warrant programme.

1.9 THE OCCWC AND THE FOREIGN OFFICE (II): THE MILITARY

Although the IMT's acquittal of the General Staff and High Command was not consonant with the conspiracy-criminal organization vision, the accompanying opinion was encouraging and left the Americans with considerable latitude in pursuing individual members of the armed forces. The IMT declared that, though they were not a group as such, 'they were certainly a ruthless military caste', and that 'where the facts warrant it, these men should be brought to trial

---

[123] PRO, FO 937/143, FO minute, 17 Oct. 1946; Burns to Wilberforce, 14 Apr. 1947; Hilton to Brown, 1 Dec. 1947; PRO, FO 371/66564, Shawcross to Sargeant, 2 Jan. 1947.

[124] Report in PRO, FO 937/143. On the revelations about the Holocaust in the Farben trial, see Andrzej Pankowicz, 'Das KL Auschwitz in den Nürnberger Prozessen', *Hefte von Auschwitz*, 18 (1990), 247–367.

[125] PRO, FO 937/143, Hilton to Brown, 1 Dec. 1947.

[126] Sprecher papers, box 54, file 'Foreign delegations', memo dated Nuremberg, 13 May 1948, p. 5. There was no Soviet delegation.

so that those among them who are guilty of these crimes should not escape punishment'.[127]

By October 1947, Taylor's staff considered that they had prepared a case based on 'conclusive evidence of serious and large scale violations of [the] rules of war' against a group of such men. These were the members of the High Commands of the Army, the Navy, and the Air Force, and of the separate High Command of the Wehrmacht (Oberkommando der Wehrmacht; OKW).[128] The indictment was to include counts relating to the conspiracy and the waging of aggressive war. Though it was ultimately to be a trial of thirteen individuals,[129] Taylor made it clear that he considered the men arraigned for this so-called 'High Command' trial to be representative of the institutions from which they were drawn;[130] and there was a marked similarity between many of the charges in that case and those previously levelled at Keitel and Jodl. (See Chapter 1.2, above.)

If there was one factor distinguishing the new trial from the relevant parts of the IMT case, it was the existence of substantial new evidence against the OKW. An important part of this evidence went to discredit the testimonies of three of the chief witnesses to appear in the trial of the German military before the IMT, and indeed to implicate these same men heavily.[131] These revelations were valuable ammunition in the fight against German militarism, enabling the Americans to expose the German public to the 'falseness of German military protestations of honor [and] chivalry'.[132] The three witnesses concerned were Field Marshals Walter von Brauchitsch, Gerd von Rundstedt, and Erich von Manstein, and they had featured on American provisional lists of defendants in a High Command trial since early 1947.[133] The cases against Manstein and Rundstedt were thought to be 'overwhelming'—the strongest against any potential defendants—and though marginally less complete, the chance of Brauchitsch's conviction was deemed 'as certain as the outcome of a lawsuit ever can be'.[134]

[127] *IMT*, i, 278–9.

[128] NARA, RG 153, entry 1018, Nürnberg administrative files, 1944–49, box 1, OCCWC to War Crimes Branch, 13 Oct. 1947, pp. 1–2; Taylor to Chief of Staff, OMGUS, 14 Mar. 1947, p. 3.

[129] Fourteen men were indicted in the High Command trial. One, Johannes Blaskowitz, committed suicide on 5 Feb. 1948.

[130] NARA, RG 153, entry 1018, Nürnberg administrative files, 1944–9, box 13, Taylor to Deputy Military Governor, OMGUS, 14 Mar. 1947, p. 3.

[131] NARA, RG 153, entry 1018, Nürnberg administrative files, 1944–9, box 13, OCCWC to War Crimes Branch, 13 Oct. 1947, p. 6. For a discussion of some of the evidence given by the soldiers for the IMT, see Manfred Messerschmidt, 'Vorwärtsverteidigung: Die "Denkschrift der Generäle" für den Nürnberger Gerichtshof', in Hannes Heer and Klaus Naumann (eds.), *Vernichtungskrieg: Verbrechen der Wehrmacht 1941 bis 1944* (Hamburg: HIS, 1995), 531–50.

[132] NARA, RG 153, entry 1018, Nürnberg administrative files, 1944–9, box 13, OCCWC to War Crimes Branch, 13 Oct. 1947, p. 6.

[133] NARA, RG 153, entry 1018, Nürnberg administrative files, 1944–9, box 13, Taylor to Chief of Staff, OMGUS, 14 Mar. 1947, p. 12; PRO, WO 309/1456, memo to Parker from Norma Ervin, 4 Feb. 1947. (Brauchitsch had been mooted as a military defendant in Nov. 1946; see *Stars and Stripes*, 14 Nov. 1946.)

[134] NARA, RG 153, entry 1018, Nürnberg administrative files, 1944–9, box 13, OCCWC to War Crimes Branch, 13 Oct. 1947, p. 3.

Moreover, the names of Rundstedt and Brauchitsch were considered by Taylor to be of 'far greater significance to the German people' than those of other prospective defendants, hence convictions would theoretically have a more significant impact in the re-educative process. Brauchitsch had been Commander in Chief of the German Army between February 1938 and December 1941, the occupier of the highest position that institution could offer, during the period of its most dramatic victories.[135] He was replaced by Hitler himself. Recalled from a brief retirement, before which he had been regarded by many as the 'symbolic first soldier of the Reich', Rundstedt had led the victorious invasion of Poland as Commander in Chief, East, and was chosen by Brauchitsch to lead the southernmost of the three forces designated for the invasion of the USSR. The so-called 'Army Group South' was assigned to the offensive in the region of the Ukraine.[136]

Meanwhile, Manstein, though not as senior, was regarded by the *cognoscenti* as being the outstanding military brain in the Wehrmacht, achieving universal acclaim both as a staff officer and as a field commander. In September 1941 he assumed command of the Eleventh Army, which operated independently in the extreme south of the Soviet Union. Fourteen months later, after a series of victories in the Crimea and his promotion to field marshal, Manstein took control of the newly formed Army Group 'Don', which was renamed forthwith as the reformed Army Group South.[137]

All three were heavily implicated in the issuing and distribution of criminal orders on the eastern front—in particular the so-called 'Commissar Order' and the 'Barbarossa Jurisdiction Decree'[138]—and in logistical support and assistance to the SS Einsatzgruppen, the itinerant killing squads deployed in the rear of the invading German armies to murder Jews and other 'racial' and political 'undesirables'. For our purposes, the other salient characteristic of the field marshals was that they were in British custody.[139]

The military had known of the OCCWC interest in the three since the beginning of 1947,[140] but had done little by way of investigation into their deeds. Hence, when in August 1947 Taylor forwarded some of the evidence gathered on

---

[135] Brian Bond, 'Brauchitsch', in Correlli Barnett (ed.), *Hitler's Generals* (New York: Quill and Morrow, 1989), 75–101, esp. 75–7, 94.

[136] Earl F. Ziemke, 'Rundstedt', in Correlli Barnett (ed.), *Hitler's Generals* (New York: Quill and Morrow, 1989), 179–97.

[137] Field Marshal Lord Carver, 'Manstein', in Correlli Barnett (ed.), *Hitler's Generals* (New York: Quill and Morrow, 1989), 221–48.

[138] The Commissar Order provided for the murder of the political agents attached to Red Army units; the Barbarossa Jurisdiction Decree removed the threat of punishment from German court martials for 'ideologically motivated' murders, and allowed for the immediate execution of 'suspect' elements.

[139] Rundstedt was officially an American prisoner; he had been loaned to the British for interrogation after his capture in May 1945, and had thereafter caused confusion at Nuremberg by declaring himself to be a British prisoner. For a more complete survey of the treatment of these soldiers from 1945–53, see Donald Bloxham, 'Punishing German Soldiers during the Cold War: The Case of Erich von Manstein', *Patterns of Prejudice*, 33, no. 4 (1999), 25–45.

[140] PRO, WO 309/1456, memo to Parker from Norma Ervin, 4 Feb. 1947.

the three field marshals and on one Colonel-General Adolf Strauss to Attorney General Hartley Shawcross, and General Clay did likewise to his temporary British opposite number, Air Marshal Sir Sholto Douglas,[141] it was a clear reminder of the British obligation to consider legal proceedings or, alternatively, to allow extradition to interested countries.

Taylor would probably have been happy with a positive response to either option. He favoured a third possibility above all, however. He considered that it might better serve the ethos of the zonal programme if Britain could be persuaded to participate in a joint trial, with their prisoners in the dock alongside those of the Americans. Thus the case would not only benefit from the better-known defendants, but also from the gesture of Allied solidarity in their prosecution.[142] Only one of these avenues appealed to the British Government.

The War Office Secretary, Frederick Bellenger, decided that extradition would be the most favourable solution to the problem. Financial and personnel constraints undoubtedly played their part in his decision, but Bellenger was demonstrably aware of the political connotations of the choice which faced his department in disposing of the three most notable Germans in British custody. He had quickly turned to the Foreign Office for advice, and ultimately handed over effective responsibility to that department. Bevin's officials concurred with Bellenger, as did the Lord Chancellor, William Jowitt. The tide of public opinion had turned against trials, they argued, and there was no sense in adding to an already overburdened schedule, and particularly not with a case of this magnitude.[143] A joint trial would similarly incur significant costs and a controversial embroilment. It would also associate the British with what Bellenger had disdainfully described as charges of a 'Nuremberg character';[144] the type of novel, 'political' tools which opponents of the Nuremberg trials readily seized upon.[145] Bevin's more diplomatic rebuttal suggested that he 'wished to avoid any further suggestion of collaboration with the USA to the exclusion of other countries'.[146]

Both Taylor and the British Government were to be disappointed by a decision of General Clay. Clay was under pressure to bring the Nuremberg trials to a close, and he informed the British that as the indictment in the OKW case was by this time complete, he was not inclined to prolong matters. He considered that the British had not pulled their weight in their trials programme and expressed

[141] Hoffman, 'German Field Marshals as War Criminals?', 17–18; NARA, RG 260, records of the Chief of Staff, box 1, Clay to Douglas, 19 Aug. 1947.

[142] NARA, RG 153, entry 1018, Nürnberg administrative files, 1944–9, box 1, OCCWC to War Crimes Branch, 13 Oct. 1947, pp. 2–6.

[143] Hoffman, 'German Field Marshals as War Criminals?', 18; PRO, LCO 2/2994, report of Elwyn Jones, 9 Oct. 1947; Rieu to Coldstream, 11 Oct. 1947.

[144] PRO, WO 311/648, Bellenger to Bevin, 3 Oct. 1947. Jowitt also considered it 'politically undesirable to institute trials for crimes against peace in British courts': see PRO, LCO 2/2994, Rieu to Coldstream, 11 Oct. 1947.

[145] See below, Chapter 4.

[146] PRO, LCO 2/2994, Reed to Attorney-General, 16 Oct. 1947.

concern at the fact that the decision to try the soldiers in Britain had not been made. To Taylor, he wrote the following on the impossibilities of incorporating the British prisoners in any way:

we are establishing our purpose in [the] trials of von Leeb, *et al.*, and while perhaps less known to the world, these field marshals were well known in Germany. At Nuremberg, we are establishing [a] precedent for [the] future and not aiming at specific individuals. History will make no distinction between a von Runstedt and a von Leeb.[147]

The British were thus no nearer to a solution at the end of 1947. In keeping with his attitude and that of his superior towards trials, the Deputy Military Governor Brian Robertson thought it best to drop the whole issue there and then.[148] The pressure for action once again came from Elwyn Jones and Shaw-cross. The former had examined the evidence and convinced the latter of its value, along with Bevin—who also sensed some moral imperative to trial—and the new Secretary of State for War, Emmanuel Shinwell.[149] Shawcross, more-over, felt the force of Telford Taylor's gaze upon him, the chief of counsel main-taining an active interest in the fate of the field marshals.[150]

Of the other interested parties, both the Lord Chancellor William Jowitt and the Foreign Office officials were equivocal. Appreciating that criticism might be forthcoming whatever decision was eventually made, the latter counselled only proceeding with criminal charges if convictions were likely.[151] Jowitt had begun to see trials as 'acts of vengeance rather than [the] administration of justice', and preferred to risk American criticism for not trying the men rather than running the gauntlet of domestic disapproval.[152]

It might have been possible discreetly to 'drop' the matter, but for a pair of extradition demands from Poland and the USSR, and a request from the OCCWC for the field marshals' presence at Nuremberg as witnesses in the High Command case. These all occurred in the first half of 1948 and by bringing the soldiers back into the limelight precipitated a final decision on the question of prosecution. The Polish Government wished to try von Brauchitsch and von Manstein, and the Soviets likewise von Rundstedt and von Manstein, in connec-tion with crimes committed in the invasion and occupation of those two coun-tries. In contrast to the response to the possibility of extradition to the

---

[147] NARA, RG 260, records of the Chief of Staff, Clay to Robertson, 7 Nov. 1947; PRO, LCO 2/2994, Rieu to Jowitt, 14 Oct. 1947; minutes of meeting in Jowitt's room, 15 Oct. 1947; *Clay Papers*, ed. Smith, i, 440–1, Clay to Taylor, 17 Oct. 1947. Clay was to be proved wrong here, as Chapter 4, below, illustrates.

[148] PRO, LCO 2/2994, Reed to Shawcross, 14 Nov. 1947. Robertson and Douglas saw the extent of German disdain for the trials.

[149] Hoffman, 'German Field Marshals as War Criminals?', 20–1; PRO, LCO 2/2994, Bevin to Jowitt, 2 Dec. 1947.

[150] PRO, LCO 2/2994, Taylor to Shawcross, 23 Oct. 1947.

[151] Hoffman, 'German Field Marshals as War Criminals?', 21.

[152] PRO, LCO 2/2994, Jowitt to Alexander, 3 Feb. 1948; Jowitt to Shawcross, 26 Nov. 1947; note of meeting of 22 Dec. 1947; Rieu to Coldstream, 11 Oct. 1947.

Americans, the British Government declined both of these requests. This can be attributed mainly to a legitimate distrust of Soviet legal procedure, and to more debatable concerns about Polish justice.[153] As Jowitt had put it some months earlier, and rather chauvinistically, handing the prisoners over 'to some of our eastern friends is equivalent to handing them over to be murdered'.[154]

It was, however, implicit in the official rejection of the extradition requests that the British intended to try the soldiers. The Cabinet therefore decided to proceed against them as a matter of preserving good faith.[155] This put an end to a scheme hatched in the Foreign Office under which the field marshals would have been kept in British custody until after the extradition deadline of 1 September 1948.[156] The legitimation for this prevarication would in all probability have been the medical condition of the four suspects.[157] Health considerations had been a factor in the case from early in 1948, and they still had an important role to play after the decision had been made to try.

Brauchitsch, Rundstedt, Manstein, and Strauss were all of advancing years,[158] and it was natural that they should experience some of the frailties of relative old age. Brauchitsch's health had clearly deteriorated the most and, in the light of a series of examinations in the first quarter of 1948, the Cabinet's decision to try the four had left his disposition subject to his prevailing medical state. As it transpired, he died of coronary thrombosis in October of that year.[159] The condition of each of the other three was in no way as clear cut, and in March 1948 a panel of Home Office doctors had declared them all fit for trial.[160] Yet by May 1949, as the long-winded legal preparations were still in progress, Strauss and Rundstedt were also discounted on medical grounds. In the event, Manstein alone was tried between the months of August and December 1949, two years after Taylor had forwarded the evidence concerning the officers, and three years after the conclusion of the IMT trial.

The road to the Manstein trial was long and twisted for a number of reasons. The prominence of the field marshal was clearly one, as was, relatedly, the series of pressures associated with the Cold War and, thirdly, perennial financial and personnel difficulties. Additionally, we can see a particular official and public disdain in Britain for trials of soldiers. This opposition was a subsection of a more general discontent with trials. Both forms of opposition will be expanded upon later, but they should be introduced now because they affected the shape of the British programme.

---

[153] PRO, PREM 8/1112, CM (48) 47th conclusions, 5 July 1948.

[154] PRO, LCO 2/2994, Jowitt to Alexander, 3 Feb. 1948.

[155] PRO, PREM 8/1112, CM (48) 47th conclusions, 5 July 1948.

[156] PRO, PREM 8/1112, Shinwell to Cabinet, 17 June 1948.

[157] Ibid. Shawcross to Cabinet, 22 June 1948.

[158] In June 1948 they were, respectively, 67, 73, 61, and 69 years old.

[159] PRO, PREM 8/1112, CM (48) 47th conclusions, 5 July 1948, memo to Cabinet from Shinwell, 28 Mar. 1949.

[160] Ibid. memo to Cabinet from Shawcross, 22 June 1948.

1.10 BRITISH DOMESTIC OPPOSITION TO THE TRIALS

Eleven soldiers of the rank of General or above had actually reached trial under the British before Manstein. This relatively large number may be attributed to the narrowness of the counts that could be brought under the Royal Warrant, which restricted the defendants substantially to members of Nazi military, para-military, or police formations. However, Manstein was of particular prominence, and the lateness of his trial made it a matter of import in a Germany that was re-asserting itself,[161] and in a Britain sensitive to the international climate.

One case study will serve as an illustration both of the general opposition to trials and of the nature of the specific brand of discontent with putting officers on trial. The events in question concern the fate of Field Marshal Albert Kessel-ring, formerly Commander in Chief of the German forces in Italy, who was sen-tenced to death in May 1947 by a British court in Venice for authorizing the reprisal murder of Italian citizens. A Conservative back-bencher pondered thus on Kesselring's fate: 'I suppose it is a just sentence but somehow as others it rather revolts me. It is time, I think, to end all of these trials of war criminals . . . I feel that enough has been done to show Germans how naughty they have been—more especially as the crimes they committed are no worse than those committed by the Russians.'[162]

More substantial protests began immediately after sentence had been passed. Churchill instantly telephoned Downing Street to lodge a complaint that it was too harsh. His grounds for concern in this case were an echo of those expressed by Field Marshal Alexander, that in the war as a whole 'Kesselring had fought fairly'.[163] Alexander had indeed doubted that such a 'fine and able general' was guilty of war crimes, and he asserted that 'the real people to blame were the SS of Hitler's Headquarters' (though, as he later admitted, he knew none of the details of the crime in question).[164]

Thus within two years of the end of the war, members of Britain's legislature and some of that nation's most prominent figures could argue an artificial div-ision between the criminality of the Wehrmacht and the SS, centring on the trad-itional standing of the former rather than its actions beyond the battlefield. Another politician could go further still and justify the ending of trials with an entirely spurious 'relativization' of Nazi atrocity *vis-à-vis* the actions of the So-viets. In the succeeding years, such beliefs, based upon professional military col-legiality or misapprehensions of Nazi criminality or extreme anti-Bolshevism, or any combination of these three, would only grow in strength.

---

[161] See below, Chapter 4, for an expansion of these points.

[162] Durham Records Office, Cuthbert Headlam diaries, D/He/42, fo. 127, 6 May 1947. I thank Nick Crowson for this reference.

[163] PRO, PREM 8/707, Rowan to Attlee, 6 May 1947; Alexander to Attlee, 8 May 1947; Churchill to Attlee, 13 May 1947.

[164] PRO, LCO 2/2994, Alexander to Jowitt, 3 Feb. 1948; Norman Hilton, *Alexander of Tunis: A Bio-graphical Portrait* (London: W. H. Allen, 1952), 217.

Active support for Manstein *et al.* was manifested in different ways. On a moral level, it entailed such niceties as the provision of a full-dress dinner in honour of 'Papa' Rundstedt—as he had come affectionately to be known by his British jailors—by the officers of British Army War Crimes Group, North West Europe, while he was *en route* to the venue of his aborted trial. This was the same group that had previously tried the executors of one of the criminal orders passed on by Rundstedt.[165] On a more practical plane, support involved the withdrawal of services of many of the staff of this group, so strongly did they feel against the prospective trial.[166]

In Parliament, two peers set up a public fund, to which Churchill was an early subscriber, to provide legal defence in this 'belated trial of an aged German general'. Two thousand pounds were raised in all. The lower house contributed two defence counsel free of charge. They were right-wing Labour MP Reginald Paget and one Samuel Silkin. (The latter was Jewish, a fact giving a spurious legitimacy to the claims of trial critics that legal proceedings were universally unpopular—even amongst those who could be identified with the victims of Nazism.)[167]

It seems, though, that the opposition to the Manstein trial achieved its greatest success indirectly, in the reduction of potential defendants from three to Manstein alone. It will be recalled that in March 1948 he, Runstedt, and Strauss were all found fit for trial. A year later a combined Home Office and Army board of doctors examined the three once more and found that only Manstein was now fit; and this despite the fact that a few days previously doctors at the soldiers' Münster Lager prison hospital had adjudged only Strauss unfit.[168] The conclusions of a Cabinet discussion on these findings averred that, although they had been unanimous, 'some of the details of the . . . reports were not very convincing'. Consequently, a trio consisting of Jowitt, Shawcross, and a medical expert were brought in to make the final decision as to who would be tried.[169]

That Manstein alone reached trial is to be attributed to the ultra-cautiousness of the experts. Given the proportions that the case had assumed, it would have been disastrous for the Labour Government both in domestic and foreign policy had one of the accused collapsed in the dock. This was certainly in the mind of Norman Brook of the Home Office when, in correspondence with Attlee, he questioned rhetorically whether 'the civilian doctors [would] have certified that these two Generals [*sic*] could not have stood their trial for murder in this coun-

---

[165] *News Chronicle*, 19 Feb. 1948; Bower, *Blind Eye to Murder*, 287.

[166] PRO, PREM 8/1112, Shinwell to Jowitt, 8 Nov. 1948.

[167] Reginal Paget, *Manstein: His Campaigns and His Trial* (London: William Collins, 1951), 71–4; Bower, *Blind Eye to Murder*, 293.

[168] PRO, PREM 8/1112, memo to Cabinet from Shinwell, 28 Mar. 1949: Bower, *Blind Eye to Murder*, 291.

[169] PRO, PREM 8/1112, CM (49), 24th conclusions, 31 Mar. 1949; CM (49), 32nd conclusions, 5 May 1949.

try'.[170] Likewise, Bevin confessed in the House of Commons that the 'escape' of Rundstedt and Strauss aroused in him a 'profound admiration for the medical profession'.[171] Finally, it should not be unduly surprising to learn that Rundstedt's lawyer did not consider his client's health to have deteriorated over the four and a half months since he had been officially charged;[172] nor that the field marshal lived for more than a decade after the year of his proposed trial.

So to the complex of legal, administrative, and foreign-political factors affecting the functioning of the British trial programme must be added that of a variety of 'principled' oppositions. These grew in influence in direct relation to the decline of active support for the cleansing of Germany and, as we shall see in more detail later, they shared many of their contentions with the nationalistic elements in that country in the post-war years. British policy-makers heeded both of these sets of voices, to the detriment of the purge. It remains to be asked what the comparable situation was in American trial policy.

1.11 THE POLITICS OF THE SUBSEQUENT NUREMBERG PROCEEDINGS

The OCCWC faced administrative problems in three related areas: those of time, money, and personnel. A perennial shortage of judges, combined with underestimates of the likely completion times of each trial, meant a growing backlog of cases. Budgetary pressures also built up as the series of trials dragged on. In consequence, Taylor's programme, which had grown in scope over the first six months of the existence of the OCCWC, had to be curtailed somewhat.

In May 1947, Taylor recorded his hope that the bulk of the sixteen proposed trials would be over by the end of 1947, though he considered that 'several' might continue through the early months of 1948.[173] It will be recalled that his goal was to have six tribunals functioning simultaneously, and it was upon this assumption that his time estimates were made. Clearly however, the number of tribunals in existence was itself contingent upon the supply of personnel from the US.

Judges, trial lawyers, linguists, and clerical personnel were required, and since Taylor had stipulated that the judges should be of 'high calibre', in order to command respect and to cope with the unusual nature of the proceedings,[174] adequate recruitment was by no means a foregone conclusion. It was particularly problematic given the decision by the US Chief Justice Fred Vinson that federal judges would not be granted leave to serve at Nuremberg, meaning that the state judiciaries would have to be combed for suitable candidates.[175] In fact, by May 1947 only four of the tribunals were in operation, and Taylor was waiting upon

[170] PRO, PREM 8/1112, Brook to Attlee, 30 Mar. 1949.
[171] *Hansard* (HC), col. 1590, 21 July 1949.
[172] LHCMA, LH 9/24/77, Grimm to Liddell Hart, 18 May 1949.
[173] NARA, RG 260, administrative division records, 1946–9, box 2, file 'Program—war crimes trials', Taylor to Chief of Staff, OMGUS, 20 May 1947.
[174] Ibid. file 'Conditions at Landsberg prison', Taylor to Jackson and Petersen, 2 Sept. 1946.
[175] Lucius D. Clay, *Decision in Germany* (Westport, Conn.: Westview, 1950), 251.

Washington for the remaining judges in order to start proceedings in two cases in which the indictments had already been filed.[176] By September of that year, despite the arrival of the additional judges, only seven cases were complete or in progress, with indictments filed in another three. Moreover, some of the incumbent judges had to leave for various reasons at the conclusion of the earlier trials.[177]

The number and complexity of the prospective trials and the shortage of judges made it improbable that the programme would be completed by any of the deadlines previously suggested. This threatened a considerable strain on the resources of the occupiers. The War Department had initially granted Taylor sufficient funds, by his estimate, to finance the OCCWC, the tribunals, the General Secretariat serving those tribunals, and the remainder of the IMT secretariat (*in situ* in order to supervise the publication of the records of that trial) until the end of the fiscal year 1947.[178] The pressure on the OCCWC from OMGUS increased concomitantly with the likelihood that both the funding and the time-span would prove inadequate. Thus, in the aftermath of Taylor's March outline programme, he was pointedly advised by the Deputy Military Governor Frank Keating—the man to whom he was officially responsible—of the unavailability of additional funds. 'No exceptions' could be made. Keating confessed to Clay that he issued the communication because Taylor was 'getting a bit out of hand',[179] and the subsequent removal of two projected trials from the OCCWC timetable was doubtless Taylor stepping somewhat back into line. This concession was to prove insufficient, however, for over the summer of 1947 'budgetary and time limitations' bore ever more heavily on the hard-pressed OCCWC.[180]

Clay was more accommodating than his deputy, having approved both the March and May plans.[181] Yet when he surveyed the situation in September, he acknowledged that the fulfilment of the May programme was 'impossible'. The War Department was only thought capable of providing a further six judges at the utmost; sufficient for only two more trials. A further condensation of the agenda was required, in order that the remaining cases could be opened before the end of the calendar year, in anticipation of concluding them all within that fiscal year.[182] (Even this can be interpreted as calculated generosity on Clay's part, for there was no guarantee that trials thus begun would finish in time, and no question of terminating a trial in progress; indeed, proceedings continued at

[176] NARA, RG 260, administrative division records, 1946–9, box 2, file 'Program—war crimes trials', Taylor to Chief of Staff, OMGUS, 20 May 1947.

[177] *Clay Papers*, ed. Smith, i, 420–1, Clay for Noce, 8 Sept. 1947.

[178] NARA, RG 260, administrative division records, 1946–9, box 2, file 'conditions at Landsberg prison', Clay to Taylor, 13 Sept. 1946; *Clay Papers*, ed. Smith, i, 265–9, Clay for Echols, 25 Sept. 1946.

[179] NARA, RG 260, records of the Chief of Staff, box 22, Keating to Taylor, 25 Mar. 1947; box 26, Keating to Clay, n.d.

[180] Taylor, *Final Report*, 81–2.

[181] NARA, RG 260, administrative division records, 1946–9, box 2, file 'Program—war crimes trials', Taylor to Chief of Staff, OMGUS, 20 May 1947; Taylor, *Final Report*, 81.

[182] *Clay Papers*, ed. Smith, i, 420–1, Clay for Noce, 8 Sept. 1947; 440–1, Clay for Taylor, 17 Oct. 1947; Taylor, *Final Report*, 82.

Nuremberg into 1949.) In compliance, the OCCWC culled two cases from the remaining six projected, and managed to open them in the nick of time, as the indictments were filed on 2 November, and the defendants arraigned on 20 and 30 December 1947 respectively.

Administrative difficulties impinged considerably upon the operations of the OCCWC. Not only were the later cases compressed, but neither the Milch nor the Flick trials were initially envisaged in the form they took. Rather, they materialized as the preparation of other cases ran into complications.[183] As is clear from the British case, however, logistical problems that were real enough were frequently accompanied by partisan concerns. The cutting of the OCCWC budget by Congress was certainly related to the dictates of the Cold War. Moreover, the promotion of the trial of Nazi doctors and scientists to the position of opening case of the Nuremberg subsequent proceedings was related to reluctance to begin the series with a potentially controversial trial of industrialists.[184]

Tom Bower has attributed the limitations of the British and American trial programmes almost entirely to the influence of anti-Communists, Germanophiles, and some antisemites acting within a Cold-War-oriented, if not broadly conspiratorial, agenda. While it is clear that overtly political considerations carried much weight in the British Foreign Office, and that much of the influential opposition to trials in the UK was based upon prejudices of various forms, these factors do not tell more than half the story as regards the USA. Frank Buscher has provided a more nuanced analysis of the role of constitutional and legal factors, and differing views of the aims and achievements of the trials, alongside the use by the Conservative right and media of increasingly vehement and influential anti-Soviet rhetoric.[185]

That substantial opposition emerged in the USA to the Nuremberg and Dachau trials is not in doubt. However it was not until the second half of 1947 and thereafter—parallel with the development of the 'American Cold War'— that criticism was voiced regularly and found a ready audience.[186] The critics thus had little time and opportunity to forestall further trials, for, as we know, in the second half of 1947 the shape of the subsequent proceedings programme was being finalized; and the Dachau trials were reaching their conclusion. It is none the less evident that some pressure was exerted by the War Department to bring the trials to an early close alongside the growing dissidence in the US.[187] Yet prompt completion was no more than Taylor had wished for and promised from the early days, and this pressure seems to have served only to hold him to his vow in the face of a huge and complex project which showed the potential to run on almost indefinitely.

[183] Taylor, *Final Report*, 78–9.
[184] Paul Weindling, 'Ärzte als Richter', in C. Wieseman and A. Frewer (eds.): *Medizin und Ethik im Zeichen von Auschwitz* (Erlangen: Palm and Enke, 1985), 31–44.
[185] Bower, *Blind Eye to Murder*; Buscher, *The US War Crimes Trial Program*.
[186] Bosch, *Judgment on Nuremberg*, 80.   [187] e.g. Clay, *Decision in Germany*, 252.

Moreover, the whole of the occupation was subject to strict budgetary constraints and was characterized by 'interservice rivalries and battles between the military and civilian sectors' which made any substantial project problematic.[188] By Taylor's own account it is clear that in comparison with anyone in the British camp he was given remarkable autonomy of action despite these increasing concerns. The condensation of the final six proposed cases into two resulted in the loss of thirty-five potential defendants; but he recalls that only on one occasion were his plans for the incorporation of individuals disapproved by General Clay; that was in the matter of Manstein *et al.*[189] Thus US opposition was only one of a number of circumstantial influences at work, and its impact on the form of the Nuremberg trials process was considerably less than Bower and others would have us believe. We shall see subsequently how the outcome of some of these trials and the receptivity to their messages was partially influenced by the opposition both from the Allied countries and from within Germany; here, it remains for us to draw together the strands of Allied war crimes policy between 1946 and 1949.

1.12 CONCLUSIONS

If there was one thing that the critics of 'war crimes' trials divined correctly, it was that by necessity they were political trials. The punishment strategies were conceived out of inter-departmental debate; specific legislation was drawn up to fit the respective plans; governments decided when the trials should start, and broadly—particularly in the light of the Cold War—when they should stop; and all along legislatures and bureaucracies threw in their weight on either side of the debate. Finally, unofficial political pressure was also directly applied, including that from officials 'on the ground' in Germany, to save this or that Nazi from punishment.[190]

Quite simply, and though the level of politicization varied, it was impossible completely to divorce the political from the judicial. The trial programmes themselves may only be properly considered in appreciation of this fact. Such an awareness should not, however, detract from the very real accomplishments of the individuals and groups who did ensure that trials materialized, and took place in more-or-less equitable conditions. Nor should it obscure the congeries of more mundane structural, financial, and human problems affecting substantial ventures in foreign lands, not least of which was the rapid decline in Anglo-American public enthusiasm for trials. Above all, the vast majority of the Allied actors we have considered worked according to their own conception of duty:

---

[188] David Clay Large, *Germans to the Front: West German Rearmament in the Adenauer Era* (Chapel Hill, NC: University of North Carolina Press, 1996), 32; John Gimbel, 'Cold War Historians and the Occupation of Germany', in Hans Schmitt (ed.), *US Occupation in Europe after World War II* (Kansas: University of Kansas Press, 1978), 94–6, on high occupation costs.

[189] Taylor, *Final Report*, 82–3.   [190] See below, Chapter 5.

some to the dictates of ideology; some to the requisites of the flag; and some even to the call of humanity. Thus while the limitations on the British trial programme in particular are clear, especially when we consider the lengthy and tortuous process of closure, we should not forget the considerable efforts that went into trying more than 1,000 defendants, nor the small but committed opposition to that closure. Furthermore, that the British trial programme was finally terminated in 1949, three years after the Cabinet decision for closure, bespeaks the pursuit of at least a limited justice, if for select crimes and victims.

Moreover, the occupation of Germany was not always intended to be wholly punitive. The comparatively enlightened nature of the military occupations of western Germany may be partially explained as regards the British and American authorities by their lack of experience of occupation, which both hindered full understanding of Nazi criminality and tempered the desire for vengeance. Yet 'democratization' rather than 'denazification'—broadly defined—became the cardinal aim of the project not merely out of Cold War utilitarianism, but because it was predicated upon the very reasonable assumption that the former was both worthy and humanitarian.

For both political and legal reasons, the British wartime Government had been reluctant to involve itself in the trial of the major war criminals in the first instance. (Indeed, the IMT's judgements on the conspiracy and criminal organization parts of the case show that the reservations of British, Soviet, and French officialdom about the American innovations were to an extent justified.) Yet when such a commitment appeared unavoidable, the British contribution to proceedings was a significant one. The BWCE and the two British judges played pivotal roles in the IMT showpiece, whether in David Maxwell-Fyfe's rapier penetration of Hermann Göring's defence or in Sir Geoffrey Lawrence's temperate presidency of the tribunal. Nor was it simply a question of individual contributions. Once the decision had been made to embark upon the trial venture, the British agencies concerned—the Foreign Office, the War Office, the Lord Chancellor's Office, and the Attorney General's Office—were determined to make it a success, realizing that they had become embroiled in something of considerable significance for the post-war world. Similarly, when it seemed that British honour was at stake in the negotiations preceding a second international trial, the Labour Government was prepared to forego its numerous misgivings in order to co-operate. The Foreign Office remained vigilant, however, and helped to create a loophole through which the Attorney General could escape, and the whole of the United Kingdom with him.

The ministry was not averse to war crimes trials *per se*, but rather to placing Britain in a potentially compromised position. It did not care for a second lengthy, controversial, and expensive legal involvement which it considered would have little impact—save perhaps to forestall an increasingly desirable German renaissance—on the consciousness of the rapidly changing post-war world. This line was clearly pursued up to and during the Manstein episode.

If the schism between the Foreign Office diplomats and the Soviets occurred comparatively early in the day, it was even preceded by the perceptions of the military. In combination, the force of these impulses posed a formidable challenge to the continuation of a substantial war crimes programme in the British zone. With the addition of the pressure from the broad anti-Communist, pro-military lobby specifically on behalf of the field marshals, this threat became almost irresistible. Only by force of rather perverse circumstance did von Manstein become the last British prisoner to stand in the dock for war crimes, and his lawyer Reginald Paget was correct in regard of all but a few when he surmised before the trial that 'we have rather slipped into it, and I think that everybody would be thankful if a reasonable excuse could be found for slipping out of it'.[191] In all probability this explains the widespread acquiescence in the decision not to try von Rundstedt and Strauss. The problems of the Manstein saga are the clearest indication of why the story of the Royal Warrant trials was not one of the prosecution of major war criminals.

These more traditional forms of war crimes trial were enacted ad hoc. Accordingly, their parameters were defined by the strictures of British legal precedent, and their frequency and subject-matter were greatly at the mercy of the ebb and flow of public and political opinion. These variables certainly influenced the principles applied in the prosecution of different classes of crime. It might be said that in the hunt for perpetrators of crimes against British servicemen justice took on a literal aspect, in the attempt to prosecute such deeds as extensively as possible. Conversely, the prosecution of the far more widespread and extreme crimes against non-British civilians became a matter for a more metaphorical, limited reckoning.

The scale of Nazi criminality ultimately made every trial programme a selective venture.[192] In June 1946 it had been suggested that there were 90,000 'potential war criminals' in American custody.[193] Contemporary estimates suggest there were 20,000 people in the British zone suspected of atrocities against British servicemen or of being senior staff in concentration camps and sub-camps;[194] this number did not even, therefore, include several categories of Nazi criminal. Like the British authorities, Jackson, Taylor and the American JAG all explicitly recognised the limited range of legal action, hence their attempts at 'representative' trial and punishment.

The particular focus adopted by the British mirrored the approach of most other European countries that were pre-occupied with clearing-up their own particular sphere of interest. (However the British programme *did* concern many

---

[191] LHCMA, Liddell Hart papers 1/563, Paget to Liddell Hart, 5 Nov. 1948.

[192] Hence some of the criticisms of the limited extent of the American trials. See e.g. Lutz Niethammer, *Entnazifizierung in Bayern: Säuberung und Rehabilitierung unter amerikanische Besatzung* (Frankfurt am Main: Fischer, 1972).

[193] Cited in Weindling, 'From International to Zonal Trials', 2.

[194] Dale Jones, 'Nazi Atrocities against Allied Airmen', 544, 548.

crimes against non-British nationals, a claim that few other European states could make.) Consequently, the greatest contribution made by Britain to the prosecution of major war criminals after the IMT trial was in helping inadvertently to shape the American trial programme. In terms of the 'mood of the times', not just throughout western Europe, but in the east as well,[195] that the USA continued with a venture of the scale of the Nuremberg subsequent proceedings is rather more remarkable than Britain's generally low-profile efforts. The longevity of the subsequent proceedings undertaking thus requires some explanation.

The Americans were slower than the British to anticipate the Cold War, but they were also less troubled by financial constraint,[196] and personnel shortages, though the latter point should not be overplayed.[197] It is also possible to generalize about a less conservative legal ethic amongst the American law-givers. The commitment to giving substance to the principles tentatively established by the IMT resulted in the establishment of a semi-permanent prosecuting machinery as part of the occupation set-up. This insulated Taylor's staff from the direct influence of American public and political opinion, which were to become progressively antipathetic. Thus, though pressure built up on the OCCWC to bring the Nuremberg trials to an end, that office ultimately succeeded in indicting the majority of those whom it sought to.

If the occupation structure, and within that the 'personal factor' of Lucius Clay was important in facilitating the subsequent Nuremberg proceedings, perpetual impetus was needed at the rock-face to keep them going. It is thus testament to the determination of Telford Taylor and his liberal Harvard Law School-oriented staff that the controversial 'Nuremberg trials' continued until the end of the 1940s.

These, then, are the circumstances in which the Allied prosecutors acted in pursuit of their general goals. This book should be read in that light. The processes of 'sentence review' and 'clemency' that hugely compromised the trial ventures in the 1950s with the mass early release of convicted war criminals had not yet occurred.[198] And understandable distaste fifty-five years on at the number of war criminals who were not caught, or who were caught but not tried, or who were tried but not punished severely enough—in both zones—should not obscure the influence of those delimiting factors specific to time and place. One such factor has not yet been considered in any detail, however. That is the matter of the prosecution of anti-Jewish crimes, or indeed of any criminal actions that cut across boundaries of nationality and even partisanship in the war.

[195] See Istvan Deak's introduction to Istvan Deak, Jan T. Gross, and Tony Judt (eds.), *The Politics of Retribution in Europe: World War II and Its Aftermath* (Princeton, NJ: Princeton University Press, 2000), 3–14, esp. 12.
[196] Gimbel, 'Cold War Historians and the Occupation of Germany', 95–6
[197] e.g. the problems encountered in the early days of the Dachau programme: IfZ, FG 16, p. 4. It was only in 1947 that substantially greater assistance was brought to bear: ibid. p. 50.
[198] These processes will be examined in Chapter 4, below.

To an extent the attitude of the British authorities to 'race'-specific crimes may be inferred from the terms of the Royal Warrant. However, beyond that legal yardstick other less tangible influences bore upon the way that racially oriented murder was depicted in the courtroom. Such influences were also manifest in the various 'Nuremberg trials'. They emanated from societies that had not responded to the enormity and anti-Jewish specificity of the 'final solution', and would in turn perpetuate, through the trial medium, their own particular ideological imperatives both 'at home' as well as in occupied Germany.

CHAPTER TWO

Race-Specific Crimes in Punishment and Re-Education Policy: The 'Jewish Factor'

The place of what has been called the 'Jewish Factor' in Allied war crimes policy[1] was well established before the trials began. Though the relevant surviving information on policy-making and implementation beyond the IMT trial is fragmentary at best, the general continuities of the policy may be inferred from developments in and around Allied courtrooms. The scale and extremity of Nazi genocide occasionally forced recognition of 'race'-specific crimes, but at no time were the underlying principles of Allied policy reconsidered. The overall effect was that crimes against Jews were subsumed within the general Nazi policies of repression and persecution. Legal conservatism was to some extent responsible, but the overarching framework for this refraction of Nazi persecution was formed by a combination of Allied preconceptions of Nazi criminality and the way in which Anglo-Saxon liberal culture related to Jews.

Of the three groups of trials in question, the 'Dachau', 'Nuremberg', and Royal Warrant series, the conduct of the first was most clearly articulated *vis-à-vis* victim particularity and category of crime. The trials at which 'Jewish' issues arose were mainly restricted to the six 'parent' trials against select personnel of the Dachau, Buchenwald, Mauthausen, Flossenbürg, Nordhausen/Mittelbau-Dora, and Mühldorf camps, and the 250 subsidiary cases against other members of the same institutions or their sub-camps (Aussenlager). Of the 1,672 accused in 489 trials in the Dachau series, 1,022 were in the various camp cases.[2]

After the first case against the Dachau staff themselves, the remit of the investigators and the prosecution was expanded from consideration only of the fate of nationals of countries at war with the Reich to include all non-German nationals in German custody.[3] The substantive charges revolved around traditional conceptions of breaches of the laws and customs of war, framed within the allegation of a 'common plan' to commit such crimes, and thus were chronologically restricted to the time after which the USA had entered the European war.[4] Clearly, therefore, there was no explicit recognition of the fate of ethno-religious groups,

---

[1] John P. Fox, 'The Jewish Factor in British War Crimes Policy in 1942', *English Historical Review*, 92 (1977), 82–106.

[2] Sigel, *Im Interesse der Gerechtigkeit*, 9, 38.

[3] IfZ, FG 16, pp. 63 (on German nationals), 47, 50 (on types and numbers of 'Dachau' trials). See also, Sigel, *Im Interesse der Gerechtigkeit*, 41, 105–12.

[4] Sigel, *Im Interesse der Gerechtigkeit*, 29; IfZ, FG 16, pp. 61–2, for analysis of the common plan charge.

nor of Germans persecuted within their own country; nor, indeed, of the
build-up of repressive measures and the development of the camp system prior
to 1 January 1942. (This ultimately led to at least one defendant actually claiming in cross-examination that he had not beaten any inmate since the US declaration of war!)[5]

In terms of legal restriction, the Royal Warrant trials were even more straightforward than the Dachau trials, yet the former programme requires closer attention, as is accorded towards the end of this chapter, owing to the variety of cases
it involved. The concluding section then considers the peculiar relationship of
liberal British and American politico-legal culture to questions of ethnic specificity during the occupation generally. Prior to that, we will look at the role of the
'Jewish factor' in the most important and complex ventures of all, the IMT and
subsequent Nuremberg trials. At the outset, however, consideration should be
given to the collection of the source material required in the prosecution of the
different classes of crime, and of the way in which this evidence was employed.

2.1 THE SEARCH FOR EVIDENCE

Beyond the legal and political thinking that bore directly and specifically upon
crimes against Jews, the same incidental factors that influenced the depiction of
any area of judicial investigation enjoyed a significant role. Chance was naturally
to play a part in deciding which aspects of Nazi criminality were to be uncovered,
given the vastness and complexity of the German enterprises. The hand of fortune was clearly at work in deciding that the records of the German Foreign
Office would be found in Marburg Castle, or that the correspondence of Alfred
Rosenberg would be discovered behind a false wall, in time for their incorporation in the IMT trial.[6] Conversely, there was little that the diplomats and lawyers could do about the large-scale migration from Europe of Nazis through
escape networks, and by other means, or about the destruction of incriminatory
documents. But whether the Allies maximized their potential to convict war
criminals was governed considerably by the efficiency of those bodies delegated
to gather the information in the first place.

The task of securing evidence of what were broadly termed 'war crimes' was
shared by a number of agencies that acted with little co-ordination and frequently with none of the spirit of co-operation.[7] The longest-standing such
organization, and the only genuinely multinational one, was the United Nations
War Crimes Commission. However, it did not gather information on the full
breadth of Nazi criminality, and for a number of reasons was not supported by

---

5 Sigel, *Im Interesse der Gerechtigkeit*, 53.

6 Edmund A. Walsh, *Total Power: A Footnote to History* (New York: Doubleday, 1948), 96.

7 Detailed accounts of the war crimes machinery of the Allies may be found in William F. Fratcher,
'American Organization for Prosecution of German War Criminals', *Missouri Law Review*, 13, (1948),
45–75; UNWCC, *History of the UNWCC*; Smith, *The Road to Nuremberg*; Taylor, *Anatomy*.

the governments of the 'Big Three' Allies. In the final analysis, it also failed to provide the sort of documentary evidence which the Americans in particular sought. Consequently, the UNWCC was marginalized, and contributed little to the Nuremberg proceedings in particular, or Anglo-American trials in general.[8] Likewise, the British and Americans cared little for the findings of the national war crimes commissions related to the UNWCC or which, as in the case of the Soviet commission, operated separately. Only the Soviets relied substantively on these at the IMT trial, and there is little indication that they went to form the relevant parts of the judgement; otherwise the national commissions provided information for trials in their own countries alone, barring exceptional cases such as that of von Manstein, where the charges were exclusively concerned with eastern European nationals.

As we shall see, it was German documents testifying to German crimes which the British and Americans sought, and not primarily eyewitness testimony to atrocities where such acts had taken place. Therefore the military machines of the victorious Allies became the most important investigative organizations, for they were the best positioned to collect the appropriate evidence. Moreover, it was certain that the majority of potential defendants would be living in the areas occupied by the armies, and in particular those of the western Allies because of the mass flight from the east in the face of the Soviet advance.[9] Finally, as the legal novelties of the Nuremberg trial plan were peculiarly American, the onus was upon American servicemen to substantiate the innovatory claims of their superiors.

Neither the American nor the British army were acclimatized, in the way in which some of the eastern national commission members had been, to the sort of crimes that required investigation. To the extent it had occupied them for most of the war, the 'war crimes' question consisted of a limited conception, specifically of atrocities committed against their own fellow servicemen. Their scope expanded somewhat in spring 1945, as it became evident that the far more horrific and widespread criminality of the concentration camps demanded prosecution. Nevertheless, neither army shared the philosophy of the American Nuremberg prosecution, which was to cast a broad net across the whole of the Nazi system; nor did they really possess the requisite expertise or, in some cases, enthusiasm.[10] This was never to change with regard to the British army, and even when the American JAG was commissioned to substantiate the charges of aggressive war

---

[8] The UNWCC volume exaggerates the importance of the commission, as does Kochavi's *Prelude to Nuremberg*, while Fratcher views its main contribution as giving the major powers the moral support of the minor nations. Tom Bower, in *Blind Eye to Murder*, is far more scathing, and the commission is notable by its virtual absence in the writings of Bradley Smith and Telford Taylor. Also critical is Sigel, *Im Interesse der Gerechtigkeit*, introduction.

[9] Fratcher, 'American Organization for Prosecution of German War Criminals', 55.

[10] IfZ, FG 16, p. 5; UNWCC, *The History of the UNWCC*, 349–50; Bower, *Blind Eye to Murder*, 129–31. On the ill-preparedness of the British JAG, see also Weindling, 'From International to Zonal Trials', 8.

and war crimes, some of its leading figures remained suspicious of the Nuremberg project.[11]

In his efforts to maximize the chances of the Bernays plan succeeding, Jackson called in the services of the body which he deemed to have 'given a much more exhaustive treatment to the subject of crimes than any other agency in the United States'.[12] The Office of Strategic Services (OSS; the forerunner of the CIA) was commissioned to prepare evidence on the counts of conspiracy and crimes against humanity. However, not only did the OSS have little time in which to prepare its cases—both it and the JAG were only put to their tasks in the first half of May 1945, and the trial began in November—it was apparently nowhere near as well prepared as Jackson thought for the job in hand. Bradley Smith, who as a historian both of the IMT trial and the OSS is certainly better qualified to judge on such matters, deems that for the first month and a half of its existence, the latter simply trod water, attempting to conceal its unpreparedness. The JAG was of little more use.[13]

If we add to these revelations the inter-organizational rivalries which prevented full co-operation between the OSS and the army; that the US State Department was not to be of great assistance in the furtherance of the case due to 'misgivings . . . [about] the effect of the prosecution on sentiment in neutral countries'; and that vital security-classified intelligence information was not to be made available from organizations such as the code-breakers of Bletchley Park, it becomes apparent that OCCPAC was not at first particularly well situated to justify the complex charges which the Americans had drawn up.[14] Ultimately, only the cornucopia of documentation helpfully bequeathed by the Nazi bureaucracy would provide the Nuremberg prosecutors with material with which to work.

2.2 DEPLOYING THE EVIDENCE: 'HARD DOCUMENTS' AND 'REPRESENTATIVE EXAMPLES'

Even within the American camp there was dissent over how to go about illustrating twelve years of history, including some of the most sensational, if horrific, evidence imaginable. The treasure trove of documents preserved for the prosecution had convinced the trial planners, and Jackson in particular, that everything they needed to illuminate the darkest corners of the Nazi era was in printed form.[15] This approach again owed much to the American anti-trust trials with

[11] 'Justice Jackson's story', fo. 1083.   [12] Ibid. 1082.
[13] Smith, *The Road to Nuremberg*, 235–8. On lack of preparation of the JAG's staff, see IfZ, FG 16, pp. 8–9.
[14] 'Justice Jackson's story', fos. 1046–7, 1092; on the intelligence information: *ex inf.* Peter Calvocoressi, 13 Sept. 1997; Richard Breitman, *Official Secrets: What the Nazis Planned, What the British and Americans Knew* (Harmondsworth: Penguin, 1999), 214–23.
[15] e.g. report to Truman cited in the *New York Times*, 9 Sept. 1945; see also Library of Congress, papers of Harold Leventhal, box 230, Nuremberg Trials file, Board of Review, memos 2, 3, 29 Oct.; 1 Nov. 1945.

their focus upon complex, technical issues. However, it caused a schism within OCCPAC,[16] and Jackson was eventually forced to modify his position a little.

Jackson's opponents wished to give a little 'human interest' to what would clearly be a lengthy undertaking by putting witnesses before the IMT. This was not least in the interests of maintaining a reasonable standard of press coverage.[17] Yet the Justice had already chosen the audience to which he wished chiefly to appeal: posterity. He disdained the use of any witnesses OCCPAC 'could reasonably avoid', arguing that 'the documents make dull publicity, but they [seem] to me to make the sounder foundation for the case, particularly when the record is examined by the historian'.[18]

The limitations of Jackson's vision become evident upon juxtaposition of two of his specific contentions. With regard to the potential use of four witnesses who had been involved to varying degrees with resistance movements in the Third Reich, one of his peculiar objections was that 'they saw events from different observation points. They had different personal relations to different people. They had a strong bias against the Hitler regime[!]' Conversely, he lauded the 'indisputable character' of a collection of documents, one of which was the subsequently notorious 'Hossbach memorandum'. Though now generally accepted as a reliable record of the gist of Hitler's pronouncements at the meeting in question, these 'minutes' were for some time the subject of considerable debate as to their veracity, and remain a bone of historiographical contention as to their significance. Moreover, that after the trial Jackson considered the memorandum not only provided indisputable evidence of the plan for aggressive war, but also for the 'extermination of the Jews', is testament to the extent to which the 'conspiracy' idea dominated all else: Jews are not even mentioned in the document.[19]

It took considerable pressure from several OCCPAC staff, as well as from a body of journalists bored by the relentless documentary barrage which the prosecution case had become, to persuade Jackson to put on the stand even the

---

[16] William Donovan, erstwhile head of the US Office of Strategic Services, stormed out of the prosecution, in large part in protest against the documentary approach.

[17] 'Justice Jackson's story', fos. 1336–7.

[18] Ibid. fos. 1239–40; Library of Congress, papers of Henry L. Stimson, reel 115, Jackson to Stimson, 5 June 1946.

[19] 'Justice Jackson's story', fos. 1153–6. The memorandum has been a chief bone of contention in the debate among historians of the Third Reich: some—who could be labelled 'intentionalists' in the parlance of Holocaust historiography—believing, like Jackson, that Hitler's utterances were signs of deliberate and specific intent; and others—A. J. P Taylor in the first instance, and numerous 'structuralist' or 'functionalist' historians after him—arguing that, while evidence of aggressive thought, they must not be taken at face value, because of the number of other contextual influences on the subsequent development of Hitler's thinking. For an early, critical view of the accuracy of the memorandum, see Walter Bussmann, 'Zur Entstehung und Überlieferung der "Hossbach-Niederschrift"', *VfZ*, 16 (1968), 373–84. For a more positive opinion: Bradley F. Smith, 'Die Überlieferung der Hossbach-Niederschrift im Lichte neuer Quellen', *VfZ*, 38 (1990), 329–36.

few witnesses OCCPAC did call.[20] Jackson was fearful lest the witnesses buckle under the pressure to perform publicly, and consequently retract their confessions; yet he acquiesced, feeling that 'the documentation was so well established that there could be no harm from putting on some witnesses. There were some there who had tales to tell.'[21] One of these was Otto Ohlendorf, the man who had led the mobile SS killing squad, Einsatzgruppe D, into the Crimea in 1941. Ohlendorf gave one of the most honest, quotable, and shocking performances seen at Nuremberg. His testimony, including his estimate of the 90,000 murders committed under his command, echoed throughout the pages of the newspapers of the attendant press services, and reserved him a seat at the Justizpalast in the American subsequent proceedings. It also illustrated that witnesses might have an insight that could not always be gleaned from paper records, for by that point most of the Einsatzgruppen progress reports had not been discovered.

Nevertheless, a clear hierarchy was established amongst the forms of evidence. The substance of the 'proofs' required also mirrored the theorized nature of the conspiracy-criminal organization approach. As the fundamental aim was to show how war crimes and crimes against humanity derived from a conspiracy to aggression, establishing the link became in practice more important than charting the multitude of crimes. The story of the murders and privations was reduced, in the prosecutorial lexicon, to the presentation of 'representative examples' of atrocities.

This approach was made explicit in Jackson's opening address to the IMT, where he proclaimed that his emphasis would 'not be on individual barbarities and perversions which may have occurred independently of any central plan. One of the dangers ever present is that this trial may be protracted by details of particular wrongs and that [the tribunal might] become lost in a "wilderness of single instances"'.[22] The implications of his strategy may be discerned at one of his pre-trial meetings with the BWCE and the UNWCC.

Following Jackson's lead, David Maxwell-Fyfe, Deputy Chief Prosecutor for the United Kingdom, suggested that 'with regard to torture and murder, what [the prosecution] wanted was a really bad example of one case'.[23] Thus, also in July 1945, the trial staff requested of the governments of nine United Nations countries that they 'furnish . . . three examples of war crimes or violations of international law' to be used in the prosecution of the leading Nazis. These instances should be 'typical' and the 'best evidence of the widespread and organized nature of the violations of international law'. It was thought that this would 'establish the universality and the similarity of the crimes committed and from

---

[20] Dodd papers, box 321, file 'Documents concerning trial organisation and procedure', Amen to Jackson, 1 Dec. 1945; file 'Planning Committee', Wheeler to Storey, 15 Nov. 1945.

[21] 'Justice Jackson's story', fos. 1335–7.

[22] *IMT*, ii, 104. For an earlier statement to this effect, see Jackson papers, container 111, office files—US Dept. of State, 2 July 1945, State Dept. to OCCPAC.

[23] PRO, WO 219/3585, minutes of 70th meeting of UNWCC, 18 July 1945, pp. 2–8.

this that they were all related to a common plan or enterprise'. Appropriate examples, it was suggested, would be the bombing of Rotterdam in May 1940 for the Netherlands, and the Lidice massacre in Czechoslovakia.[24]

In practice, given a limited Anglo–American comprehension of atrocities, it was impossible to say what was or was not 'typical', or even if 'types' as such did exist within groupings of diverse Nazi institutions and practices such as the camp system. It was patently incorrect of Sir Thomas Barnes of the BWCE to say that Ravensbrück 'would be worth taking as an example' of the concentration camp system as it 'appeared to be on a par with other camps', because it was exclusively a women's camp, the only such in the Nazi system.[25] The net effect of the policy was, as intended, to limit the content of American presentations on tangible crimes, because the prosecutors were chary of introducing 'cumulative' evidence.[26]

The educational intent of the IMT project was established, but it does not appear that the teachers were particularly well informed about their subject matter. Crimes that were not documented, or of which no documentation survived, were not likely to emerge at Nuremberg. And even crimes that were signified by official correspondence might remain undisclosed in the courtroom if they were not felt to be sufficiently 'representative' of whatever OCCPAC wished them to be. Meanwhile, documentation was not always as reliable as it appeared. Above all, the imposition of a legalistic framework onto Nazi criminality decreed that everything, even substantive crimes, was to be explained in the terms of an untested theory.

2.3 APPLYING 'WAR CRIMES' AND 'CRIMES AGAINST HUMANITY'

Naturally, many of the same considerations of fortune and circumstance applied to the procedures for the selection of evidence as affected the choosing of defendants. Yet in that aspect of the former in which we are interested, there was a more consistent underlying trend which was not consonant with a comprehensive treatment of the fate of the European Jews. This concerned the categorization of the crimes committed against Jews and the attitude of the trial policy-makers and implementers. The innovation of the charge of 'crimes against humanity' was a helpful initiative, but its value was limited by the nature of its use, and the context in which it was considered.

Though ultimately the decision as to what constituted a 'crime against humanity' was a judicial one, it was necessarily defined and circumscribed by the

---

[24] PRO, LCO 2/2980, undated BWCE correspondence. See also memo on trials of major war criminals by Patrick Dean, 14 Aug. 1945, printed in *Documents on British Policy Overseas, 11 August–31 December 1945*, 34–43, point 9.

[25] PRO, LCO 2/2980, minutes of 4th meeting of BWCE, 14 June 1945, p. 3.

[26] *IMT*, iii, 569; iv, 365–6, for instances of the limiting effect of the policy on the representation of crimes against the Jews.

wording of any given indictment.[27] Consequently, the salient ruling that the
IMT had to make was whether or not 'persecutions on political, racial or religious grounds' enacted before the commencement of war in 1939 could be adjudged crimes against humanity, and hence deserved judicial attention. The
narrow interpretation chosen by the Tribunal was that they could not, given that
it had not been 'satisfactorily proved' that such persecutions were done 'in execution of, or in connection with' the conspiracy to commit crimes against peace.[28]

Following suit, the subsequent Nuremberg tribunals that were confronted
with the question ruled similarly to the IMT, despite the fact that CCL10 dif-
fered from the London Charter over the definition of crimes against humanity:[29]
it did not imply that a link had to be made between such crimes and a conspiracy
to commit crimes against peace. Thus in a strict legal sense, the Americans'
broad conspiratorial approach failed to establish the relevance of the build-up of
Nazi antisemitic ideas, and their early consummation into practice as embodied
in the Nuremberg Laws or the Kristallnacht pogrom and related persecutory
measures. However, such a legalistic approach does not account for the fact that
judgement was only the final act in the story of each trial, preceded as it was by
the collection of evidence and its presentation and consequent entry into the
records for use by historians and, albeit less critically, in contemporary press reports of the proceedings.[30]

For instance, much of the evidence on the antisemitic propagandist Julius
Streicher concerned the pre-war period. He was primarily included in the trial
in a sort of early attempt at prosecuting incitement to racial hatred, for his porno-
graphic, racist publications.[31] As the only defendant indicted exclusively for his
anti-Jewish influence, Streicher was also alone in being charged with the peculiar
combination of conspiracy and crimes against humanity. His presence suggests
that the Allies recognized the need to account on some level for the virulence of

---

[27] Numerous texts describe the genesis and life of the 'crimes against humanity' count; a selection
varying in detail and perspective includes James T. Brand, 'Crimes against Humanity and the Nuernberg
Trials', *Oregon Law Review*, 28 (1949), 93–119; Ginsburgs and Kudriavtsev (eds.), *The Nuremberg Trial
and International Law*; Jacob Robinson, 'The International Military Tribunal and the Holocaust: Some
Legal Reflections', in Michael R. Marrus (ed.), *The Nazi Holocaust*, 9 pts (London: Meckler, 1989), pt 9,
608–20; Marrus, 'The Holocaust at Nuremberg'. The last three in particular concern themselves with the
confusion during the drawing-up of the London Charter over the presence of a semi-colon (rather than a
comma) midway through the text of the crimes against humanity definition. (See below, Appendix A.)
The semi-colon appears to have been mistakenly introduced, but nevertheless it restricted the tribunal's
ambit regarding pre-war atrocities against German groups—including Jews—to cases where such brutality and discrimination were ostensibly connected with the conspiracy for aggressive war. However, as we
shall see, the Nuremberg prosecutions still attempted to introduce much evidence that, though not accepted as connected with the conspiracy count, was still entered into the historical record.

[28] *IMT*, i, 254–5.

[29] In both the Ministries and Flick trials the tribunals deemed the matter beyond their competence.

[30] For instance, Major Walsh's presentation on the persecution of the Jews contained much on pre-war
measures. See *IMT*, iii, 519 ff.

[31] Dean memo, 14 Aug. 1945, printed in *Documents on British Policy Overseas, 11 August–31 December
1945*, 34–43, point 4, in which Streicher was described as 'representative' of Nazi 'anti-Semitic organisations'.

the Nazi hatred of Jews, though—clearly under American influence—within the context of the plan for aggressive warfare. (Parenthetically, Streicher did not fit into the latter picture at all, as he was progressively marginalized in Nazi circles of power after the early years of rule.) Yet the formulation of 'crimes against humanity' and the indictment of a Streicher should not blind us to the realities of the national and international politics of the era.

On the part of the UK, we know that the Royal Warrant contained nothing about 'conspiracy', 'crimes against peace', or crimes by Germans against Germans who happened to be Jewish.[32] The trials that ensued were to be differentiated from proceedings conducted in the British zone before Control Commission or German tribunals. These courts were part of the governmental machinery, and employed the 'crimes against humanity' clause of CCL10 in cases where it was deemed that the deeds in question were illegal by civilized standards when they were committed.[33] Such crimes were inevitably confined to acts of direct commission or incitement, and, unlike the Americans, the British did not see war crimes and crimes against humanity as necessarily related.[34] Even the proposition, which was given substance by the judgement of the IMT, about the inherent criminality of the Gestapo and the SS did not carry any weight—at least not formally—in British courts.[35]

The British and American prosecutions, both at the IMT trial and in the subsequent proceedings displayed, albeit in a watered-down fashion, many of the ambiguities characterizing the responses of the liberal democracies to the Holocaust while it was taking place. At base, the accepted view of antisemitic activity was a quintessentially liberal one: though violence against a minority group was despised, outbreaks of antisemitism were interpreted as reactions to Jewish 'difference', or what Tony Kushner has called 'the irritant of Jewish particularity'. As Kushner argues, however, this classic, assimilationist theory could not account for the level of Nazi antisemitism. Initially, therefore, responses featured ambivalence towards reports of atrocities in the USSR based on experience of

[32] The Royal Warrant did contain a clause stating that 'where there is evidence that a war crime has been the result of concerted action upon the part of a unit or group of men, then evidence given upon any charge relating to that crime against any member of such unit or group may be received as *prima-facie* evidence of the responsibility of each member of that unit or group for that crime'. However, 'concerted action' was not synonymous (*nicht gleichbedeutend*) with the American conspiracy charge. For an embellishment of this point, see Honig, 'Kriegsverbrecher vor englischen Militärgerichten', 31–2.

[33] PRO, FO 371/70822, CG3534/34/184, Marsden-Smedley to Reed, 1 Sept. 1948.

[34] Thus, whereas British Control Commission courts and German courts in the British zone considered crimes against humanity, they never judged on war crimes *stricto sensu*. See PRO FO 371/70822, CG3534/34/184, also FO 371/77047, CG417/15/184, Newton to Brand, 18 Feb. 1949. Conversely, the US authorities did not allow German courts in their zone to adjudicate over either war crimes strictly defined or crimes against humanity, except where the offence in question was also a crime under German law, in which case the German penal code was the governing statute anyway. See PRO FO 371/70823, CG4306/34/184, O'Grady minute, 5 Nov. 1948; Mercer to O'Grady, 30 Oct. 1948.

[35] One of the many instances of criticism of the idea of prosecuting 'criminal organizations' may be found in PRO, LCO 2/2984, Shawcross to Atlee, 17 Jan. 1946; for comment on the subsequent attitudes of British courts to the issue, see Kudriavtsev and Ginsburgs (eds.), *The Nuremberg Trial and International Law*, 279.

atrocity stories in previous wars, but also on a suspicion of the vagaries of 'Slav imaginations' and a belief in the inclination of Jews to 'magnify their persecutions'.[36] Subsequently, there was an unwillingness to commit to any strategy either of rescue for the victims or punishment for the perpetrators, despite the verification of atrocity reports and the issuance of general declarations pertaining to the Axis and its crimes. Allied reticence was characterized by denials— many grounded again in a liberal-universalist refusal to single out the treatment of any group as unique—that the Jewish fate required any specific consideration over and above that of other groups or of the universal aim of winning the war. There was also fear on either side of the Atlantic about the consequences in terms of the post-war world of allowing Jews to air their grievances: it was felt that anti-semitism would be stirred up in those countries whose nationals were to be subjected to what might be attributed to Jewish vengeance; and, relatedly, that a strong moral claim might result for a separate Jewish state.[37]

The Roosevelt administration realized, however, that with the strength of Jewish opinion in America it could not afford not to confront the Jewish catastrophe in some measure[38] (and the legal considerations of pre-war atrocities and acts against Axis nationals were very much framed as 'Jewish' issues in debate). Without the pressure from bodies equivalent to the War Refugee Board or the US Treasury Department, the legally conservative British law officers and Foreign Office strove to downplay 'racially' specific crimes. Yet that the American political consensus of 1944–5 did incorporate some of the aspirations of what were broadly and incorrectly conceived of as Jewish pressure groups should not, however, suggest that the former was dictated by the latter. There remained striking similarities in the underlying principles of the legal ways in which each nation approached the Jewish 'question'.

There were clear controls on the use of the leeway given to the Nuremberg prosecutors. The unwritten rule that the Nuremberg case could in no way be seen to be influenced by Jewry appears to have been a pre-eminent check, a view buttressed explicitly by the long-standing mistrust of the 'objectivity' of 'Jewish' evidence and the traditional Christian stereotype of the vengeful Jew, and implicitly by continuing fears over potential Jewish emigration to Palestine. Secretary of War Stimson's opinion of Morgenthau was that 'a man of his race'—he was Jewish—should not be involved in dealing with Germany.[39] Additionally, both

---

[36] See esp. p. 251 of Tony Kushner, 'Different Worlds: British Perceptions of the Final Solution during the Second World War', in David Cesarani (ed.), *The Final Solution: Origins and Implementation* (London: Routledge, 1994), 246–67; Dale Jones, 'British Policy', 340–1; and, more generally, Tony Kushner, *The Holocaust and the Liberal Imagination: A Social and Cultural History* (Oxford: Blackwell, 1994); Martin Gilbert, *Auschwitz and the Allies* (London: Michael Joseph, 1981); Walter Laqueur, *The Terrible Secret* (London: Weidenfeld and Nicolson, 1980); Breitman, *Official Secrets*.

[37] Bernard Wasserstein, *Britain and the Jews of Europe, 1939–1945* (Oxford: Clarendon Press, 1979).

[38] See above, Chapter 1. For Jewish pressure on OCCPAC to promote the Jewish case, see Aronson, 'Preparations for the Nuremberg Trial'.

[39] Kochavi, *Prelude to Nuremberg*.

the man who invented the conspiracy-criminal organization plan and the man entrusted with implementing it saw the sections of the case devoted to the fate of the Jews as unsuitable for presentation by Jews.

When confronted with Jewish organizations requesting representation on the prosecution, the Chief of Counsel refused, but not on the grounds given in reply to a similar request by the Polish Government, namely, that it was logistically impossible to give time and space to all interested parties.[40] Rather, Jackson argued that he wished to 'get away from the racial aspects of the situation': 'we didn't want to exaggerate racial tensions [in countries where Jews still existed]'. 'The only thing to do about that was to avoid making [Nuremberg] a vengeance trial',[41] he claimed, thus playing unfortunately into the stereotype of the vengeful Jew. Jackson was prepared to admit Chaim Weizmann, the later President of Israel, as an expert witness for the prosecution on the murder of the Jews, but only on the condition of prior presentation of a carefully prepared statement; Weizmann demurred. The British remained faithful to their perennial line in insisting that it would be preferable to have non-Jews testify.[42] Murray Bernays went a little further than both, and suggested that it would give 'added authority' to the American case if 'the Jewish problem [was] assigned to a group of high churchmen' for presentation in court.[43]

These passages are not meant to imply an overt antisemitism amongst the trial-planners of either nation: though there were instances of distinctly prejudiced official observations on the role of Jews in the trials,[44] we also see individuals such as the American prosecutor, Micky Marcus, who were particularly sympathetic to the Jewish cause.[45] Rather, they are intended to signify the difficulties, peculiar perhaps to Jewish–non-Jewish relations, that official representatives of the liberal democracies encountered in confronting 'race-specific' crimes.[46] Thus Jackson was happy to have Jewish lawyers on his team, as long as

---

[40] Tusa and Tusa, *Nuremberg*, 103–4.

[41] 'Justice Jackson's story', fos. 1075–7.

[42] Ibid. 1076–7; Robinson, 'The International Military Tribunal and the Holocaust', 610; Marrus, 'The Holocaust at Nuremberg', 13. For an example of specific suspicion of Jewish evidence by a British legal official—the judge advocate in the 'Belsen' trial—see *The Trial of Josef Kramer and Forty-Four Others*, ed. Raymond Phillips (London: William Hodge, 1949), 116.

[43] Jackson papers, container 107, 'Office files, US Chief-of-Counsel: pre-trial planning', Bernays to Jackson, 3 July 1945.

[44] See e.g. the note by Mr Pink, 'Some impressions of the Nuremberg trial', transmitted to FO 29 Nov. 1945, printed in *Documents on British Policy Overseas, 11 August—31 December 1945*, 405–8, point 6. Such references will be familiar to students of Whitehall's response to the plight of Europe's Jews (on this, see recently and most impressively Louise London, *Whitehall and the Jews*, Cambridge: Cambridge University Press, 2000), and the very fact that this sort of language was deemed acceptable for official correspondence is indicative of an ingrained ambivalence on the subject. Relatedly, Bradley Smith also describes Stimson as 'a social anti-Semite, as were the vast majority of old-family New York aristocrats in the 1940s': *The Road to Nuremberg*, 31.

[45] He himself held Zionist convictions and employed Raphael Lemkin, the Polish-Jewish jurist who first attempted to codify the crime of genocide in the light of the Shoah, as a consultant.

[46] Kushner, *The Holocaust and the Liberal Imagination*, 197–201.

they were not involved in presenting the Jewish case. As he said, 'we thought it would be just as bad not to let any appear as it would be to let too many appear.'[47] Likewise, both Jackson and the BWCE were prepared to seek information pertaining to the Holocaust from Jewish sources, provided, as the British put it, they were 'reliable' conduits (which presumably implied them not being stridently Zionist).[48] But Jews could not be allowed to be seen to describe the fate of their kin; this was the task of the 'objective' Nazi documentation on the one hand, and the voice of universal opinion—personified in US Supreme Court Justice Jackson—on the other.

Beyond the perceived ideological dangers of allowing Jews to present 'their' case, there was the more real threat of the potential of a full exposition of the Shoah to distract attention from the theoretically based conspiracy charge. Whether based upon a genuine understanding that Nazi antisemitism had its own dynamics which were not always consonant with the plan for European domination (which is unlikely),[49] or merely an inability on behalf of OCCPAC to see beyond the boundaries of the conspiracy plan (as Bradley Smith implies), it was certainly not in the interests of the Americans to give too much attention to the fate of the Jews.

Put another way, the establishment of the long chronology of Nazi antisemitism was vital to the integrity of the conspiracy idea, but was not in itself of primary importance: witness the Streicher indictment. Although Jackson was aware that Jewry were the Nazis' principal victims, he had clearly not apprehended the peculiar nature of their persecution (for which he can scarcely be blamed), and consequently thought that their treatment merely provided the best example of the logical outcome of Nazi thinking and practice. This is all the more pertinent because the conspiracy idea as originally conceived by Bernays had actually had the treatment of the Jews outside the context of war as one of its prime focuses.[50] The Justice was not being true to Bernays's principles, or those of Herbert Pell and Bohuslav Ecer in the UNWCC, even when he was adamant that the indictment should include mention of 'persecution . . . of Jews and

---

[47] 'Justice Jackson's story', fo. 1077.

[48] PRO, WO 311/39, BWCE to FO, 8 Apr. 1946, requesting details of estimated numbers of Jewish dead, to be used in the cross-examination of Julius Streicher. The statistics were to be provided by the Board of Deputies of British Jews or 'other reliable Jewish organisations'. The famous Jewish jurist, Jacob Robinson, assisted Jackson's staff in the preparation of the Jewish case, and much of the work done on the relationship between the 'conspiracy' and crimes against the Jews was done by a pair of Jewish men—Hans Nathan and Isaac Stone—seconded from the OSS. For further comments as to the relative merits of different Jewish organizations, see PRO, FO 371/57561, Henderson to FO, 10 Jan. 1946, where, the author favours representation at the IMT trial of the Board of Deputies over that of 'the more extreme bodies such as the [World Jewish] Congress'. On the work of Charles Dwork of the OSS on the Holocaust in preparation for the IMT case, see Aronson, 'Preparations for the Nuremberg Trial'.

[49] Marrus suggests that the failure to realize the genuinely ideological, rather than 'structural', nature of Nazi antisemitism was due to the absence of any convincing ideologues from the witness-stand. Marrus, 'The Holocaust at Nuremberg', 40. Rosenberg and Streicher were hardly to be taken seriously, while Hitler, Himmler, and Heydrich were all unavailable.

[50] Aronson, 'Preparations for the Nuremberg Trial', 261–4.

others in Germany as well as outside of it, and before as well as after commencement of the war'.[51]

2.4 THE 'CONSPIRACY' TO INITIATE WAR: THE TYRANNY OF A CONSTRUCT

For Bernays, Jackson, and Taylor, it was the charges of conspiracy and crimes against peace which set the IMT trial and the subsequent proceedings apart from other 'war crimes' trials. Specific 'war crimes', and even 'common designs' thereto, could be charged under the more restricted series of proceedings taking place simultaneously at Dachau. Nuremberg was the theatre in which to recreate the full sweep of the Nazi drama. Indeed, it could be said that the Dachau trials, the trials under the Royal Warrant, and the vast majority of national trials were directed at the symptoms of Nazi criminality (the actual implementation of murder and cruelty), while the Nuremberg trials were generally concerned with the causes of it.

Yet it was the subordination of the tangible crimes of persecution and murder to the theoretical concept of conspiracy which not only baffled the French and Soviets at the IMT trial, but helped to increase cynicism about, and turn public attention away from, those proceedings.[52] Nor did the conspiracy–criminal organization plan contribute a great deal to the prosecution of Axis criminality. Of those individuals convicted by the IMT, only one, Rudolf Hess, was sentenced for guilt on the conspiracy and aggressive war counts alone. Moreover, no one convicted of aggressive warfare was condemned to death as a result of that finding alone.[53] Finally, the idea of guilt by association with an organization involved with the criminal conspiracy was so tightly circumscribed by the IMT's judgement that in effect no blanket pronouncements were made about group criminality.[54] In an attempt to substantiate a considerable portion of its *raison d'être*, however, the OCCWC persevered with the conspiracy–criminal organisation plan in the subsequent proceedings. It was ultimately to meet with even less success than its predecessor organization, gaining no convictions at all on the conspiracy charge, and only securing five out of fifty-two for crimes against peace.

Jonathan Bush has posited that the pursuit of judicial condemnation of aggressive warfare was the chief driving force behind the choice of subsequent

---

[51] Jackson papers, container 95, 'Protocol file: Jackson's personal file of draft arrangements', notes on proposed definition of war crimes, 31 July 1945.

[52] Michael Biddiss, 'The Nuremberg Trial: Two Exercises in Judgement', *Journal of Contemporary History*, 16 (1981), 601, 607–8; Smith, *The Road to Nuremberg*, conclusion.

[53] Peter R. Black, *Ernst Kaltenbrunner: Ideological Soldier of the Third Reich* (Princeton, NJ: Princeton University Press, 1984), 274.

[54] On the British non-implementation of the criminal organization idea, see PRO, WO 267/601, report for the quarter ended 31 Dec. 1947. Apparently, even the holding of senior SS positions did not 'make an impression on a court, unless concrete evidence of mis-doings of the accused [was] also produced'.

proceedings.[55] Yet it is impossible to separate 'crimes against peace' from the conspiracy charge, as the former were always accompanied by the latter, and the evidence adduced for the aggressive war count was inevitably submitted for the umbrella accusation also.[56] In the Farben and Krupp trials these counts were presented virtually coterminously. Indeed, it is hard for the layman to comprehend the difference between the charge of planning and preparing for aggressive war and that of conspiring to commit it. Clearly, the judges of the NMTs agreed, casting the two charges out together in both of these proceedings.

Bush's contention is, however, helpful in establishing the emphasis that should be given within the broad conspiracy charge to the pursuit of aggressive war. Both in the mind of the judges and, this chapter contends, of the OCCWC policy-makers, the idea of a conspiracy to commit war crimes and crimes against humanity was secondary. This is demonstrably the case with respect to the Nuremberg judiciary, which, neither in the IMT trial nor in any of the subsequent proceedings, allowed consideration in judgements of crimes against humanity committed before 1939 because, despite the altered definition of such acts in CCL10, the NMT judges agreed with their predecessors that the conspiracy charge was not applicable to any act except the planning of aggressive war prior to the outbreak of such wars.[57]

As has been described elsewhere, for the OCCWC to prove the conspiracy–criminal organization theory entailed sealing the gaps left by the IMT trial. More specifically, it implied gaining condemnations of what Dwight Eisenhower called the 'military-industrial complex'. This intention was a major impetus to the establishment of the OCCWC, and its realization formed the core of the subsequent proceedings, with three of the four cases in which conspiracy and crimes against peace were charged involving industrialists and military figures.[58] Telford Taylor had been involved during the war with the British code-decrypters at Bletchley Park, and in consequence of their extensive (if secret) findings about German genocide, was aware of some of the dimensions of Nazi criminality.[59] The investigation of war crimes and crimes against humanity was, however, to remain subordinated in the subsequent proceedings for structural reasons: the prosecution of criminal groupings rather than of classes of crime remained OCCWC's aim.[60]

---

[55] Jonathan Bush, conference paper, ('Nuremberg and Its Impact: Fifty Years Later'; United States Holocaust Memorial Museum, 17 Nov. 1996).

[56] The four subsequent proceedings in which crimes against peace were charged were the Farben, Krupp, High Command, and Ministries trials.

[57] This decision was reached in a joint session of Tribunals I–V on 9 July 1947. SUA, MSS 200, NMT 13/1.

[58] The fourth was the multi-faceted Ministries case.

[59] Conot, *Justice at Nuremberg*, 16, shows how Taylor expressed the need to obtain the help of British intelligence in the prosecution of the German police and military, contrary to Breitman's position in *Official Secrets*, 187–91.

[60] Taylor, *Final Report*, appendix B, 160–1.

The wish to emphasize the conspiracy count continued to prevail, despite the lack of enthusiasm for it on behalf of some of the OCCWC personnel. For example, amongst the prosecutors at the Farben trial the opinion was voiced that, rather than attempting to establish from first principles the collaboration of the conglomerate with the expansionist drives of the Reich, it would have been to the advantage of the prosecution to begin by proving the connection with the atrocities of the regime (pre-eminently in this case the use of slave labour at Auschwitz), thus establishing in the minds of the Tribunal the character of the defendants as more than simply businessmen and scientists.[61] In the event, the only convictions in the case arose from the charges of plunder and spoliation, and slavery and mass murder; the charges that had been presented last. Even the judge seemingly most sympathetic to the prosecution's case, Paul Hebert, who filed an opinion dissenting from the small number of convictions and the lightness of the sentences handed down, agreed that an adequate case for the participation in a conspiracy of conquest had not been made.[62]

Additionally, it was made clear to the OCCWC that there were few in Washington who agreed with the continued use of the conspiracy count. The previous chapter outlined the general opposition to the trial of military figures, and this disdain frequently focused on the charges which, Field Marshal Montgomery thought, made the waging of unsuccessful war a crime—the 'political' charges of conspiracy and aggression. There was a more considered disapproval in the American ranks concerning the trial of industrialists. The War Department, which was ultimately answerable for occupation policy, made it clear that it did not support the use of such charges against this class of suspect, for it in no way wanted to discourage American industrialists from supplying the US military with *matériel* for fear of having similar accusations levelled at them in the aftermath of future conflicts.[63] In anticipation of the Flick trial Taylor was informed that it would be preferable to concentrate on the less controversial charges of war crimes and crimes against humanity, rather than on the abstract principles of 'cartelization' and the like.[64] For 'cartelization', 'conspiracy' may be read, since the aggressive pre-war expansion towards monopoly status of German industry was a prime subject of the larger charge in the Farben case. (It is, incidentally, indicative of their ignorance of goings-on in Germany that the War Department feared the use of a conspiracy count against Flick; this had not been proposed.)

It is testament to the autonomy with which Taylor operated, and to the sway still held by the conspiracy idea, that the former continued to endorse the latter

---

[61] Josiah DuBois, *The Devil's Chemists: 24 Conspirators of the International Farben Cartel Who Manufacture Wars* (Boston, Mass.: Beacon, 1952), 99–103; Borkin, *The Crime and Punishment of I. G. Farben*, 135–56.

[62] *TWC*, viii, 1211–12, 1311–22.   [63] DuBois, *The Devil's Chemists*, 21–2.

[64] NARA, RG 153, entry 1018, Nürnberg administrative files, 1944–9, box 13, memo for the Assistant Secretary of War from Damon Gunn, 6 and 7 Mar. 1947.

in the years 1946–9 in the face of such opposition. He was happy to jettison certain aspects of Jackson's approach, such as the utter mistrust of eyewitness evidence; he called several survivors of the Holocaust to the stand when it was deemed necessary, as it was not in the trial of the Einsatzgruppen leaders. He was prepared also to use Jewish prosecutors in cases of Jewish concern. However, it is apparent that Taylor still viewed Nazi criminality in the same way as Jackson, seeing the murder of the Jews as an offshoot of the ambition for conquest, colonization, and tyranny—the 'conspiracy', within which the planning and initiation of aggressive war was the supreme crime. A survey of the OCCWC's plans for the subsequent proceedings reveals that this perception of the acts of the Reich led not only to a hierarchy of charges, but consequently to a hierarchy of cases, the relative importance of each determined by the nature of the defendants and the counts which could be levelled at them.

Taylor recalled that the trial of Erhard Milch was not particularly important in achieving the wider aims of the subsequent proceedings. Rather, it was initiated because it was a small and fairly compact case, ready for presentation at a time when the more substantial proceedings—for instance, the vital one against Alfried Krupp—still required far more preparation.[65] Likewise, Taylor subsequently regretted the trial of five of the Flick concern by themselves, musing that they would better have been indicted alongside other industrial defendants to make a bigger and more comprehensive case.[66] When he submitted his projected trial programme to OMGUS in March 1947, the Chief of Counsel denoted those cases which he considered non-essential to the programme; one of these was the Einsatzgruppen trial, that which above all others brought the Jewish fate to the fore.[67] General Clay, the Military Governor, concurred in this analysis, declaring that other cases in the pipeline (such as a planned trial of prominent members of various German banks) would have been more germane to American aims than would another trial of SS men.[68] There was manifestly no antisemitism at play here, but rather a feeling that the planned trial would re-establish what was already known in general terms about the Shoah and Nazi criminality. It would not, just as the other trials mentioned in this connection would not, aid in establishing the conspiracy-aggressive war theory, for the common factor in each of them was the absence of both of the relevant counts.

That proceedings were enacted against the Einsatzgruppen leaders at Nuremberg is attributable only to the attractiveness of the case on technical grounds.[69] It was pared down greatly by the elimination of the need to examine

[65] The Krupp case was also probably delayed because of its potentially controversial nature. See Weindling, 'From International to Zonal Trials'.

[66] Taylor, Final Report, 78–9.

[67] NARA, RG 153, entry 1018, Nürnberg administrative files, 1944–9, box 13, memo from Taylor to Deputy Military Governor, 14 Mar. 1947.

[68] Clay Papers, ed. Smith, i, 420–1, Clay for Noce, 8 Sept. 1947.

[69] Robert Kempner, Ankläger einer Epoche: Lebenserinnerungen (Frankfurt am Main: Fischer, 1983), 293.

the multi-faceted guilt of the Gestapo, the Kriminalpolizei, and the Sicherheitsdienst (SD), for the killing squad leaders were originally supposed to be indicted
alongside representatives of the whole of the Reich Security Head Office
(Reichssicherheitshauptamt; RSHA).[70] The bigger trial did not transpire, and
the wealth of documentation pertaining to the activities of the Einsatzgruppen
promised, and ultimately resulted in, the most straightforward and shortest of
the Nuremberg prosecution presentations, based upon the type of evidence most
favoured by the Americans. No witnesses were produced by the OCCWC, meaning no troublesome cross-examinations, no verifications of contradictory recollections of events, and no debates over the identification of the accused.
Parenthetically, it also meant that no colour was added to the proceedings, that
the victims remained mute and two dimensional, without agency or humanity,
simply statistics presented in an abstract, racist context.

The Einsatzgruppen case was an exception that highlighted the rule. It was a
trial in which the OCCWC deviated from the principle of viewing the Shoah as
providing some of the best examples of the effects of Nazism. In the other proceedings Taylor was happy to divide coverage of the genocide between cases,
picking and choosing from its component parts in order to prove the guilt of the
different groups he chose to indict, rather than seeing the broader picture of the
crime itself as motivation for its commission (whether as a result of ideological
imperative or as a prize in the struggle for power in the Nazi hierarchy).[71] When
other anti-Jewish collectives were clearly identifiable, the imperative of trial was
superseded by the pre-conceived requirements of the Subsequent Proceedings
Programme. This was illustrated in 1947, in the aftermath of the discovery of the
minutes of the Wannsee conference amongst the plethora of Nazi documentation.

For our purposes this document must be taken purely at face value, as this
is how it was read by the American investigators. It may well be, as Eberhard
Jäckel has argued, that the conference was called by Heydrich simply in order to
establish his pre-eminence in the murder of the Jews, in the aftermath of
Göring's commissioning of him above his rivals to direct a 'total solution'—
Gesamtlösung—of the Jewish question.[72] Nevertheless, the protocols are still a
crucial insight into the orchestration of complicity in the Holocaust. To the
OCCWC the document inevitably appeared to confirm the prevailing suspicion

[70] A study of either Taylor's Mar. 1947 or May 1947 programmes indicates this. See also Taylor, *Final Report*, 80.

[71] For more extensive discussion of interpretations of the development of the 'final solution', see below, Chapter 5.

[72] Göring to Heydrich, 31 July 1941, Nuremberg Document PS-710, reproduced in *Documents on the Holocaust*, ed. Yitzhak Arad *et al.* (Oxford: Pergamon, 1981), 233. For Eberhard Jäckel's view of the Wannsee conference, see his 'On the Purpose of the Wannsee Conference', in James S. Pacy and Alan P. Wertheimer (eds.), *Perspectives on the Holocaust: Essays in Honor of Raul Hilberg* (Oxford: Westview, 1995), 39–49. For a more recent, more comprehensive analysis of the conference, see Peter Longerich, *Die Wannsee-Konferenz vom 20 Januar 1942: Planung und Beginn des Genozids an den europäischen Juden* (Ber-lin: Gedenk- und Bildungsstätte Haus der Wannsee-Konferenz, 1998).

about a broad conspiracy to commit war crimes and crimes against humanity, with the SS, and more specifically the head of the infamous RSHA, at the helm. In many ways this was the sort of evidence which the Americans had always assumed did exist about the murder of the Jews, and which was to be compared conceptually to other documents attesting to different aspects of the putative conspiracy, such as the 'Hossbach memorandum'. To Jewish observers, the Wannsee minutes crystallized Nazi antisemitism, and provided a workable basis for the initiation of criminal proceedings against the participants in that conference as significant representatives of the perpetrators of what has come to be known as 'the Holocaust'.

Yet the two conference participants tried at Nuremberg were indicted in separate cases, indicating that once again the crime of the Holocaust was to be divided between proceedings, and hence subordinated. Equally importantly, two other participants who were held by the Americans were not brought to trial at all. In November 1947 Rabbi Stephen Wise petitioned the OCCWC and the Army in the latter matter on behalf of the World Jewish Congress. His memorandum requested that these men be included in the forthcoming 'Ministries' case. As the combination of a number of planned trials which time restrictions forbade, the Ministries trial was the broadest of the US proceedings since those conducted before the IMT. It thus had the potential to consider crimes perpetrated by a variety of agencies. Wise realized that it was impossible by that time to begin 'a special Jewish trial', but observed pointedly that 'there should be no legal or practical impediment in bringing to justice, within the framework of the present plans and program, those of the chief criminals responsible for the Jewish debacle'. Further, he argued that since the trial dealt, amongst other issues, 'with crimes against humanity and specifically with the meeting of January 20, 1942, it would lend itself excellently to the inclusion of the highest German officials responsible for crimes against Jews, most prominent among them being those who participated in the afore-mentioned meeting'.[73]

At that time, nineteen defendants were involved in the Ministries case, and only one—State Secretary Stuckart of the Ministry of the Interior—had been at the conference. There were two other surviving participants of the meeting who were in the Nuremberg jail but were not contemporaneously facing charges: these were Erich Neumann, the State Secretary for the Four Year Plan; and Georg Leibbrandt, a State Secretary in Rosenberg's Ministry for the Occupied Eastern Territories. A third, Otto Hofmann, was under indictment in the 'RuSHA' trial. (It is instructive that at no time in Hofmann's cross-examination during the trial was he questioned about his participation in the Wannsee conference. His culpability in this regard was explicitly a factor in his condemnation to twenty-five years imprisonment, so we are presumably to conclude that once again documents were being taken at face value, with little or no investigation

---

[73] NARA, RG 153, entry 1018, Nürnberg administrative files, 1944–9, box 1, folder 4, Wise to Kenneth Royall and Telford Taylor, 19 Nov. 1947.

into their context, however ostensibly important.)[74] Taylor voiced two related objections to the inclusion of Neumann and Leibbrandt. He cited the need to accelerate the trial programme in the face of pressure from Washington, and the logistical problem of fitting any more defendants into the courtroom.[75] It is enlightening to juxtapose two facts here. First, at the end of the trials Taylor was to confess that the relative importance of the defendants was not a factor in deciding to omit certain 'former high-ranking Reich officials who were closely connected with the program for extermination of Jews'.[76] And secondly, that by the time of Taylor's riposte to Wise's enquiry, the number of defendants in the Ministries case had already risen from nineteen to twenty-one, without the inclusion of any additional Wannsee participants in the enlargement.

Though 'Jewish' issues, and indeed war crimes and crimes against humanity as a whole, were secondary concerns to the OCCWC, it must be recognized that when aspects of the 'final solution' were touched upon in the subsequent proceedings, they were generally dealt with in some depth, even if the interpretations imposed upon them do not always stand up to historical scrutiny. Moreover, the degree of independence of action possessed by Telford Taylor ensured that some attention remained on almost all areas of Nazi criminality, and to an extent on the Holocaust, when the weight of American opinion was increasingly against trials as a whole. The historiography of the Third Reich in general, and within this that of the persecution and murder of the Jews, certainly owes a considerable amount to Taylor's and Clay's interest in seeing at least some 'representative' justice done.

In comparison with the subsequent Nuremberg trials, the governing principles of British war crimes trials policy, aside from the period of involvement with the IMT proceedings, are remarkably clear. The Jewish factor was manifested almost entirely negatively, in a refusal to differentiate along ethno-religious lines between victim groups. That policy was entirely consistent with the long-standing view of the Foreign Office that Britain's interests were served 'little by emphasizing which racial minorities . . . have suffered most'.[77]

2.5 THE 'JEWISH FACTOR' IN THE ROYAL WARRANT TRIALS

The refusal to identify specific victim groups was reflected in the phrasing of the counts under the Royal Warrant, which in prosaic and formulaic fashion charged

[74] Hofmann's cross-examination, NMT Case 8. The explanation for the failure to cross-examine on the conference is supported if we consider that, in his direct examination, Hofmann claimed that the minutes were 'an incorrect representation; especially Heydrich did not mention anything about the fact that Jews should experience a natural reduction in their number by slave labor, and that the remaining Jews were to be subjected to a corresponding treatment'. (NMT Case 8).

[75] NARA, RG 153, entry 1018, Nürnberg administrative files, 1944–9, box 1, folder 4, tele-conference, 26 Nov. 1947.   [76] Taylor, *Final Report*, 94.

[77] PRO, FO 371/46796, c2865, paper of 5 June 1945 from Political Intelligence Dept. FO on the 'Treatment of atrocities and war guilt in information services for Germany'. I thank Kirsty Buckthorpe for this reference.

merely the perpetration of 'a war crime' in a given place at a given time by the commission of a proscribed act against 'nationals' of given countries. This one categorization of the afflicted was appropriate for transmitting the universality of, for instance, death, but it failed to encompass the diverse reasons for the kil-ling of different members of the same nation. Clearly and intentionally it also prevented explicit jurisprudential recognition of the scale of the Jewish fate. Thus the defendants in the 'Zyklon B case'—the trial of Bruno Tesch and two other members of his chemicals firm—were accused, 'in violation of the laws and usages of war' of supplying 'poison gas used for the extermination of allied nationals interned in concentration camps'.[78]

The policy of non-differentiation was compounded, as most of the concentra-tion camp cases that the British presided over concerned a multitude of victim groups, incarcerated and maltreated for many different 'crimes'. Many of the in-mates in these camps were Jewish, but that made no difference in principle; they could all be described by their nationhood. (The population of Belsen was roughly 70 per cent Jewish owing to its earlier status as an exchange camp for 'privileged' Jews. The other camps had a greater inmate mixture; indeed, prior to the final months of the war they were predominantly non-Jewish.) Moreover, in the matter of the 'Belsen' trial, it was by no means certain that Jews qua Jews would find representation at a case of such obvious significance in their history. The strictly military nature of the tribunals clearly proscribed any 'Jewish' par-ticipation in any of the prosecutions under the Royal Warrant. This right was only obtained through pressure exerted by the British section of the World Jew-ish Congress.[79]

In terms of concrete results, Jewish pressure was to provide little more than this sort of tokenism.[80] The taste remained for pursuing Nazis such as the mur-derers of the Stalag Luft III airmen on an imperative encapsulated in the remark of a Foreign Office official that 'for every man who demands to know why we are continuing to grind the faces of our former enemies, there is another who asks why we have not yet traced and arrested his son's murderer'.[81] But British Jews could no longer exert emotional leverage of this degree, and besides any sort of political vociferousness on their behalf gradually became more problematic as the levels of British antisemitism increased over Palestine and other issues in the post-war years.[82] On the legal plane, the machinery in the British zone for deal-ing with crimes against the Jews was being eroded anyway, and the requisites of

[78] UNWCC, Law Reports of Trials of War Criminals, i (London: HMSO, 1947), 93.

[79] Jewish Gazette (2 Nov. 1945); Jewish Telegraphic Agency report (18 Sept. 1945).

[80] By Nov. 1946 the Cabinet was seeking to end all trials as swiftly as possible. Much earlier, JAG jetti-soned responsibility for concentration camps not in the British zone. PRO, WO 309/1, cable, WO to HQ 21st Army Group BAOR, 19 June 1945.

[81] PRO, FO 371/64723, c15911/7675/180, Barratt to O'Grady, 9 Dec. 1947.

[82] For an exposition of the motivations of antisemitic behaviour at that time in Britain going beyond the simple formula of events in Palestine as the cause, see Tony Kushner, 'Antisemitism and Austerity: The Aug. 1947 Riots in Britain', in Panikos Panayi (ed.), Racial Violence in Britain, 1840–1950 (Leicester: Leicester University Press, 1993), 149–68.

British foreign policy had even determined that no more cases of crimes against humanity could be tried in control commission courts after October 1948.[83]

Trials of Jewish interest were periodically required throughout the British programme, but were never initiated as a result of Jewish influence, the vengeful 'pinchbeck God' that a poet of the era depicted.[84] Rather, impetuses varied from pure moral indignation, as in the case of Belsen, to foreign diplomatic pressure, as with Manstein. And though the sheer amount of Jewish suffering in the camps and the specifically anti-Jewish context of some of the orders transmitted on the eastern front made it impossible for the prosecutors to avoid confronting the Jewish fate in some measure (as again in those two cases), there was no medium to convey coherently the relative magnitudes of the crimes with which the courts were dealing, for the tribunals were not entitled to submit a written opinion substantiating their judgements. Indeed, to what extent the judges—at the coal-face of the whole war crimes issue—were influenced, on the one hand, by the evidence and, on the other, by the prevailing political and legal agendas of the policy-makers and law givers can never be adequately assessed. In the absence of evidence to the contrary, it may be assumed that within their narrow remit the members of the tribunals were no better equipped to ignore the mood of the times than was anyone else.

We may gain a rare insight into the implementation of the policy of victim non-differentiation in the trial of Field Marshal Albert Kesselring. His appearance in 1947 before a British court in Venice concerned massive German 'reprisal' actions against the Italian population,[85] and specifically his role in the murder of 335 civilians in the Ardeatine caves outside Rome in 1944 in retaliation for the death in a partisan attack of thirty-three German soldiers. Kesselring admitted in court that he considered the general policy of reprisals in the ratio of ten to one 'just and fair', and had consequently acquiesced in the transmission of an order to this effect from Hitler to the Fourteenth Army in Rome. (The additional murder of five men more than the intended 330 was apparently an administrative oversight.)[86] However, in the matter of the Ardeantine caves massacre, the defence contended that the action was entirely an SD responsibility over which the Wehrmacht had no responsibility. The court must have found this proposition impossible to believe, for Kesselring was convicted on both counts.

Implicit in the judgement was the rejection of the idea that reprisal killings, at least in this ratio and these circumstances, could be justified in wartime. The

---

[83] PRO, FO 1060/267, minute by Deputy Legal Advisor (Political), 16 Feb. 1950.

[84] This poem by Vivien Bulkley appeared in *Poetry Review*, 38, no. 4 (1947). It was exceptional amongst poems in the 1940s in addressing issues of war criminality and the Jewish fate.

[85] See Martin Seckendorf, 'Ein williges und fügsames Instrument: Die Wehrmacht in Italien—1943 bis 1945', in Johannes Klotz (ed.), *Vorbild Wehrmacht: Wehrmachtsverbrechen, Rechtsextremismus und Bundeswehr* (Cologne: Papy Rossa, 1998), 66–95, on Kesselring's responsibility for the harshness of the measures introduced.

[86] LHCMA, Hakewill Smith 1, transcripts of Kesselring trial, day 4, p. 7.

legality or otherwise of reprisals was by no means a clear-cut issue, as the Judge Advocate pointed out in his summary of the case to the court.[87] Indeed, when Kesselring's sentence of death was commuted to one of life imprisonment, one of the reasons forwarded by the confirming officer was 'the uncertainty surrounding limitations imposed on reprisals by law'.[88] References were made throughout by both sides in the trial to British, German, and American authorities on the laws of war, including the British manual of military law, and the most generous interpretation which may be derived therefrom regarding the permissibility of reprisal executions may be summarized as follows. The actions must be initiated if possible against the actual perpetrators, and may only be selected from the local geographical area if it is clear that the general populace supported the insurgent measures; killings must be as deterrent rather than revenge; they must not be in an excessive ratio (whatever that may be); and they must be humanely carried out. The intentional execution of non-combatant innocents from outside the geographical area does not appear to be condoned under any circumstances.[89]

As Christopher Browning has pointed out in a study of Wehrmacht reprisal policy in Serbia, based in part upon the Nuremberg Balkan generals' case, since the American tribunal considered that the army had failed to conform to these approximate legal standards, it declared all the reprisals which it was asked to consider to be criminal. Thus no differentiation was made between the categories of victims; a ruling which, Browning implies, blurred the considerable differences between the fates of—for example—Serbs and Serbian Jews under the German military regime.[90] In a matter that was in some ways a microcosm of the Balkan generals' trial, the Kesselring tribunal also failed to distinguish between groupings which had been the victims of German reprisals in Italy.

The variety of individuals comprising the 335 murdered in the Ardeantine caves shared one common feature: each person was considered, in the words of the local SD commander Kappler, 'todeswürdig', or 'worthy of death'. Some had actually been condemned to death, many to terms of imprisonment, and some were awaiting trial in Roman prisons for offences against the occupying forces;[91] indeed, it was a contention of Kesselring that he would never have consented to

---

[87] LHCMA, Hakewill Smith 9, p. 7. The Judge Advocate advised that if Kesselring was ultimately responsible for the killings, he would then as a minimum be guilty of the murder of the five people executed above the established quota of 330 (p. 6). There was thus a potential scenario in which Kesselring would be sentenced merely for the murder of a handful of individuals beyond the arbitrarily prescribed ratio of ten Italians for one German.

[88] PRO, PREM 8/707, TACGHQ to War Office, 29 June 1947.

[89] These conditions are the combined conclusions of the British Judge Advocate-General, Henry MacGeah (in his correspondence on the Kesselring case with C.-in-C., Central Mediterranean Forces, 23 June 1947, in PRO, FO 1060/260) and the tribunal in the Nuremberg Case 7, the Balkan generals' trial.

[90] Christopher R. Browning, *Fateful Months: Essays on the Emergence of the Final Solution* (New York: Holmes and Meier, 1991), 94.

[91] LHCMA, Hakewill Smith 1, transcripts of the Kesselring trial, day 3, unnumbered pages.

the killing of innocents as reprisal.[92] This claim was not entirely consonant with the general thrust of the field marshal's defence that an 'iron curtain . . . separated the Wehrmacht from the SD',[93] and nor was it consistent with the fact that between fifty-seven and seventy-two completely innocent Jews had been killed in the caves.[94] By Kappler's admission these people had been incarcerated as a result of a general order and were awaiting deportation to Mauthausen concentration camp; and as the army knew, they were 'todeswürdig' for no other reason than that they were Jews.[95] As Browning has written of reprisal policy in Serbia:

all interned Serbs were at high risk; but the interned male Jews were doomed. The German military could conceive of innocent Serbs but not innocent Jews . . . it was axiomatic that all Jews were anti-German and thus a legitimate target of a professional organisation dedicated to defending Germany against its enemies.[96]

Given both the doubt over the legal status of reprisals, and the leeway given to the court by the Judge Advocate's proposition that, if Kesselring was deemed ultimately responsible for the massacre, they could 'take into account both the killing and the manner of it', it is clear that the substantive difference between the reasons for the selection of the Jews and of the other victims carried significant potential weight. However, at no time in his notes on the case did the president of the court, Brigadier General Hakewill Smith, mention the Jews, even when discussing the theoretical position of 'innocent' victims.[97] Not much remains to be said, for once again Jews were notable by their absence, and once again the specific was submerged within the general. Nor was any effort made to amend the second count on which Kesselring was found guilty. That count charged the murder of 335 Italian nationals, though it had transpired during the trial that as many as six of the murdered Jews were not Italian.[98]

Finally, Kesselring's sentence was commuted on the basis of a few finely balanced legal arguments that found their most complete rebuttal in the death of the Jews in the Ardeatine caves: uncertainties around the law. That a totally innocent group, which counted among its number individuals from nowhere near the geographic locality, and which by the very fact of its incarceration could not have had anything to do with partisan incidents, could be sacrificed without objection under the authority of a military commander who had a reputed affinity with the Italian people was a clear illustration of why the Jewish fate was 'different'. And

92 LHCMA, Hakewill Smith 9, p. 6.

93 LHCMA, Hakewill Smith 1, transcripts of the Kesselring trial, day 13, p. 9.

94 Kappler provided the lower number, and Stefano Lidonitti, Secretary General to the Committee of Martyrs, the higher. LHCMA, Hakewill Smith 1, transcripts of the Kesselring trial, day 3; day 6, pp. 7–9.

95 LHCMA, Hakewill Smith 1, transcripts of the Kesselring trial, day 3; day 4, p. 2.

96 Browning, *Fateful Months*, 55–6.

97 LHCMA, Hakewill Smith, notes on the first charge.

98 Lidonitti, who had apparently researched the matter in some detail, stated that one of the Jews was Dutch, one Russian, one German, and that three were of unknown nationality. LHCMA, Hakewill Smith 1, transcripts of the Kesselring trial, day 6, p. 9.

if the death of these fifty-seven to seventy-two Jews was in reality a part of the Holocaust, in Venice it was treated as a standard component in a legal debate about a war crime *stricto sensu*.

An ostensibly marginal consideration such as the identity of a few of the Ardeatine caves victims becomes more relevant when we consider the significance of the legal process. The trials were the chief means by which Nazism was examined in depth; they were the scalpel to the bludgeon of the larger occupation and re-education policy, the foil to generalities. Nuances that they did not investigate were likely to remain uninvestigated during the post-war period.

What then was the general context within which the trials functioned? This matter is taken up in greater detail in the following section of the book, which explains the failure of the trials to impact in an informative way either in Britain and the USA or in western Germany. It serves to conclude this section and to introduce the next to show that beyond the courtroom, unbound by the fetters of jurisprudential judiciousness, the British and the American authorities would go even further in sculpting the profile of victimhood that would be presented to the post-war world. The murder of the Jews was de-emphasized more firmly and explicitly in general occupation policy. In other words, *the dominant official interpretation* of Nazism in occupied western Germany accorded a distinctly diminished role to the Nazis' chief genocidal project. For a number of reasons that had nothing to do with proportional historical representation, the British and the American occupiers chose to build their re-educational edifices on the foundation-stone of 'Aryan' suffering.

2.6 OCCUPATION POLICY, VICTIM SPECIFICITY AND SYMBOLS OF SUFFERING

Despite the steady flow of information out of occupied Europe on the plight of the Jews from mid-1942 at the latest, the force of the reports and imagery from the concentration camps uncovered during the Allied advance in 1945 made those institutions the prime symbols of Nazi atrocity for the west. For the British public and occupiers, we know that Bergen-Belsen in particular was emblematic; the pre-occupation with the place went beyond the initial horror at its discovery, stretching to a concern several months later with the fate of orphaned inmate children.[99] The camp was incorporated into a series of generalistic British meta-narratives about the triumph of good over evil and the liberation of humanity from Nazism, but the reportage of the liberation was remarkable for avoiding reference to the Jews who formed the majority of the inmates.[100]

---

[99] Cf. *British Paramount News* issue of Nov. 1945, *Belsen Children Find Refuge Here*.

[100] David Cesarani, '"Le crime contre l'Occident": Les réactions brittaniques à la libération des camps de concentration nazis en 1945', in Marie-Anne Matard-Bonucci and Edouard Lynch (eds.), *La libération des camps et le retour des déportés: L'histoire en souffrance* (Brussels: Éditions Complexe, 1995), 238–49, esp. 238; Joanne Reilly, *Belsen: The Liberation of a Concentration Camp* (London: Routledge, 1998), 1–2.

Buchenwald and Dachau held similar places in the American consciousness of Nazi atrocity. In contrast to Belsen, however, the majority of their prisoners—approximately four-fifths—were not Jewish, but were instead prisoners from Germany and other European countries held on political grounds. As Peter Novick has suggested, these were therefore not representative of the 'Holocaust' as we understand it today, and the American reportage accordingly either did not mention or did not privilege the fate of the Jews.[101]

In terms, then, of apprehension of the racial focus of the most extreme Nazi crimes, the liberation period was not at all helpful. One of the singular features of the Holocaust is that the majority of its victims were murdered outside the perpetrating country, to the east of Germany. The German concentration camps themselves, the only camps with which the western Allies came into direct contact, were of a different order, with different histories and functions, from the extermination facilities constructed in Poland with apparatus for mass gassing. The former were generally institutions of political repression, the latter of outright genocide. Thus, though it was to be expected that in 1945–6 in the immediate vicinity of Belsen the place would serve both as didactic tool and stick with which to beat the locals,[102] it served simply to perpetuate a circumscribed British conception of the past when, two years later, the only licensed book from England in the Hamburg region dealing directly with Nazi genocide concerned that camp.[103] Of western occupation policies generally, it is evident that while the early policies of forcing the native populations to visit and clean the western concentration camps, and public displays of photographs of those places, confronted German civilians with the depravity of their erstwhile society,[104] the public screenings in the midst of the IMT trial period of the American-made *Todesmühlen* was a reiteration which did not encourage differentiation between the institutions or the objects of oppression. The twenty-minute-long *Todesmühlen (The Mills of Death)*, consisted in the main of a compilation of images of death from institutions in western and eastern Europe alike. It was

---

[101] Novick, *The Holocaust in American Life*, 63–5.

[102] Rainer Schulze, 'A Difficult Interlude: Relations between British Military Government and the German Population and Their Effects for the Constitution of a Democratic Society', in Alan Bance (ed.), *The Cultural Legacy of the British Occupation in Germany* (Stuttgart: Hans-Dieter Heinz Akademischer Verlag, 1997), 67–109, esp. 70–2.

[103] Moreover, this book was written from the perspective of a liberator rather than one of the liberated. It was a translation of Derek Sington's *Belsen Uncovered* (London: Duckworth, 1946). For a reproduction of the licensed book lists, see the appendix to Rhys Williams's, '"The Selections of the Committee Are not in Accord with the Requirements of Germany": Contemporary English Literature and the Selected Book Scheme in the British Zone of Germany (1945–1950)', in Alan Bance (ed.), *The Cultural Legacy of the British Occupation in Germany* (Stuttgart: Hans-Dieter Heinz Akademischer Verlag, 1997), 110–38, esp. 126–34.

[104] See e.g. Karl Jaspers, *Die Schuldfrage: Von der Politischen Haftung Deutschlands* (Munich: Piper, 1987), 29. On American policies of forcing Germans to see Buchenwald, and the refusal of the local population to admit knowledge of what had occurred practically on their doorstep, see Manfred Overesch, *Buchenwald und die DDR; oder, Die Suche nach Selbstlegitimation* (Göttingen: Vandenhoeck und Ruprecht, 1995), 106–9.

problematic because at no point in the narration were Jews, or any other victim group, singled out.[105] Indeed, the film ended with a Christianization of suffering: a reference to a calvary of the murdered.

Equally deficient were the hour-long OCCPAC production *Nazi Concentration Camps*,[106] prepared for the IMT, and the short documentary culled from it, entitled *KZ* (*Konzentrationslager*; 1945) and tested in Erlangen. A similarly titled edition of the occupation *Welt im Film*, shown in June 1945, dwelt entirely on concentration and labour camps, erroneously describing the Hadamar 'mercy-killing' institution in this category, and describing victims only in terms of their nationality.[107] (We also know that the word 'Jews' was specifically edited out of *Your Job in Germany*, a 1944 propaganda film shown to the occupying American troops, and subsequently in a revamped form to US audiences.[108] Jews had been the only non-national victim group mentioned in the original narration.) This type of visual imagery was recognized early on as being particularly influential as part of the re-education process in laying bare the concentration camps *per se*,[109] so the dearth of photographs of Auschwitz, and the poor pictorial presentation of Majdanek in the illustrated Allied press, when compared with, say, the de-judaized Belsen, logically contributed towards keeping the extermination centres in obscurity in the western mind.[110]

As, over time, distinctions between persecutions were becoming somewhat more precise before the IMT and other courts, it was still a matter of chance as to the types of atrocities—and thus the victim groups—to which the average German was most exposed. Thus recipients of the occupation newspaper *Hamburger Nachrichtenblatt der Militärregierung* in May 1945 met with the death camp (*Todeslager*) Majdanek, and the qualitative and quantitative differences between that place and the other camps of which so much had previously been written. But four days later the same organ conflated 'Maideneck [*sic*] und

---

[105] For the failure of the film to instil a sense of collective responsibility, see Brewster S. Chamberlin, 'Todesmühlen: Ein früher Versuch zur Massen "Umerziehung" in besetzten Deutschland 1945–1946', *VfZ*, 29 (1981), 420–36. As the film had to be reduced in length, everything on the earlier history of the camp was removed, accommodating only the images of horror from the end of the war. *Süddeutsche Zeitung* (15 Apr. 1985). The inexactitude of the film was replicated in the popular press. For example, *Die Neue Zeitung* (15 Feb. 1946) reproduced a very incomplete map of the concentration camp network.

[106] Douglas, 'Film as Witness', on *Nazi Concentration Camps* and its use both during the IMT trial and subsequently, notably in the Eichmann trial.

[107] Imperial War Museum film archive.

[108] David Culbert, 'American Film Policy in the Re-Education of Germany after 1945', in Nicholas Pronay and Keith Wilson (eds.), *The Political Re-Education of Germany and Her Allies after World War II* (London: Croom Helm, 1985), 173–202, esp. 190, 202.

[109] Chamberlin, 'Todesmühlen'; Culbert, 'American Film Policy'.

[110] For details of the representations of the extermination camps, see Ute Wrocklage, 'Majdanek und Auschwitz in der internationalen Bildpresse 1945', in Yasmin Doosry (ed.), *Representations of Auschwitz* (Auschwitz: Auschwitz State Museum, 1995). Also Dan Diner, 'Massenverbrechen im 20. Jahrhundert: Über Nationalsozialismus und Stalinismus', in Rolf Steininger (ed.), *Der Umgang mit dem Holocaust: Europa—USA—Israel* (Cologne: Böhlau, 1994), 468–81, esp. 468–9. This coverage should be contrasted with that of Belsen, to which whole newsreel articles were devoted in spring 1945: for instance, the 'Horror in Our Time' issue of *Gaumont British News* (Apr. 1945); and the 'Belsen Goes up in Smoke' edition of *British Paramount News* (May 1945).

Theresienstadt, Belsen und Auschwitz, Dachau und Nordhausen, Mauthausen und Ebensee, Kiel und Neuengamme, Buchenwald und Oranienburg'.[111]

Likewise, readers of the left-wing *Telegraf* were confronted daily for three weeks in mid-1946 with moving extracts from the diary of a Ravensbrück inmate; but this was the only consistent coverage given to a 'camp' in the early years of that newspaper.[112] Alternatively, subscribers to the liberal *Frankfurter Rundschau* could find themselves reading in some detail on Auschwitz (from coverage of the trials), the 'euthanasia' centre Hadamar, or alternatively on 'the Hell of Treblinka', with the massive omission of the specifically Jewish fate at the third of these.[113]

Even the proliferation of inmate memoirs encouraged by the Allies in 1945 and 1946 constituted an unbalanced picture of camp life. The vast majority were penned by non-Jewish political prisoners of various sorts, and again related chiefly to camps from within the Reich. Only three of the forty-two released in the British and American zones concerned Auschwitz (none described the pure extermination centres). Of these, only one was written by a (German) Jew, and he had spent comparatively little time at the camp. Moreover, he appears to have been overtly political. The others were again written by political prisoners, one by an exiled German. All three writers had been incarcerated at Auschwitz I, the original concentration camp, as opposed to Auschwitz-Birkenau, the extermination facility. Furthermore, all three of these accounts were coincidentally published in 1948, when the Allies were seeking to end their trial programmes with the minimum of friction out of politically motivated consideration for German sensibilities about the Hitler era.[114]

To portray predominantly regular, western concentration and labour camps, with the concomitant absence of Jews, was not only unrepresentative in itself, it was problematic in the context of the early Allied collective guilt accusations. That large numbers of the inmate populations of these camps were themselves German was seized upon by opponents of collective measures.[115] It was an obvious inconsistency in Allied propaganda, but was in fact encouraged in what

---

[111] Issues of 29 May, 2 June 1945.   [112] *Telegraf* (23 May–14 June 1946).

[113] *Frankfurter Rundschau* (3 Dec., 5 Feb. 1946). Wassili Grossmann's article on Treblinka recalled only 'Polish' victims.

[114] Helmut Peitsch, '*Deutschlands Gedächtnis an seine dunkelste Zeit*': Zur Funktion der Autobiographik in den Westzonen Deutschlands und den Westsektoren von Berlin 1945 bis 1949 (Berlin: Edition Sigma, 1990), 101–2, 173–7; the books penned by the regular political prisoners were, Emil de Martini, *4 Millionen Tote klagen an! Erlebnisse im Todeslager Auschwitz* (Munich: von Weber, 1948); Zenon Rozanski, *Mützen ab . . . Eine Reportage aus der Strafkompanie des KZ Auschwitz* (Hanover: Verlag des anderen Deutschland, 1948); that by the sole Jew was Rudolf Weinstock, '*Das wahre Gesicht Hitler-Deutschlands*': Häftling Nr. 59000 erzählt von dem Schicksal der 10000 Juden aus Baden, aus der Pfalz und aus dem Saargebiet in den Höllen von Dachau, Gurs-Drancy, Auschwitz, Jawischowitz, Buchenwald (Singen: Volksverlag, 1948). Peitsch makes nothing of the different identities of the victims, and little of the differences between the camps. On the development of concerted German opposition to occupation measures and the beginning of the distortion and displacement of the Nazi past, see below, Chapter 4.

[115] Alfred Grosser, *Germany in Our Time* (New York: Praeger, 1971), 41; Victor Gollancz, *What Buchenwald Really Means* (London: Gollancz, 1945).

was to become the dominant theme of occupation 'information' policy in West Germany.[116] Thus a report produced in April 1945 by the influential Psychological Warfare Department of the joint Allied supreme command SHAEF[117] on the making of a documentary on the concentration camps aimed to 'promote German acceptance of the justice of the Allied occupiers by reminding Germans of their past acquiescence' and, therefore, their 'responsibility'. However, it also aimed to show specific crimes committed in the German name to rouse the populace against the Nazis. The latter was to be accomplished specifically by focusing upon German victims of atrocities and, if possible, establishing their individual identities.[118] The special June 1945 edition of *Welt im Film* duly pinpointed German resistance fighters. Jews, again, were not mentioned at all.

Finding iconic 'good' Germans who had been mistreated by the Nazis was naturally an important part of leading the country towards democracy in illustrating by example the existence of political alternatives and moral choice: one such was Kurt Schumacher, who went on to lead the SPD, the Social Democratic Party of the BRD. Yet in many instances the straightforward message was compounded by a number of sub-texts. Most notable in this context was the military 'resistance' in Germany, whose most ostentatious act was the bomb plot on their leader's life on 20 July 1944. Their actions provided apparent testimony to the rift between the established order and Nazism and 20 July remains to this day a touchstone of all those wishing to mitigate German guilt, regardless of the true impetus to revolt.[119] There is evidence that the moderating of American public opinion on the former enemy was aided by the publication in 1947 of Allen Dulles's *Germany's Underground*, an overblown account of resistance,[120] just as the appearance of volumes such as Hans Bernd Gisevius's *Bis zum bitteren Ende* nourished German apologia.[121] (Simultaneously in Britain, the film *Frieda* explored with some popularity the idea that there were after all 'good' Germans, or that there might be again in the future.) Yet the resisters were in truth a varied

[116] Kurt Koszyk, *Pressepolitik für Deutsche 1945–49. Geschichte der deutschen Presse*, pt 4 (Berlin: Colloquium, 1986), chs. 2, 3, on the development of this policy over time. See Reilly, *Belsen*, 71, for an example of a conflicting directive from around the same time.

[117] On the function of the Psychological Warfare Division in forming information policy in Germany, see Koszyk, *Pressepolitik für Deutsche*, 21–3.

[118] University of Warwick, Modern Records Centre, Crossman papers, MSS 154/3/PW/1/1–211, SHAEF PWD report, 25 Apr. 1945. Part of the rationale for distinguishing between Germans at this juncture was to discourage widespread participation in the feared 'Werewolf' guerrilla movement, or a resort to a national redoubt.

[119] For the inflation of the resistance, see the *Times* (20 July 1963). On the use of the 20 July as an educational tool in modern Germany, see Ian Buruma, *Wages of Guilt: Memories of War in Germany and Japan* (London: Jonathan Cape, 1994), 187; on the ambivalence of Germans towards the plot in the early years of the BRD, David Clay Large, '"A Beacon in the German Darkness": The Anti-Nazi Resistance Legacy in West German Politics', *Journal of Modern History*, 164 (1992), suppl., 173–86.

[120] Allen W. Dulles, *Germany's Underground* (New York: Macmillan, 1947); Schwartz, *America's Germany*, 158.

[121] Hans Bernd Gisevius, *Bis zum bitteren Ende*, i. *Vom Reichstagsbrand zur Fritschkrise*, ii. *Vom Münchener Abkommen zum 20 Juli 1944* (Darmstadt: Claasen, 1947/8); Peitsch, 'Deutschlands Gedächtnis an seine dunkelste Zeit', 48–9.

selection, many of them conspiring out of fear of what Hitler's wars would bring down on Germany, not out of any sense of moral indignation at his means of conquest. They had not carped when alongside the attempt to conquer the USSR itinerant police units massacred nearly 2 million Soviet and Polish Jews. Indeed, a minor plotter had been Artur Nebe, erstwhile head of the killing squad Einsatzgruppe B.

Consider also the 28 May 1945 issue of the two-sided British Military Government newspaper the *Hamburger Nachrichtenblatt*. This was one of the only printed sources available in a zone starved of information and short of newsprint.[122] The issue confronted the reader with a short article from an anonymous observer who had simplistically equated the Wehrmacht with the SS, thus attributing responsibility for Germany's crimes to one of the most revered institutions of German society as well as the more obvious malefactors. Overleaf, the scene was dominated by a German who was ostensibly above reproach: 'thus spake Pastor Niemöller' ran the headline of an article on Germany's moral and spiritual crisis, the messianic Nietzschean allusion unmistakeable.[123]

Martin Niemöller is worthy of closer examination, as for comparative purposes is another of the Allies' totemic victims, Eugen Kogon. Niemöller was the founder member of the 'Pastor's Emergency League', a precursor of the Protestant Confessing Church, which was established in 1934 in reaction to the pro-Nazi 'German Christian' movement. He was incarcerated in a concentration camp in 1938 on a Hitler order after official release from state imprisonment for anti-Nazi activity. Kogon, an admirer of Niemöller,[124] was a sociologist on the other side of the confessional divide. Kogon was interned by the Nazis immediately upon the annexation of Austria. In the post-war period both were given platforms to discuss the issue of German guilt. Niemöller was one of the best-known victims of Nazism, and toured western Germany as a prominent public speaker and preacher; he featured regularly in both the organs of the Allied occupation press and the licensed media.[125] Kogon was commissioned—by the Psychological Warfare Department of SHAEF—to write a treatise on the concentration camp system,[126] and was made the licensed editor of the journal *Frankfurter Hefte* which, after its foundation early in 1946, swiftly achieved an unparalleled popularity.[127] He was also used as an expert witness in various war crimes trials.

[122] For the importance of the Allied publications, see Morris Janowitz, 'German Reactions to Nazi Atrocities', *American Journal of Sociology*, 52 (1946), 141–6, esp. 143.

[123] *Hamburger Nachrichtenblatt* (28 May 1945): 'Generale mit Gestapo-Methoden'; 'Also sprach Pastor Niemöller'.

[124] Michael Kogon (ed.), *Eugen Kogon: Ideologie und Praxis der Unmenschlichkeit: Erfahrungen mit dem Nationalsozialismus* (Berlin: Quadriga, 1995), 198.

[125] For instance, *Frankfurter Rundschau*, hereafter '*FR*' (15, 25 Jan. 1946; 5 Mar. 1946; 30 Apr. 1946).

[126] Hubert Habicht (ed.), *Eugen Kogon—ein politischer Publizist in Hessen: Essays, Aufsätze, Reden zwischen 1946 und 1982* (Frankfurt am Main: Insel, 1982), 7.

[127] Karl Prümm, *Walter Dirks und Eugen Kogon als katholische Publizisten der Weimarer Republik* (Heidelberg: Karl Winter, 1984), 11, 17–18.

Inherent to their stories of opposition and victimization was, again, an emphasis on the German concentration camps and the plight of political opponents of Nazism: Niemöller had been imprisoned in Sachsenhausen and Dachau, Kogon in Buchenwald. Kogon's book, *Der SS-Staat*, was indeed based extensively on his own experiences of incarceration and accordingly the fate of the Jews is the subject of only a small subsection.[128] But Niemöller and Kogon were also particular sorts of German opponents and victims. First, they represented each of the leading Christian traditions. The church was the only pillar of public life to retain its influence after the German collapse, and its influence in re-spiritualizing Germany, not least in the forthcoming struggle against Communism, was considered essential by characters as diverse as Heinrich Böll, Konrad Adenauer, and the Allied leaderships. (As the one institution entrusted with 'self-denazification' by the occupiers, however, the church signally failed to purge its own body, casting its ills in the form of the scapegoat of the German Christian movement.)[129] In itself this was not unproblematic, for the church had largely remained silent in the face of the war and Nazi genocide, and Christian teaching more generally had established the 'culture of contempt' towards Jews in which Hitler's antisemitism flourished. Of equal import to the Allies as Kogon's and Niemöller's Christianity, however, was the negative connotation of that identity: the very fact that they were not Jews.

We might extrapolate here from the pre-war period, when the coverage given in the UK to the fate of Niemöller and the German churches was already widespread, probably more so than that of the Jews. In late October 1939 the British Government published a White Paper on German atrocities, partially in response to German propaganda on the British use of concentration camps during the Boer War. Consistent with the contemporary distrust of Jewish sources and the reluctance to appear publicly to connect the war effort with the protection of Jews, this document was deliberately angled to downplay Jewish suffering. It was decided to emphasize in 'the first few documents [cases] which are not so sensational as the Jewish ones *but which show that perfectly good Aryans such as Niemöller and the German Catholics have also had to suffer*'.[130]

Not only were Niemöller and Kogon good symbols as non-Jews for polities that remained unwilling to stress Jewish suffering, it clearly did not deter the Allies that both men had revealed attitudes to Jews that were, at the least, ambivalent. If Kogon had only infrequently allowed his anti-capitalist views to lapse explicitly into antisemitism in the pre-war period,[131] and was to examine the

---

[128] Kogon, *Der SS-Staat*.

[129] Doris L. Bergen, *Twisted Cross: The German Christian Movement in the Third Reich* (Chapel Hill, NC: University of North Carolina Press, 1996), 207–12.

[130] PRO, FO 371/23105, c16788, Roberts to Stevens, 16 Oct. 1939. Emphasis added. For contextualization of this document and the perpetuation of such attitudes during wartime, see Kushner, 'Different Worlds', 249–51.

[131] Prümm, *Dirks und Kogon*, 65–8.

Holocaust in some depth later in life,[132] Niemöller had been more forthright, most notoriously expressing his regret that Jesus had been born a Jew.[133] Finally, and perhaps relatedly, the two were attractive to the western Allies because of their anti-Communism.[134] Niemöller's was again more vociferous,[135] but we might also examine the second German edition of Kogon's *Der SS-Staat* and the first edition in English translation in 1948 with the title *The Theory and Practice of Hell*. Their final chapters are given over to a comparative examination of the use of prison camps in the USSR under Stalin. This nourished the parallel Allied trend towards using the concentration camps as generic symbols of totalitarian domination rather than specific manifestations of Nazism: an approach that was officially adopted in British information policy May 1948, when it was decided for anti-Communist reasons to broadcast information in Germany on Soviet camps and deportations.[136]

The appropriation of Nazi imagery for use in the post-war environment was not always as crude (and unsuccessful) as Churchill's suggestion that the election of the 1945 Labour Government would introduce a Gestapo into British society.[137] US Secretary of War Stimson's support for the organizational section of the IMT case was partially predicated on the apprehension that a trial of the Gestapo would serve as a useful weapon in discrediting other secret police forces, and specifically the Soviet NKVD.[138] The Nazi camps had obvious potential in this connection, and would be used accordingly and with increasing force from 1945.[139] Indeed, as western popular comprehension relied to an extent on those 'liberated' within the German boundaries, and also on their pre-war incarnations, the 'totalitarian' comparison had a certain weight; these were, after all, institutions that had been invented for the incarceration and terrorization of political opponents. It was no mere coincidence, however, that their non-Jewish inmates were the victims on whom the western Allies preferred to concentrate.

---

[132] e.g. Hermann Langbein *et al.*, (eds.), *Nationalsozialistischen Massentötungen durch Gifigas: Eine Dokumentation* (Frankfurt am Main: Fischer, 1983).

[133] The best and most recent examination of Niemöller's anti-Jewishness, and the failure of many observers to take this into account when assessing his opposition to Nazism, is an unpublished chapter of an ongoing Ph.D. thesis at the University of Southampton: Thomas Lawson, '"The Splendid Image of a Christian Conscience Unbowed": The Development and Implications of the Myth of Martin Niemöller'.

[134] On the oft-made connection between Jews and Communism, see Novick, *The Holocaust in American Life*, 92–3. On Kogon's anti-Communism, Prümm, *Dirks und Kogon*, 61.

[135] Lawson, 'The Myth of Martin Niemöller'. For a rare contemporary observation—from Sept. 1947—that Niemöller's antisemitism, amongst other things, might render him inappropriate as a point of reference, see Christof Schneider, *Nationalsozialismus als Thema im Programm des Nordwestdeutschen Rundfunks (1945–1948)* (Potsdam: Verlag für Berlin-Brandenburg, 1999), 141–2.

[136] Koszyk, *Pressepolitik für Deutsche*, 233.

[137] Martin Gilbert, *Winston S. Churchill*, viii (London: Heinemann, 1988), 32; A. J. Davies, *To Build a New Jerusalem* (London: Abacus, 1996), 219.

[138] Smith, *The Road to Nuremberg*, 61–2.

[139] Novick, *The Holocaust in American Life*, 86–8. At the beginning of the IMT trial, in fact, an observer from the FO Political Dept. equated the Soviet 'concentration camps in Siberia or the Urals' with 'similar establishments in Germany'. See note by Mr Pink, undated, reproduced in *Documents on British Policy Overseas, 11 August—31 December 1945*, 405–8.

2.7 CONCLUSIONS

For our purposes here, it is important to understand that 're-education' was the tool with which British and American perceptions of German-ness and Germanism were foisted on the German people. Even in the ostensibly crime- and perpetrator-specific war crimes trials and denazification proceedings these generalistic trends were evident. Hence, for instance, the indictment of the General Staff and High Command at Nuremberg in a juxtaposition of the comparable dangers of German militarism and Nazism. The equation was mirrored in the attempts to include both in the extreme category in the denazification scheme.[140] Undoubtedly, if it had been possible to quantify 'Prussianism' during the war, this too would have been a prominent charge.[141]

Just as the war had been entirely devoted to defeating the Axis, and at no point specifically to halting mass murder, so the peace was all about reforming Germany. To the extent that the latter required recourse to some of the 'facts' of Nazism, these were supplied, but only to the end of moulding Germans into the image the Allies wished of them. To illustrate this point the Nuremberg trials are a helpful microcosm. In both the narrower and the broader media 'representative' crimes against humanity were seen as almost interchangeable in establishing the base outcome of aggression and racism in which the vast majority of German people were seen by their silence to be at least tacitly complicit.

Draconian measures against Germany had been the intention of the founders of occupation policy—particularly the Americans—from before the 'liberation' of the concentration camps; these places served simply to confirm beyond all doubt the necessity of a redirection of that society. And as the Allies gathered this evidence and developed their own general ideas of Nazi criminality, they were quite happy to transmit these perceptions back to the Germans. In other words, occupation officials, who may have been less well informed about their subject matter than the population they were supposed to be informing chose the symbols with which they were most familiar, and which most suited their aims, regardless of how unrepresentative these totems actually were. The presence of the 'Jewish factor', however, meant that Jewish victimhood was particularly susceptible to misrepresentation.

The 'Jewish factor' in OCCPAC and OCCWC policy was, measured in terms of its negative ramifications, a relatively constant one. If during the war it became important to play down claims to recognition of the specificity of anti-Jewish crimes, afterwards it was de rigueur to emphasize how even-handed the prosecuting agencies were in pursuing all classes of criminal for all types of crime—though as the pre-eminence of the conspiracy theory shows, this was manifestly

---

[140] PRO, FO 371/55439/c12776, CCG to COGA, Oct. 1946.
[141] Barbro Eberan, *Luther? Friedrich 'der Grosse'? Wagner? Nietzsche?...?....? Wer war an Hitler schuld? Die Debatte um die Schuldfrage 1945–1949* (Munich: Minerva, 1983) 19.

not the case. As Telford Taylor wrote, it would not 'have been fair or wise to favor or discriminate against any particular occupation, profession or other category of persons'.[142] The result was that the American jurists created a distorted representation of Nazi crimes by the very act of trying to standardize the prosecution of an unevenly distributed cruelty. Over and above this, they also diminished real, specific crimes by attempting to cram them into the space left after the consideration of the theory of aggressive war within the broad and imaginary conspiracy framework.

For the British, the fate of the Jews was even less of an impetus to trial. As the only other 'western' nation whose trial programme had any claim to being genuinely international in its scope, the UK remained extremely parochial in its concerns. While the Americans, hailing from an increasingly pluralistic liberal culture (although this development was being forced along from within), translated 'universalism' into approaching the Jewish tragedy alongside that of other groups, they went further than the British who were predisposed not even to recognize explicitly that Jews had suffered as a collective.

Though the weight of evidence on the murder of the Jews drew attention to itself during some trials, this was by no means always so; thus, for instance, in the Kesselring case, which has already been juxtaposed with the Nuremberg Balkan Generals' trial. Although both courts reached similar decisions on the illegality of reprisal killings and consequently did not differentiate qualitatively between groups as victims of such murder, the tribunal in the Balkan Generals' case saw fit to list Jews as constituting numerically one of the largest classes of dead; there is no evidence to suggest that an opinion penned by Kesselring's judges would even have mentioned Jews.

The situation could not be amended in the period in question because at no time were Jews allowed a voice with which to draw attention to the extreme fate of their kin. They were reliant upon the offices of others whose attention was divided between many interests, and for whom the weight of evidence about the Shoah was not always compelling, even if it was apparent. Jews were not alone in this anguish, however, nor was their situation even extreme. The Sinti and Roma were all but forgotten at Nuremberg and elsewhere, and their wartime fate remains a marginalized chapter of the twentieth century, as the history of those peoples has always been in the shadow of supposedly greater 'civilizations' and more 'important' international developments. Furthermore, owing to suspicion of Soviet evidence (or indeed any evidence not gathered by Anglo–American forces) and, not infrequently, to a thinly disguised chauvinism towards the eastern Europeans, little attention was paid by the western Allies to the slaughter and indirect killing of millions of Slavs, both civilians and prisoners of war.

The translation of these Allied socio-cultural, political, and legal priorities to the trial transcript and thence to wider representations and perceptions of

---

[142] Cited in *Final Report*, appendix B, 160.

Nazi criminality brings us to the second section of this book. The next chapter examines much more extensively the way that the Allies examined the depths of German criminality. It considers the legal accounting for the eastern extermination centres within the context of the investigation of the camp system as a whole.

Part II: Post-War Representations and Perceptions

CHAPTER THREE

The Limits of the Legal Imagination: Plumbing the Depths of Nazi Criminality

If the concentration camp has been the *signifier* of Nazi atrocity from the liberation period down to the contemporary focus on Auschwitz, the nature of the *signified*, the referent, has not always been apparent. Neither has this received wisdom been uniform. For the Nazis the camp system was a stratified one, with particular sorts of institution reserved for particular categories of inmate and subject to particular authorities.[1] The 'concentration camp' *per se* was a specific designation,[2] and the generic use of the term in the post-war world has done nothing to aid scientific analysis of the Nazi system of repression and murder.

Interpretations of the camp system have been as varied as national experiences of the Hitler era. The French focused on camps in their proximity, but also on those institutions where members of the French resistance had been incarcerated. This was characteristic of a post-war regime that sought to locate all of the blame for the chequered French war record on the Nazis, and grossly exaggerated the part of the French resistance.[3] Not by chance were heroes of the resistance prominent on the IMT bench and amongst the French prosecutors.[4] In the official Soviet comprehension of Nazism, Auschwitz, and to a greater extent Majdanek, were promoted as symbols of the 'martyrdom' of the international 'victims of fascism' rather than any particular group. Under Soviet influence, in the eastern zone of Germany and then the DDR, Buchenwald, Ravensbrück, and Sachsenhausen were similarly used, with grossly disproportional emphasis

---

[1] For a taxonomic study of the camp system with particular reference to the Jewish fate, see Donald Bloxham, '"Extermination through Work": Jewish Slave Labour under the Third Reich', *Holocaust Educational Trust Research Papers*, 1, no. 1 (1999–2000), 3–7; for general consideration of the other major categories of camp, see Ulrich Herbert, Karin Orth, and Christoph Dieckmann (eds.), *Die nationalsozialistischen Konzentrationslager. Entwicklung und Struktur*, 2 vols. (Göttingen: Wallstein, 1998); for Soviet POWs, see Christian Streit, *Keine Kameraden: Die Wehrmacht und die sowjetischen Kriegsgefangenen* (Stuttgart: Deutsche Verlags-Anstalt, 1981); for forced non-Jewish labourers, see Herbert, *Hitler's Foreign Workers*.

[2] Werner Johe, *Neuengamme: Zur Geschichte der Konzentrationslager in Hamburg* (Hamburg: Landeszentrale für politische Bildung, 1986), 15–30.

[3] Henri Rousso, *The Vichy Syndrome: History and Memory in France since 1944* (Cambridge, Mass.: Harvard University Press, 1991); Gerhard Kiersch and Annette Kleszcz-Wagner, 'Frankreichs verfehlte Vergangenheitsbewältigung', in Jürgen Weber and Peter Steinbach (eds.), *Vergangenheitsbewältigung durch Strafverfahren? NS-Prozesse in der Bundesrepublik Deutschland* (Munich: Olzog, 1984), 164–76.

[4] 'Justice Jackson's Story', fos. 1345–7.

on the resistance movements within these camps, and little or none on Jews, homosexuals, or 'gypsies'.[5]

For the liberal democracies, we know that the camps of Dachau, Buchenwald, and Belsen, with all their complex inherent and potential meanings, were the vital symbols. It was no accident that the first major trial to be conducted at Dachau, between 15 November and 13 December 1945, concerned the former commandant of that camp and several of his staff; nor that the parallel British Royal Warrant trial, spanning 17 September to 17 November 1945, dealt with Josef Kramer and many of his accomplices. If these camps were the 'ultimate metaphor of evil',[6] then settling accounts with their most notorious staff suggested catharsis. Little interest or patience would be reserved for the more detailed and nuanced findings of the subsequent Nuremberg tribunals, just as the Germans themselves would not really be forced to confront the trials that succeeded that of the major war criminals.[7] This brings us to the crux of the present chapter: what role did the early trials play in the formation of representations of 'the camp'?

The focus in the first three sections will be upon the IMT and the 'Belsen'[8] cases and, to a lesser extent, on the first Dachau trial. As a consequence both of their timing and their subject-matter, and in Germany in part as a result of the Allied control of the news media, these three commanded the most widespread attention of any trials of the period. The chapter culminates, however, in an examination of what was effectively a non-representation at the trials: that of the Polish extermination centres of Belzec, Sobibor, and Treblinka. Besides the IMT trial, it brings in consideration of the first and fourth of the subsequent Nuremberg proceedings. These were, respectively, the Medical trial and the Pohl trial against members of the SS Business Administration Head Office,

---

[5] Fulbrook, *German National Identity after the Holocaust*, 28–35. See also Peter Reichel, *Politik mit der Erinnerung: Gedächtnisorte im Streit um die nationalsozialistische Vergangenheit* (Munich: Hanser, 1995).

[6] Cited in Kushner, *The Holocaust and the Liberal Imagination*, 221; see also Jon Bridgman, *The End of the Holocaust: The Liberation of the Camps* (London: Batsford, 1990), 34–53.

[7] Newspaper reporting of the subsequent Nuremberg trials was fragmentary at best, and only two of the twelve judgements were published. See Joachim Perels, 'Verpasste Chancen: Zur Bedeutung der Nürnberger Nachfolgeprozesse vor dem Hintergrund der ungenügenden Strafverfolgung von NS-Tätern in der BRD', in KZ-Gedenkstätte Neuengamme (ed.), *Die frühen Nachkriegsprozesse: Beiträge zur Geschichte der nationalsozialistischen Verfolgung in Norddeutschland*, iii (Bremen: Edition Temmen, 1997), 30–7, esp. 30, on the judgements in the Farben and Ministries trials. Only the judgement in the Einsatzgruppen trial appears to have received a mention on the official radio station in the British zone. Schneider, *Nationalsozialismus als Thema im Programm des Nordwestdeutschen Rundfunks*, 161, 170.

[8] Entitled the 'Belsen' trial because, as we shall see, Auschwitz was an important subject of the proceedings also. A note of explanation for this immensely complex set of institutions is required. After a reorganization order of 22 Nov. 1943, Auschwitz was officially divided into Auschwitz I (the original concentration camp, with one converted gas chamber and crematorium), Auschwitz II (also known as Birkenau, the major killing centre), and Auschwitz III (also known as Monowitz, which was in fact only one of ten labour camps; these had no killing facilities). Auschwitz as a whole was also often referred to by its Polish name, Oswiecim, adding to the confusion. The contingent parts of the camp will be differentiated as needed during this chapter.

the organization that administered the concentration camps from March 1942 onwards.

The study will show how the trials avoided consideration of the clearest signifier of Nazi genocidal antisemitism. Trial policy was implicated in the process of conflation and homogenization that characterized occupation policy as a whole and that created the enduring camp trope. This process was one that would have wide-ranging ramifications in a world where victimhood was fast becoming ready political currency.

3.1 THE DACHAU TRIAL

The start of the first trial at the former concentration camp Dachau, concerning the very staff that had formerly ruled supreme there, coincided with the beginning of the IMT trial. Though observers from eleven countries were present for the Dachau proceedings, the Nuremberg trial had attracted some 250 journalists and radio reporters, as well as numerous photographers and film operators.[9] In terms of global attention the latter would steal all of the headlines outside the USA[10] (and, indeed, many of those within it), and thus the Dachau trial was primarily of relevance in the formation of American opinion.

For one vital reason the American press went even further than its British counterpart in spring 1945 in distorting the role of the concentration camps 'liberated' by that country. Dachau had what appears to have been a small experimental gas chamber, as well as a substantial crematorium. Historiographical consensus suggests that if any gassings did in fact take place there, they were on a small, exploratory level.[11] However, in the light of wartime rumours of mass gassings, the apparently concrete evidence of these facilities and the report of the US investigating team suggested to many that they had discovered one of the very worst camps. Many of the early reports contained information on the gas chambers.[12]

This was an enduring feature. Thus though the proceedings established that the gas chambers had only been experimental,[13] a report in the *New York Times* on the relevant testimony sensationally revealed 'the wholesale execution of Russian prisoners in a gas chamber'.[14] *Todesmühlen* would also refer to mass gassings at Dachau. Not only did this elide the difference between concentration camps and extermination facilities, it also exaggerated the use of gas in the mass

---

[9] Sigel, *Im Interesse der Gerechtigkeit*, 41; *FR* (30 Nov. 1945).
[10] According to Jürgen Wilke, *Nürnberger Nachrichten* carried more than 700 articles on the IMT trial; *Tagesspiegel* 500; *Frankfurter Rundschau* 300; *Süddeutsche Zeitung* more than 200. See Wilke, 'Ein früher Beginn der "Vergangenheitsbewältigung"', 14.
[11] Langbein *et al.* (eds.), *Nationalsozialistische Massentötungen durch Giftgas*, 277–80.
[12] Norbert Frei, '"Wir waren blind, ungläubig und langsam: Buchenwald, Dachau und die amerikanischen Medien im Frünjahr 1945', *VFZ*, 35 (1987), 385–401, esp. 391. For the report of US Investigating Team 6823, 30 Apr.–31 Aug. 1945, see NARA, microfilm no. 00049103, USA versus Martin Gottfried Weiss *et al.*, 1945 (hereafter, 'USA v. Weiss'), roll 1, target 6.
[13] Ibid. roll 2, trial transcript, pp. 129–132.   [14] *NYT* (17 Nov. 1945).

murder of groups other than Jews. These impressions could perhaps have been tempered from within the courtroom, for the dock contained Friedrich Wilhelm Ruppert, formerly of the Majdanek concentration-extermination centre. However, his experiences there were irrelevant chronologically and geographically to the charges marshalled in the Dachau case.

The extreme vision of Dachau was compounded by the first exchanges of the trial. The two counts of the indictment were irrefutable, at least in moral terms. They charged the defendants with acting in pursuit of a 'common design' to subject nationals of countries with whom Germany was at war, and prisoners-of-war, to 'cruelties and mistreatment', including 'killings and beatings'.[15] This 'common design' was not analogous to the 'conspiracy' charge used at Nuremberg but was rather a device to show that concentration camps were inherently criminal enterprises and that individual guards must therefore have been criminal parties irrespective of participation in specific, substantive criminal acts.[16] However, the prosecution proclaimed in its opening statement that it was seeking to prove the defendants were actually engaged in a scheme of outright extermination in Dachau, the chief methods of which were starvation and overwork.[17]

There is no indication or whether of not the court concurred with the idea of planned extermination, for the judgement was not accompanied by an opinion. Prior to announcing sentences the tribunal made the very reasonable declaration that the regime of Dachau and its sub-camps 'subjected its inmates to killings, beatings, tortures, indignities and starvation to an extent and to a degree that necessitates the indictment of everyone, high and low, who had anything to do with the conduct or operation of the camp'.[18] The press coverage of the trial and its aftermath went well beyond this measured statement, however.

Even at the end of 1945, when much had been revealed about more extensive atrocities during the IMT trial, the *New York Times* adjudged of the Dachau trial that it was 'one of the most odious and feared of the concentration camps set up by the Hitler regime'.[19] The *Washington Star* was also sufficiently obsessed to find one and a half pages for a diary extract on the 'Horror Camp' of Dachau. And it was simply unfortunate when, midway through 1946, the *Times Herald* printed an estimate of the dead at the camp which was between six and ten times too large.[20]

---

[15] USA v. Weiss, roll 2, introduction.

[16] Sigel, *Im Interesse der Gerechtigkeit*, 44. The use of the (apparently reasonable) common design count is perhaps another indication of the less conservative American approach to the prosecution of war crimes. Indeed, in its closing statement the prosecution at the Dachau trial went so far as to emphasize 'the fact that the offense with which these 40 men stand charged is not killing, beating and torturing these prisoners but the offense is aiding, abetting, encouraging and participating in a common design to kill, to beat, to torture and to subject these people to starvation' (ibid. 55).

[17] USA v. Weiss, roll 2, trial transcript, p. 53.

[18] Ibid. roll 3, trial transcript, p. 1981.   [19] *NYT* (13 Dec. 1945).

[20] *Washington Star* (16 Dec. 1945); *Times Herald* (29 May 1946)—the estimate was 300,000.

The Dachau programme went on to consider institutions lower down the scale of depravity than that of the eponymous camp. A series of trials against the personnel of Mauthausen, and proceedings concerning the Hadamar 'mercy-killing' institution, touched respectively the worst of the chief penal camps and one of the nerve-centres of the most successful Nazi genocide—the murder of the mentally and physically 'handicapped'. With regard to the Jewish fate, several of the sub-camps of Dachau were worse than the main camp itself (though comparatively little time was allocated to them at the first, most visible trial), and, indeed, places of greater Jewish suffering such as Mühldorf would be considered later in the programme.[21] The paramount place of Dachau alongside Buchenwald[22] in the American memory of the Nazi 'camps' was, however, assured. The 'Belsen' trial similarly did little to contextualize that camp within the system of terror for the British public.

3.2 THE 'BELSEN' TRIAL

The beginning of the trial of Josef Kramer *et al.* set the tone for the case. The indictment made no mention of Jews, and that part of it devoted to 'war crimes' at Auschwitz, at which Kramer and several of the other SS personnel had served in addition to Belsen, did not refer to either gas chambers or mass murder. An article published on the first day of the trial in *The Times* referred to the trial as the 'Belsen trial'—the epithet had already been adopted—but omitted Auschwitz.[23] The only licensed German newspaper in the western zones, the liberal *Frankfurter Rundschau*, was happy to reproduce the British description of Kramer as 'the Beast of Belsen', thus accepting and reflecting the bias towards that camp.[24] The *New York Times* promised revelations of a 'gas death chamber' in 'Oswiecim' (Auschwitz), but failed to mention Jews.[25] The opening speech for the prosecution included only one reference to Jews—the near-precise estimate of 45,000 Greek Jews—taken to Auschwitz, of whom it was noted only sixty survived.

The prosecutor Colonel Backhouse did, however, differentiate between Auschwitz and Belsen, stating that conditions at the former were the result of 'a policy of deliberate extermination', whereas at the latter they were brought about by 'criminal neglect, . . . deliberate starvation and ill-treatment.' He introduced the idea of millions of deaths at Auschwitz, promising to bring forward a witness who would testify to 4 million murders at the camp[26] (a number far in

---

[21] On the greater number of Jews incarcerated at Mühldorf and the other Dachau sub-camp of Kaufering, see Edith Raim, *Die Dachauer KZ-Aussenkommandos Kaufering und Mühldorf: Rüstungsbauten und Zwangsarbeit im letzten Kriegsjahr 1944/5* (Landsberg am Lech: Landsberger Verlagsanstalt Martin Neumeyer, 1992), 176–8.

[22] Lawrence Douglas, 'The Shrunken Head of Buchenwald: Icons of Atrocity at Nuremberg', *Representations*, no. 63 (1998), 39–64.

[23] *The Trial of Josef Kramer*, ed. Phillips, 4; *The Times* (17 Sept. 1945).

[24] *FR* (19 Sept. 1945).　　　　[25] *NYT* (17 Sept. 1945).

[26] *Trial of Josef Kramer*, ed. Phillips, 13–30.

excess of current expert estimates of the total of dead at Auschwitz-Birkenau),[27] but the *Frankfurter Rundschau* was again true to the tone of the proceedings when, amidst its detailing of the scale of the Auschwitz gas chambers, the Jews were notable by their absence.[28] When Backhouse's witness subsequently arrived, she did reveal that the Auschwitz victims were predominantly Jews.[29] Yet some of the reporting of the opening speech distorted Backhouse's message: focusing on Belsen, then describing Auschwitz as a camp with 'very much the same routine as Belsen'. The 4 million figure was faithfully reported in the *New York Times* and *The Times*, but again they referred only to 'people' cremated.[30]

Alongside her estimate of the number of Jews killed at Auschwitz, the witness in question, a Polish–Jewish doctor, Ada Bimko, told of the operations of the gas chambers, and the techniques used to get the bodies to the crematoria, including the operations of the Jewish Sonderkommando. Her testimony actually seized the headline in *The Times*, and constituted one of the clearest assertions of the nature of Auschwitz throughout the course of the reporting of the trial; indeed, it was only in the context of her appearance that the *Frankfurter Rundschau* got to grips substantially with the Jewish aspect of the trial.[31] The two other witnesses to give competent testimonies about the gas chambers at Auschwitz were also Jewish.

In a moving and informative appearance, Sophia Litwinska described a horrific ordeal when she was on the verge of being gassed. Charles Bendel had been deported from Drancy (Paris) to Monowitz in December 1943. From January 1944 his services as a doctor were required in the 'Gypsy camp' in Birkenau. He was thus in a position to observe the arrival of transports of Jews, the 'selections', and the consequent gassings. He witnessed the delivery of the gas in Red Cross vans, and was one of the first to provide what by now is a staple of death-camp testimony, in his recollections of the 'basalt-like' appearance of the intertwined corpses in the Birkenau gas chambers.[32] Most of this detail was related in *The Times*, though that newspaper concentrated more on the sensational 'near-death' experience of Litwinska than on the remainder of her testimony.[33] The information was all but absent from the *Frankfurter Rundschau* and the *New York Times*.

---

[27] The most authoritative minimum estimate is 1.1 million total dead, including around 960,000 Jews: Franciszek Piper, *Die Zahl die Opfer von Auschwitz* (Auschwitz: Auschwitz State Museum, 1993), 166–7.

[28] *FR* (22 Sept. 1945); ibid. (17 Oct. 1945) for Russian film evidence on Auschwitz, in which, without comment, the concluding words of the narration were reported: 'Vier millionen Menschen sind in diesem Lager ermordet werden' [4 million *people* were murdered in this camp]. Emphasis added.

[29] *Trial of Josef Kramer*, ed. Phillips, 68.

[30] *The Times*, *NYT* (both 18 Sept. 1945).

[31] *The Times* (22 Sept. 1945); an article on 24 Sept. disclosed Bimko's revelation that 'the gas chamber [*sic*] was used exclusively for Jews and gypsies [*sic*]'. Bimko claimed to have received the figure from one of the workers in the Sonderkommando. See *FR* (26 Sept. 1945); ibid. (10 Oct. 1945), for the remaining small appreciation of Jewish issues. *NYT* was slightly less clear in its report of 22 Sept., implying that 'selections' of Jews for mass murder also went on at Belsen.

[32] *Trial of Josef Kramer*, ed. Phillips, 81, 131–5.   [33] *The Times* (25 Sept. 1945; 2 Oct. 1945).

Consistent with the prejudices of the British, however, the first witnesses for the prosecution were members of the British Army involved in the liberation of Belsen and in its subsequent administration. The first survivor of Belsen to be examined was illustrative of an equally judgmental selection: Harold Osmond Le Druillenec, a Jersey schoolmaster, was reported to be the only Briton known to have survived Belsen.[34] (Le Druillenec appears to have been something of a star witness for the British, who utilized him again at the trials of staff of the Neuengamme camp.)[35] The Jewish witnesses, who had seen far worse than had Le Druillenec, or indeed the British soldiers, were relegated to later appearances, when the initial impact of the trial had diminished.

The capricious nature of press reporting ensured that substantial attention was only paid in most British national newspapers to the first of the two months of the trial proceedings, hindering correction of any early misconceptions stemming from the first days of the case. In addition, the press coverage of those early phases was far from unproblematic. On at least one occasion, evidence about Auschwitz was confused with that on Belsen. Dora Szafran had been moved from the former to the latter in January 1945, but her testimony was reported in such a way as to give the impression that selections for the gas chamber at the former had in fact occurred at the latter.[36] Such misapprehensions clearly contributed to the later description in the liberal American publication *PM* of the 'tortures and gas-chamber deaths at the Belsen and Oswiecim camps'; or the *New York Times*' invocation of the 'Belsen gas chamber'.[37]

Elsewhere in the Anglo-American press, the *Jewish Chronicle* had allowed itself to be distracted from the evidence produced at the trial by the pronouncements of the British defence counsel. Though it was scandalous to announce in mitigation of the defendants that concentration camps were 'the common form in Europe'; that they were little different in nature to Allied treatment of the Germans; and that they contained 'the dregs of the ghettos of Central Europe', the expression of the newspaper's righteous indignation at the expense of factual reporting was not helpful in the interests of the popular record.[38]

The dramatic decline in British and American press coverage began directly after the testimony of the chief defendant, Josef Kramer. Kramer had been commandant of Belsen at the time of its liberation, and previously commandant of Birkenau, so the Auschwitz connection in his case was by far the most significant of any of the defendants. His knowledge of the gassing of the Jews and his role in the selections for the gas chamber were the crucial issues pertaining to Auschwitz, to which much time was devoted in his cross-examination. He revealed that 'as a rule' Jews were the only people required to attend selections. Yet the report in *The Times* made no mention of Jews and concentrated more on Kramer's

---

[34] *Trial of Josef Kramer*, ed. Phillips, 30–66; *The Times* (21 Sept. 1945).
[35] *Telegraf* (31 Mar. 1946).   [36] *Trial of Josef Kramer*, ed. Phillips, 116.
[37] *PM* (15 Nov. 1945); *NYT* (27 Sept. 1945).
[38] *Jewish Chronicle* (12, 19 Oct., 23 Nov. 1945).

denials than his admissions.[39] The *Frankfurter Rundschau*, on the other hand, continued to report throughout the closing months of the trial; yet it contrived to concentrate largely on Belsen, and even when considering the cross-examinations of Kramer and Irma Grese, or Auschwitz specifically, avoided the subject of Jews.[40]

The summing-up of the arguments of the defence and the prosecution by the judge advocate in the Belsen case was an approximation to a justification of the verdicts. It contained a fair representation of the evidence forwarded during the course of the trial concerning Auschwitz, Belsen, the differences between these two camps, and the fate of the Jews.[41] Of course, there was no indication of which of the arguments of the Judge Advocate were accepted and which rejected by the court. Perhaps in recognition of the limited influence of the summing-up on the verdicts reached, it received as little press coverage as had become the norm since midway through the trial. The proceedings of the last four days of the first British war crimes trial after the Second World War were received with virtual silence in *The Times* and the *New York Times*. In both, the verdicts were mechanically reproduced alongside either reflections on technical issues of the trial or consideration of the reactions of the defendants.[42]

The reading of the indictment and the judgement at the beginning and end respectively of the trial of the major war criminals attracted an enormous amount of press coverage. The judgement was particularly important, in that it summed up, to the best of the abilities of the judges, the evidence introduced in the trial. In the 'Belsen' trial, however, neither the indictment nor the judgement shed light on the broad sweeps of Nazi policy. The indictment was necessarily restricted to individual acts of cruelty on the part of the defendants, and did not introduce the mass murder of the Jews. The judgement, in the tradition of military courts martial, was not accompanied by an opinion of the tribunal detailing the reasons for the verdicts and the sentences.

In sum, if the trial of Kramer *et al.* did go some way towards challenging 'narrow British parochialism with regard to the war and the Jews',[43] it did not go very far. In western Germany, Anglo-American preconceptions about the camp system were in turn transmitted through the Allied-controlled press, while the licensed German press did not show itself capable of or willing to break down the evidence from the courtroom. The majority of the defendants were drawn from Belsen, and even those who had played significant roles at Auschwitz remained connected primarily with Belsen. It remained 'the Belsen trial', and the majority of newspaper reports on issues pertaining to Auschwitz had either come after, or

---

[39] *Trial of Josef Kramer*, ed. Phillips, 421; *The Times* (9 Oct. 1945).

[40] *FR* (13, 17, 19 Oct. 1945).   [41] *Trial of Josef Kramer*, ed. Phillips, 630–45.

[42] *The Times* (14–17 Nov. 1945); *NYT* (18 Nov. 1945). *FR* (16, 20 Nov. 1945) again devoted more time to the sentences and the closing briefs of the prosecution, but did not correct the misleading picture that it had established.

[43] Kushner, *The Holocaust and the Liberal Imagination*, 226.

in the context of, discussion of Belsen. The name of Auschwitz was introduced but there was certainly no consistent differentiation between the extermination camp and the concentration camps to counteract the barrage of photographs and reports of the latter at the close of the war in Europe. This lack of clarity was perpetuated at Nuremberg in the greatest single forum for the investigation of Nazi criminality.

3.3 THE IMT TRIAL AND THE CAMP SYSTEM

The inequities of the French and Soviet cases before the IMT resulted from a combination of the desire of their representatives to downplay Jewish particularity whilst emphasizing their own national suffering and heroism. Indeed, they were given *carte blanche* to concentrate upon whichever symbols of suffering they chose by the prevailing emphasis on 'representative' illustrations of Nazi criminality. Additionally, the paucity of French and Soviet documentary resources meant that they did not make any real investigation of the Nazi administration of murder.

Neither team made proper enquiries into chains of command, spheres of authority, or the way in which institutions fitted into the scheme of policy. Often the information they propagated was simply incorrect: Soviet Chief Prosecutor Rudenko described Dachau as 'a camp of extermination';[44] the French claimed they had evidence to the effect that 'about seven million *persons* died in [Auschwitz].'[45] The omission of Jews from the Auschwitz story—indeed from almost everything in these presentations—was repeated in the closing address of the French Chief Prosecutor, de Menthon.[46]

Nevertheless, the French did bring forth a witness to testify to conditions at Auschwitz. Marie-Claude Vaillant-Couturier had been transported there from Ravensbrück, and she became acquainted with many of the horrors of Auschwitz. An eyewitness to selections, she described on more than one occasion how Jews were singled out for murder. She provided a concise layperson's account of the gassing process and established that Birkenau was a part of Auschwitz. The memory of this formidable witness proved accurate in every regard except those in which she could only speculate; thus she overestimated the number of Hungarian Jews arriving in the camp in 1944 as around 700,000.[47]

The quality and integrity of this account was not necessarily transferred to the wider publics of the world, however. For though, in consequence of her appearance at Nuremberg, Vaillant-Couturier was interviewed by the *Frankfurter Rundschau*, the reporter chose not to ask her anything about her experiences at Auschwitz. The newspaper opted instead to get her opinion on the issue of the

---

[44] *IMT*, xxii, 324; v, 178.
[45] *IMT*, xix, 550; vi, 323 (Nuremberg document RF-140). Emphasis added.
[46] *IMT*, v, 368–426.   [47] *IMT*, vi, 203–27. The number was approximately 438,000.

'general guilt'—*Gesamtschuld*—of the German people.[48] Moreover, in addition
to her strength of character and memory, Vaillant-Couturier had one quality as a
witness that made her attractive to the French, who, like the British with Le
Druillenec, used her in other contexts.[49] She had been deported to Auschwitz as
a member of the French Resistance, and not, as was the case with the vast majority of the rest of her compatriots so treated, as a Jew. The route to Auschwitz via
Ravensbrück was not nearly as common a one from France as that via Drancy, so
she represented the small glory of France rather than the great shame.

In fact the French made no mention at all of Drancy, the Parisian internment
centre which had served as a holding-place for Jews on their way to Auschwitz.
They did, however, bring a witness to testify about conditions in the Natzweiler-
Struthof camp in Alsace, but this was a rather different proposition for them. In
the preparations for the IMT trial when it was decided that individual examples
of generic actions were needed as illustrations, Professor André Gros of the
UNWCC had surmised that the 'Struthof camp would typify the concentration
camp atrocities'.[50] Struthof held a similar position in the French mind to that of
Belsen in the British,[51] but its selection was almost certainly a concomitant of the
use of the camp by the Nazis for the internment of suspected members of the
French resistance under the 'Night and Fog Decree', the *Nacht- und Nebelerlass*.
The witness concerned, one Cappelen, made no mention of the 150 Jews who
were gassed in Natzweiler's experimental gas chamber in order to provide skel-
etons for the Strasbourg University Institute of Anatomy.[52]

The press coverage reflected the bias of the French evidence towards the mal-
treatment of 'political prisoners'. All that *The Times* could write of Vaillant-Couturier was that 'her evidence on conditions [at Auschwitz] bore out the hideous
tale already heard at the Belsen trial'. In a separate issue, evidence was discussed
about gassing at Auschwitz, including the vastly inflated estimate of 7 million
dead, but Jews were not singled out. Rather, the talk was of 'a general system of
extermination . . . in all camps'. *The Times* suggested after some of the French
evidence that 'the world already knows enough of the Belsen and Dachau trials,
for example, to need any detailed repetition of these monstrous war crimes
now'.[53] (It is instructive to note that in the period from the beginning of the trial
to the Christmas recess, the name of Auschwitz was only mentioned once in *The
Times*, in a brief reference to the Soviet part of the indictment.)

[48] *FR* (15 Feb. 1945). The expression *Gesamtschuld* appears to have been coined by Thomas Mann. See
his *Deutsche Hörer! Radiosendungen nach Deutschland aus dem Jahren 1940–1945* (Frankfurt am Main: Fischer Taschenbuch, 1987), 154.

[49] On a specific use by the French of Vaillant-Couturier in the representation of the camps, see
Wiewiorka, 'La construction de la mémoire du génocide en France', 24–6.

[50] PRO, WO 219/3585, minutes of 70th meeting of UNWCC, 18 July 1945, pp. 8–9.

[51] Muriel Klein-Zolty, 'Perception du Génocide juif dans les "DNA" et dans Le Monde de 1944 à
1946', *Le Monde Juif*, no. 150 (1994), 109–20.

[52] *IMT*, vi, 278–88. On the Strasbourg Institute, see Alexander Mitscherlich and Fred Mielke, *Medizin ohne Menschlichkeit: Dokumente des Nürnberger Ärzteprozesse* (Frankfurt am Main: Fischer, 1960), 13.

[53] *The Times* (25–30 Jan. 1946).

The massive destruction wrought on Soviet territory meant that the USSR did have a very legitimate claim to a sympathetic hearing. Yet, possibly as a result of the lack of evidence to hand, they attempted to inflate death tolls and appropriate suffering at certain camps. At one point the Soviets claimed that '840,000 Russian prisoners of war in Sachsenhausen were annihilated at one time'.[54] Their opening and closing addresses were replete with references to shattering statistics of the damage inflicted upon eastern Europe; and while western observers were dubious about the veracity of these figures, 'the Russians admitted to no doubts. Their figures were confidently stated and satisfyingly round.'[55] Their estimate of the numbers killed at Auschwitz was attained scientifically, they claimed. By employing 'rectified co-efficients for the part-time use of the crematorium ovens and for the periods when they stood empty', a Soviet extraordinary state commission concluded that the camp had consumed 'four million *citizens* of the USSR, Poland, France, Yugoslavia, Czechoslovakia, Romania, Hungary, Bulgaria, Holland, Belgium and other countries'.[56] This figure was considerably greater than the actual total. Though it is unclear, political motives must be suspected for the posting of such a high estimate. What was patently not an honest error was the failure to mention that the victims of Auschwitz were primarily Jewish; this failure was duplicated in the Russian references to Treblinka and, uniquely in the Allied presentations, the extermination centre Chelmno in the 'Warthegau' area of western Poland annexed to the Reich.

These omissions were mitigated by the one witness whom the Russians did introduce with experience of Auschwitz. Severina Smaglevskaya, a non-Jewish Russian national singled out the Jews at Birkenau, who 'were driven directly to the crematory, were not registered, were not tattooed, and very often were not even counted'. Her evidence, when taken in conjunction with that of the detailed Soviet commission report, painted a picture of Auschwitz which was surprisingly accurate given the circumstances under which it was delivered.[57] Predictably, however, the full insight of Smaglevskaya's testimony was not passed on to a wider audience. The information which was relayed in *The Times* about Auschwitz included the 4 million over-estimate and mention of gas chambers, but the victims were not recognized as Jews.'[58]

In its broad treatment under the conspiracy count of war crimes and crimes against humanity, the American prosecution team was predisposed to emphasize the concentration camps liberated by its countrymen as 'representative examples'. Jackson's opening address, which was also the first set-piece of the trial, included no references to camps in the section 'crimes against the Jews';[59] Thomas Dodd's presentation on 'concentration camps' included reference to

[54] *IMT*, vii, 586; this estimate was faithfully repeated in *FR* (8 Mar. 1946). The real total was probably a little in excess of 12,000. See Reinhard Otto, *Wehrmacht, Gestapo und sowjetische Kriegsgefangene im deutschen Reichsgebiet 1941/42* (Munich: Oldenbourg, 1998), 265–6.

[55] Tusa and Tusa, *The Nuremberg Trial*, 194.

[56] *IMT*, viii, 322. Emphasis added.   [57] Ibid. viii, 318–22; vii, 174–5.

[58] *The Times* (9–28 Feb. 1946).   [59] *IMT*, ii, 118–27.

'the infamous Auschwitz', but also to Mauthausen as 'one of the most notorious extermination centers', and to Flossenbürg as 'a factory dealing in death'.[60]

Auschwitz would be used only sparingly and inconsistently as an illustration. The film footage shown of the concentration camps by the Americans featured only those which they had liberated. It purported misleadingly to show 'mass execution gas chambers and furnaces'.[61] In the introduction of the case against the SS, most of the examples came from Dachau; Auschwitz was only mentioned in the context of a document drawn up in 1940, when it was still a regulation concentration camp.[62] Mauthausen was similarly given precedence over Auschwitz in the presentation of the cases against Ernst Kaltenbrunner and those organizations under his command provisionally from May 1942 and permanently from January 1943—the Gestapo and the SD.

Mauthausen assumed particular importance in this context for three main reasons. First, there was 'unequivocal' documentary evidence of the harshness of the camp's regime, according to a directive drawn up in January 1941 which categorized it separately from every other German camp as the harshest of all the penal institutions.[63] (It must be noted that this document was drawn up prior to the inception of the extermination camps.) Secondly, gas chambers—again small and experimental, although greater killing capacity could easily have been improvised—had been discovered at Mauthausen. Thirdly, Mauthausen had been vital in the implementation of the infamous 'Bullet Decree', or *Kugelerlass*. This was an order to execute Allied airmen who had been caught attempting to escape, and like the murders of the Stalag Luft III airmen, it aroused as much anger in the ranks of the Anglo-Americans as any of the Nazi horrors did. Though Mauthausen was perhaps the worst of the concentration camps, with a death toll of approximately 119,000, in terms of scale and victim profile, and the systematization of murder, it was of a different order to the eastern extermination centres.[64]

The only American presentation to grasp the importance of the death camps in the murder process was Major William Walsh's exposition on the 'persecution of Jews'. He referred to reports of Polish origin on 'Auschwitz *concentration camp*' and on 'the *concentration camp* at Treblinka'. Both detailed the production-line murder of thousands of Jews, though the report on Treblinka erroneously referred to the use of steam in the murders.[65] The remaining document produced dealing directly with Auschwitz was the now-famous 'Auschwitz escapees

---

[60] *IMT*, iii, 508, 512, 513.

[61] Ibid. iii, 512. Dachau and Mauthausen had small gas chambers, Buchenwald had none.

[62] Ibid. iv, 286–311, 189–91, 202–7, 225 (Nuremberg document PS-1352).

[63] Ibid. 264–5 (Nuremberg documents PS-1063(a), PS-1063(b)).

[64] Gordon J. Horowitz, *In the Shadow of Death: Living outside the gates of Mauthausen* (London: Tauris, 1991), 18, 22. The gas chamber accounted for approximately 4,000 of an estimated 119,000 victims of the Mauthausen complex of camps, 38,906 of whom were Jews.

[65] *IMT*, iii, 566–8 (Nuremberg documents L-161, PS-3311). Emphases added. The recurrence of reports about the use of steam for murder at Treblinka will be discussed below, Chapter 3.6.

report' compiled by two former Birkenau inmates, Rudolf Vrba and Alfred Wetzler. Walsh quoted the number 'gassed in Birkenau in the two-year period between April 1942 and April 1944' as 1,765,000.[66] The final item of interest in his presentation was an affidavit of an RSHA official, Wilhelm Höttl. It reported a conversation with Eichmann, in which the latter had estimated that the Nazis had murdered 6 million Jews in total, 'approximately four million . . . in the various concentration camps' and 2 million 'in other ways'.[67]

Yet Walsh's presentation was only one of many, and given the conflicting representations of Nazi crimes available from the other Americans and from the other prosecution teams, there was no reason for any observer to be more convinced by his words than those of anyone else. Indeed, readers of the *Frankfurter Rundschau* would not even encounter the names of any of the camps, or any specific methods of killing, from the reporting of Walsh's presentation. The only time the death of millions of *human beings*—'Menschen'—was recounted was in the context of Höttl's affidavit, which the newspaper was quick to point out was only hearsay evidence.[68]

The press reporting fairly reflected the evidence presented during the trial, concentrating on the 'standard' concentration camps when war crimes and crimes against humanity were at issue, and on better-known issues of Jewish persecution such as the destruction of the Warsaw Ghetto. Höttl's estimate was cited, yet no names were suggested for the 'various extermination camps' where 4 million Jews had been killed.[69] In its 'review of the year', The Times made no mention of Auschwitz in any capacity, though it did refer to 'the unspeakable infamies of such concentration camps as Belsen and Dachau, where thousands of victims were put to death or allowed to die'.[70]

The prosecution witness SS-Hauptsturmführer Dieter Wisliceny, a subordinate of Adolf Eichmann, introduced the name and assignment of his superior into the proceedings. He also addressed the deportations from the Balkans to Auschwitz, and went into detail about the Hungarian deportations. In the *Times* report of Wisliceny's testimony, however, though the idea was finally conveyed of the mass murder of Jews in gas chambers, Eichmann's name was given as 'Aichamann', and Auschwitz as 'Oswiecim', without comment that the latter two were synonymous.[71] Incredibly though, the most significant eyewitness to the Auschwitz destruction process was summoned in Ernst Kaltenbrunner's defence.

Rudolf Höss, the former commandant of Auschwitz had revealed all he knew of the camp in a series of interrogations by the Americans in the weeks prior to Kaltenbrunner's testimony, yet he was not selected as a witness against Kaltenbrunner, probably because the American prosecution thought that it had established enough about conditions in the camps. Hartley Shawcross suggests that Höss was called in—in a move of staggering naïvety by Kaltenbrunner and

---

[66] *IMT*, iii, 568.   [67] Ibid. 569.   [68] *FR* (18 Dec. 1945).
[69] *The Times* (15 Dec. 1945).   [70] Ibid. (2 Jan. 1946).   [71] Ibid. (4 Jan. 1946).

his counsel—'in a half-hearted attempt to counter the charge of conspiracy by showing that the defendants did not know what happened in the concentration camps [*sic*]'.[72] Smith concurs in this explanation of Höss's presence, when he suggests: 'that [Kaltenbrunner and his counsel] could have so completely misjudged public opinion and believed that Höss's cold-blooded chronicle of mass suffering and death would be an asset to the defence indicates the degree to which the American prosecution's fixation with conspiracy had come to dominate the whole trial.'[73] In fact Höss *was* prepared to testify that the murders had been carried out in secret and that they were not part of a common plan, but his honesty as to the functioning of the camp ensured that Kaltenbrunner and his department took their enormous shares of the blame.

As with each witness's appearance, Höss's direct testimony temporarily revived the journalistic attention that wilted under Jackson's documentary approach.[74] Yet his cross-examination left much unsaid. It was conducted in short order, and very much in the tradition of the adversarial trial system, with the American Colonel Amen restricting Höss to confirmation or retraction of statements cited from an affidavit with which he had earlier supplied the prosecution. The problem with this approach was that Höss, as he had shown in his interrogations, was not interested in obfuscating anything; he had been resigned to his fate since capture in March 1946. The affidavit against which he was cross-examined has become one of the most quoted documents concerning the 'final solution', detailing the 'improvements' Höss had made at Auschwitz over the killing process at Treblinka and the other extermination camps in the Generalgouvernement, and concluding that he had presided over the gassing of 2.5 million people (more than double the probable number), mainly Jews of various nationalities, with another half-million dying from starvation and disease.[75] It was damning enough and certainly incriminated Kaltenbrunner, but it considered only a fraction of the detail which Höss had provided during his interrogations.[76]

[72] Hartley Shawcross, *Life Sentence: The Memoirs of Lord Shawcross* (London: Constable, 1995), 117.

[73] Smith, *Reaching Judgment at Nuremberg*, 89; cf. Tusa and Tusa, *The Nuremberg Trial*, 319–20.

[74] However, the *Jewish Chronicle* all but ignored Höss, as it had many other issues of the trial (perhaps as part of the general silence of Anglo-Jewry after the war, examined in Kushner, 'Different Worlds', 253), and the *NYT* considered his appearance only in the separate context of Alfred Rosenberg's defence, and reported again that 3 million *people* had died at Auschwitz.

[75] *IMT*, xi, 412–18.

[76] During the course of these interrogations Höss had given a concise history of the construction and extension of Auschwitz I, the creation of Birkenau originally as a massive concentration camp and its subsequent designation as the focal point of the plans of Himmler (and the Führer) for the extermination of the Jews. The building of the gas chambers and crematoria, together with their capacity, and Höss's liaison with Eichmann were also described (meetings which have been used as vital evidence in the debate about the timing of a decision for the 'final solution'). Equally importantly, he provided remarkably accurate estimates of the numbers of Jews 'received' from Hungary, Belgium, Slovakia, France, Holland, Germany (via Theresienstadt), Greece, the General/gouvernement, and Upper Silesia. The total thus constituted —1.125 million—is comparable with some of the most realistic recent estimates. (See pre-trial interrogation of Obersturmführer Rudolf Höss, Apr. 1, 2, 1946. Höss produced the same figures before his trial in Cracow, Nov. 1946. *Faschismus—Ghetto—Massenmord: Dokumentation über Ausrottung und Widerstand der Juden in Polen während des zweiten Weltkrieges*, ed. Tatiana Berenstein *et al.* (Berlin: Rütten and

Höss's fortuitous appearance aside, few facets of 'Auschwitz'—either as a camp or as a concept—were given substantive treatment at the trial of the major war criminals. Issues concerning the camp that did arise did so as much by luck as design, and were dealt with in scatter-gun fashion. 'Auschwitz' was largely restricted to the activities of Kaltenbrunner, and to a much lesser extent, Hans Frank, with occasional prosecution side-swipes at Göring and Wilhelm Frick.

There is no indication that the accumulated evidence about Auschwitz imposed itself on the consciousness of the non-Soviet judges as constituting anything other than a particularly bad example of a 'concentration camp', which was exactly how the Americans had portrayed it. The American judge Biddle actually queried who Eichmann was during the compilation of an early draft of the judgement.[77] The judges may have shown 'a strong emotional response to the atrocities from the first film of the concentration camps down to the often jumbled testimony of the few victims called as witnesses by the Soviets and the French',[78] neither of which were unreservedly helpful, but they did not draw out the implications of what they had seen.

During the cross-examination of von Ribbentrop, the British judge Birkett pondered 'does the Tribunal really need any further evidence about the German attitude to Jews? It has been dealt with exhaustively.'[79] This was priorts the cases of Kaltenbrunner and the Gestapo. Further, the detailed testimony of Vaillant-Couturier on her experiences at Auschwitz and Ravensbrück was described by a British Foreign Office observer as being 'a bright spot . . . Her evidence which was horrifying in the extreme caused a deep impression';[80] yet the President could only observe that 'the details of the witness' evidence as to Ravensbrück seem to be very much like, if not the same, as at Auschwitz'. He asked whether it would be possible 'to deal with the matter more generally, unless there [was] some substantial difference between Ravensbrück and Auschwitz'.[81]

A primitive analysis was the best that could realistically be hoped for, and this is what was delivered. Ultimately, the IMT went for the 'safe' option, and formulated that part of its judgement directly concerning Auschwitz from the testimonies of two of the Nazis involved: Höss and Wisliceny. As Franciszek Piper has observed, the Tribunal did not address the question of how many were killed at the camp. It satisfied itself with reiterating the figures provided by Höss: namely that during his time in command (1 May 1940 to 1 December 1943), 2.5 million *persons* were murdered at Auschwitz, and a further 500,000 died from

Loening, 1960), 374–7.) The discrepancy between these figures and the 3 million number he suggested in his affidavit resulted from the fact that Höss—forever the humble functionary—resorted then to the number which Eichmann had suggested to him must be correct.

[77] Smith, *Reaching Judgment at Nuremberg*, 115.   [78] Ibid. 89.
[79] H. Montgomery Hyde, *Norman Birkett* (London: Hamish Hamilton, 1964), 513.
[80] PRO, FO 1019/97, Dean to Foreign Office, 31 Jan. 1945. Samuel Rajzmann's later testimony on Treblinka likewise 'made a shattering impression' on proceedings. *The Death Camp Treblinka: A Documentary*, ed. Alexander Donat (New York: Holocaust Library, 1979), 231.
[81] *IMT*, vi, 227.

disease and starvation.[82] Wisliceny's testimony was used concerning the role of Eichmann's office in seeking out and rounding up Jews in the German satellites. Examples were cited of the evacuation of 400,000 from Hungary and 110,000 from Rumania. Höttl's report on the total number of Jewish dead also featured.[83]

Press coverage of the judgement remained largely faithful to the text of the trial. The technique employed in each nation was simply to quote long passages verbatim, though the left-wing German *Telegraf* reflected a widespread trend by concentrating more on the personalities of the individual defendants, and their examinations, than on wider historical questions.[84] The evidence was selected judiciously in *The Times* and in the *Frankfurter Rundschau*, which gave over two special editions to the judgement, and the balance remained the same as in the tribunal's written opinion.[85] Yet lest it be thought that the material referred to here represents a substantial quantity, its volume should be set against the vast mass of the remainder of the proceedings.

The evidence on war crimes and crimes against humanity was considerably outweighed by that pertaining to the first two counts of the indictment. The ratio was reflected in the judgement; the above pronouncements upon Auschwitz and the murder of the Jews were buried in a document running to 170 pages. In simple statistical terms, the judgement devoted as much time each to Mauthausen and Flossenbürg as to Auschwitz.[86] Nearly as much space was required to sum up the evidence on the pillage of public and private property as to pronounce upon the persecution of the Jews.[87]

Interestingly, the names of two 'camps' were entirely absent from the judgement. Belzec and Sobibor, which between them may have accounted for the deaths of nearly 1 million Polish Jews, were nowhere to be seen. The institution completing the genocidal triumvirate instrumental in the murder of the majority of Polish Jewry—the death camp Treblinka—only received one fleeting reference in the tribunal's final reckoning on 'the persecution of the Jews'. Thus the following imprecise account:

Part of the 'final solution' was the gathering of Jews from all German occupied Europe in *concentration camps*. Their physical condition was the test of life or death. All who were fit to work were used as slave labourers in the concentration camps; all who were not fit to

[82] Piper, *Die Zahl der Opfer von Auschwitz*, 9.

[83] *IMT*, i, 250–3. On the statistics of Jewish dead at Nuremberg, see William Seltzer, 'Population Statistics, the Holocaust, and the Nuremberg Trials', *Population and Development Review*, 24 (1998), 511–52, esp. 532–6.

[84] Cf. e.g. the consistent coverage of the defendants from the inception of the newspaper (22 Mar. 1946) with the reduced attention to the organization cases after 28 July 1946, followed by the upsurge in column space, and the promotion of the story to the front page, as the closing statements of the accused were reported (1 Sept. 1946). For more on the specific focus on the criminals rather than their crimes, see below, Chapter 4.

[85] *The Times* (1, 2 Oct. 1946); *FR* (1, 2 Oct. 1946).

[86] *IMT*, i, 228–9, 234–5, 292.   [87] Ibid. i, 238–43, cf. 247–53.

work were destroyed in gas chambers and their bodies burnt. Certain *concentration camps* such as Treblinka and Auschwitz were set aside for this main purpose.[88]

3.4 THE SIGNIFICANCE OF BELZEC, SOBIBOR AND TREBLINKA

The representation—or rather the non-representation—of Belzec, Sobibor, and Treblinka has particular significance when considering the depiction of the Holocaust as a whole. The three killing centres, in the Generalgouvernement, were the site of the murder of approximately 1.7 million Jews from that region of central and southern Poland, and from the Bialystok district to the north-east. They were an integral part of what came to be known as Aktion(operation) Reinhard, a larger scheme of murdering and expropriating the Jews from the aforementoined areas. (Recent research suggests that the code-name may also have been used to designate operations at Auschwitz.)[89] The three centres were almost completely successful, killing the vast majority of the Jews in their sphere of operations, then closing. The first gassings occurred at Belzec in March 1942, the last at Sobibor in October 1943.[90] The development of the murder process in the Generalgouvernement was key to the radicalization of the 'final solution' asa whole; for our purposes the operations of the killing centres therein became the clearest early expression of the nature of Nazi intentions towards the Jews.

This thesis is in contrast to that implicit in Martin Gilbert's *Auschwitz and the Allies*, which posits that Auschwitz was the prime signifier of the Holocaust.[91] For although Belzec, Sobibor, and Treblinka were predominantly concerned with the Jews of former Poland, and thus lacked the pan-European aspect of Auschwitz, it should not be forgotten that half of the Jews who perished under Nazism were Polish. Further, while Auschwitz has become symbolic of the Holocaust, it only achieved major importance in the Nazi killing programme from 1943 onwards, and owes its particular notoriety to the well-publicized murder of Hungarian Jewry in 1944, and to the comparatively large number of survivors who remained to testify to its horrors. The peak killing period of the

---

[88] Ibid. xxii, 466. Emphases added. The complicated question of Jewish labour use under specific circumstances will be taken up in the Chapter 5, below.

[89] The name 'Aktion Reinhard' was in all likelihood given in honour of Reinhard Heydrich, who was killed by a Czech partisan in May 1942. See e.g. Yitzhak Arad, *Belzec, Sobibor, Treblinka: The Operation Reinhard Death Camps* (Bloomington, Indianapolis: University of Indiana Press, 1987), 13. On Auschwitz, see Bertrand Perz and Thomas Sandkühler, 'Auschwitz und die "Aktion Reinhard" 1942–5. Judenmord und Raubpraxis in neuer Sicht,' *Zeitgeschichte*, 26 (1999), 283–316.

[90] For a recent breakdown of the murder totals of each centre, see Thomas Sandkühler, 'Die Täter des Holocaust: Neuere Ueberlegungen und Kontroversen', in Karl Heinrich Pohl (ed.), *Wehrmacht und Vernichtungspolitik: Militär im nationalsozialistischen System* (Göttingen: Vandenhoeck und Ruprecht, 1999), 39–66, esp. 47. Although the victims of Belzec, Sobibor, and Treblinka were overwhelmingly Jews from the regions of Pland, groups of Jews from elsewhere in Europe were also murdered there. For details, see Arad, *Belzec, Sobibor, Treblinka*, 396–8; *Nazism, 1919–1945: A Documentary Reader*, iii, ed. Jeremy Noakes and Geoffrey Pridham (Exeter: Exeter University Press, 1988), 1153–6.

[91] Gilbert, *Auschwitz and the Allies*.

Holocaust was the year from March 1942, a time of widespread localized massacres in Poland and the Soviet Union, and the operation in tandem of the gas chambers Belzec, Sobibor, and Treblinka.

These three centres were three of the four 'pure' extermination centres employed by the Nazis. Functioning in tandem and under the same authority, these institutions were unique even within the Nazi apparatus of murder. They were clearly of a different nature to the 'normal' concentration camps: lacking the facilities to support streams of labourers, 'their sole purpose was to kill as many people as quickly and smoothly as possible'.[92] Additionally, the victims of the centres were almost exclusively Jewish,[93] while this was not so in the case of the extermination centres at Auschwitz-Birkenau and Majdanek.[94]

The absence of Belzec, Sobibor, and Treblinka from the post-war trials,[95] with its implications for popular appreciation of the Jewish fate,[96] may only be explained with reference to a combination of factors. It was in part a function of the faith in 'representative examples'; the prosecutions believed they had enough information about Jewish deaths in the camps, or simply did not wish to furnish more. Additionally, there were qualitative and quantitative deficiencies in the documentary and eyewitness evidence available on the camps. We also see the interplay of the preconceptions and prejudices of the legal actors, the requirements of the legal process, and suspicion of eyewitness testimony.

3.5 THE ABSENCE OF AKTION REINHARD (I): AN EXPROPRIATION EXERCISE?

The cloak of official secrecy had been drawn particularly tight around Belzec, Sobibor, and Treblinka. SS and Police Leader Odilo Globocnik, the director them of their operations, ensured at the beginning of 1944 that the documents dealing with it were obliterated; 'after all,' he wrote to Himmler, 'the other basic works concerning this matter have already been destroyed'.[97] Amongst these 'basic works' were the camps themselves. Comparatively small, and of light construction, after they had completed their task they were dismantled, and farms built on the killing grounds.

---

[92] Michael Burleigh, *Death and Deliverance: 'Euthanasia' in Germany, 1900–1945* (Cambridge: Cambridge University Press, 1994), 232. The fourth 'pure' extermination establishment, Chelmno in the Warthegau, did not have permanent gassing installations but the more primitive gas vans; the total number of deaths there was smaller than at any of the other three centres.

[93] A small number of gypsies were murdered in Treblinka. *Nazism*, iii, ed. Noakes and Pridham, 1156.

[94] Perhaps 140,000 non-Jews were murdered in the Auschwitz complex. Of the 200,000 victims of Majdanek, approximately 60,000 were Jews, the remainder being Poles and Russian POWs. An estimated 160,000 people were murdered in the two killing phases at Chelmno, which ran from Dec. 1941 to Jan. 1943 and from June to July 1944. Though the majority of these were Jews, several thousand Gypsies, Poles, and Russians were also murdered.

[95] This was the case until a series of trials of the various camp staffs in the 1960s, which provided must of the source material for Yitzhak Arad's *Belzec, Sobibor, Treblinka*.

[96] The first comprehensive study, by Yitzhak Arad, was only published in 1987.

[97] Nuremberg document PS-4024. Yitzhak Arad's translation, used here, differs slightly from the official Nuremberg translation. See Arad, *Belzec, Sobibor, Treblinka*, 376.

The series of correspondence, of which this document was the last, was a rare survivor of the Nazi purges, since it was *the* major documentary source used before the IMT concerning Aktion Reinhard *per se*. Few documents concerning this coded process were actually drawn up anyway,[98] thus any investigation of the operation was heavily dependent upon eyewitness testimony. Yet there were distinct problems in obtaining such evidence. The chief on-the-spot perpetrators managed, one way or another, to avoid contributing their testimonies to the Allied records.[99] Survivors were few, testament to the near-total success of the campaign: only one inmate of Belzec outlived the camp; thirty Jews survived Sobibor, having escaped in the uprising; and sixty-seven survived Treblinka, again as a result of a revolt. Nevertheless, there remained sufficient material to build up a realistic picture of the camps from survivor testimony. The problem was the Anglo-American preference at Nuremberg for 'hard' Nazi documentary evidence rather than what were seen as unreliable and possibly exaggerated eyewitness accounts.

A further generic difficulty was of particular importance in the case of Aktion Reinhard: terminology. Perhaps the most obvious example of this involved Höss's testimony, in which alongside correct citation of Treblinka and Belzec he named Sobibor as 'Wolzek',[100] a mistake replicated in many accounts of the commandant's appearance, and in memoirs of the IMT trial.[101] Vitally, the connection was not made at Nuremberg between the name 'Aktion Reinhard', which had not been widely known before the trials, and the murder of the Jews of the Polish territories, of which general knowledge had long been available. This was more than a semantic problem, for names are the first and clearest terms of reference, giving shape to a concept and shaping the understanding of it.[102] The absence of an appellation meant that latent knowledge of mass killings in Poland was less easily transformed into awareness of the distinct boundaries and exact nature of this murder campaign. It contributed to the failure to differentiate the death of a Polish Jew in the Generalgouvernement from a murder in the Warthegau or in the 'Occupied Eastern Territories'. It also blurred the lines of enquiry into the specific chains of command and dynamics of the Aktion, and into its ultimate, special function. It is undoubtedly no coincidence that the earliest historians of the Holocaust, who misapprehended the meaning of the name Reinhard, failed to differentiate between killing systems in Poland.

---

[98] Ibid. 16.

[99] Ibid. 399–400. Globocnik was captured by the British but subsequently committed suicide; Christian Wirth, commander of the team of gassing specialists, and inspector of the Reinhard camps, was killed by partisans in Trieste before the end of the war; Hermann Höfle, commander of the Head Office of the Aktion, was only arrested in 1961—he subsequently committed suicide; Franz Stangl, one-time commandant of Sobibor and Treblinka, was arrested as late as 1967; and Friedrich Wilhelm Krüger, the HSSPF in the Generalgouvernement, disappeared without trace after the war.

[100] A mistake for which there is no apparent explanation.

[101] Nuremberg document PS-3868.

[102] As critical theory has shown, the process of naming is not an unadorned aid to clarity.

Gerald Reitlinger considered that the operation was directed against the Jews of all Poland, which it was not. Consequently, he erroneously established Chelmno as part of the Aktion.[103] Raul Hilberg, Leon Poliakov, and Joseph Tennenbaum, in their histories of the murder of the Jews, and even Martin Broszat, in his later study of Nazi Polish policy, mistook the operation solely for a looting exercise, which was only the lesser part of the activity.[104] In these accounts we also see confusion—which has yet to be entirely resolved—over the relationship of Majdanek to the Reinhard camps. Certainly Majdanek was situated within, and helped in the murder of the Jews of, the Generalgouvernement,[105] but it was not directly under Globocnik's control, and functioned in large part as a slave labour reservoir for non-Jews and Jews, and as an administration centre for the loot accruing from the Belzec, Sobibor, and Treblinka murders. It seems to have had a more explicitly economic function in Aktion Reinhard than an exterminatory one;[106] the same might be speculated about Auschwitz.

The name 'Reinhard' was first appropriated at Nuremberg for use solely in reference to the expropriation campaign. Before the defeat of Germany, there were only limited clues available as to the true nature of the operation. Those that did exist had only come to the attention of the Allies through Polish channels, and they consisted of half-truths, progressively distorted under the duress of their passage across Europe. We shall consider two. The first is in an announcement made on 22 November 1943 in London by Dr Ignacy Schwarzbart, Jewish representative in the Polish government-in-exile. He revealed the names of ten members of the German administration in Poland considered to be primarily responsible for the slaughter of Jews in Poland. Fourth on his list was an individual named *Reinhard*,

chief of the 'Annihilation Squad' (*Vernichtungskommando*) a unit known as '*Einsatz-Reinhardt*'. As commander-in-chief of the 'Annihilation Squad' [Reinhardt] supervised sixteen SS sub-leaders specially trained in the Lublin area in exterminating the Jewish population . . . After training in the Lublin area, where the Ghetto was first liquidated by them, these members of the annihilation squad were sent to take charge of the extermination in the Radom, Otwock, Lwow, Falenica and many other ghettos and are responsible for the killing of many hundreds of thousands of Jews.[107]

---

[103] Gerald Reitlinger, *The Final Solution* (London: Valentine, Mitchell and Co., 1953), 244–51.

[104] Raul Hilberg, *The Destruction of the European Jews* (New York: Harper, 1961), 630; Joseph Tennenbaum, *Race and Reich: The Story of an Epoch* (Westport, Conn.: Greenwood Press, 1956), 189–91. Leon Poliakov, *Harvest of Hate* (London: Elek, 1956), simply states that 'for the most part the convoys of Jews from the Government General were sent to one of the three' camps in the territory. See also Martin Broszat, *Nationalsozialistische Polenpolitik* (Frankfurt am Main: Fischer, 1965), 68–9.

[105] See e.g. C. Rajca and A. Wisniewska, *Majdanek: Nazilager in Lublin* (Lublin: Majdanek State Museum, 1986), 10.

[106] On Globocnik's influence over Majdanek, which co-existed with that of the WVHA, and on Majdanek's relation to the 'final solution', see Tomasz Kranz, 'Das KL Lublin—zwischen Planung und Realisierung', in Ulrich Herbert, Karin Orth, and Christoph Dieckmann (eds.), *Die nationalsozialistischen Konzentrationslager: Entwicklung und Struktur*, 2 vols. (Göttingen: Wallstein, 1998), 363–89, esp. 371–3.

[107] Address of 22 Nov., 1943 from Queensway, London, cited in the *Polish Jewish Observer* (26 Nov. 1943).

This association probably sprang from the murderous 'man-hunts' which Globocnik and his men orchestrated through the streets of Lublin immediately prior to the beginning of the deportations.

The second instance concerns a Polish war crimes commission report compiled in the second half of 1945. In a discussion of the role of the Einsatzgruppen in exterminating the Jews, the report concluded that 'one of these groups, the Reinhard group famous for its crimes, dealt with the province[s] of Warsaw, Lublin, Cracow and Lwow [Galicia], in the General Government'.[108]

The association between the name Reinhard and the murder of the Jews, which these reports suggested, was ignored at Nuremberg, for they were corroborated there by a sole voice, that of one Georg Konrad Morgen, an SS 'judge of the reserve'. Morgen's investigations into corruption in the concentration camps had led him to a meeting with Christian Wirth. Morgen recounted this meeting in an affidavit used in the defence of the SS before the IMT; he also testified at the trial of the SS as a criminal organization. As will be seen later, he went into much valuable detail about the mechanics of the killing procedure; what is important here is that he recalled Wirth's men operated under the name 'Einsatz Reinhard'.[109] However, the Nuremberg prosecutors took their lead from the surviving documentation which ostensibly suggested that Aktion Reinhard was purely an economic concern.

The machinery set up to facilitate the expropriation of the murdered, and to plough the valuables thus gained into the Reich, was vast. Particularly implicated in this process was the SS Business Administration Main Office (Wirtschafts-Verwaltungshauptamt or WVHA), the subject of the fourth subsequent Nuremberg proceeding, the Pohl trial. The WVHA received much of the Jewish property, and channelled money, gold—some of it extracted from the victims' teeth—and jewellery into an account in the Reichsbank. Significantly, the name Reinhard came to have many well-known applications and associations in the expropriation process. Those members of the WVHA involved in the process came to be known as 'Special Staff Reinhard', and the abbreviation 'Reinh.' appeared at the foot of documents pertaining to the expropriation process.[110] Moreover, money stolen from the Jews could be called upon by the SS in the nature of loans to support economic ventures; these funds were known as 'Reinhardfunds'.

In the proceedings of the IMT there were only two documentary sources used which referred to Aktion Reinhard by name. One of these was unremarkable, a straightforward reference to the economic aspect of the operation.[111] The other

---

[108] *German Crimes in Poland*, ed. Central Commission for the Investigation of German Crimes in Poland, 2 vols. in 1 (New York: Fertig, 1982), i, 135. These volumes were researched in the immediate aftermath of the war and first published in 1946–7.

[109] Morgen's affidavit, Nuremberg document SS-65. The explicit link between the name and the murder operation was also established by Kurt Gerstein (below, Chapter 3.6). The information does not appear to have been transmitted to Nuremberg. See George Wellers, 'Encore sur le "Témoignage Gerstein"', *Le Monde Juif*, no. 97 (1980–1), 23–34.

[110] e.g. Nuremberg document NO-725.　　　[111] Nuremberg document L-18.

was the aforementioned series of correspondence between Himmler and Globocnik on the winding-up of the economic side of the enterprise. The treatment of this set of documents is an example of a vital source of information being poorly used; for within these communications lay many clues as to the murderous side of the operation.

Despite Globocnik's admission, recorded within these documents, that 'the entire Aktion Reinhard is divided into four spheres' (namely, the expulsion itself, the employment of labour, the exploitation of property, and the seizure of hidden goods and landed property), there was no enquiry as to the non-economic aspects. Moreover, the deeper indications within this material of the nature of the operation were ignored. One such signifier was a claim by Globocnik that 'the Action Reinhard was . . . too dangerous'. The second was Globocnik's request to Himmler that 'a few iron crosses might be awarded for the special performances of this difficult task'. Thirdly, we see a series of allusions to the suppression of the Warsaw ghetto uprising, which had well-known associations, established before the IMT, with the extermination process.[112]

Notwithstanding the evidence suggesting the wider implications of the exercise, this series of documents was used only for its economic aspect at the IMT trial.[113] It was utilized in the trial of the SS as a criminal organization in order to implicate the WVHA, and again in the case against Walther Funk, President of the Reichsbank after 1939.[114] The subsequent Nuremberg trial at which the name Aktion Reinhard was heard most frequently was the Pohl case, throughout which confusion reigned regarding our subject. At various stages the component threads of the Aktion, including the murder campaign, were teased out in court, but ultimately the whole was judged to be an economic affair. Thus while it was contended early in the trial that the operation was 'a coldly premeditated program of mass murder and gigantic theft visited upon a people whose only crime was that of failure to be born an Aryan', the tribunal eventually decreed that it was only instituted after the murder of these people to 'marshal their resources'.[115] Conceptions of Aktion Reinhard also varied from prosecutor to prosecutor.[116]

OCCWC knew that Globocnik was intimately associated with the murder of the Jews,[117] as was stated at the beginning of the trial.[118] The prosecution also

---

[112] The issue of the Warsaw ghetto uprising and its suppression became a major issue at the IMT trial. The report by Jürgen Stroop, 'The Warsaw Ghetto is no more' (Nuremberg document PS-1061) actually noted that of 14,000 Jews captured during the operation, 6,929 were deported to 'T.II'. This is a reference to Treblinka II, or Treblinka B, the location of the extermination centre, and was established as such before the IMT: see Syracuse University Archive, papers of Francis Biddle, hereafter 'Biddle papers', box 3, vols. 1–3, 'Notes on evidence', p. 172A.

[113] For the text of the document, and another incomplete interpretation of it, see 'Pillages: "L'action Reinhardt"', *Le Monde Juif*, no. 17 (1949), 17–18.

[114] *IMT*, xx, 314–18, 421; xxii, 230; xxi, 239.   [115] NMT, Case 4, pp. 83, 8076.

[116] Ibid. pp. 1027, 1062.   [117] Ibid. pp. 74–5.

[118] Ibid. opening address of the prosecution, p. 3.

spent much time trying to establish Oswald Pohl's jurisdiction at Auschwitz.[119] Both Auschwitz and Majdanek were in fact placed under the jurisdiction of the Inspectorate of Concentration Camps—which was shortly to become office group D of the WVHA—by a Himmler decree of February 1942. However, the authority for the mass gassings came directly from the RSHA, not from the WVHA (though members of the inspectorate did have to oversee the gassings in the camps and were entirely complicit); moreover, the WVHA had no jurisdiction at all over the operation of Belzec, Sobibor or Treblinka. The connection OCCWC had between the WVHA and Globocnik concerned the transfer of decentralized forced labour camps for Jews in the Lublin district to their joint, direct control in September 1943 as part of an attempt to centralize the exploitation of the remaining Jewish labourers in the Generalgouvernement.[120]

As the final judgements in the Pohl trial show, convictions were based on the defendants' involvement in the expropriation of Jews from the occupied territories, and on their involvement in the murderous slave labour programmes in the concentration camps wherein victims from many groups perished. This comes as no great surprise, given that the WVHA was concerned with the administration and inspection of concentration camps, and with the finances of the SS. Some of the WVHA men were convicted partially on the basis of their knowledge of the 'final solution',[121] and undoubtedly they all knew of it. However, the concrete link with the genocide of the Jews was not established because it was not a direct one at the highest levels.

This must have dawned on the OCCWC prosecutors during the trial. What must also have become clear is that the chief connection between the WVHA men and the 'final solution' as such was the theft from the murdered; so in many cases it became the chief aim of the prosecution to establish whether the defendants knew where the loot came from.[122] Thus, in all probability, the narrow interpretation of Aktion Reinhard at the trials: as the limited role of the WVHA in the murder of the Jews became more obvious, it was in the interests of the prosecution to concentrate on the economic aspects of the genocide in pursuit of the primary goal of conviction of the defendants in the dock. The definition of the operation settled upon during the Pohl trial came to be widely accepted, and not just by Poliakov and Hilberg. When the Aktion was cited at the later RuSHA trial, it was described as the 'administrative task of collecting and distributing the property confiscated from murdered and enslaved Jews'.[123]

[119] See e.g. the questioning of a witness (ibid. p. 6687), the opening speech of prosecutor McHaney (pp. 72–4), and throughout Pohl's testimony (pp. 1253–2040).
[120] Nuremberg document NO-599. For discussion of the context of these negotiations, and the ultimate failure of the WVHA-Globocnik venture, see Bloxham, '"Extermination through Work"', 13–14; below, Chapter 5.
[121] e.g. defendant Franz Eirenschmalz, judgement NMT, Case 4, pp. 8140–50.
[122] Ibid. pp. 8091–6, for that part of the judgement dealing with Aktion Reinhard and the Eastern Industries Company.
[123] NMT, Case 8, p. 92.

3.6 THE ABSENCE OF AKTION REINHARD (II): BYPASSING THE CAMPS

The name Reinhard was thus divorced from the murder of the Polish Jews. It remains to chart the early historiography of the murder process itself. An investigation of the representation at the trials of any subject necessarily begins with the question of what was known beforehand. With the murder of the Jews of the Generalgouvernement, as with the continent-wide genocide, it would be a fair generalization to answer that sufficient information about the essence of Nazi policy was available from early days, though little detail was known and much misinformation was transmitted from occupied Europe. Let us first consider the information available in Britain, home of the Polish Government-in-exile, during the war.

David Cesarani suggests that by 1943, readers of the *Jewish Chronicle* had 'learned the approximate meaning of Treblinka, Sobibor [and] Belzec'.[124] This was certainly true of readers of most organs of the British Jewish press or publications dealing with Poland[125] and would seem to be a fair summary of the state of knowledge concerning these camps of anyone interested in the Jewish situation. 'A comprehensive report, which described . . . the operation of the gas chambers in western [*sic*] Poland, and which unequivocally related these developments to a systematic German plan to murder all of Polish Jewry, [appears] to have reached the [Polish] government-in-exile [by] the end of May [1942].'[126] This report came from the underground Bund leadership in Warsaw,[127] and announced that 'the extermination of the Jews in the territory of the so-called Government-General started in February 1942 . . . In March, some 25,000 Jews were carried off in "an unknown direction" out of Lublin in sealed railway cars.' The 'gist' of this report was broadcast to Europe by the BBC on 2 June 1942; the

[124] David Cesarani, *The Jewish Chronicle and Anglo-Jewry, 1841–1991* (Cambridge: Cambridge University Press, 1994), 179.

[125] The *Polish Fortnightly Review*, organ of the government in exile, carried an article (1 July 1942) on the deportation of the Lublin Jews to their death in the locality of Sobibor; 'Extermination of the Polish Jewry' (1 Dec. 1942), described 'electrocutions' at Belzec. The *Polish Jewish Observer* published articles (21 May 1943; 24, 30 Mar. 1944) on 'electrocutions' at Belzec and death by steam at Treblinka. It contained an accurate topographical account of Treblinka (11 June 1943); between 27 Oct. and 17 Nov. 1944, it published two eyewitness accounts of the camp. Interestingly, both of the contributors, Jacob Vernik/ Yankiel Wiernik and Samuel Rajzmann, were used in the Soviet presentation to the IMT. The *Jewish Chronicle* (27 Nov. 1942) carried an article '2 million Jews slaughtered', again mentioning electrocution at Belzec, while the *Zionist Review* of the same date claimed that 'the methods applied in the mass extermination are, apart from execution by firing squads, electrocution and lethal gas chambers'. A *Jewish Telegraphic Agency* report (12 Aug. 1943) published details of a report from Poland on the 'mass executions of Jews in the Tremblinka [*sic*] Death Camp', including fairly accurate procedural details in addition to the idea of mass 'asphyxiation by liquid gas'. In Nov. 1943, the *Jewish Chronicle* published details of deportations from the Vilna ghetto to Sobibor. The inmate uprising at Treblinka also held some attention in Sept. 1943: see *Jewish Telegraphic Agency* report (23 Sept.); *Zionist Review* (29 Sept.). In the closing weeks of the war, even *The Times* mentioned the 'torture chambers of Belszec [*sic*], Majdanek, Oswiecim, and Treblinka' (24 May 1945).

[126] Engel, *In the Shadow of Auschwitz*, 175.

[127] The 'General Jewish Worker's Union' in Poland.

Daily Telegraph also carried details of the report on 25 June, and again on 27 June.[128]

More importantly, at the end of November a report by Jan Karski, a courier for the Polish Government, was publicized after being submitted to western leaders. It relayed the information that, on the basis of a Himmler order of March 1942, Jews were being deported to

special 'exterminating camps' near the townships of Treblinka, Belzec and Sobibor where they were murdered in wholesale massacres [and] since the story of the deportations [to Treblinka] from the Warsaw ghetto had now broken in the West, and Jewish circles had begun finally to absorb the notion that Polish Jewry was being subjected . . . to a deliberate program of total biological annihilation, the [Polish Government-in-exile] had to take some official cognizance of events'.[129]

This 'cognizance' took the form of a note, dated 10 December, by the Polish Government to the governments of the United Nations concerning the extermination of the Polish Jews. This note elicited a speedy response from the Allied nations in the form of a joint declaration condemning Germany's 'policy of cold-blooded extermination' and naming Poland as 'the principal Nazi slaughter-house'.[130] For the purposes of this study, the important element of the Polish Government's note was its reiteration of the report naming Belzec, Sobibor, and Treblinka together as extermination camps in Poland, and the claim that these camps were not only the recipients of the Jews from the Warsaw ghetto, but also of the Jews from 'other ghettos in Central Poland'.

Reports on the murder of the Polish Jews came amidst much other news about the war, and even the Jewish and Polish publications had other priorities ranking alongside and often above transmitting information about Nazi atrocities in Poland. Also, Karski's report was in the main devoted to purely Polish issues. Yet despite its scrappy nature, it is evident that sufficient information had come to light for those so inclined to compile surprisingly accurate accounts of the General gouvernement killing centres, which were marred only by persistent and peculiar misconceptions regarding the methods of killing. In any case, it was the prosecutorial and judicial task, as well as that of the Polish Government-in-exile and of subsequent historians, to separate 'fact' from fiction, detail from generality.

The Black Book of Polish Jewry: An Account of the Martyrdom of Polish Jewry under the Nazi Occupation, published in New York in 1943, was an example of what could be made of the information coming out of Poland. Pulling together various Polish accounts, this publication, which was sponsored by Eleanor Roosevelt and Albert Einstein amongst others, detailed the murder of the Jews of

---

[128] Yehuda Bauer, 'When Did They Know?', *Midstream*, 14 (1968), 51–8.

[129] Engel, *In the Shadow of Auschwitz*, 198.

[130] The World Jewish Congress had actually been pressing for this Allied Declaration for some time, but the Polish government note was the catalyst. See Kushner, *The Holocaust and the Liberal Imagination*, 168–9.

the Warthegau by 'a special gas-chamber car' at Chelmno.[131] More relevantly, *The Black Book* included a detailed chapter on Treblinka.[132]

The report contained only one substantial error, involving the method of murder at Treblinka: after correctly describing the cramming of Jews into special chambers disguised as bath-houses, and the fact that the doors of the chambers were then hermetically sealed, the report declared that 'the slow suffocation of living people [began], brought about by the steam issuing from numerous vents in [the chamber]'. In fact, the murders at Belzec, Sobibor, and Treblinka involved the use of carbon monoxide exhaust fumes, generated from a diesel engine. However, the nature of the actual substance used to murder the Jews within the gas chambers was intelligence to which very few were privy. The rest of the information outlined here regarding the gas chambers of the three camps, and Treblinka in particular, was more widely disseminated. We shall consider some of the material directly and explicitly available at Nuremberg.

At the end of 1945, the reformed Polish government submitted a symbolic indictment to the IMT listing evidence under all four counts pertaining to that country. It contained extensive details on the extermination camps, including their Jewish specificity.[133] Perhaps most importantly, OCCPAC had at its disposal analysts who had consulted much of the aforementioned evidence, in addition to reports from the US War Refugee Board. In particular, OSS agents had been deployed to seek out information germane to the broad conspiracy charge, including that on the persecution and extermination of the Jews. The resultant studies not only included perhaps the earliest investigations of Eichmann's 'Referat für die Judenfrage', and proper differentiation between the concentration camps as the Americans perceived them and the annihilation centres; they also established a hierarchy of the latter category. The largest they recognized as Auschwitz-Birkenau, establishing also the Polish name Oswiecim; below that they listed Majdanek, Treblinka, Belzec, and Sobibor. A detailed Polish government report on Chelmno also featured.[134]

Polish war crimes commission reports, compiled in much the same way as *The Black Book*, were the chief repository of survivor and bystander testimony on the Reinhard camps at the trial of the major war criminals. The most relevant such report was an indictment by the Polish Government of Hans Frank, for the establishment in his territory of the 'extermination camp at Treblinka, intended

---

[131] Jacob Apenszlak (ed.), *The Black Book of Polish Jewry: An Account of the Martyrdom of Polish Jewry under the Nazi Occupation* (New York: Roy, 1943), 115–18.

[132] Ibid, 141–7.

[133] Bodleian Library, Goodhart papers, hereafter 'Goodhart papers', reel 30, fos. 83 ff.

[134] On the Gestapo and differentiation between types of camp, see NARA, RG 238 (NM66), entry 52l, box 1, files of Lt. Col. Wheeler, Wheeler to Storey, 25 Aug. 1945; RG 238 (UD), entry 66, box 98, article on 'responsibility' for the Jewish persecution, pp. 25–6; box 95, report on Gestapo. On the OSS and the 'Jewish case' at Nuremberg, see Aronson, 'Preparations for the Nuremberg Trial'. On extermination camps, see NARA, RG 238 (UD), entry 66, box 97, report on Hans Frank; box 98, folder 'Mass annihilation of Jews', pp. 15–16; RG 226, entry 191, boxes 1–4, also contain much on the plight of Jewry, including eyewitness accounts of Belzec and Treblinka.

for mass killing of Jews'.[135] Containing much of the same information about Treblinka as *The Black Book*, this report detailed the progression in the persecution of the Polish Jews, culminating in the decision about 'a complete annihilation of the ghettos'. It declared that

The Jews had simply ceased to exist. Special camps were established for this purpose, where the destruction of human lives was carried on by mechanized means. The best known of these death camps are those of Treblinka, Belzec and Sobiber [*sic*] in the Lublin district . . . The victims were recruited chiefly from the General Government, and particularly from the following districts: Warsaw, Radom, Lublin, Krakow and Lwow, but Jews from outside the General Government were also sent there, particularly from the Bialystok district.

These details are all accurate. The only inexactitude again involved the methods of murder. Links with the stories emerging from occupied Poland are obvious, when we see that the report stated that the victims of Belzec, Sobibor, and Treblinka 'were put to death . . . by hitherto unknown, new methods, gas and steam chambers as well as electric current employed on a large scale'. However, it was not possible for reports such as this to relate the mechanics of the murder process; expert testimony would be needed for that. Rather, these reports served to establish the existence of the extermination centres.[136]

Aside from the words of Höss, expert testimony *was* available at Nuremberg courtesy of two SS men, who by various means had gained first-hand experience of the extermination centres. Moreover, as non-victims, the weight of their testimony was ostensibly greater, to OCCPAC at least, than that contained in the war crimes commission reports. The first witness was the aforementioned SS judge Konrad Morgen, whose wartime investigations had led him on one occasion to Auschwitz, and on another occasion to an encounter with Christian Wirth, inspector of the Reinhard camps. Morgen's testimony, as a witness for the defence in the trial of the SS as a criminal organization, recounted that meeting. Wirth had described the method of gassing which he claimed to have developed, using the exhaust fumes from internal combustion engines, and, importantly, the implication of personnel used in the 'euthanasia' campaign, killers who had gained their experience with lethal gas in the murder of Germany's physically and mentally disabled.[137]

---

[135] Nuremberg document PS-3311.

[136] There was a second Polish commission report of relevance which was not entered into the tribunal's records. Nuremberg document USSR-93, pp. 41–5 devoted five pages to the various types of camp. Under the title 'execution camps' (*Hinrichtungslager*), the camps were separated into two categories. Auschwitz, Majdanek, and Treblinka were described as the 'graveyards of millions of human beings'. Belzec and Sobibor were classified alongside Chelmno, and Kosow-Podlaski camps. After a potted history of the camp, the report stated that the Jews of Sobibor were murdered in gas chambers. It also went on correctly to claim that some foreign Jews, particularly Dutch and French, went to Sobibor. Once again we can see the continuation of a trend, as the report claimed that the victims of Belzec were murdered by electric shocks.

[137] *IMT*, xx, 487–515; Nuremberg document SS-65.

The second expert witness to the Reinhard murders contributed his testimony to the trials posthumously. This was Kurt Gerstein, head of the 'Technical Disinfection Services' of the SS, and expert on Zyklon B, the gas used in the murder process at Auschwitz. He was qualified to report on the Reinhard camps because in August 1942, as part of a mission to research the possibilities of using Zyklon B instead of diesel-exhaust fumes in the murder process, he visited Belzec and Treblinka, and the construction site of Majdanek. His comprehensive report on the mission, written in May 1945, included mention of the location of each Reinhard centre. The section on Belzec covered every aspect of the killing process and has become one of the best-known eyewitness accounts of the Holocaust.[138] As Saul Friedländer points out, it was accurate in every detail except those that Gerstein could only surmise, such as his huge over-estimate of the number of victims of the campaign.[139] Moreover, in order to add greater weight to his statement, Gerstein handed over to the Allied troops to whom he had surrendered a series of bills for the large-scale purchase of Zyklon-B by the RSHA, which were written in his name.

So the seeds were sown for an investigation into the killing centres. Though not always accurate in detail, the Polish commission reports provided a good overview, and gave ample basis for further investigation. The Gerstein and Morgen testimonies provided concise accounts of the camps, their processes, and administration. However, none of these pieces of evidence was used in the formation of the judgement.

The case of Governor-General Hans Frank was the most obvious arena amongst those of the individual defendants in which to seek information concerning the murder of the Polish Jews. It was true, as Frank protested, that the camps were not run under his authority but under that of the SS and Police, but his acquiescent awareness of their existence within his territory cannot be doubted.

The camp in the Generalgouvernement receiving most frequent mention was Majdanek;[140] Sobibor was entirely absent; and Belzec had only a passing reference, by the defendant, as he tried to illustrate his innocence in the 'final solution'.[141] While the IMT conceded that Frank was 'a willing and knowing participant . . . in a programme involving the murder of at least three million Jews', there was no mention of where the Jews were killed. And though the judgement concluded that 'the concentration camp system was introduced in the Government General by the establishment of the notorious Treblinka and Midanek [*sic*] camps', this statement was in the context of a paragraph dealing with the repression of the Polish population, rather than with the extermination of the Jews.[142]

---

[138] Nuremberg document PS-1553.
[139] Saul Friedlander, *Counterfeit Nazi: The Ambiguity of Good* (London: Weidenfeld and Nicolson, 1969), 114.
[140] *IMT*, xii, 17–18.   [141] Ibid.   [142] *IMT*, xxii, 497–8.

The Polish war crimes commission report on Hans Frank was used once by the American prosecution in an introductory presentation on the persecution of the Jews,[143] but not in the direct case against him. Its absence from the latter certainly sprang from the consensus that, while the report would serve to illustrate some general points, it was not reliable enough to use as evidence to help convict a defendant. More surprisingly, given that it came from the side of the perpetrators, neither Morgen's nor Gerstein's evidence was used by OCCPAC, nor by the IMT or the subsequent Nuremberg tribunals.

We have already seen how Aktion Reinhard figured in the Pohl trial. The link with the first subsequent Nuremberg trial, the Medical trial, involved those 'euthanasia' specialists who had lent their expertise to Odilo Globocnik to help murder the Polish Jews. As *the* major source of information then available on that link,[144] Gerstein's affidavit was introduced by OCCWC and was accorded 'judicial notice' by the tribunal. The President, however, declared that, owing to the importance of the matter, all efforts should be made to bring Gerstein to Nuremberg to testify in person;[145] unfortunately, Gerstein had committed suicide in the summer of 1945 while a prisoner of war in a French jail.

It is evident from the indictment that the prosecution had some idea of the connection between the defendants and the 'final solution',[146] but owing to the lack of 'hard' documentation, the (infrequent) discussion of the matter revolved largely around assertion and counter-assertion.[147] Nothing was heard of the 'final solution' in the judgement on the relevant defendant, Viktor Brack.[148] Some of the reasoning behind the omission was made explicit in the pronouncement on his co-defendant Karl Brandt (who did not in any case have a direct connection with the extermination camps): quite simply, sufficient incriminating evidence existed on other counts to gain convictions without reference to the genocide of the Jews.[149]

At least in the Medical trial the Gerstein report received judicial consideration, however. In the IMT trial, it was not even brought to the attention of the judges. Both the American and the French prosecutors knew of it, but the French, to whom Gerstein's information was initially entrusted, ironically chose only to emphasize the invoices for Zyklon-B which, it will be remembered, were attached by Gerstein to his statement to add authority to the latter.[150] A small

---

[143] *IMT*, iii, 566–9. Presenting this document, Major Walsh failed to cite the paragraph claiming that 'the erection of [Treblinka] was closely connected with the German plans aiming at a complete destruction of the Jewish population in Poland', as well as the sentence coupling Belzec with Sobibor and Treblinka. Moreover, his coverage of the camps focused mainly on concentration camps rather than extermination centres.

[144] Reitlinger, *The Final Solution*, 129; Poliakov, *Harvest of Hate*, 191.

[145] NMT, Case 1, pp. 1797–1808.   [146] NMT, Case 1, p. 11.

[147] Brack's affidavit, Nuremberg document NO-426; NMT, Case 1, pp. 1525–30, 7509–25; see also Nuremberg Document NO-426; NMT, Case 1, p. 2418.

[148] On Brack's complicity, see Arad, *Belzec, Sobibor, Treblinka*, 9, 16–17; Burleigh, *Death and Deliverance, passim*.

[149] NMT, Case 1, pp. 11505–15, 11394.   [150] *IMT*, vi, 332–3; 363.

industry has grown up around the question of why the report was not allowed more attention, given not only its importance, but the extent to which Gerstein and his associates, and the French authorities after them, had gone to establish his credentials.[151] Some of these have been linked with Gerstein's own wartime experience, which was in many ways as remarkable as his testimony. At one extreme there is the conspiratorial suggestion that French Catholics were keen to obscure his story, and thus the fact of his failed attempt to elicit a reaction from the Papacy to the detail of the ongoing Holocaust.[152] Adalbert Rückerl has suggested alternatively that the report was dismissed as 'gross exaggeration, if not entirely the fabrication of a sick mind'.[153] Perhaps the French simply did not observe the correct procedure for entering a document into the record—but then they could simply have re-entered it if it was thought of sufficient importance.[154] OCCPAC considered it but clearly did not think it merited use,[155] whether in line with the general distrust of eyewitness evidence or the more specific distrust of evidence from anti-Nazi sources.

In a hierarchical evidentiary system of evidence it took more than the word of a dead man, whoever he was, to establish the terrible truths that Gerstein had sought to transmit. The Zyklon-B bills, though no less astonishing in their own way than his story, were more appropriate, it was thought, for the courtroom. The prosecution before the IMT was 'playing it safe' again, as would the tribunal itself in the judgement on Frank and in the pronouncement on Auschwitz, and as would the subsequent Nuremberg tribunal in the case of Brack.

This is not to imply criticism of the prosecutions or the tribunals, but rather to highlight the differences between legal and historical evidence. Reitlinger, Poliakov, and Hilberg could all use Gerstein accurately for their own ends, but they had a very different interpretation of 'doubt' to that of the Nuremberg jurists.[156] In tribute perhaps to their profession, the outstanding quality that these historians all displayed was a propensity to penetrate the dense web of preconception which had been spun around Nazi camp criminality during and after World War II. Such prejudice invalidated the unique insights of Konrad Morgen as a

---

[151] For some of the verifications and the history of the report, see Leon Poliakov, 'Le dossier Kurt Gerstein', *Le Monde Juif*, no. 36 (1964), 4–20; 'Augenzeugenbericht zu den Massenvergasungen', repr. in *VfZ*, 2 (1953), 177–94; George Wellers, 'Les chambres à gaz et le témoignage Gerstein', *Le Monde Juif*, no. 86 (1976–7), 46–62; Georges Wellers, 'A propos d'une thèse de doctorat "explosive" sur le "Rapport Gerstein"', *Le Monde Juif*, no. 121 (1986), 1–17.

[152] For this theory, and others, see Pierre Joffroy, *A Spy for God: The Ordeal of Kurt Gerstein* (London: Collins, 1971), 267–71.

[153] Adalbert Rückerl, *NS-Vernichtungslager im Spiegel deutscher Strafprozesse* (Munich: Deutscher Taschenbuch Verlag, 1977), 14.

[154] This can be deduced from study of Joffroy, *A Spy for God*, and the Biddle papers, box 3, notes on evidence, 2, pp. 47–51.

[155] Dodd papers, box 321, file 'Board of Review documents 1945 Oct.', shows that OCCPAC at one time was thinking of using the affidavit.

[156] Nevertheless, it should be noted that the judgement of a German trial of the suppliers of Zyklon B in Mar. 1949 referred to Gerstein's report. See Rückerl, *NS-Verbrechen vor Gericht*, 122–3.

defence witness for the SS. Though he went on to testify in the 'subsequent' trials, his words continued to arouse scepticism.

Doubts over Morgen's testimony arose chiefly from his attempt to differentiate the management of the extermination centres from those of the orthodox concentration camps. (Obviously in terms of the case in hand he was fighting a losing battle, because the SS in some form had a hand in both of these groupings.) But the detail and nuances of Morgen's testimony were lost because he spoke truths that no one was yet ready to hear. He described visits to Dachau and Buchenwald in the course of his duties, and his relatively pleasant depiction of these camps, which had for some time been established in the western mind as examples of the worst of Nazi atrocity,[157] cast all of his testimony into doubt. While summarizing the evidence against the SS, the British prosecutor David Maxwell-Fyfe declared with vitriol to the IMT that

On the face of it, the evidence which has been given by almost all the witnesses called before your Commissioners [in the organization cases] is untrue. You yourselves have seen and heard some of the witnesses, selected by Defence Counsel . . . The witness Morgen described the variety theatre, the cinema, the bookstalls, and the other amenities of Buchenwald. Dachau, he said, was a recreation camp.[158]

Yet it is evident that Morgen visited the camps long before they descended into the state of complete disrepair and depravity in which they were discovered by Allied troops. Besides, we know from the evidence of Eugen Kogon, formerly an inmate at Buchenwald, that that camp did indeed have the facilities described above,[159] though for privileged inmates and for a restricted period. Furthermore, it is not surprising that the camp administration would have attempted to give as favourable an impression as possible to an investigating judge. Finally, it is evident with hindsight, given Morgen's later testimony at the Pohl trial, that he was speaking of the camps in relative terms. In the latter case, Morgen stated that after he had heard about the establishment of the extermination facilities at Birkenau, and 'in the General Government under the Eastern Territory [*sic*]', he had tried to find out whether gassing took place in other concentration camps as well: he 'really did not find anything like it'.[160]

At the Pohl trial Morgen also tried to establish the differences between Auschwitz I and Auschwitz II (Birkenau), as between a concentration camp and an extermination facility. Asked by the judge whether he would apply the same reasoning to Dachau, 'where the gas chamber was actually within the compound of the concentration camp', he denied the existence of a gas chamber at Dachau. The judge responded with the claim that 'we know about the false shower bath, and we know about the crematoria, so don't . . . try to tell us there were no

[157] On the particular use of gruesome evidence from Buchenwald, in a way that detracted from the systemization of the Nazi system of persecution and focused attention on its bestial acts, see Douglas, 'The Shrunken Head of Buchenwald'.
[158] *IMT*, xxii, 175–6. [159] Kogon, *Der SS-Staat*, 131–7.
[160] *NMT*, Case 4, pp. 6687–9.

exterminations at Dachau . . . There is not any question about it.' Morgen could only point out, before the defence was told to move on, that 'the presence of a crematory does not necessarily prove that people were being gassed before being taken to [that] crematory'.[161] On this particular question, however, the ignorance of the IMT, the tribunal in the Pohl trial, and the various prosecutors of the nuances in the system of Nazi atrocity, led to scepticism as to the value of the whole of Morgen's testimony.[162] At the IMT trial counsel for the defence was instructed not to waste time, and the final statement of the prosecution on the indicted organizations labelled Morgen a 'famous perjurer'.[163]

This episode illustrates better than any other that trials faced many of the same pitfalls as broader occupation policy. It traces a peculiar circularity as a mission to inform about the past was itself shaped by influences prohibiting full understanding of that past. The Allied mission was not simply historical, however; it was overtly political. As such, the particular nature of the past it recreated would have an immediate relevance as well as importance for posterity.

3.7 CONCLUSIONS

The decision not to document the murder process Aktion Reinhard resulted in a certain posthumous triumph for Nazism. The cynical prediction that in the absence of obvious physical evidence no one would believe the survivors proved substantially true. There was a distinct failure at any of the Nuremberg trials to confront the murder of the Polish Jews. Belzec and Sobibor barely received a mention in the proceedings of the trials, despite much anecdotal evidence as to their existence and role. Treblinka appeared scarcely more often, with the exception of the eyewitness accounts provided by the Soviets at the IMT Trial. The total of 6 million Jewish dead was promoted at Nuremberg, but in an atmosphere where statistics were hurled around with abandon and where false equivalencies were regularly drawn—both unconsciously and wilfully—between victim groups. The press coverage of the trials served only to magnify the distortions of the courtroom.

The popular record of the 'camps' which the trials helped to form consisted of a mixture of inflated accounts of the better-known establishments and, in as far as Auschwitz was described, uncertainty about the numbers killed there or the identity of the murdered. OCCPAC never really got to grips with Auschwitz as anything other than a particularly bad concentration camp and the Dachau and Royal Warrant series focused upon western camps, their sub-camps; and 'labour-education' camps. OCCWC did conduct trials of direct relevance to Auschwitz, in the Farben, Krupp, and the Pohl cases.[164] By that time, however, through 1947

---

[161] *NMT*, Case 4, pp. 6687–9.
[162] For the dismissive reaction of the American judge, see Francis Biddle, *In Brief Authority* (New York: Doubleday, 1962), 464.
[163] *IMT*, xxii, 323.   [164] Pankowicz, 'Das KL Auschwitz in den Nürnberger Prozessen'.

and 1948, the trials were receiving minimal attention other than as objects of adverse criticism. Moreover, the Pohl trial dwelt significantly on the western concentration camps alongside Auschwitz, and the institutions that were examined in the Milch case and the Medical case respectively were predominantly the German concentration centres. In the French zone, of the twenty-seven most prominent trials, the 'grands procès', those pertaining to camp criminality concerned Ravensbrück, the Wurttemberg and Neckar complexes, and a series of smaller institutions all in Germany.[165] Finally, of the myriad small cases of 'crimes against humanity' tried in the western zones under control council law and often by German jurists between 1945 and 1951, the concentration camp subjects were Buchenwald, Ravensbrück, and Kaufering, and in one sole instance an eastern extermination centre: Sobibor.[166]

The slant of knowledge passed down is reflected even in the work of one as acutely concerned with Germany's war record as Heinrich Böll.[167] His first full novel, *Wo warst du, Adam?*, conceived and written in the late 1940s and published in 1951, was exceptional amongst contemporary literature anywhere in considering the fate of the Jews. Yet the picture is confused. The camp to which sixty-seven Hungarian Jews are brought, in murderous conditions, towards the end of the war, is a small, 'northern' concentration camp rather than an eastern extermination camp.[168] That all the current inmates must be killed is a reflection of the reality of the final period of the war—the lack of railway facilities with which to deport them deeper into the Reich in the face of the advancing enemy.[169] The regular 'selection' procedure for the living and dying is based upon a gradation of the singing ability of the new arrivals. The best, scoring zero, are safe, entering the camp choir; the worst, scoring ten, are given little chance of surviving longer than two days.[170] This is not the stuff of systematic murder, but of capricious individual killings enacted at the behest of that beloved stock-figure of post-war caricature, the tyrannical and perverse SS commandant. Beyond these problems, the one Hungarian with whom the reader is asked to

---

[165] Pendaries, *Les procès de Rastatt*, 149–232, 265–90.

[166] Ibid. 94–6; Rückerl, *NS-Verbrechen vor Gericht*, 122. Other groupings of these trials concerned the personnel of the former 'euthanasia' institutions, the perpetrators of crimes during *Kristallnacht*, the Röhm *putsch* and other political murders, denunciators, and the *Endphaseverbrecher*. These smaller cases, against low-ranking personnel, were accorded virtually no public attention.

[167] On Böll and the war in general, see Wilhelm H. Grothmann's 'Das Menschenbild bei Heinrich Böll', Ph.D. thesis (Kansas, 1968). Böll had a particular interest in the Holocaust, modifying Adorno's classic denunciation of poetry to the declaration that 'after Auschwitz, one can no longer breathe, eat, love, read . . .': Heinrich Böll, *Frankfurter Vorlesungen* (Cologne: Verlag Kiepenheuer and Witsch, 1966), 26.

[168] It has been suggested that Jews were gassed at Böll's fictitious camp. See J. H. Reid, *Heinrich Böll: A German for His Time* (Oxford: Berg, 1988), 88. However, in the passage to which Reid alludes, there is no mention of gas chambers. Nor does Reid mention the fate of those with moderate singing ability; all the evidence points to murders within the camp being conducted individually with the gun, rather than *en masse*.

[169] Böll, *Wo warst du, Adam?*, 96.

[170] Ibid.: 'Wer zehn hatte, hatte wenig Aussicht, länger als zwei Tage am Leben zu bleiben'.

identify—the emblematic victim of this novel—is a converted Catholic Jew, Ilona.[171]

If Böll, like Eugen Kogon, and like OCCPAC, the IMT, and the Pohl tribunal could not bring out the full spectrum of the qualities of murder practised by the Third Reich, how, it might be asked, could the average bystander? It is certain both that the professional researcher could discover in some detail the 'truth' about the extent and intent of Nazi genocide, and that many Germans unfortunately did not need to be told it by the new authorities. But there was a substantial remainder of Germans who could be discerned by their passivity on either side of the defeat, and this is to say nothing of the Allied publics. If the darkest deed of Nazism, the murder of the Jews, was to be comprehended, to transmit to *these* people the nuances of the camp system was vital. The earlier study of Allied occupation policy, however, suggests that such revelation was thought neither necessary nor particularly desirable.

None of this is intended to diminish the concentration camps, or the fate of non-Jewish peoples. Nor should it support German apologia of ignorance by suggesting that the majority were unaware of the brutal Nazi repression of the Jews.[172] (Interestingly in this connection, knowledge of the early shooting massacres in Soviet territory may have been more widespread than the more systematized murders in extermination centres.)[173] It is, however, testament to the poor quality of the information available *vis-à-vis* the grades and direction of persecution. Besides, all Germans knew of 'the concentration camps', if only as a concept enforcing civil obedience—the very reason they were instituted; educationally, the eastern extermination camps were more important, for they had been somewhat veiled by distance, secrecy, and rumour.

Barely a month after VE Day, when the western concentration camps were still on many lips, the regulation German response upon the mention of atrocities was 'we have already heard much about this'.[174] The Germans—and the British and Americans—were only to hear more of the same. The failure to differentiate between Dachau and Treblinka or between Auschwitz I and Birkenau was a failure to distinguish murderous persecution from outright genocide, the Nazi oppression of political opponents from the decimation of European Jewry.

---

[171] Anyone acquainted with the shrill latter-day rhetorical conflict over the commemoration of the Auschwitz victim Edith Stein will appreciate the particular representational issues thus raised. Stein was a German Jew who converted to Catholicism and became a Carmelite nun, but was deported and murdered as a Jew. She has, however, been adopted by the Catholic Church as a Christian martyr, and was beatified and then, in 1998, canonized. See e.g. Isabel Wollaston, 'Auschwitz and the Politics of Commemoration: The Christianisation of the Holocaust', *Holocaust Educational Trust Research Papers*, 1, no. 5 (1999–2000).

[172] See e.g. Werner Bergmann, 'Die Reaktion auf den Holocaust in Westdeutschland von 1945 bis 1989', *Geschichte in Wissenschaft und Unterricht*, 43 (1992), 327–50, esp. 328.

[173] Wolfgang Benz, 'The Persecution and Extermination of the Jews in the German Consciousness', in John Milfull (ed.), *Why Germany? National Socialist Anti-Semitism and the European Context* (Providence: Berg, 1993), 91–104, esp. 100.

[174] Janowitz, 'German Reactions to Nazi Atrocities', 143.

And while capable historians could make the distinction, as they could cut through most of the veil of secrecy surrounding Aktion Reinhard, it is in the vagaries of popular perception that such potential confusions find their most fertile soil.[175] Moreover, in a post-war world where the automatic reflex of every nation that fell under the Nazi yoke was to stress erstwhile distance from and resistance to Nazism, whatever the truth of the matter,[176] a prevailing emphasis on institutions where non-Jewish Germans had been incarcerated in some numbers was an invitation to German self-exculpation. Thus to the next chapter, and the role of the trials in establishing consciousness of the extent to which German society had been subverted by Nazism.

As an addendum, however, it is worth considering a philosophical question: namely, whether any one crime or institution can be 'representative' of the murder of the Jews, as the Nuremberg prosecutors thought. Auschwitz—that which has entered the popular consciousness as metonym for the Holocaust—could not be representative of anything other than itself, for the simple reason that nothing was the same as Auschwitz. Majdanek was perhaps the most comparable institution, combining aspects of the extermination camp and the labour camp, yet Majdanek was not a place of primarily Jewish suffering. Auschwitz probably consumed more victims than any other individual camp, but this should not suggest that the gassing of a Jew at Auschwitz was in any way typical of the deaths of Jews in other extermination camps, and not simply because the number of Jews murdered in other such camps was in total much greater than the 1 million of Auschwitz. The consideration of the murder of approximately 1.8 million Jews in shooting massacres is another matter again. If anything, the 'pure' extermination centres of Belzec, Sobibor, Treblinka (and Chelmno) were, as Pierre Vidal-Naquet has suggested, a closer approximation to 'absolute negativity' than was Auschwitz.[177]

Moreover, while Auschwitz became the epicentre of the genocide from 1943, before then that dubious distinction belonged, first, to the western areas of Soviet territory, then to the Lublin district of Poland. This leads us on to a sociological consideration of greater representational importance than the bare topography of the killing process. The vast majority of Holocaust victims (five-sixths) were not westernized, assimilated Jews, transported half-way across Europe; they were not Anne Frank, or the German Weiss family from the Hollywood soap-opera *Holocaust*, nor were they the Americanized Hungarians carefully selected for Steven Spielberg's film *The Last Days*; they were primarily Yiddish speakers from in and around the Pale of Settlement who were murdered in the lands of their birth. It was of such people that Gerald Reitlinger, one of the

---

[175] See e.g. on the controversies over commemoration of the Auschwitz sites, and related French incidents, Wieviorka, 'La construction de la mémoire du génocide en France', 31 and *passim*. Also noteworthy in this connection is the great play David Irving made of the differences between the Auschwitz camps in his recent libel case against Penguin Books and Deborah Lipstadt.

[176] See the essays in Deak, Gross, and Judt, *The Politics of Retribution*; Rousso, *The Vichy Syndrome*.

[177] Pierre Vidal-Naquet, *Assassins of Memory* (New York: Columbia University Press, 1992), 97.

earliest historians of the 'final solution', wrote the following: 'the Eastern European Jew is a natural rhetorician, speaking in flowery similes . . . sometimes the imagery [thus conjured] transcends credibility'.[178] This instructive and unfortunate remark could have come straight from the mouth of Robert Jackson, and is a suitable epitaph to the oft-displaced memory of the murder of Polish Jewry.

[178] Reitlinger, *The Final Solution*, 531.

CHAPTER FOUR

The Failure of the Trial Medium: Charting the Breadth of Nazi Criminality

If the war crimes trials did not convey the depths to which Nazism had sunk, what then of the breadth of German malfeasance? Despite blurring the forms and subjects of persecution, the trials and other media, and pre-existing forms of German and Allied popular knowledge, contributed to a general awareness of German atrocity. Who was blamed for these crimes?

The locus of blame varied according to time and place. On one level, in the liberal democracies, and particularly Britain, Germans as a whole were held responsible. The remarkable durability of wartime stereotypes down to the present—as manifested at international football matches and in much of the rhetoric against further European integration—is testament to popular identification with Ernest Bevin's vitriolic 'I hates [sic] those Germans'. This type of blanket association of Nazism with the whole of German society finds some reflection in remarks made by the Israeli ambassador at the opening of a touring exhibition in Aachen in April 1998.

The exhibition was the well-known and self-explanatory 'War of Annihilation [Vernichtungskrieg]: The Crimes of the Wehrmacht from 1941 to 1944', and the ambassador declared that 'hardly anyone in Israel is interested in it because no one can understand what it has to say that is new'.[1] The Israeli reaction to the exhibition, it seems, differs remarkably from the German, which has been one of outrage and right-wing terrorism at one extreme and of cathartic eye-opening and apology at the other, but certainly of great general interest.

The explanations are easy enough to ascertain. A nation that can be identified with the victims is less conscious of differentiation between groups acting in the name of the perpetrator nation; conversely, 15–18 million Germans served in some capacity during the Hitlerzeit, so the legacy of military service is a matter of concern for a large proportion of the population. The record of the Wehrmacht is in many ways the record of the German people of the Hitlerzeit as a whole. Moreover, the existence of the Wehrmacht predated Nazism, and thus congeries of psychological considerations come into play around dichotomies of Germanism and Nazism, continuity and rupture, traditionalism and

---

[1] 'Ansprache des Botschafters des Staates Israel, A. Primor anlässlich der Eröffnung der Ausstellung "Vernichtungskrieg, Verbrechen der Wehrmacht von 1941 bis 1944" am 17 Apr. 1998 in Aachen', ed. Ulrich Wisser (World Wide Web: www Verlag Ulrich Wisser, 1998), 1–2.

usurpation, and, more specifically, ideological responsibility and 'apolitical' soldierly obedience. Conversely, and apparently paradoxically, the German record of early victory and later stubborn resistance against the vast armies of the USSR and, thereby, Bolshevism, was a source of pride for many Germans, and the POWs who eventually returned from the Soviet Union were regarded as heroic symbols of the German war effort. The immediate post-war world, as a crucial formative period for modern German identity in general, was a key time in the establishment of powerful mythologies: the battle over the record of the Wehrmacht was integral to the self-image of a nation.

The real debate about the Wehrmacht exhibition is psychological, since there is no legitimate historiographical dispute in specialist circles that the German army contributed fulsomely to Nazi genocide.[2] Though the Wehrmacht was not involved in the planning of the 'final solution of the Jewish question', it was instrumental in facilitating that murder by conquest, and by the logistical support and protection of the Einsatzgruppen, and also in implementing it with their own 'shooters'. Wehrmacht murderousness in Serbia and White Russia was particularly extensive, while the ideologically informed, Manichaean nature of the war with the Soviet Union radicalized the German war effort so that 'partisan warfare' everywhere from 1941 would be met with the most extreme violence. Greece and Italy, for instance, would feel the massive force of an often-indiscriminate 'reprisal' policy. The military was also directly involved in the genocidal planning for the policies of enforced starvation of vast areas of eastern Europe. In the connection of food provision for the invading forces, the military leadership smoothed the ground for the intentional neglect and ensuing death of in excess of 3 million Soviet POWs. Finally, military culpability extended to the murder of the mentally ill and the 'gypsies'.

The last twenty-five years have witnessed a flourishing of impressive, scholarly studies that have established a hard core of Wehrmacht complicity in Nazi crimes. The pioneering work of Christian Streit, Omer Bartov, Helmut Krausnick, and Jürgen Förster in particular focused attention on the willingness of military commanders to issue to their armies, and even radicalize, criminal orders and incitements to genocidal activity.[3] An even more recent crop of literature has depicted a rank and file that was in touch to some degree with the ideological priorities of the political regime and hence was receptive to the idea of 'atrocity by policy'. Walther Manoscheck has gone as far as to suggest that

---

[2] Peter Steinbach, 'Krieg, Verbrechen, Widerstand', in Karl Heinrich Pohl (ed.), *Wehrmacht und Vernichtungspolitik: Militär in nationalsozialistischen System* (Göttingen: Vandenhoeck and Ruprecht, 1999), 11–37, esp. 13.

[3] Streit, *Keine Kameraden*; Omer Bartov, *The Eastern Front, 1941–1945: German Troops and the Barbarization of Warfare* (New York: St. Martin's Press, 1985); id., *Hitler's Army: Soldiers, Nazis and War in the Third Reich* (Oxford: Oxford University Press, 1992); Helmut Krausnick and Hans-Heinrich Wilhelm, *Die Truppe des Weltanschauungskrieges: Die Einsatzgruppen der Sicherheitspolizei und des SD 1938–1942* (Stuttgart: Deutsche Verlags-Anstalt, 1981).

criminal orders and criminal acts are part of a *Kriegsalltag*—the 'everyday history' of the Wehrmacht at war in the east.[4]

While the most damning recent research is based upon more recently discovered, or hitherto obscure source material, the framework of military criminality was discerned at Nuremberg.[5] The Commissar Order and the Barbarossa Jurisdiction Decree were cited, as was the Einsatzgruppen connection. The Wehrmacht was of course one of Jackson's and Taylor's prime targets as they attempted to illustrate the connection between the various criminal enterprises of the Third Reich. However, as reactions to the exhibition suggest, the awareness of military actions that OCCPAC and OCCWC tried to foster did not materialize. The Barbarossa campaign, the invasion that precipitated the murder first of Soviet Jewry and then of Jews from all of Europe, was not associated with the concentration camps, however the latter were comprehended. The enduring vision, in Germany and the 'West' generally, has been of an 'upstanding Wehrmacht'.[6] A plethora of English and American war films focusing on the conflict in western Europe and Africa have perpetuated the image of a hard-fighting but honourable foe. Erwin Rommel, 'the Desert Fox', in particular has been promoted as an exemplar.[7] This chapter seeks to explain within the context of general reactions to the trials why they did little to revise conceptions of the nature of the Wehrmacht's war.

The salient political context in the propagation of the Wehrmacht's clean image was again the Cold War. It altered the agenda to the point of reversal of many of the principles of occupation policy, including the dismantling of the Allied trial machinery. Ultimately, from around 1949, it lead to the process of rearming Germany as an intrinsic part of a western European defence system. The leaders of the liberal democracies lost concern for examining the war record of their new ally, and their counterparts in the BRD proved adept at exploiting the situation to whitewash the record of German soldiery. The process was consummated symbolically when in 1951 Dwight Eisenhower publicly withdrew any general accusation against the Wehrmacht.[8]

---

[4] Walter Manoschek, 'Verbrecherische Befehle—Verbrecherische Taten: Sie gehörten zum Kriegsalltag der Wehrmacht', *Mittelweg*, 36 (1992/3), 137–44. Bartov's works overlap with this category; see also the essays in Hannes Heer and Klaus Naumann (eds.), *Vernichtungskrieg: Verbrechen der Wehrmacht 1941 bis 1944* (Hamburg: HIS, 1995); Christian Gerlach, 'Verbrechen deutscher Fronttruppen in Weissrussland 1941–1944', in Karl Heinrich Pohl (ed.), *Wehrmacht und Vernichtungspolitik: Militär in nationalsozialistischen System* (Göttingen: Vandenhoeck and Ruprecht, 1999), 89–114.

[5] Perels, 'Verpasste Chancen', 32, on the details of Wehrmacht-Einsatzgruppen co-operation in the High Command case.

[6] Alfred Streim, 'Saubere Wehrmacht?', in Hannes Heer and Klaus Naumann (eds.), *Vernichtungskrieg: Verbrechen der Wehrmacht 1941 bis 1944* (Hamburg: HIS, 1995), 569–97.

[7] On German films, see Claus Seidl, *Der deutsche Film der fünfziger Jahre* (Munich: Wilhelm Heyne, 1987), 36–7; Bärbel Westermann, *Nationale Identität im Spielfilm der fünfziger Jahre* (Frankfurt am Main: Lang, 1990), 34–6.

[8] Wolfram Wette, 'Wehrmachtstraditionen und Bundeswehr', in Johannes Klotz (ed.), *Vorbild Wehrmacht: Wehrmachtsverbrechen, Rechtsextremismus und Bundeswehr* (Cologne: Papy Rossa, 1998), 126–54, esp. 130.

The trials themselves therefore became victims of broader occupation policy. As the latter metamorphosed, the former remained isolated and vulnerable, symbols of resented Allied hegemony and out-dated accusations of guilt. Indeed, some of the anti-Communist noises emanating from London and Washington were utterly incongruous with the messages of those cases that touched upon the Wehrmacht's Vernichtungskrieg in eastern Europe.

The trials were attacked as German nationalism reasserted itself, and eventually Britain and the USA compromised their own previous legal commitments by the widespread early release of convicted war criminals. To an extent, Jeffrey Herf's juxtaposition of the competing demands of justice on the one hand and democracy on the other is helpful. Meaningful confrontation with the past gave way in the face of the need to establish a new order based on the common consent of a population that did not look favourably upon trials. Decisively important was the role of the various German élites—politicians, the clergy, bureaucrats, and, indeed, military officers—in discrediting the trials as Allied impositions. For the reasons outlined above, imprisoned soldiers were vital chattels in the game. Thus, after charting the general growth in discontent with the trials, this chapter will culminate in a case study of the treatment of a single, very significant officer—Erich von Manstein.

This is not simply a tale of power politics subverting justice. Nor was outspoken defence of the Wehrmacht on grounds of misplaced conviction an entirely German phenomenon. The following analysis seeks to examine German responses to the trials in two contexts. It argues that the Allies did not prepare the ground for acceptance of the true breadth of German guilt and, furthermore, suggests that the German rejection of the criminal nature of the Soviet conflict should be seen alongside broader 'occidental' re-evaluations of the war. First then, the chapter places German reactions to the trial in relation to the comparatively intense Allied 're-education' programmes of the early post-war period, discussing the reactions to the issue of 'guilt' in its many guises. Secondly, it compares German attitudes to trials with attitudes in the USA and, particularly, Britain.

We know that even at the height of the re-educational campaigns the trials were complemented by didactic frameworks that accorded little priority to the victims. It is argued here that the introspection which was the key aim of this 're-education' prompted only sterile consideration of guilt, and that only in a select few. With its emphasis on German society and, in so far as specific crimes were pinpointed, the problematic German concentration camps, the ground was prepared for responses that omitted Germany's most extensive crimes: those committed to the east of Germany and against non-Germans. The self-reflectivity that was encouraged was taken to extremes and ignored those that had been cast as 'racial other' by the Third Reich: the Jews and the Slavs.

If the unsullied image of the German army in the liberal democracies is attributable in large part to ignorance, because the war fought against their armies was of a comparatively 'civilized' nature, there were also better-informed and influential voices in Britain and America who were sympathetic to the Wehrmacht soldiers from the eastern front. Their attitudes stemmed on one side from identification with the anti-Bolshevik nature of the conflict with the USSR, and that stance would become more and more popular as the post-war world developed. But within what was effectively a community of shared interest with other Christian European nations against the forces of Communism in the 'east', in whose interest it was to 'relativize' German actions in the Soviet Union, there was a more active and closely defined interest-group: military professionals and their admirers, whose political agenda was as little concealed as that of the Wehrmacht in the east.

American and British absolution of the Wehrmacht was an important aspiration in Adenauer's Germany, as the Eisenhower declaration showed. Some of the key elements in what was a highly effective transnational public relations campaign on behalf of the German military have been summarized by Jürgen Förster as follows:

for far too long the memoirs of German generals, quickly translated into English during the Cold War, shaped the public's image of the Wehrmacht's record in the Second World War. Many a historian relied on such accounts as *Lost Victories* by Erich von Manstein . . . Moreover with his book *On the Other Side of the Hill* (1951), B. H. Liddell Hart had already provided them with a large audience to whom they could talk about their campaigns in Europe and Africa and their purely professional part in them. From Nuremberg onwards, the notion has existed of separating the Führer from his followers, the generals from their supreme commander, and the Wehrmacht from the crimes of the SS.[9]

The Manstein case study will detail the complicity of Basil Liddell Hart and many other Allied citizens with the burgeoning German movement that pressed to distort the nature of the Soviet war and to exonerate convicted war criminals.

4.1 GENOCIDE IN THE CONSCIOUSNESS OF THE POST-WAR WORLD: AN OVERVIEW

'Never again' was indeed the *motif* of post-war British society but, as Peter Hennessy has shown, in real terms it concerned aspirations to a better Britain.[10] Reforming the world may have occupied a tiny minority as a possibility, and a slightly larger number as an abstract concept, but to the mass of people, the problems were of social security, housing, employment, health, education, and simply getting on with the peace. The solution was a democratic socialist welfare state, and if Britain's needs were served by importing the labour of displaced

---

[9] Jürgen Förster, 'The Relation between Operation Barbarossa as an Ideological War of Extermination and the Final Solution', in David Cesarani (ed.), *The Final Solution: Origins and Implementation* (London: Routledge, 1994), 85–102, esp. 85–6.

[10] Peter Hennessy, *Never Again: Britain, 1945–51* (London: Jonathan Cape, 1992).

persons from the Baltic States with known fascist, even genocidal, pasts, then this would come to pass. The episode of labour recruitment under the 'European Voluntary Worker' scheme is a good indicator of the lack of sensitivity with which surviving Jews were treated by a population and government who were unclear about the exact fate of their kin, and were uninterested in clarification.[11]

After the war, the 'average American' also 'knew and cared little about what went on in Germany. Isolationism, for a while at least, was once again the prevailing mood of the United States. Bringing the boys back home and reintegrating them into America's life and economy had first priority.'[12] For many of those concerned with broader developments, particularly on the West coast, the war with Japan supplanted the German conflict. It lasted longer; for US troops, it had been more brutal, and for the population at a less comfortable distance, than the European engagement.[13] Again, the evidence is of a lack of engagement with the fate of the Jews.

None of the above should detract from the vilification of Germany in Britain and America. The latter had long been subject to the anti–German, and particularly anti–Prussian, influence of Roosevelt, while the official policy of the former since the Casablanca conference of January 1943 was effectively to equate all Germans with Nazis.[14] This animosity reached a peak as the concentration camps were revealed; but it was hatred on the same continuum as had existed previously when reports came through about the Malmédy massacre or the murder of Allied pilots or POWs.[15] Moreover, the excess of Anglo-American Germanophobia was arguably unloaded in 1945. We have also seen that for various reasons the symbol of the 'concentration camps' did not signify the murder of the Jews, while the available wartime intelligence on the development of the 'final solution' appears to have made little popular impact. Widespread knowledge of the Holocaust in the USA developed in the 1970s, and in Britain later even than that.[16]

The relative prevalence of awareness of the Holocaust in the Federal Republic (BRD) and now the united Germany is in part testament to the recent success of educational initiatives within a more open approach to the most sensitive period of that nation's past. In order to put the argument of this book into perspective, scholarly consensus suggests that the seminal stage in the development of West

---

[11] David Cesarani, *Justice Delayed* (London: Mandarin, 1992).
[12] Hans W. Gatze, *Germany and the United States: A 'Special Relationship'?* (Cambridge, Mass.: Harvard University Press, 1980), 162.
[13] Michael Schaller, *The American Occupation of Japan: The Origins of the Cold War in Asia* (Oxford: Oxford University Press, 1985), 3–4, 26.
[14] Eberan, *Wer war an Hitler schuld?*, 19–20.
[15] In 1943, 70% of Britons polled registered either hatred, bitterness, anger, blame, dislike, contempt, or disgust for the German people. *The Gallup International Public opinion Polls: Great Britain 1937–1975*, i, *1937–1964*, ed. George Gallup (New York: Random House, 1976), 82.
[16] Kushner, *The Holocaust and the Liberal Imagination*, ch. 7.

German popular consciousness of Nazi genocide was certainly not the Nuremberg trials; nor was it the opening in 1958, and the consequent operations, of a national centre for the investigation of Nazi capital crimes; nor, indeed, the capture and trial of Adolf Eichmann by Israel at the beginning of the 1960s. The student movement of the late 1960s, in which the 'guilt of the fathers' was brought to the fore, and the popularization of the story of Anne Frank were vital,[17] but were surpassed by the screening in 1979 on national television of the American mini-series *Holocaust*. As one critic has observed dryly, the masses were stirred by this soap-opera to a crescendo of self-questioning—and banal apologia—while the small circle of acknowledged experts remained for the most part confined to debating the timing of a 'Hitler-order' for the 'final solution'.[18]

Though in the IMT era the citizens of the Soviet zone were prevented from genuine slumber by the educative programmes complementing the trials, the infiltration of Marxist-Leninist theory ensured that the question, 'Wie konnte es geschehen?'—how could it happen?—was never directed at the murder of Europe's Jews.[19] It was certainly a function of this instruction that marchers protesting in Dresden about the acquittals and more lenient sentences in the IMT trial employed the motif 'Auschwitz demands the death penalty';[20] but the invocation of the name and the understanding of the phenomenon were worlds apart in the domain of Communist propaganda. Nevertheless, in whatever form it was conceived, 'Auschwitz' remained largely the property of the Soviet sphere until the osmosis began nearly two decades later with a series of trials of camp personnel in Frankfurt. Little prior adjustment to the nuances of the Nazi murder campaigns was manifest in the west. Thus of a group of forty Cologne schoolchildren questioned in 1954 on their knowledge of the war, none admitted to awareness of the genocide of the Jews, or of Auschwitz, Treblinka, or Majdanek,[21] the extermination centres that received any attention in the Allied trials. This should not imply that repression of the Holocaust was uniform in the BRD, but it does point to the absence of accurate public discourse.

Shortly after its establishment, the BRD's Justice Ministry set about creating a centralized office providing the best legal assistance for the inhabitants of the Allied prisons.[22] The government followed this up with sustained pressure on the British and Americans to commute death sentences and release

---

[17] Bergmann, 'Die Reaktion auf den Holocaust', 329, 332, 350.

[18] Henryk M. Broder, *Volk und Wahn* (Hamburg: Spiegel Buchverlag, 1996), 215–16.

[19] Hans Otto Gericke, 'Die Presseberichterstattung über den Nürnberger Prozess und die Überwindung des faschistischen Geschichtsbildes', *Zeitschrift für Geschichtswissenschaft*, 33 (1985), 917, 920–1, for the educative programmes; Erich Goldhagen, 'Der Holocaust in der Sowjetischen Propaganda und Geschichtsschreibung', *VfZ*, 28 (1980), 502–7, for the nature of the initiatives.

[20] *FR* (12 Oct. 1946).

[21] *Heinrich Böll: Werke. Essayistische Schriften und Reden*, i, ed. Bernd Balzer (Cologne: Verlag Antje Kunstmann, 1978), 133.

[22] Norbert Frei, *Vergangenheitspolitik: Die Anfänge der Bundesrepublik und die NS-Vergangenheit* (Munich: Verlag C. H. Beck, 1996), 21–2.

prisoners. However, the murder of the Jews was virtually absent from school textbooks.[23] Likewise, no German film of that era concerned itself directly with Nazi persecution or murder.[24] The list could go on. At best, political efforts on behalf of the Nazis' victims were 'half-hearted' in comparison with those 'victims' of the Allies, the war criminals.[25] Difficult though it may now seem for us to believe, the self-image of German victimization was real enough at the time, with the vast influx of refugees expelled from the formerly German-occupied territories, the division of Germany, and, before their return, the legions of POWs in Soviet hands.[26] Conversely, the 'restitution' payments made to Israel in the 1950s can be interpreted as Chancellor Konrad Adenauer choosing a line of reconciliation 'less threatening' to his constituents than the trial of Nazis.[27]

With Adenauer's canny exploitation of the Anglo-American moves toward collaboration with west Germany after 1949, the political vista was not conducive to official meditation on the criminal Nazi past.[28] His coalition government policy reflected his long-held rhetoric about breaking with the past.[29] Even Schumacher's SPD came to argue for closure, believing that to be the route to electoral success. After 1949 we see only a number of socialist activists and Communist party supporters—a very small minority of the West German public—in opposition.[30]

Yet the window of opportunity for moral re-education was narrower even than all of this implies. The circumstantial and psychological factors enabling the victory of forgetfulness, as the political scientist Dolf Sternberger described it[31]— though it would better be characterized as a victory of displacement—were established well before the formation of the Federal Republic. Not only in the course of 1946–7 did the Americans influentially moderate their intentions from 're-education' to 're-orientation', and substitute the more lenient occupation

---

[23] Falk Pingel, 'Nationalsozialismus und Holocaust in westdeutschen Schulbüchern', in Rolf Steininger (ed.), *Der Umgang mit dem Holocaust: Europa—USA—Israel* (Cologne: Böhlau Verlag, 1994), 221–32.

[24] *Die Mörder sind unter uns* (discussed below) came closest to this subject.

[25] Frei, *Vergangenheitspolitik*, 21; Buscher, *The US War Crimes Trial Program*, 92, 110. On false victim equivalencies, see also Fulbrook, *German National Identity after the Holocaust*, 148.

[26] Robert Moeller, 'Writing the History of West Germany', in id. (ed.), *West Germany under Construction* (Ann Arbor, MI: University of Michigan Press, 1997), 1–30, esp. 14–15, 17–18; id., 'War Stories: The Search for a Usable Past in the Federal Republic of Germany', *American Historical Review*, 101 (1996), 1008–48.

[27] Herf, *Divided Memory*, 209.

[28] Norbert Frei, '"Vergangenheitsbewältigung" or "Renazification"? The American Perspective on Germany's Confrontation of the Nazi Past in the Early Years of the Adenauer Era', in Michael Ermath (ed.), *America and the Shaping of German Society, 1945–1955* (Providence: Berg, 1993), 57; Gatze, *Germany and the United States*, 182.

[29] Herf, *Divided Memory*.

[30] Thomas Alan Schwartz, 'Die Begnadigung deutscher Kriegsverbrecher: John J. McCloy und die Häftlinge von Landsberg', *VfZ*, 38 (1990), 375–414, esp.382–3; Frank Buscher, 'Kurt Schumacher, German Social Democracy and the Punishment of Nazi Crimes', *Holocaust and Genocide Studies*, 5 (1990), 261–73.

[31] Cited in Frei, *Vergangenheitspolitik*, 15.

statute JCS 1779 for JCS 1079,[32] it also seems that by the latter year the general impetus in West German society to 'draw a final line' under the recent past—or at least on the suffering that they had caused, if not that which they felt—was in the ascendant.[33] By 1948, as we have seen, the Allies were even drawing attention to Soviet 'crimes against humanity'. The flow of published accounts of the concentration camps by victims dried up after 1947, and public discussion about that side of Nazi history was silenced, paving the way for the new master narratives of silence or obfuscation or emphasis on German victimhood, or, indeed, of continued antisemitism.[34] This was attributable to a number of factors including growing assertiveness as the war distanced itself, mass discontent with the ill-managed and inequitable 'denazification' policies, and, relatedly, disdain for the authorities as Allied infighting and difficulties in running the country removed their 'aura of moral superiority'.[35]

What though of the period of closest proximity to the war, before Allied outrage had dissipated? A consideration of the discourses imposed on and promoted in Germany in 1945–6 shows that even at the time of the most concentrated propaganda, the extent of German criminality was not apparent.

4.2 AN EDUCATION IN GERMAN GUILT

Anyone acquainted with the German 'literature of the ruins', or with journals of the native population or of their occupiers, cannot but appreciate the poverty of the soil in which the Allies were attempting to sow the seeds of 're-education'. The imperative of survival and the prosaic concerns of reconstruction and re-alignment to peacetime existence necessarily occupied the majority of German civilians in the direct aftermath of conflict.[36] For a famished people, of whom the town-dwellers at least were frequently freezing in winter, and in summer were engulfed by the fetid stench of corpses lying amongst the as-yet uncleared rubble, Brecht's aphorism from his reworking of *The Beggar's Opera* was entirely apt: 'Erst kommt das Fressen, dann kommt die Moral': 'First grub, then morality'.[37]

---

[32] James F. Tent, *Mission on the Rhine: Reeducation and Denazification in American-Occupied Germany* (Chicago, Iu.: University of Chicago Press, 1982), 254–318. The British had generally been less demonstrative in 're-education', and less strict with 'denazification' anyway.

[33] Frei, *Vergangenheitspolitik*, 14.

[34] Peitsch, '*Deutschlands Gedächtnis an seine dunkelste Zeit*'; Frank Stern, 'The Historic Triangle', and Constantin Goschler, 'The Attitude towards Jews in Bavaria after the Second World War', both in Robert Moeller (ed.), *West Germany under Construction* (Ann Arbor, Mich.: University of Michigan Press, 1997), 199–230, 231–50.

[35] Herbert Frey, 'The German Guilt Question after the Second World War: An Overview', Ph.D. thesis (Washington, 1979), 229.

[36] For a typical, brief but poignant, literary evocation of the situation, see Hans Bender, *Die Hostie* (Munich: Carl Haenser, n.d.).

[37] Cited in Constantine Fitzgibbon, *Denazification* (London: Michael Joseph, 1969), 11; Grosser, *Germany in Our Time*, ch. 3.

Even the ability of the fortunate to concern themselves with broader questions than their immediate well-being was no guarantee of attentiveness to Allied pedagogy.[38] The huge resentment of the occupation regimes[39] was in no way tempered by the imagery of atrocity: as the German metaphor has it, a young dog is likely to resent having its nose rubbed in its own excrement.[40] Thus concentration camp photographs often caused disgust and distrust rather than contemplation; conversely, the repetitive visions of mountains of corpses, lacking in any identity, could even lack emotional impact,[41] save, as has been heretofore described, if they actually suggested *German* suffering.

A further swathe of Germans, cutting across these cleavages, included all those who would close their ears to the screams of the past out of feelings of culpability, or at least fear of retribution. Amongst their number were the hundreds of thousands directly or indirectly involved in the campaigns of racial extermination and repression, and many of the 8 million former members of the Nazi party. This braune Erbe ('brown legacy') formed a formidable constituency which was in the main implacably opposed to Allied occupation, punishment, and re-education, and is of less interest to this study than the remainder of German post-war society.[42]

Again multifarious, but probably more numerous, were those conscious of the role of propaganda in the preceding decade. These were naturally suspicious of anything that bore its scent.[43] Educational measures would therefore have to combine a message of sufficient power to make an impact on the German consciousness with the judiciousness required to make the lesson palatable. The first of these requirements was met, in the short term at least, because the Allies had at their disposal the photographic evidence of the 'liberated' concentration camps. However, and related to the way in which that evidence was employed, the second criterion was certainly not fulfilled.

---

[38] e.g. Maria Höhn has shown how after the war, German women were often pre-occupied with regaining their pre-1933 status: 'Frau im Haus und Girl im *Spiegel*: Discourse on Women in the Interregnum Period of 1945–1949 and the Question of German Identity', *Central European History*, 26 (1993), 57–90.

[39] On the way discontent with the occupation served to repress guilt in Germany, see Josef Foschepath, 'German Reaction to Defeat and Occupation', in Robert Moeller (ed.), *West Germany under Construction* (Ann Arbor, Mich.: University of Michigan Press, 1997), 73–89. See *Befreier und Befreite: Krieg, Vergewaltigungen, Kinder*, ed. Helke Sander and Barbara Johr (Munich: Verlag Antje Kunstmann, 1992), esp. 61–4, on rape by troops in the western zones—a feature which scarcely gave the occupiers moral authority.

[40] Cited in Chamberlin, 'Todesmühlen', 420.

[41] Bergmann, 'Die Reaktion auf den Holocaust', 332.

[42] On this 'inheritance', including discussion of the double-edged term 'restitution' (*Wiedergutmachung*), see Norbert Frei, 'Das Problem der NS-Vergangenheit in der Ära Adenauer', and Herbert Obenaus, '"Man spielt so gern mit dem Begriff Opfer": Wiedergutmachung und Annahme der NS-Vergangenheit in Niedersachsen bis zum Anfang der fünfziger Jahre', both in Bernd Weisbrod (ed.), *Rechtradikalismus in der politischen Kultur der Nachkriegszeit: Die verzögerte Normalisierung in Niedersachsen* (Hanover: Hahnsche Buchhandlung, 1995), 19–31, 33–64.

[43] Chamberlin, 'Todesmühlen', 432–4.

In its initial, atavistic form, the re-educational imperative was expressed via the formula of collective guilt—in the post-war German lexicon the *Kollektiv-schuldthese*. This concept was most notoriously articulated in Roosevelt's pronouncements about the principles of occupation policy, and consequently in the occupation statute JCS 1067.[44] It was less popular with the British planners, featuring more in their rhetoric than in their policies;[45] and at the opening of the IMT trial Justice Jackson disavowed the principle.[46] Moreover, we know that JCS 1067 was never fully implemented, the severest provisions ignored.[47] Yet it was in the spirit of the theory, at a time of Allied non-fraternization with the local populations, that the earliest and most concerted efforts at mass instruction were enacted. Concomitantly, the collective guilt charge occupied Germans even after it had been dropped by the Allies. Nothing could change the fact that Germany had been forced to surrender unconditionally, with the implicit message that there was no group who the Allies considered to be untainted; nor, in, say, 1947, could the considerable remaining restrictions on the freedoms of the populace be ignored.[48]

Putting aside for the moment the question of precise intent, the early wave of re-educative material was certainly substantial. Anyone in western Germany between 1945 and 1946 sufficiently concerned with current affairs to attend the screenings of *Welt im Film*, or to read any of the organs of the military government or licensed press would have been confronted consistently with information, polemic, and considered reflection about the issues of, and responsibility for, 'war crimes' and 'war guilt'. Furthermore, there is evidence to show that awareness of the existence of propagandist aims did not necessarily preclude trust in information originating from the Allies. Thus research conducted by the Deutsches Institut für psychologische Forschung und Psychotherapie early in 1946 on Bavarian viewers of the concentration camp documentary, *Todesmühlen*, revealed that although two-thirds of respondents considered the film to be partially or wholly propaganda driven, a majority (56.3 per cent) still believed it to be factually accurate.[49] Newspaper readers recorded a similar faith in reporting of the trial of the major war criminals.[50]

Yet faith did not equate to contrition, or even undue concern. *Der Tagesspiegel* ascribed the relatively low turn-out for *Todesmühlen* at Berlin cinemas to 'fear of

---

[44] Hoffmann, *Stunden Null?*, 96.

[45] Jill Jones, 'Eradicating Nazism from the British Zone of Germany: Early Policy and Practice', *German History*, 8 (1990), 145–62. See Hermann Weiss, 'Dachau und die internationale Öffentlichkeit', in *Dachauer Hefte, 1. Die Befreiung* (Munich: Deutscher Taschenbuch Verlag, 1993), 12–38, esp. 37, for the influence of the discovery of the concentration camps in stirring up general anti-German feeling.

[46] *IMT*, ii, 102–3.   [47] Gatze, *Germany and the United States*, 165.

[48] Eberan, *Wer war an Hitler schuld?*.   [49] Chamberlin, 'Todesmühlen', 433–4.

[50] *Public Opinion in Occupied Germany: The OMGUS Surveys, 1945–1949*, ed. Anna J. Merritt and Richard Merritt (Chicago, Ill.: University of Illinois Press, 1970), report no. 33 (18 Dec. 1946), 'The Trend of Public Reactions to the Nuremberg Trials', 121.

the truth'. In all probability, they resulted simply from apathy.[51] Very few Germans felt any responsibility at all when confronted with the concentration camps, as the statistics emerging from the *Todesmühlen* questionnaires testify.[52] Those who did were predictably those with least to be ashamed of.[53] Feelings of collective unworthiness stemming from shame caused other, predominantly leftist intellectuals to withdraw from political engagement; much as the body of self-conscious writers, pre-eminent amongst which was the *Gruppe '47*, retreated to the short story form—*Kurzgeschichte*—thinking the corrupted German language incapable of sustaining the traditional novel.

For most of its recipients, the *Kollektivschuldthese* was anathema, however.[54] Undoubtedly it was applied to make all Germans contemplate their own particular responsibilities; but in the crudeness of its presentation it seemingly equated the whole with its most criminal elements. Nor was it officially and publicly retracted in the sense in which it had been levelled. As the philosopher Karl Jaspers implied, the only explicit notion imparted by the widely distributed concentration camp photographs and reports was: 'this is your fault.'[55] We have seen that it was not at all clear exactly what these images represented; equally, it was difficult to ascertain from them in what precise ways the ordinary German was culpable. It was left to individuals to decipher for themselves the difference between 'guilt', 'responsibility', 'liability', and 'shame'—which in the early Allied usage were almost interchangeable—and between degrees of each. Most did not try. Those who did were likely to face the prospect of either being ignored or condemned as treacherous,[56] and this despite the fact that no one who really considered it accepted the charge as the Allies had apparently framed it, discerning different levels of guilt, not all of which were liable to punishment, and some of which were international, indeed universal in scope.[57]

Unsurprisingly, the apologia averred that ultimate and complete responsibility lay with the Nazi leaders, and perhaps also with the Allied powers for failing to forestall Hitler. Two chief claims could be made on the Germans' behalf: lack of knowledge of Nazi policy and lack of power to influence it.[58] The second of

---

[51] *Der Tagesspiegel* (9 Apr. 1946). The article stated that of approximately 630,000 inhabitants of the American zone of Berlin eligible and able to see the film, only 157,120 had done so, meaning (it deduced) 75% of the population were afraid of the truth.

[52] Chamberlin, 'Todesmühlen', 433, which reveals that, although 62.8% of viewers responding recorded the strong impression made on them, and 56.3% believed the film to be factually accurate, 87.9% felt no personal responsibility for the images they had seen.

[53] See e.g. Walter Dirks, 'Der Weg zur Freiheit: Ein Beitrag zur deutschen Selbsterkenntnis', *Frankfurter Hefte*, hereafter '*FH*', 1 (July 1946), 50–60, esp. 53.

[54] OMGUS report no. 33, *The OMGUS Surveys*, 122.   [55] Jaspers, *Die Schuldfrage*, 29.

[56] For disavowal of guilt, see Bance's introduction to his *Cultural Legacy*, 20–1; Fitzgibbon, *Denazification*, 99; for condemnation of its proponents: Frey, 'The German Guilt Question', 142; more generally, on resentment of former victims and opponents of the Nazis: Obenaus, '"Man spielt so gern mit dem Begriff Opfer"', 33.

[57] *The question of Schuldfrage* was a case in point. On Adenauer's stance, see Herf, *Divided Memory*, 213–14.

[58] Janowitz, 'German Reactions to Nazi Atrocities', 144.

these is at least problematic, and the first is simply wrong in the majority of cases. Some of the individual claims warrant direct consideration.

A former war correspondent who had been on the eastern front with the Waffen-SS 'Wiking' Division declared his willingness to testify before the IMT against Göring, Fritzsche, and the Reich Cabinet, on the grounds that they had lied to the German people, leading them into a criminal war, of the nature of which even his SS superiors were unaware.[59] This was a crude and duplicitous attempt to exculpate the organizations, which were shortly to come under the tribunal's scrutiny; for no one associated with the ideological indoctrination of SS troops could be anything but clear about their virulent fanaticism.[60]

In more general terms, that 57 per cent of the German population responding to an OMGUS survey on the IMT trial claimed that those proceedings revealed to them for the first time the existence of concentration camps has been taken at face value by scholars seeking to establish that the trial genuinely contributed to an early beginning of the process of working through the past.[61] The OMGUS question is of course indicative of the Allied failure to differentiate between 'camps'; but given that the orthodox concentration camps had been reported even in the western press since the mid 1930s,[62] and that 'Dachau' had entered the pre-war German consciousness to the extent of its incorporation in Kindergarten rhymes, the claims of ignorance regarding them were invariably self-serving.[63]

Ludwig Linnhoff, erstwhile Berlin policeman, attempted to disperse blame even further into the ether with a peculiar tale of obedience to senior orders. He began by confessing to the IMT court contact committee that subordinate members of the SS and party had indeed decided upon the disposition of Jews and 'half-breeds' (*Mischlinge*). However, higher officials could do nothing to alter the situation, because their juniors were working under the weight of instructions from the party offices or Hitler himself. The conclusion: Hitler, Himmler, Goebbels, and Bormann were ultimately responsible—and they were all either dead or missing.[64]

As an evasion of guilt such recourse to putative powerlessness is more complex. Acts of commission were excused by the alleged imperative to obey orders, or at best by the claim of continued tenancy in an important position in order to mitigate the severity of decreed measures. Standing by in the face of criminal activity was justified with reference to the inexorability of such measures and

---

[59] PRO, FO 1019/55, correspondence of Walter Kalweit, 24 Apr. 1946.

[60] Dieter Pohl, 'Die Einsatzgruppe C', in Peter Klein (ed.), *Die Einsatzgruppen in der besetzten Sowjetunion 1941/42* (Berlin: Gedenk- und Bildungsstätte Haus der Wannsee-Konferenz, 1997), 71–87, refers specifically to the crimes of the 'Wiking' division.

[61] Wilke, 'Ein früher Beginn der "Vergangenheitsbewältigung"'.

[62] Weiss, 'Dachau und die internationale Öffentlichkeit', 12.

[63] 'Lieber Herr Gott, mach mich stumm,/Das ich nicht nach Dachau komm [Dear God, make me dumb, so that I may not be sent to Dachau]'. See Janowitz, 'German Reactions to Nazi Atrocities', 141.

[64] PRO, FO 1019/55, correspondence of Ludwig Linnhoff, 21 May 1946.

the likelihood of punishment for attempting to intervene. The first argument, adopted by soldiers, industrialists, and diplomats alike, suggested that they were part of the system whether they liked it or not, but that the real blame lay with the political leaders.[65] Despite Allied rejection of this defence in the law courts (though it could be used in mitigation), it retained great currency amongst the former servants of Nazism. The second contention, adopted by many clergymen, and more representative of popular thought, was predicated upon the claim that most Germans were not part of the system at all; vague allegations were then made against 'leading Nazis', 'Hitler and the Nazi party', or the 'Nazi government'.[66]

A prime illustration of the latter device is the Stuttgart Declaration of Guilt (*Schuldbekenntnis*) of October 1945, made by representatives of the German Protestant churches. The declaration was as close as any public institution came to professing moral taint. However, it bears the marks of the reactionary stone from which it was hewn by Martin Niemöller, Bishops Wurm and Dibelius, and others who were themselves not free of some form of guilt.[67]

The language of the Declaration was opaque and evasive, making no mention of specific episodes or victims—a story that will already be familiar.[68] It declared:

we have struggled for many years in the name of Jesus Christ against the spirit which has found its terrible expression in the National Socialist regime of violence, but we accuse ourselves for not being more courageous, for not praying more faithfully, for not believing more joyously and for not loving more ardently.

The barely disguised implication was that those who were 'truly' guilty by commission of the undisclosed crimes were set apart; and alongside the 'solidarity of guilt' which the churches shared with the people was, inevitably, 'a great company of suffering'.[69]

It is also instructive to note the reflections of those with whom the allegations of guilt could be said to have encouraged constructive engagement, those who served to interpret the ways in which ordinary Germans could be deemed responsible for 'the concentration camps'. To this end, we will consider three

---

[65] For some of the arguments cited or advanced in contemporary texts, see Otto Nelte, *Die Generale: Das Nürnberger Urteil und die Schuld der Generale* (Hanover: Verlag des anderen Deutschlands, 1947); Tilo von Wilmowsky, *Warum wurde Krupp verurteilt? Legende und Justizirrtum* (Stuttgart: Friedrich Vorwerk, 1950); Margret Boveri, *Der Diplomat vor Gericht* (Berlin: Minerva, 1948).

[66] Janowitz, 'German Reactions to Nazi Atrocities', 144.

[67] For the 'compromise-character' of the Stuttgart Declaration, see Axel Schildt, 'Solidarisch mit der Schuld des Volkes: Die öffentliche Schulddebatte und das Integrationsgebot der Kirchen in Niedersachsen nach dem Zweiten Weltkrieg', in Bernd Weisbrod (ed.), *Rechtradikalismus in der politischen Kultur der Nachkriegszeit: Die verzögerte Normalisierung in Niedersachsen* (Hanover: Hahnsche Buchhandlung, 1995), 269–295, esp. 272; R. C. D. Jasper, *George Bell—Bishop of Chichester* (London: Oxford University Press, 1967), 291–4.

[68] The Catholic equivalent of Aug. 1945 from Fulda was similarly deficient. See Schildt, 'Solidarisch mit der Schuld des Volkes', 278–9.

[69] Text of the Declaration in Jasper, *George Bell*, 294.

influential German media organs of the early post-war years: the liberal *Frank-furter Rundschau* the first licensed German-published newspaper in the US zone; the left-wing *Telegraf*, published in Berlin and enjoying the highest circulation of any newspaper in the British zone; and *Frankfurter Hefte*, the journal co-edited by Eugen Kogon, and credited as being 'intensively concerned with the guilt question in its broadest sense'.[70]

From the pages of these three, there is evidence of a considerable preparedness to examine all facets of German public and political life. We see dissertations on the dangers of fusing the branches of state, and particularly the police, with overtly political organizations;[71] the role and responsibilities of the military;[72] the freedom of the press;[73] the conflict between unquestioning obedience to criminal orders and 'civil courage'.[74] Numerous slants, and particularly those of Niemöller and Jaspers, were sought on the broad guilt question.[75] The only noticeable absence from these undeniably reflective writings was also the crucial one. The victims find no place amongst all these discussions of structures and abstractions of guilt. We know that even when Marie Claude Vaillant-Couturier was brought forth in the *Frankfurter Rundschau* to discuss the 'German question', the way in which the German question manifested itself, in all its brutal reality, was absent.[76]

The same is true of Jaspers' *Die Schuldfrage*, as it is again of Wolfgang Staudte's *Die Mörder sind unter uns* (*The Murderers are amongst Us*, 1945) This film is unique in early post-war German cinema in confronting the issues of guilt and wartime criminality, having as the chief malefactor a commanding officer of the army who is shown to have ordered the execution of 100 men, women, and children in Poland. It has become a classic, and remains a powerful, haunting vision of post-war Germany. However, the victims are recalled only in flashback, with all the associations of characterlessness and lack of agency that that implies. The chief dynamic of the film involves an embittered former subordinate of the officer who wishes to exact his own justice, and the perpetrator himself, now back in his comfortable family setting.

One of the contentions of this and the previous chapters is that in the absence of adequate information about the misdeeds for which guilt was to be felt, it would never be properly allocated or fully accepted. The failure of Allied guilt

---

[70] Eberan, *Wer war an Hitler schuld?*, 63; circulation of the *Telegraf* gleaned from PRO, FO 1056/239, press reviews in the German zone.

[71] *FR* (11 Dec. 1945); Rudolf Schäfer, 'Die Polizei', *FH*, 1 (Oct. 1946), 590–2; Walter Dirks, 'Partei und Staat', *FH*, 1 (Dec. 1946), 820–32.

[72] Rudolf Schäfer, 'Soldaten und Militaristen', *FH*, 1 (Sept. 1946), 8–9.

[73] Walter Dirks, 'Die Freiheit der Presse', *FH*, 2 (Jan. 1947), 12–13.

[74] *Telegraf* (22 Mar. 1946). For miscellaneous discussions of guilt omitting reference to the victims, see Dirks, 'Der Weg zur Freiheit'; F. Hayek, 'Die Fronten', *FH*, 1 (Nov. 1946), 689–91; Eugen Kogon, 'Ärtzte als Knechte des Todes', *FH*, 2 (Feb. 1947), 123–4; Heinrich Scholz, 'Zur Deutschen Kollektiv-Verantwortlichkeit', *FH*, 2 (Apr. 1947), 357–73.

[75] *FR* (15 Jan. 1946, 25 Jan. 1946, 5 Mar. 1946, 2 Apr. 1946, 30 Apr. 1946).

[76] *FR* (15 Febraury 1946).

propaganda in focusing solely upon the perpetrator society was inadvertently illustrated in the words of Kogon and his fellow editor, Walter Dirks, when discussing the IMT trial as a historical event: 'in this connection we are not interested in the contents of the proceedings', they wrote, 'but rather the proceedings as such'.[77] Thus to Kogon and Dirks, the fact of the message rather than the detail was important; but, as the issue of 'concentration camp' representation and Kogon's own *Der SS-Staat* shows, it was impossible to divorce detail from interpretation. This was Raul Hilberg's meaning when he described his *magnum opus, The Destruction of the European Jews*, as a compilation of minutiae.[78]

It seems that ordinary Germans could meet the Allied accusations with one of four responses, the latter three of which were actually accommodated by Allied policy. Automatic rejection of any guilt springing from a desire to flee outright from the truth was an unalterable reaction of many, particularly of the more-or-less active Nazis. But there is evidence that in numerous other Germans such a reaction derived from the shock of the *Kollektivschuldthese* and the numbing effect of the concentration camp images.[79] The response of considered rejection—whether genuine or self-exculpatory—was provided for, because of the way the Allies had framed their propaganda. The 'Jewish factor' in occupation policy and the use of totemic German victims is sufficient illustration that even the most desirable answer to the *Schuldfrage*—acceptance of some form of responsibility—did not equate to true knowledge either of the self or of the war, for the most heinous acts were not promoted by the occupiers.

From the re-establishment of mass communications, no authoritative voice had transmitted a sense of what had actually been done in the German name. The occupiers were neither clear about the dynamics of mass murder, nor particularly concerned to find out. Even in their heyday, the broad Allied educational programmes consisted of undifferentiated images of crimes; similarly, the broadest punitive measure, denazification, centred on 'political guilt' without describing its source. Concomitantly, even the most sensitive discussions of the *Schuldfrage* did not consider German crimes *per se*, leaving the reason for guilt an abstraction open to manipulation: the following sections will show the sort of manipulations that ensued.

Committed leftist and liberal organs and intellectuals were solely concerned with the 'German crisis' and not with what that crisis meant for the Nazis' largest victim groups. The average German was confronted by a series of confusing newsreel images and photographs, unrepresentative literature, conflicting and inadequate newspaper accounts, and by blanket accusations followed by contradictory efforts to distinguish between 'Nazis' and 'Germans'. If the blunt ac-

---

[77] 'Nürnberg und die Geschichte', *FH*, 1 (Apr. 1946), 3–5.
[78] Hilberg makes the statement in Lanzmann's film *Shoah*.
[79] E. Kogon, 'Gericht und Gewissen' *FH*, 1 (Apr. 1946), 28; Dolf Sternberger, K. H. Rengstorf, 'Crime and Atonement', *Wiener Library Bulletin*, 3 (May–July 1949), 20; implicitly, in Hans Ehard's article in *Süddeutsche Juristen-Zeitung*, 3 (1948), cols. 353–68.

cusations even succeeded in making him (or her) question his responsibility, the poverty of the evidence adduced allowed him to deny it, and the subsequent withdrawal of the charges confirmed him in his denial. As Kogon wrote, many Germans thought they had disposed of their individual guilt, indeed all guilt, simply by knocking down the straw man of collective guilt.[80] And in the absence of Jews and non-German victims generally, it was all too easy for ordinary Germans to develop the myth of a victimized nation being persecuted yet further by the Anglo-Saxons. This tendency even went as far as comparing occupied Germany with a vast concentration camp—the supreme subversion of that symbol.[81]

War crimes trials outlasted the *Kollektivschuldthese*, the concentration camp propaganda, and denazification, and were seen by the Germans as the last vestige of re-education policy in its initial form. Thus they demanded a specific response over and above the general reactions of 1945–6, and in time they became a primary target for opponents of the occupation.[82]

4.3 WEST GERMAN RESPONSES TO THE IMT TRIAL

Within the context of reaction to the occupation, one factor was specific to the institution of trial: tedium. After the initial excitement at the instance of legal proceedings in 1945, there was a significant ebbing of interest in every country.[83] It is unreasonable to expect the concern shown at the time of the Nuremberg indictment by intellectuals like Erich Kästner to be replicated in, say, the fourteen-year-old girl from Krefeld, whose comment after a pleasant visit to the cinema in August 1946 was that the newsreel had not been too bad either, for there was no mention of the Nuremberg Trial, which she found terribly dull.[84]

Boredom affected many more directly concerned with the IMT than the young movie-goer. The British alternate judge, Norman Birkett, could do nothing but 'chafe in impotent despair' at 'the uselessness of acres of paper and thousands of words and [the fact] that life is slipping away'.[85] And the brief liaison between the writer and reporter, Rebecca West, and the American judge, Francis Biddle, was seemingly of greater interest to either of them than the trial, the

---

[80] Cited in Frey, 'The German Guilt Question', 232.

[81] PRO, FO 1056/93, draft report on German public opinion, 21 July–25 Aug. 1947; German reaction report, period ending 28 Jan. 1947.

[82] Trials became a *vergangenheitspolitische Obsession*. See Frei, *Vergangenheitspolitik*, section 2.

[83] OMGUS report no. 33, *The OMGUS Surveys*, 93; Warwick University, Modern Records Centre, papers of Victor Gollancz (hereafter 'Gollancz papers'), MSS 157/3/GE/1/17/6, Land Nordrhein-Westphalia reaction report, July 1946; University of Sussex Library, Mass-Observation Archive (hereafter 'M-O A'), file report 2424 A, 27 Sept. 1946.

[84] Erich Kästner, 'Streiflichter aus Nürnberg', in Hans Rauschning (ed.), *Das Jahr '45: Dichtung, Bericht, Protokoll deutscher Autoren* (Munich: Wilhelm Heyne Verlag, 1985), 295–303; 'Tagebuch Renate C.', in Sybil Schönfeld (ed.), *Der Krieg ist aus—und nun? Sommer '45 Berichte, Erfahrungen, Bekenntnisse* (Munich: Deutscher Taschenbuch Verlag, 1985), 189–93.

[85] Hyde, *Norman Birkett*, 518.

latter commenting that in West's absence, life in Nuremberg was no longer 'fun'. She in turn described Nuremberg as 'a citadel of boredom'.[86] If these key players could fail to summon up enthusiasm for the central event in their lives, it is of little surprise that those beyond the *cognoscenti* were alienated by the lengthy proceedings. It is equally understandable, even in isolation from the changing political and psychological state of the post-war world, that the hundreds of trials conducted beyond that of the 'major war criminals' were accorded hardly any space in mainstream German or Allied newspapers, and that when reports did feature, they were generally restricted to brief recounting of the events of the courtroom, with no editorial comment.

The pattern of 'boredom' and attention around the IMT trial is in itself instructive, indicating as much about the perceived relevance of each component part of the proceedings as its objective value. In Germany, such fluctuations are a difficult phenomenon to gauge, however, as the power held over the press by the occupying authorities was considerable, even late into 1946. There were clearly frequent and considerable divergences of opinion on and interest in the trials: we have reports of whistling and cat-calling in a Cologne theatre in response to newsreel footage of the Malmédy trial; whereas elsewhere meditation ensued. Likewise, widespread indifference is to be juxtaposed with unconditional condemnation or acceptance of the IMT proceedings.[87] These differences were not dependent upon class, age, or political preference, though there are indications that women were less engaged than men in the whole question.[88] Furthermore, city dwellers were likely to be better informed than their rural counterparts: when questioned in November 1946, a group of elderly villagers in the British zone confessed surprise that the trial had come to an end, assuming the accused had been executed months previously.[89]

The one constant unearthed by all the polls of the period was the dissipation of attention as the trial progressed, after the initial months of relative excitement. Indeed, we only read of interest escalating again when the twenty-two defendants made their own concluding addresses to the court; the final act before judgement.[90] The period of that attention lapse encompassed much of the substance of the trials: the cross-examinations of the defendants; the organization hearings; and a good part of the presentation of the Soviet case.

---

[86] Carl Rollyson, *Rebecca West: A Saga of the Century* (London: Hodder and Stoughton, 1995), 214–15.

[87] Gollancz papers, MSS 157/3/GE/1/4/1–21, CCG(BE) Intelligence Division review, Nov. 1946, fos. 6–8; MSS 157/3/GE/1/17/6, Land Nordrhein-Westphalia reaction report, Sept. 1946, fo. 11.

[88] Gollancz papers, MSS 157/3/GE/1/4/1–21, fos. 6–8; MSS 157/3/GE/1/17/6, Land Nordrhein-Westphalia reaction report, July 1946; PRO, FO 1056/93, survey of German public opinion to 1 Dec. 1946.

[89] Gollancz papers, MSS 157/3/GE/1/4/1–21, fos. 6–8.

[90] OMGUS Report no. 33, 18 Dec. 1946, *The OMGUS Surveys*, 121–2. This revealed a particular decline from Feb. 1946 onwards. OMGUS also recorded a reduction (within the general decline in attention) in the numbers of people reading trial reports in their entirety. See *The OMGUS Surveys*, 34. For the beginning of the decline, see *NYT* (16 Dec. 1945; 2 Jan. 1946).

Here we encounter the interface between 'boredom', as in a lack of interest, and a somewhat different quality, a lack of concern. One group was certainly keen to monitor the progress of the organization cases: the fate of most of the inmates of the civilian internment camps hinged upon their outcome.[91] The implication is that most of the remainder of the population was divided, in whatever ratio, between those who saw nothing of relevance in that part of the trial, and those who deafened themselves to it. The part of Jackson's opening speech in which he differentiated between Nazis and the mass of Germans met with much enthusiasm, as did those closing statements of the individual defendants which defended the German people. Indeed, there was a clamour for more substantial press coverage of the latter.[92] This interpretation of the evidence is corroborated by the general absence of reaction to the verdicts on the organizations amidst a hail of criticism about the acquittals of individuals.[93]

That the British people were not interested in the minutiae of the prosecution and defence of, say, the Reich Cabinet was perhaps predictable. The BBC had taken away its reporter before the Soviet presentation at the beginning of 1946, and in February Hartley Shawcross had pleaded with the media magnate Lord Beaverbrook to allocate more column space in the latter's newspapers to the non-British cases.[94] The Anglo-centrism of the British media was consistent with the belief that war crimes and war criminals were a product of Germanism, with no moral implications for Britain; boredom, it was thought, was acceptable for the Allies.[95] But by the same token it was entirely understandable that many would think, as did a columnist of the *Telegraf* in May 1946, that the eyes of the world were on Germany's reaction to the trial.[96] Such responses were orchestrated in the Soviet zone, at the conclusion of the case, yet, consistent with Communist thinking, these protests were specifically aimed at the acquitted Schacht, Papen, and Fritzsche as aristocratic or bourgeois enemies of the German people. That the same reflexes should be demonstrated spontaneously in the west indicates the extent to which Germans as a whole conceived of the prominent Nazis as other, or at least wished to give this impression. Thus, no matter how many criticized the IMT trial on grounds of legitimacy,[97] at the time clear majorities always averred that their former leaders deserved punishment.[98]

Of his listeners from east and west alike, Markus Wolf, then of Berlin radio, commented that the majority wished to close their ears to the IMT proceedings,

[91] Gollancz papers, MSS 157/3/GE/1/4/1–21, fo. 7.

[92] *NYT* (2 Jan. 1946); MRC, Gollancz papers, MSS 157/3/GE/1/17/6, Land Nordrhein-Westphalia reaction report, Sept. 1946, fos. 6–7, 22–3.

[93] PRO, FO 946/43, 'German reactions to the Nuremberg sentences', in Hanover, Schleswig-Holstein, Düsseldorf, the Ruhr, and Hamburg.

[94] House of Lords Record Office, Beaverbrook papers, c/294, Shawcross to Beaverbrook, 21 Feb. 1946.

[95] See *NYT* (21 Feb. 1946), on the necessity of paying attention to the Soviet prosecution case, in response to the lack of interest manifested. For the similar reaction of the British press, see PRO FO 1049/426, 2, Dean report on IMT trial 11 Feb.–21 Apr. 1946.

[96] *Telegraf* (4 May 1946).   [97] Kogon, 'Nürnberg und die Geschichte', 3.

[98] Polls in *NYT* (2 Jan., 10 Nov. 1946).

feeling jointly accused with the major war criminals.[99] He was incorrect. Even into 1949 reasonable audiences were turning out in Bizonia to watch *Nürnberg und seine Lehren*, a documentary of the trial focusing on the individual convicts.[100] Yet this attention should not imply any empathy with the major war criminals,[101] nor widespread reflection on the questions confronting the IMT. The attendance figures for the documentary may be a reflection of a shallow curiosity after a time-lag from the Nazi years, but they are also indicative of a detachment of the populace from the actions of their leaders like the reaction to the *Kollektivschuldthese*.

The same stimulus that provoked mass demonstrations against the acquittals by the IMT also induced an entire row of the audience to abandon the most expensive seats in a Frankfurt cinema in protest against the passage of *Nürnberg und seine Lehren* showing the concentration camp footage.[102] The events in the film theatre in turn bear a distinct resemblance to the response of Hjalmar Schacht when the concentration camp film was actually shown to the IMT: he 'ostentatiously turned away' and sat 'with his head held high in defiance'.[103] For all these actors, the registering of disgust was a public expression of the perceived moral vacuum separating them from the criminals; and it is a further illustration of the ineffectuality of this brutal imagery in education.

The only real sympathy—and, arguably, the related sentiment of empathy—with any of the 'major war criminals' concerned those whom it was felt were not the highest initiators of Nazi policy. Hence, amidst the general satisfaction displayed by the contemporary German public at the equity of the IMT proceedings and judgement, the most oft-voiced reservations concerned the fate of the service chiefs. Many did not feel that a soldier or sailor, no matter how deeply complicit, should share the sentence of the overtly political grouping that had compromised him. Thus the frequently made contrast between the IMT acquittals and the death sentences for Jodl and Keitel. On its most basic level, the principle of differentiation suggested that a general should be executed by the bullet rather than the rope.[104]

In these early responses lay some of the seeds that would grow within a short while to full-blown condemnation of the trials that so many Germans had recently accepted. In October 1950, the reactions analysis staff of the US High Commission encountered the greatest shift in German societal attitudes ever recorded to that time. Only 38 per cent of a sample of 2,000 people regarded the

---

[99] Cited in Gericke, 'Die Presseberichterstattung über den Nürnberger Prozess', 917.

[100] Wanda von Baeyer, 'Das Publikum im Film "Nürnberg und seine Lehren"', *FH*, 4 (Apr. 1949), 360–1. The author of a report for the American documentary unit claimed that the film on the trials achieved 'amazing' success in the larger cities, but not in lesser towns. See Culbert, 'American Film Policy', 188.

[101] Schwartz, 'Die Begnadigung deutscher Kriegsverbrecher', 379.

[102] Von Baeyer, 'Das Publikum', 360.   [103] *NYT* (30 Nov. 1945).

[104] A plea supported in the case of Jodl by the American and French judges. PRO, FO 945/332, CCG-COGA, 10 Oct. 1946. See also PRO, FO 946/43, 'German reactions to the Nuremberg sentences'.

IMT trial as having been conducted fairly, compared to the 78 per cent registered four years earlier.[105] How had this come to be?

4.4 TOWARDS THE 'FINAL SOLUTION OF THE WAR CRIMINALS QUESTION'[106]

With the rapid diminishment of public information on 'war crimes' and trials from 1946 the path was gradually becoming clearer for those with a vested interest in rewriting recent history. A combination of politicized Protestant and Catholic churchmen, lawyers, politicians, bureaucrats, and service veterans associations, who were representative of the surviving German societal élites, were such a collective. Some of their number had set to work even during the IMT trial, and they benefited from the general desire to evade responsibility.

These groups were resentful of the Allied occupation, and particularly its attempts to re-educate the masses and label many of the pillars of pre-war German society as inherently flawed, and they sought to undermine its foundations. Thus they tried to minimize the crimes that Germany had committed, and to compare these deeds with acts of the Allies. (With the many hardships that Germans were then experiencing there were superficial grounds for such comparisons, though they were not predicated upon any recognition of cause and effect.) The occupation could then be seen as the imposition of the victor's will alone, rather than a moral necessity. Concomitantly in this world-view, the war crimes trials were a vindictive, arbitrary act of the oppressors, and the fact that the Allies had had to stretch existing international law to cope with the unprecedented brutality of the Third Reich was exploited to the full.[107] Thus arose the revisionist vocabulary which was to gain popular currency in Germany, of the *Kriegsschuldige* ('war-guilty') and the *Kriegsverurteilten* ('war-convicted'). And thus arose also the imperative finally to discredit the trials by overturning the verdicts, or at the very least by securing the freedom of those convicted. This was effectively a move towards the 'decriminalisation of the Nazi perpetrators'.[108] It acquired the epithet of the 'Endlösung der Kriegsverbrecherfrage'—the 'final solution of the war criminals question'.

The arguments and aims now were of a different nature from the early popular excuses of ignorance and powerlessness, but they fed off their precursors. The shrewdest move made by the élites was to link the two strands in the identification of all war criminals (aside perhaps from some of the 'majors') with the

[105] *Public Opinion in Semisovereign Germany: The HICOG Surveys, 1949–1955*, ed. Anna J. Merritt and Richard Merritt (Chicago, Ill.: university of Illinois Press, 1980), 101, report no. 57. In Aug. 1949, a cross-section of West German university students—the potential leaders of that nation—refuted 7 : 1 the right of the Allies to judge war criminals; *Public Opinion, 1935–1971*, 1, i, ed. Gallup, 842.

[106] Cited in Alfred Streim's foreword to Hoffmann's *Stunden Null*, 10.

[107] Buscher, *The US War Crimes Trial Program*, 92, 100–101, 109–10, 162–3; Frei, *Vergangenheitspolitik, passim*. See also Streim, 'Saubere Wehrmacht?', 575, on some of the spurious *tu quoque* arguments.

[108] Heiner Lichtenstein, 'NS-Prozesse', in Andreas Nachama and Julius Schoeps (eds.), *Aufbau nach dem Untergang: Deutsche-Judische Geschichte nach 1945* (Berlin: Argon, 1992), 141–9, esp. 144.

ethic of service to the state.[109] Service, or 'duty' was equated at the time with obedience to senior orders. As Lord Wright of the UNWCC observed, it was the unanimous rejection by the various 'war crimes' courts of this principle as a defence which underpinned much of the objection to the trials.[110]

The best-known instances, and perhaps the most emotive, of these rejections occurred in the trials of high-ranking soldiers,[111] and so it is not surprising to note that, when in the summer of 1946 a group of antisemitic students and faculty members of the University of Erlangen launched an attack on the Nuremberg trials, they threatened to form veterans' associations to discourage 'by word and deed' slurs on officerhood.[112] Six years later, the *Institut für Demoskopie* enquired of Germans in the western zones which of the following group they considered justly imprisoned, and which unjustly: Kesselring, Dönitz, Speer, Hess, and Schirach. The aggregate of respondents reserved the greatest sympathy for the service chiefs.[113]

A reservoir of sympathy had been tapped into for Keitel and Jodl, and it was exploited much more heavily as the new rhetoric identified all convicts with German soldiers, regardless of their crime or the organization to which they belonged.[114] And if these prisoners were servants of the Fatherland, not only was it unfair to keep them incarcerated, it was an outright slur on the German nation. In turn, this logic assisted millions of Germans to identify with the victimized *Kriegsverurteilten*—and hence to reject collective guilt once more—just as did Heinrich Böll's narrator in the short story *Geschäft ist Geschäft (Business is Business)*. He described how he was 'denazified a bit—as one goes to the barber to have an irritating beard removed', then discussed decorations, wounds, and heroic acts, and concluded that he was a decent enough chap, having done no more than his duty.[115]

In combination, these contentions underpinned the *Vergangenheitspolitik* that was ultimately adopted by most West German political parties. The revisionist

---

[109] Buscher, *The US War Crimes Trial Program*, 126, 163.

[110] Goodhart papers, reel 21, Wright to Goodhart, 5 Aug. 1952. See also Peter Steinbach, 'Nationalsozialistische Gewaltverbrechen in der deutschen Öffentlichkeit nach 1945', in Jürgen Weber and Peter Steinbach (eds.), *Vergangenheitsbewältigung durch Strafverfahren? NS-Prozesse in der Bundesrepublik Deutschland* (Munich: Olzog, 1984), 13–39, esp. 17–18, 21.

[111] For the reportage of the defence arguments of the soldiers and the High Command and General Staff at Nuremberg, see e.g. Schneider, *Nationalsozialismus als Thema im Programm des Nordwestdeutschen Rundfunks*, 165.

[112] Cited in Tent, *Mission on the Rhine*, 92.

[113] *The Germans: Public Opinion Polls, 1947–1966*, ed. Elisabeth Noelle and Erich Peter Neumann (Westport, Conn.: Greenwood Press, 1981), 202. Of the interviewees 6% thought Kesselring justly imprisoned, 65% thought not. The corresponding figures for Hess were 22% and 43%. A poll conducted the following Aug. showed that 55% of respondents did not consider German soldiers should be reproached for their conduct in the war, while 21% thought 'in some cases' that 'reproach' was required.

[114] B. Boll, 'Wehrmacht vor Gericht: Kriegsverbrecherprozesse der Vier Mächte nach 1945', *Geschichte und Gesellschaft*, 24 (1998), 592–3; Frei, *Vergangenheitspolitik*, 268–96.

[115] Heinrich Böll, 'Geschäft ist Geschäft', (1950), in *Heinrich Böll. Werke: Romane und Erzählungen, i: 1947–1951*, ed. Bernd Balzer (Cologne: Gertraud Middelhauve Verlag, n.d. [1977]), 255–60, at 258.

line was much more palatable for the majority of the population, too,[116] and as in the formation or re-formation of all national communities, a mythologizing re-writing of the past was perhaps inevitable—Nazi genocide could certainly not fit any 'optimistic theory' about the present or future.[117] Clearly, the development of these attitudes had nothing whatsoever to do with historical reality, rather being predicated upon forthright, if not overtly atavistic nationalism.

By the second-half of 1947, the second-largest-selling newspaper in the British zone, the Christian Democrat *Westfalenpost*, said of the defendants in the Nuremberg Doctor's trial that they were murderers and 'public torturers', but that 'doubtless the interest of the German people in the trial would have been greater if an objective professional German judge had sat on the bench'.[118] If the Germans had to wait until 1958, when the last inmate was released from Landsberg, for the consummation of the 'final solution to the war criminals question', the real genesis of the problem—the acts of these criminals—was being squeezed out of public debate, and the readers of the *Westfalenpost* were half-way home. This explains why Adenauer could come to campaign against the death sentences passed against Oswald Pohl and four Einsatzgruppen leaders, or why Niemöller could petition on behalf of such men as Erich Koch, the notorious Reichskommissar of the Ukraine:[119] Pohl, Ohlendorf, and Koch were fellow Germans to be saved rather than criminals to be punished.

The discourse within west Germany was intentionally shifted from the subject-matter of the war criminals cases to the legitimacy of the trials themselves: from the actions of Germany to the actions of the Allies. Though the ultimate responsibility for this sophistry remains with Germany, once again the shift in perspective was accommodated by the nature of Allied propaganda and the 'guilt' reflections that it helped precipitate. If introspection—literally 'looking inwards'—was to be expected from the defeated population,[120] it was not that far from what the psychological warfare department of SHAEF had planned in the early months of the peace. Indeed, introspection for change was what Britain and America ultimately wanted of the Germans. They applied the principle very literally, however: the focus was on Germany and German society, with German concentration camps as the prime illustrations. When ordinary Germans were encouraged by their own leaders, and finally also by Allied

---

[116] A survey of 1,000 letters sent to US High Commissioner John McCloy in 1951 requesting release of imprisoned war criminals was divided into three chief categories of argument: Christian forgiveness/brotherhood; political contentions (including the influence of the war criminals issue on German–American relations, the relevance of Soviet crimes against humanity, and the justification of harsh German military measures in the face of 'partisans'); and legal concerns. See Ulrich Brochhagen, 'Vergangene Vergangenheitsbewältigung: zum umgang mit der NS-Vergangenheit während der fünfziger und frühen sechziger Jahre', *Mittelweg*, 36 (1992/1993), 145–54, esp. 149.

[117] Herf, *Divided Memory*, 392.

[118] PRO, FO 1056/239, German press review, 15 Aug.–15 Sept. 1947.

[119] Lambeth Palace Library, Bell Papers, 49, fo. 273, Bell to Niemöller, 2 Jan. 1950.

[120] This is proposed in Alexander Mitscherlich and Margarete Mitscherlich, *Die Unfähigkeit zu trauern: Grundlagen kollektiven Verhaltens* (Munich: Piper, 1967).

information policy, to look eastward beyond the parapets it was not to contemplate the catastrophe that they had helped to bring about, but rather to see the forces of Communism as a threat again, and eventually even to contemplate the suffering of their brethren at the hands of Slavs.

That the German response to the trials must be seen in the light of the conduct of those trials and of the occupation is only logical. By their very essence the trials were perpetrator-centric and accusatory, and hence engendered defensiveness and/or narcissism. Moreover, as one of the justifications for trials was that they illuminated the democratic virtue of due legal process, they rather invited legalistic criticism of the *tu quoque* variety, and also lobbying for the 'rights' of the accused and convicted. The orientation away from the horrific and tragic reality of Nazi genocide was emphasized by the document-centred IMT trial and the 'failure of the legal imagination' that left the eastern extermination centres in the shadows. Put more simply, the Allies helped to keep the destruction that the Germans had wrought in the abstract.

A consideration of the course of Holocaust remembrance shows that the common factor in attracting popular interest is identification with the victims. The key to the success of the diary of Anne Frank, and of the *Holocaust* series, and of the Eichmann trial, which was as much about the Jewish tragedy as the fate of one of its perpetrators, was in the telling of the tales of the afflicted.[121] In the decade after the war this did not happen in any substantial measure in Britain, the USA, or western Germany. Norbert Frei has revealed how none of the initiatives to 'master the past' in the early years of the BRD took cognisance of those who had genuinely suffered under the Nazis.[122] This trend was actually established at the outset of the occupation; furthermore, the trial venture which towered above all others was equally the one most singularly bereft of balance. Not only did the IMT trial confront the world with huge criminals, it also presented enormous crimes, but in doing so it neglected to ensure that the victims were given the stage. In consequence, few non-German and no Jewish names, faces, or stories were engraved on the collective consciousness.

The effect when the focus is put on the perpetrator can be illustrated by a few latter-day instances in the UK. The decision to submit the cases of the Belarussian war criminal Anthony Sawoniuk and the former Chilean dictator Augustine Pinochet for judicial consideration instantly provoked debate about the propriety of trying elderly men at a late stage. Infirmity, particularly in the case of Pinochet, strengthened the case against trial. Correct though it may have been to identify factors prejudicial to due process, it loaded the emotional dice in favour of these men, who were suddenly given personalities and physical conditions with which the public could identify. In contrast to their victims and alleged victims, these were now three-dimensional characters over whose disposition it was possible to discuss the self-ascribed British characteristic of 'fair play'.

---

[121] Bergmann, 'Die Reaktion auf den Holocaust', 332.
[122] Frei, *Vergangenheitspolitik*, 14.

In terms of the post-war trials the German public could either identify themselves *against* war criminals or *with* them. In the first instance, as with the 'Belsen', Dachau, and IMT trials, these criminals could then be induced to bear the
sins of the whole, in *exactly* the same way that many Anglo-Americans initially
related to them. In the second, it was necessary to claim that there had been no
sin, or at least to 'relativize' that sin; over time this became the dominant trend in
the BRD. From this point, within the context of occupation policy, appropriat-
ing the imagery of victimhood for Germans as a whole, war criminals included,
was not a large conceptual leap.

If the distortion of the concept of the victim was accommodated by Allied occupation policy in Germany, it was also admitted into the liberal democracies
themselves. Interestingly, in light of the outcome of the IMT trial, the editor of
the liberal American journal *PM* took issue with the hanging of Kaltenbrunner
and Frank. These two, he observed, like the two soldiers (but unlike Papen, who
had been acquitted), had only followed orders.[123] His reaction featured a common blend of misapprehension of the executive powers of the men concerned, as
well as a less understandable elision of the moral, and indeed in most circumstances legal, imperative to disobey patently criminal orders. It is also difficult to believe that he would have maintained this position in the full knowledge of Frank's
and Kaltenbrunner's records. Yet, but for his choice of case study, his stance was
shared by many who had also been duly outraged on the liberation of the concentration camps. Parliament and Congress, as well as the Bundestag, became
forums for far more serious apologists than this journalist.

For obvious reasons, the war criminals issue would never assume the significance for the constituencies of the liberal democracies that it did in Germany.
Nevertheless, in so far as popular responses can be measured, their development
mirrors in microcosm the reactions that we have just encountered.

4.5 THE BYSTANDERS JUDGE NUREMBERG

In Britain, despite the growing frustration with the IMT trial over the length of
time it took to reach seemingly self-evident conclusions, when judgement day
loomed, public interest in the proceedings was substantially restored. Many of
those who considered the trial to be unnecessary apparently still regarded it with
interest—at least as a concept—and confessed a degree of admiration. Thus in
September 1946, 60 per cent of those interviewed by the societal monitoring organization Mass Observation hazarded guesses as to the date of the forthcoming
verdicts, and all but two of these were accurate to within a week. Perhaps more
tellingly, three out of five of the total interviewed still maintained that all of those
on trial were guilty, regardless of whether or not they agreed with the principle
of trial. That attitudes towards the major war criminals had not softened greatly

---

[123] George S. Wheeler, *Die amerikanische Politik in Deutschland* (Berlin: Kongress, 1958), 127.

is evidenced by the results of a smaller survey in September 1946 that actually suggested methods by which the death sentences should be carried out.[124]

It was, however, apparent from the September survey that beyond the disposition of the 'major war criminals' there was little desire for more substantial purges of actors whose deeds were not directly relevant to Britain. It may well have been imagined that all of the really important Nazi malefactors had been dealt with by the IMT, as Churchill implied at the time.[125] In any case, the large investment of time and money at Nuremberg had been commented on even by convinced supporters of the trial, and it was seen as a one-off, designed to establish a precedent for the future, rather than as the beginning of a process as some Americans would have it.[126] Of the few pushing for further trials, or at least punishment, there was a general differentiation between the direct perpetrators of atrocities and all others, particularly servicemen. Thus a Mrs A. P. R. was keen to distinguish war as a crime from trials—which were 'obviously justifiable'—of 'sadists and concentration camp gaolers'. Her opinion was shared by Mr D. A., who deemed that trials should be limited to the likes of Josef Kramer: 'leaders like generals and members of the [High Command of the Wehrmacht]', he considered, 'are not guilty of any crime other than the "crime" of making war effectively'.[127]

By the end of 1947 things had moved on apace. Another Mass Observation study showed that the proportion of those questioned showing absolutely no pity for, or outright antagonism towards, the German people, had halved over the previous eighteen months to a quarter. Approximately half now expressed 'no ill feeling' or varying degrees of sympathy. More importantly in the trial connection, three-quarters of the same group considered that German prisoners of war should be repatriated immediately.[128] Further evidence that 'forget', if not necessarily 'forgive', was now the order of the day is provided by the results of a survey on public attitudes towards Palestine and the Jews which concluded that 'Jewish suffering in concentration camps is now for most people an outworn theme with, if anything, unpleasant war associations'.[129] British officialdom had showed itself to be quite responsive to popular sentiment on the question of war criminals, so this was the sort of environment in which concerted opposition to the trial of such figures as Manstein and Rundstedt could exert influence.[130]

American dissidents had to wait slightly longer for their time. Disillusionment with US occupation policy both benefited from and contributed to the

---

[124] M-O A, file report 2424 A, 27 Sept. 1946; directive replies, Sept. 1946.

[125] Gilbert, *Churchill*, 8, p. 284.

[126] M-O A, file report 2424 A, 27 Sept. 1946; directive replies, Sept. 1946. See also the collection of letters from the public on the IMT trial in FO 371/57562, 57563 on arguments reflecting a wide range of opinions about trial, many of them ambivalent.

[127] M-O A, directive replies, Sept. 1946 (directive respondents DR 3119 and DR 1264 cited).

[128] M-O A, file report 2565, 23 Feb. 1948; directive replies, Sept. 1946.

[129] M-O A, file report 2515, Sept. 1947.

[130] See below, n. 264, for British official sensitivity to popular opinion.

resumption of full-scale party-political enmity after the war,[131] as the more radical elements of the Republican opposition played out their agendas. Controversies over the Dachau trial programme at the end of 1948 and through 1949[132] not only encouraged German opposition to the trials, they caused considerable cynicism in the USA about the merits of the occupation methods. Buscher contends that 'by the end of the 1940s, many in the United States had come to accept the conservative argument that the convicted Nazi perpetrators were not criminals, but were instead the victims of the Allied war crimes program'.[133]

A sea change had therefore taken place in public attitudes towards war crimes trials since the trial of the major war criminals, and it requires some explanation. During the winter of 1945–6 a public opinion survey revealed that 'almost no American . . . thought that the program of denazification and punishment was too harsh', and this feeling was mirrored in the national press. A year later, still only 4 per cent of a sample polled considered the IMT sentences too severe.[134] Though, as in Britain, there was not thought to be any need for judicial process in disposing of the leading Nazis,[135] when the trial option was decided upon, it received overwhelming support across party-political lines. Americans in the ratio of fifteen to one considered justice to have been done by the IMT.[136]

William Bosch, the presenter of some of these facts and figures, argues that this general alignment behind the trial concept was due to an American proclivity for what the diplomat George Kennan once called the 'legalistic-moralistic approach to international problems'. The idea that in championing the trial the US was playing the role of standard-bearer, introducing a universally applicable and enforceable code of law designed to bring order from international chaos, cohered with the general public and Rooseveltian assumptions of the role of that nation in the world. The pure motives of the US would not be tainted by association with the Soviets in the trial, but rather the partnership would set a precedent for international co-operation.

Idealistic also was the prevailing explanation of the causes of the war and of the locus of guilt amongst a small, definable group of top Nazis, the extirpation of whom would swiftly re-establish sanity and balance. The obverse side of this naïvety was an equally profound disenchantment with the trials for their failure to deliver as the Cold War became a reality, and as a proliferation of dull legal proceedings illustrated the considerable depth of criminality in German society.[137]

---

[131] Gimbel, 'Cold War Historians and the Occupation of Germany', 95.

[132] These are outlined in chapter 4.6, below.

[133] Buscher, *The US War Crimes Trial Program*, 29–44.

[134] *Public Opinion Quarterly* (winter 1946–7), 645.

[135] Ibid. (summer 1945), 247, showed that only 4% of a sample thought Göring should be tried, whereas 78% opted rather for arbitrary punishment, most of them favouring death.

[136] William Bosch, *Judgment on Nuremberg: American Attitudes toward the Major German War-Crime Trials* (Chapel Hill, NC: University of North Carolina Press, 1970), 90–109; Backer, 'From Morgenthau Plan to Marshall Plan', 159.

[137] Bosch, *Judgment on Nuremberg*, 25–6, 36–9, 109–16; see also George Kennan, *American Diplomacy, 1900–1950* (Chicago, Ill.: University of Chicago Press, 1953), 95.

Thus a ready audience was again provided for those who could simplistically explain away the ills of the new world; this time with reference to Communism.

Additionally, we know that most American vitriol on wartime criminality was reserved for the Japanese, an attitude springing undoubtedly in part from racism.[138] Such a mind-set could accommodate the image propounded by German nationalists, and by right-wingers in Britain and the USA, of western Germany upholding the 'Christian-occidental' tradition against the 'East'.[139] As in Germany, with the passage of the horrors of war further into history, these ideas and others related to them would wield greater influence.

4.6 BRITISH AND AMERICAN 'REVISIONISM'

Orchestrated opposition to the trials never achieved anything like mass proportions in the USA or Britain. Nevertheless, it involved some very influential figures who brought with them the power of their positions. At the end of the 1940s its champions in Parliament alone could count amongst their number Winston Churchill at the Conservative helm; the peer George Bell, Bishop of Chichester; Richard Stokes, a right-wing, pro-German Labour MP; Reginald Paget; and Lord Maurice Hankey, a Secretary of the War Cabinet in the 1914–18 conflict, now sitting in the Upper House. Many others, representing each political party in both Houses of Parliament, as well as in the Allied military machines, would share in the dissent that crystallized around the Manstein trial.[140] Of those not directly involved in domestic politics, opponents included the Judaeo-Christian publisher Victor Gollancz, the writer T. S. Eliot, and the aforementioned Captain Basil Liddell Hart.

The variety of their stances ensured that not all of the arguments forwarded by these individuals were harmonious. Nevertheless, the degree of abstraction from the deeds of the war criminals that each achieved in their rhetoric was a common factor and was quite as extreme as anything managed in Germany. This was true even of the most humanitarian form of dissidence, as displayed by Bell and Gollancz with their Christian emphasis on reconciliation. Their views were in part founded on the role of the German resistance as illustrative of widespread opposition to Nazism, and they focused exclusively on the sufferings of the German population—in anticipation of mass reprisals against what they saw as an innocent public—where before they had concerned refugees from

[138] A Gallup poll conducted in Apr. and May 1943 ascertained that 70% of American whites thought the USA could get on better with Germany after the war than Japan. The contrary view was upheld only by 7%. The corresponding figures for American blacks were 30% and 22%. Two years later, 82% of an undifferentiated sample of Americans considered the Japanese 'more cruel at heart' than the Germans. *The Gallup Polls: Public Opinion 1935–1971*, i. *1935–1948*, ed. George Gallup (New York: Random House, 1972), 509.

[139] Werner Jochmann, *Gesellschaftskrise und Judenfeindschaft in Deutschland 1870–1945* (Hamburg: Hans Christians Verlag, 1988), 336.

[140] See Liddell Hart's correspondence in the LHCMA, for the names of the several parliamentarians and others involved in opposition to the trials who are not mentioned below.

Germany.[141] When voices such as theirs were silent on the fate of the genuine victims of the Nazis, it may be pondered who was to speak up. Their agendas, alongside those of Kogon and Niemöller in Germany, only facilitated the narrow approaches to the past of West Germany's emerging leaders.

Neither could Bell's downplaying of Nazi crimes be attributed to ignorance. Indeed, there is evidence of a calculated removal of the more extreme crimes against humanity in an attempt to draw the spurious parallels, beloved of dissenters everywhere, between Allied and German atrocities. The best illustration of this process came in spring 1949 when Bell enlisted Liddell Hart's assistance in editing one of his anti-trial speeches in the House of Lords: in order, in Liddell Hart's words, to focus upon 'cases where similar charges could be brought against the Allies', Bell removed reference in the final version to German 'murder and ill-treatment of civilian populations of or in occupied territory on a vast scale in concentration camps and elsewhere' and 'deportation for slave labour'.[142]

Liddell Hart's broader correspondence reveals the extent of exchange of ideas and information to the end of upsetting the whole process of trial and imprisonment. The members of an informal network centred around the military historian and Lord Hankey continuously updated each other on foreign-political and domestic developments that bore on the war criminals issue, several of them gathering periodically in the 1950s for conspiratorial dinners.[143] Hankey, Paget, and Stokes used their political and diplomatic contacts to press for 'a constructive solution'. On the fringes was Field Marshal Alexander, who was to become Minister of Defence on the Conservatives' resumption of power in 1951, and Churchill himself was a recipient of some of their correspondence, via Paget. The group also extended to Lord Pakenham, who had served from 1947–8 as 'Minister for Germany' in COGA.

Beyond the displacement of the victims, the other commonalities in the rhetoric of these men can be deduced from a survey of some of the leading published protest tracts of the period. Hankey's *Politics, Trials and Errors*, Paget's *Manstein: His Campaigns and his Trial*, and the work of two of the other 'anti-Nuremberg diners', Montgomery Belgion's *Epitaph on Nuremberg*, and F. J. P. Veale's *Advance to Barbarism*, are cases in point.[144] Overall, there is little internal coherence to their arguments, which read like anglicized versions of many of the

---

[141] For their pre-war and wartime concerns respectively, see Bell's published lecture to the Jewish Historical Society of England on 1 Feb. 1939, *Humanity and the Refugees* (London: Woburn Press, 1939); Gollancz, *Let My People Go* (London: Gollancz, 1942); Jasper, *George Bell*, 256–314; Gollancz, *In Darkest Germany* (London: Gollancz, 1947), and *What Buchenwald Really Means*.

[142] LHCMA, LH 9/24/178, draft speech sent to Liddell Hart, 19 Apr. 1949; text of speech (5 May 1949), in *Hansard* (HL), 162 (1948–9), cols. 376–85.

[143] LHCMA, LH 1/57, Belgion to Liddell Hart, 24 Jan. 1952; Bell papers, 43, fo. 123, Hankey to Bell, 22 Feb. 1952.

[144] Lord Hankey, *Politics, Trials and Errors* (Oxford: Pen-in-Hand, 1950); Montgomery Belgion, *Epitaph on Nuremberg* (London: Falcon, 1946); F. J. P. Veale, *Advance to Barbarism: How the Reversion to Barbarism in Warfare and War-Trials Menaces our Future* (Appleton, Wis.: Nelson, 1948); Paget, *Manstein*. See also J. F. C. Fuller, *Armament and History* (London: Eyre and Spottiswoode, 1946), H. A. Smith, *The*

self-contradictory Nuremberg defences: either the classic, 'I knew nothing about atrocities and anyway I always opposed them'; or the modified, 'I was powerless to intervene and yet always helped when I could'.

First, these critics failed to make clear the distinctions between the Nuremberg and the Royal Warrant trials. The arguments concerning the two distinct generic charges of 'crimes against peace' and 'war crimes' then merged in the minds of the partisan, and the more established concept became inextricably associated with the other more novel and debatable contribution of the Americans. 'Nuremberg' became a byword for the politicization of all war crimes trials. Thus the frequent claim that the Allied courts were trying their enemies for losing the war,[145] when in fact they were trying them for common crimes committed during warfare.

Emphasizing both the *tu quoque*—'you did it too'; with reference to such Allied actions as the bombing of German cities, and to Soviet crimes—and *ex post facto* criticisms of the trials, these polemics neglect to consider the extremities of Nazi policies while condemning unreservedly 'victor's justice'. (In this vein Richard Stokes could state of the Germans that 'whatever they have done in the way of breaking the laws of war we committed similar acts by indiscriminate bombing and generally parachuting people in behind the military lines for espionage purposes'.[146]) They blame Allied demands for unconditional surrender and threats of post-war retribution for drawing out the conflict and, ignoring the real chronology of Nazi genocide, for themselves contributing to the perpetration of atrocities in the desperate struggle towards the end of the war. Replete with factual inaccuracies, the inadequacies of these works are compounded by clear biases involving anti-Bolshevism and, in as much as they are mentioned at all, Jews.

For these and other critics, the prosecution of prominent soldiers generally raised issues more problematic than those involved in the trial of concentration camp guards, or even of the military rank-and-file, for the direct commission of atrocities. The latter categories prompted no exacting moral or political questions for those who could believe that such acts were the preserve of fanatics and monsters—as the SS and police organizations were frequently and crudely portrayed—or spontaneous actions caused by hot blood in the field. Few could be found to stand up for such as Joseph Kramer and Irma Grese of Belsen, and though Hankey wanted a general amnesty, he was prepared to forego releasing prisoners convicted of 'sheer sadism';[147] apparently, he realized that having

---

Crisis in the Law of Nations (London: Stevens and Sons Ltd., 1947); J. H. Morgan, *The Great Assize* (London: John Murray, 1948); Edward Glover, *War, Sadism and Pacifism* (London: George Allen and Unwin, 1947); Gallieri Gallus, *Nuremberg and After* (Newtown: The Montgomeryshire Printing and Stationery Co., 1946).

[145] Cited in Veale, *Advance to Barbarism*, 195. On the conflation in Germany of the different sorts of trial, see Rückerl, *NS-Verbrechen vor Gericht*, 112.

[146] LHCMA, LH 9/24/178, Stokes to Liddell Hart, 29 Nov. 1948.

[147] Hankey, *Politics, Trials and Errors*, 145.

'scamps' like concentration camp guards let loose in Germany might be undesirable even for Adenauer.[148] Likewise Churchill, who by 1948 was a convinced opponent of the further purging of Nazi Germany, announced during an attack on the proposed Manstein trial that there were exceptional cases 'such as the slaughter of the men of the Norfolk Regiment . . . [which] it was right to pursue, as one would pursue a common case of murder, even after fifteen years had passed before it came to light'.[149]

It was another matter entirely to try internationally recognized and respected officers for ordering, inciting, or at the least acquiescing in the perpetration by their troops of 'atrocity by policy'. In a way that is stereotypically attributed to Germans (and which probably accounts for Manstein's participation in genocide),[150] unquestioning obedience and discipline seem to have been the admirable qualities of soldiery for these critics. Even the observers who accepted the guilt of the major war criminals appear to have differentiated between the soldiers convicted by the IMT and the rest of the military. Airey Neave, the British officer in charge of the commission which collected evidence pertaining to the organization cases at Nuremberg, prided himself on understanding the difference between a 'Nazified' officer like Keitel, who had worked directly with Hitler, and the 'handsome' field commanders who appeared to testify in defence of the General Staff and High Command. For Neave, Keitel could be found guilty of all the charges in the indictment, but German officerhood in general should not be blamed for atrocities committed by SS 'thugs'.[151]

Military opposition to the trials was the earliest form of concerted protest in the USA, and it was, if anything, more publicly expressed than its British counterpart during the immediate post-war period. The IMT was attacked repeatedly in the *Army and Navy Journal* for the indictment of the General Staff and High Command. That organ, a non-official Washington based publication that had acted as a mouthpiece for several discontented American officers in Germany, considered that the only legitimate subjects for trial were individuals who had gone beyond the remit of their orders to commit or condone outrages.[152] These criticisms were initially rebutted by a national press aware of the political role of top soldiers, and of the ordinary soldier's obligation to refuse to obey blatantly criminal orders.[153] However, over time they contributed to the growing nationwide antipathy towards US occupation policies.

The general 'political justice' argument had been championed in the USA since the end of the IMT trial by the Republican Senator Robert Taft. However, such was the contemporary moralistic surge in the USA that his criticisms met

[148] Bell papers, 43, fos. 107–8, Hankey to Bell, 27 Nov. 1951.
[149] Gilbert, *Churchill*, viii, 441–2.
[150] Erich Kosthorst, *Die Geburt der Tragödie aus dem Geist des Gehorsams: Deutschlands Generäle und Hitler—Erfahrungen und Reflexionen eines Frontoffiziers* (Bonn: Bouvier, 1998), 178–203.
[151] Neave, *Nuremberg*, 28, 357.
[152] *NYT* (5 Dec. 1945), for Jackson's rebuttal of some of the journal's charges.
[153] Bosch, *Judgment on Nuremberg*, 167–82; Taylor, *Anatomy*, 238–9.

with almost universal condemnation.[154] They were only given force early in
1948 by the public criticism of the subsequent proceedings by the former presid-
ing judge in the Nuremberg Balkan generals' case, Iowa supreme court justice
Charles Wennerstrum. This was followed up with a campaign by the right-wing
Chicago Tribune to oust Telford Taylor. A series of hardline Republican Senators, prominent among whom were William Langer and, later, Joseph Mc-
Carthy, seized the opportunity to criticize the 'Communist-inspired' trial
process, which they viewed as an illustration of the Truman administration's leniency towards the USSR. A golden opportunity for such dissidents came in the
second half of 1948 and in 1949, as information came to light about the use of im-
proper interrogation techniques before the trial at Dachau of seventy-four members of the Waffen-SS for their part in the Malmédy massacre.

Given the underlying political agenda of some of the Republican critics of the
trials, it is not surprising that they particularly targeted the proceedings against
the industrialists; Telford Taylor was, after all, a convinced new dealer heading a
team of largely like-minded prosecutors, and so it was in the area of economic
policy that a divergence of opinion was most evident. Rather bewilderingly
though, given the moves by the western Allies to distance themselves from the
Soviets after the IMT trial, Senator Langer asserted in the aftermath of the war
crimes trial programme that it was a Communist instrument designed to attack
property rights, with the aim of destroying capitalism.[155] More specifically, at
the beginning of the Farben trial, Representative George Dondero of Michigan
hysterically accused the chief prosecutor in that case, Josiah DuBois, of belong-
ing to a group of men with strong Communist sympathies who had obtained important posts in the military occupation. A crude Judaeo–Bolshevik stereotype
was also introduced into the tirade, as Congressman John Rankin of Mississippi
ranted against 'this saturnalia of persecution' perpetrated by a 'racial minority
[who], two and a half years after the war closed, are in Nuremberg not only hanging German soldiers but trying German businessmen in the name of the United
States'.[156]

James Byrnes's concerns, voiced the previous year to Bevin in Paris, were now
being borne out. We have seen previously the Foreign Office's concern with
developments in the Farben trial *vis-à-vis* British business interest; and it is not
surprising to note that Dondero's constituency housed the headquarters of the
Dow Chemical Company, which had from 1938 enjoyed close relations with the
IG Farben combine.[157] The 'rumblings of discontent' by and on behalf of the
international business and financial community were to redouble with the onset
of the Krupp trial at the end of 1947, and Taylor was fortunate to have Clay's
steadfast support in pressing on with the industrialists' cases.[158]

---

[154] *NYT* (8, 10 Oct. 1946).   [155] Buscher, *The US War Crimes Trial Program*, 37.
[156] Borkin, *The Crime and Punishment of I. G. Farben*, 139–40; Bosch, *Judgment on Nuremberg*, 82–3.
[157] DuBois, *The Devil's Chemists*, 69; Borkin, *The Crime and Punishment of I. G. Farben*, 81–2.
[158] Manchester, *The Arms of Krupp*, 707–8.

There was a hierarchy of concern amongst critics of the trials similar to the distinction frequently made in Britain between military defendants and others, though there were of course some in every country who made blanket condemnations of any type of trial. The objections to the trials of soldiers centred mainly around variants of the 'superior orders' debate, and the related, hackneyed view of the armed forces as merely tools of the politicians. We have seen that John Rankin was just as indignant about the trials of soldiers as about those of industrialists. Dondero's prime concern was the former: he objected vehemently to what he saw as the potential demoralization of Allied soldiers by attacks at Nuremberg on the mythical sanctity of the defence of superior orders.

Dondero interpreted the Nuremberg venture as encouraging 'mass disobedience to superior officers' and suggested that 'implied therein is the threat that if the forces of international communism are victorious, ruthless vengeance will be meted out to those who dare defend their country and its interests'.[159] His views were shared in differing forms by the Democrat Senator Burton Wheeler of Montana, by Admiral Leahy, formerly Chief of Staff to Roosevelt, and by a majority of the American officer corps, save for the few who appreciated the role of military 'executives' in policy-making and recognized the nuances of the court case and the particular, ordered nature of Nazi atrocities.[160]

Nuremberg prosecutor Theodor Fenstermacher recalls that military disapprobation about the trial of German soldiers was still being made known during the Balkan generals' trial which lasted through the second half of 1947 and into 1948.[161] Ironically, such protests only seem to have strengthened Taylor's desire to include Manstein *et al.* in the High Command trial in order both to prove that he was not succumbing to military pressure, and to strengthen the case he was attempting to make that the OCCWC was not 'prosecuting German Generals for "Losing the war" or for [doing the] same things our own Generals did'.[162]

The debate with the potential to disrupt the trial of soldiers most seriously had not by that time emerged, however. The issue of some sort of western German contribution to western European defence in the developing Cold War was tentatively raised in 1947, but it did not become a major issue in Allied political debate until 1949 and even more so thereafter.[163] When it did materialize, it decisively reinforced the position of the critics of trial, compounding it with the dictates of *realpolitik*.

---

[159] Bosch, *Judgment on Nuremberg*, 83, 178.

[160] Ibid. 167, 172, 178; *NYT* (6 Dec. 1945). Taylor, *Anatomy*, 148, on General William Donovan, then head of the US Office of Strategic Services and a member of OCCPAC, distinguishing between the duty-bound field commanders and the complicit staff officers at the Wehrmacht High Command.

[161] *Ex inf.* Theodor Fenstermacher, 16 Nov. 1996.

[162] NARA, RG 153, entry 1018, Nürnberg administrative files, 1944–9, box 1, OCCWC to War Crimes Branch, Army Dept., 13 Oct. 1947, p. 6.

[163] Large, *Germans to the Front*, 35–8.

4.7 NEGATING ALLIED PUNISHMENT POLICY: PREMATURE RELEASES AND
POLITICAL EXPEDIENCY

As Germany aligned itself increasingly against the Allied punishment policies, the conditions of trial and punishment came under ever closer scrutiny. Whatever the motives of many of the critics, there were procedural inconsistencies and inadequacies in the British and American programmes that legitimately came to the fore. The unprecedented nature of their legal endeavours was manifest as they failed to anticipate the necessity of proper appellate machinery, and as the allocation of sentences over time and between courts featured considerable divergences. Confronting these deficiencies was important if the integrity of the trial mission was to be preserved and, as some US jurists pointed out, the constitutional guarantee of due process was not to be infringed.

However, the political pressure in the late 1940s and early 1950s was such that it was difficult to discern the exact motivation for the first concerted moves towards sentence review and 'equalization'. There was even some disagreement between former confederates in the prosecution of war criminals. Thus Telford Taylor suggested that the first widespread revisions of sentences, instituted and carried through in 1950 and 1951 by the US High Commissioner in Germany, John J. McCloy, on the convicts from the subsequent Nuremberg proceedings,[164] were 'the embodiment of political expediency . . . [dealing] a blow to the principles of international law and concepts of humanity for which we fought the war'.[165] Contrarily, Benjamin Ferencz, who had led the prosecution of the Einsatzgruppen leaders, accepted that McCloy's early actions stemmed from genuine moral concern over the propriety of some of the existing punishments, and others have discerned a belief in the educational value of exposing the German people to the legal safeguards built into the democratic system.[166]

Nevertheless, Ferencz's magnanimity was not boundless. A sense of the frustration and bitterness engendered by the reduction of sentences in a case that was considered open and shut can be gleaned from a letter to Taylor in December 1951:

I notice in this morning's paper that a group of our Landsberg friends have been given their freedom as a Christmas present. These include . . . three Einsatzgruppen boys, Schubert, Jost and Nosske. Schubert confessed to personally supervising the execution

---

[164] McCloy and his predecessor Clay were also responsible for reviewing the Dachau sentences.

[165] Telford Taylor, 'The Nazis go Free', *Nation* (24 Feb. 1951), 170–2; Manchester, *The Arms of Krupp*. On the pressure exerted on McCloy in Jan. 1951 from within Germany *vis-à-vis* European security, see Ulrich Brochhagen, *Nach Nürnberg: Vergangenheitsbewältigung und Westintegration in der Ära Adenauer* (Hamburg: Junius, 1994), 40.

[166] United States Holocaust Memorial Museum, hereafter 'USHMM', record group 12.002.02*05, Benjamin B. Ferencz papers, 1924, war crimes trials and war crimes related records, 1945–94, war crimes trials related records, 1949–94, file 'Nürnberg to Landsberg', Ferencz to Peter Maguire, 23 Feb. 1990; see also Schwartz's contentions in 'Die Begnadigung deutscher Kriegsverbrecher'.

of about 800 Jews in a humane manner to avoid the moral strain on the execution squad. You may recall that the deadline for cleaning up Simferopol was Christmas 1941 and that Schubert managed to kill all the Jews by then. So for Christmas ten years later he goes Scot free. Who says there is no Santa Klaus? Nosske was the one whom the other defendants called the biggest bloodhound of all the day after the sentences were imposed and [he] only received twenty years. Now Nosske is free to join former Gen. Jost whose command ordered a fourth gas van when the three in operation executing women and children were insufficient to do the job properly. Noel, Noel, what the hell.[167]

Even McCloy's defenders have conceded that, after the 1951 reviews, the overriding theme in US punishment policy was concession in the bargaining process of rebuilding relations with West Germany.[168] By 1953 the Anglo-Americans had long since concluded that the BRD would have to contribute in some way to a system of European defence against the perceived Communist threat, and the wartime alliances had been turned on their heads.[169] At the beginning of that year, President Truman asked his Secretary of State Dean Acheson to rid the US of the troublesome burden of war criminals;[170] and within half a decade, this had been achieved. Contributions from the US High Commission, the US Army, and the jurists and politicians of the BRD ensured that the last war criminal left the Landsberg jail in 1958.[171]

In terms of chronology, the British record is even less impressive than that of the Americans—the British jail at Werl was emptied completely of war criminals by 1957. And though all but absent from the historiography of the period, this programme of release entailed two of the most celebrated convicts held by any country: Manstein, imprisoned for eighteen years at the end of 1949, and Kesselring, serving the life sentence imposed in 1947. The cases of the two field marshals are not only emblematic examples of German attitudes towards the *Kriegsverurteilten* after the early years of Allied occupation, they also illustrate the extent to which mythologies and misconceptions of the war on both sides of the English Channel contributed to and benefited from the commission of an injustice by the British Government.

Importantly, neither criminal benefited from sentence reviews *per se*. Manstein missed the first wave in 1949, in which no grounds were found to alter Kesselring's term.[172] Thus, while the peculiar German methods of dealing with

---

[167] USHMM, record group 12.001.03*02, Ferencz papers, 1924, Ferencz family background information, 1919–93, general correspondence, 1944–94, personal correspondence 1946–54, Ferencz to Taylor, 17 Dec. 1951.

[168] Buscher, *The US War Crimes Program*, 161.

[169] On the issues of rearmament, see Large, *Germans to the Front*; Schwartz, *America's Germany*.

[170] Buscher, *The US War Crimes Program*, 161.

[171] The process of sentence review in the American case is admirably covered in Buscher, *The US War Crimes Program*, and Schwartz, 'Die Begnadigung deutscher Kriegsverbrecher'.

[172] LHCMA, Wade I, final report by No. 1 War Crimes Review of Sentences Board, Appendix C. Kesselring's sentence, like those of his two subordinate generals, was not reduced from life imprisonment—the quantum of which was 21 years—despite the arguments of the JAG.

the Nazi past did place some strain on relations with the Allies,[173] both Britain and the USA, either officially or unofficially, contrived to meet the demands of the Federal Republic's *Vergangenheitspolitik*. The personal role of Churchill and his parliamentary contacts in and around the 'anti-Nuremberg diners' circle appears to have been of particular importance from 1951 onwards.

We have seen how the imagery of soldierhood was superimposed by the West German élites upon the whole war criminals issue. Two factors ensured that over and above this generalistic trend, genuine, high-ranking soldiers were singled out in the German protests against 'victor's justice'. Since the élites were concerned with the reputation of their professions and interest groups, as well as with the wider control of German society,[174] the most prominent convicts received the most vocal and orchestrated support of all. Secondly, the issue of rearmament inevitably brought with it the invocation of Germany's former military leaders.

A prominent military historian has put Manstein and Kesselring in the 'very front rank of commanders'.[175] Manstein was called 'the most brilliant strategist among all our Generals' by General von Blumentritt, and 'the most dangerous military opponent of the Allies' by Liddell Hart.[176] Moreover, Kesselring was the highest-ranking military prisoner outside Spandau where the IMT convicts were housed under quadripartite authority. Both were also field commanders, and thus not compromised in the minds of such as Airey Neave by their physical proximity to Hitler. Their names, cited both together and separately, became synonymous after their convictions with the 'defamation' of the armed forces. As one young German officer said in 1950, 'I cannot serve as a soldier in order to guard . . . von Manstein's cell'.[177] Finally, a survey of the press reporting of the Manstein trial suggests that it was of significantly greater interest than the Nuremberg High Command trial that covered similar ground.[178] This was partly due to the timing of the case, and partly to the absence of any really famous names and the highest ranks from the latter in the absence of Brauchitsch, Rundstedt, and, of course, Manstein.[179]

Manstein's eighteen-year sentence had caused much consternation in West Germany. The CDU's official press organ proclaimed it a further British

---

[173] Brochhagen, *Nach Nürnberg*.

[174] Frei, *Vergangenheitspolitik*, 194.

[175] Richard Brett-Smith (ed.), *Hitler's Generals* (San Rafael, Calif.: Presidio, 1977), 7.

[176] Cited in Christian Schneider, 'Denkmal Manstein: Psychoprogramm eines Befehlshabers', in Hannes Heer and Klaus Naumann (eds.), *Vernichtungskrieg: Verbrechen der Wehrmacht 1941 bis 1944* (Hamburg: HIS, 1995), 402–17, esp. 402–3; Boll, 'Wehrmacht vor Gericht', 584.

[177] Cited in Frei, *Vergangenheitspolitik*, 207; see also 202, 249, 292; Hans Speier, *From the Ashes of Disgrace: A Journal from Germany, 1945–1955* (Amherst, Mass.: University of Massachusetts Press, 1981), 112–13; Alastair Horne, *Back into Power* (London: Max Parrish, 1955), 66–8.

[178] See also Paul Leverkühn, *Verteidigung Manstein* (Hamburg: Nölke, 1950), introduction.

[179] As Jonathan Bush suggests (paper for 'Nuremberg and Its Impact' conference, 1996), the High Command trial was not 'really meaningful' in terms of achieving its ends because of the profile of the defendants.

condemnation of the Wehrmacht. August Haussleiter from the Bavarian section of that party reflected the popular equation of different victimhoods when he suggested that such proceedings struck the Germans as 'witchcraft trials' (*Hexenprozesse*) if there was also no possibility of investigating and punishing under international jurisdiction those crimes committed on the invasion of Germany and during the expulsion of Germans from eastern Europe.[180] A contemporary political essayist criticized the judgement thus: '[t]he time for historical objectivity in viewing the events of the last war has still not arrived. History did not have the last word with the Manstein verdict, but politics made a move intended to retard developments.'[181] 'Politics', however, would soon undo what the law had done.

Adenauer was fully seized of the symbolic importance of Manstein and Kesselring. In June 1952 he met with Liddell Hart in Bonn, and told him of the difficulties he was having with Wehrmacht veterans' associations. They refused to support German rearmament in the form of ratification of the European Defence Community Treaty as long as the nation's military honour was impugned by the continued imprisonment of former soldiers. (One such veterans' organization, the 'Stahlhelm', had actually elected Kesselring as its president while he was in British custody.)[182] Moreover, such soldiers would be needed to take a lead in Germany, where the officers who had opposed Hitler were held in considerable mistrust.[183] The most vehement demands for release concerned the two best-known soldiers in Allied custody—Kesselring and Manstein—and Adenauer suggested that such an action would be considered a gesture of goodwill in the run-up to the ratification debates in the Bundestag.[184] Barely a month after this encounter, as the culmination of a series of clandestine political developments, the Chancellor's wish was effectively granted.

The end of the Manstein trial heralded not only the first full year of the existence of the nascent republic—under the Allied High Commission rather than military government—but also the year when the prospect of rearming West Germany first loomed large. The war in Korea had established the relevance of building up the defences of a segregated country in the face of Communism, and the reflexes of the western Allies were by now finely attuned to the dictates of the post-war world. If Germany was to be asked to bear arms again, it was inevitable that the disposition of its master-soldiers would have some influence on the terms and conditions under which it responded. Thus, to the military lobbies

---

[180] e.g. *Frankfurter Allgemeine Zeitung* (20, and esp., 21 Dec. 1949).

[181] *Merkur*, 4 (1950), 460. *Merkur* was established in the French zone early in 1947, and claimed to be broadly European rather than Germano-centric in tone. See Eberan, *Wer war an Hitler schuld?*, 59.

[182] Volker R. Berghahn, *Der Stahlhelm: Bund der Frontsoldaten 1918–1935* (Düsseldorf: Droste, 1966), 279. The organization was briefly reformed post-1945 after its dissolution in 1935; but its activity in this second period is not considered significant.

[183] On Manstein's influential and condemnatory view of the 20 July plotters, see e.g. Wette, 'Wehrmachtstradition und Bundeswehr', 133.

[184] LHCMA, Liddell Hart 11/1952/8, note on talk with Adenauer, 7 June 1952.

that campaigned on behalf of their interest-group, and to the large part of the political élite of the BRD, were added numerous 'realist' politicians from the English-speaking countries who realized now, if they had not done so before, that concessions would have to be made.

Prophetic in this final category was Winston Churchill. Though he had initially supported the idea of punishment, immediately after the surrender he had made it clear that he was prepared to 'write off' assistance rendered by war criminals in the re-establishment of order in Germany against the crimes committed. In June 1945 he confessed that he 'did not like to see the German admirals and generals, with whom [the British] had made arrangements, being made to stand with their hands above their heads'. In October 1948, in the context of the heated debates on the possible trial of Manstein *et al.* he described as foolish the desire 'to make a feature of such squalid long-drawn vengeance [as trials] when the mind and soul of Germany may once again be hanging in the balance'.[185]

The alliance of what Ernest Bevin called the 'trades union of Generals'[186] with the political 'realists' manifested itself on the confirmation of Manstein's sentence. The confirming officer was the Commander-in-Chief of the British Army of the Rhine, General Keightley. Keightley appears to have shared the professional biases of his predecessor, General Harding, who commuted the death sentences on Kesselring and two of his subordinates, for he accepted at face value the key contentions of the defence on the dictates of military security and the distance between the SS and the army. On the basis of two petitions from Manstein pointing out the importance of the trial 'both judicially and politically', Keightley reduced the sentence to twelve years, despite the advice of the Deputy Judge Advocate-General that the arguments disclosed 'no *legal* reason why he should not confirm the findings *and* the sentence'.[187] Apparently, Keightley

had formed the opinion that the Court had given too little consideration to the abnormal conditions prevailing on the Russian front. The organisation by the Russians of sabotage and acts of terrorism was unparalleled by anything that happened elsewhere. All the rules for the decent conduct of warfare had already been ignored by the Russians. The savage counter-measures taken by the Germans were directed from Berlin chiefly by Himmler, and Manstein, who was much pre-occupied with his military problems, played mainly a passive part in the atrocities committed against the civil inhabitants.[188]

Much of this was demonstrably untrue contemporaneously; the remainder was a distinctly partial portrait of Manstein's behaviour. Even ignoring his many proven acts of neglect, which included allowing the Einsatzgruppen to murder

[185] Gilbert, *Churchill*, viii, 14–15, 31, 438–9.
[186] *Hansard* (HC), col. 1590, 21 July 1949.
[187] PRO, FO 371/85914, CG786/48/184, Shinwell to Bevin, 13 Feb. 1950. Emphasis added.
[188] PRO, FO 371/85913, CG522/48/184, Robertson to Kirkpatrick, 1 Feb. 1950.

'over sixty eight thousand Soviet citizens, mostly Jews', and the continued operation of the Barbarossa jurisdiction decree, he had been convicted of issuing the 'Commissar Order' permitting the killing without trial of suspected Bolshevik party agents attached to Red Army units.[189]

A few months later, in anticipation of the gravity of the rearmament question, Adenauer restated that two of the necessary conditions for such action were 'cessation of the defamation of the German soldier and a satisfactory settlement of sentences for war crimes'.[190] Ivone Kirkpatrick, the British High Commissioner in Germany, took the point and pushed for the review of sentences on German officers because in December 1950 the NATO foreign ministers were to meet in Brussels to make concrete proposals on a German contribution to European defence.[191]

Kirkpatrick, a Foreign Office diplomat, shared with his military predecessor, Brian Robertson, the view that it was essential at the earliest possible juncture to reintegrate Germany, and hence to assuage German opinion. He also shared some of the prejudices common in British officialdom of the period: in a different capacity three years earlier, as part of the general Allied move towards hardline anti-Communist propaganda, he had recommended that German Jews no longer be employed in prominent positions within the information services control unit in the British zone.[192] He was now in the optimum position to influence British policy, for with the post of High Commissioner came the power of clemency under the Royal Warrant, delegated first by the War Office and then the Foreign Office. At the beginning of 1951 Kirkpatrick declared his intention to begin a second round of sentence reviews. The first review series, initiated in January 1949, had been designated as 'final', with 'no further reviews, except under exceptional circumstances . . . permitted'.[193]

Kirkpatrick made no attempt to conceal his overtly political motives for reconsidering sentences, and a report issued in his defence by his Foreign Office colleagues reiterated them.[194] As Hartley Shawcross immediately divined, the obvious beneficiaries of review would be the most prominent of Britain's prisoners: the leading soldiers. The tone and substance of Kirkpatrick's pronouncements, like McCloy's comparable actions around the same time, antagonized some, such as Shawcross, who had been involved in the prosecution of war criminals. They also aroused the ire of Attlee's Cabinet, as well as much of the

---

[189] Ibid. CG 496/48/184, Russell of Liverpool to FO, 28 Jan. 1950. Manstein was also found guilty of ordering both the murder as 'hostages' of innocent civilians and the mass deportations of Soviet citizens for use as slave labour.

[190] Konrad Adenauer, *Memoirs* (London: Weidenfeld and Nicolson, 1966), 300.

[191] PRO, FO 371/85914, CG3702/48/184, minute by member of the German Political Dept. (signature illegible), 24 Nov. 1950; Large, *Germans to the Front*, 104–7.

[192] Koszyk, *Pressepolitik für Deutsche*, 227.

[193] Jack Fishman, *Long Knives and Short Memories: The Spandau Prison Story* (London: Souvenir Press, 1986), 323–4, 343.

[194] Ibid. 329.

rank-and-file of the Labour Party. The material result was the withdrawal of the High Commissioners' powers *vis-à-vis* war criminals, and some consternation about how a civil servant had been invested with such extensive authority in the first place.[195]

The issue took on a different hue when the Conservatives returned to office under Churchill in October 1951. They had been less enthusiastic towards the IMT trial than the Labour party when they were previously in government.[196] Free from the responsibilities of power when the vexed question of Manstein's trial arose, they had also benefited from the discomfort of the Labour Government, and were not necessarily bound by moral commitment to the cause of his continued punishment. Several of their prominent members had actively opposed it, as—albeit more discreetly—they had the Kesselring verdict and sentence. Immediately upon his re-accession Churchill moved to release all of the remaining officers in British custody.[197]

Foreign Secretary Anthony Eden, with whom the authority to recommend clemency now lay after its withdrawal from the UK High Commission, stressed that this power could only be exercised in cases where it was justified.[198] He was subsequently criticized by Reginald Paget for his 'woolly liberalism', and his purported belief that trials were 'part of a noble experiment to establish universal law under a universal authority and such bilge of that sort'.[199] It is doubtful if Paget's analysis of Eden was accurate, for the Foreign Secretary was still prepared to use every legal device at his command to alleviate the perceived problem. In December 1951 he persuaded the Cabinet to accept his recommendation that pre-trial custody be counted against sentences handed down on war criminals. With the exploitation of a semantic loophole, this decision meant much more than the equitable principle for which it appeared to stand, for in certain cases it effectively doubled a reduction already made. Such a sentence was that passed on Manstein.

In anticipation of the need for clarity, the Court had decreed at the end of the trial that Manstein's sentence 'will date from today (19 December 1949). The period during which the accused has been in custody has been taken into account.'[200] This was drawn to Eden's attention, yet he argued that in such cases the judicial qualification 'taken into account' did not necessarily mean that pre-trial custody had been fully 'reckoned towards [the] sentence'. Despite instances such as Manstein's when the intention of the court had been obvious and unequivocal, if the judgement had not stated explicitly the formula that time

[195] Jack Fishman, *Long Knives and Short Memories*, 326–34.
[196] Aronson, 'Preparations for the Nuremberg Trial', 263.
[197] Birmingham University Archives, hereafter, 'BUA', FO 800/846, fo. 2, Churchill to Eden, 29 Nov. 1951; fo. 12, Churchill to Eden, 8 June 1952.
[198] Ibid. fos. 20–3, Eden to Churchill, 29 Aug. 1952.
[199] LHCMA, Liddell Hart 1/563, Paget to Liddell Hart, 13 Jan. 1953.
[200] PRO, FO 371/104159, CW1663/13, Kirkpatrick to Eden, 23 Apr. 1953.

previously served would be 'set off in its entirety', it was considered legitimate to subtract this time from the total number of years decreed.[201]

The pressure to finish with the war criminals issue for good was increased on Eden and the government in the summer of 1952 when the question of German ratification of the European Defence Community Treaty loomed large. Upon informing his parliamentary confederates—Paget, Hankey, and Field Marshal Alexander, now Minister of Defence—of his conversation with Adenauer in Bonn, Liddell Hart received from Paget the assurance that the message would be brought to 'Winston's' attention, and the confidence that the concerned individuals in the government were now anxious to obtain a pretext on which to release the field marshals. They were arranging for a negative medical assessment of Manstein, which, as we know from the prolonged prelude to the field marshal's trial, was the safest method of diffusing political protest, a basis that even the Labour cabinet had conceded would be unlikely to spawn extensive difficulties.[202] The tactic of this particular report was to emphasize Manstein's long-standing eye trouble and, almost incredibly, the feelings of melancholy that he was experiencing in prison.[203]

The scheme may have been attempted before, but, as Alexander complained, the doctor sent to inspect Manstein had not been adequately primed as to which aspects of the prisoner's disposition to concentrate on.[204] Nevertheless, both Kesselring and Manstein had complaints that, in varying degrees of seriousness, necessitated hospital treatment. Thus in July 1952 it was decided that Kesselring be given medical parole for an 'exploratory operation' on a throat cancer, and in August Manstein was also temporarily released to have an operation on his cataracts. Neither man would see the inside of a prison cell again, because following their operations they were scheduled to remain at liberty for an indefinite convalescence period.[205] This plan had been devised at the highest levels of the Foreign Office, and certainly with the knowledge of Churchill and the British High Commission.[206] To be sure that the true significance of the operation was not lost in the BRD, Kirkpatrick assured Adenauer that 'no one temporarily released on grounds of health would be taken back into custody'. Adenauer proceeded to recommend this system to the US High Commission.[207]

Though it was considered that Germany was not overly concerned with the terms on which the field marshals were freed, an outright act of clemency was 'more clear cut and would presumably be clearer to German public opinion'.[208] Thus the remainder of Kesselring's sentence was officially remitted in October

[201] PRO, CAB 129/48, C (51) 54, Foreign Secretary's note to Cabinet, 18 Dec. 1951.
[202] Fishman, *Long Knives and Short Memories*, 334.
[203] LHCMA, Liddell Hart 11/1952/8, Liddell Hart's notes on London visit, 1–3 July 1952.
[204] Ibid.
[205] LHCMA, Liddell Hart 1/563, Paget to Liddell Hart, 1 Aug. 1952.
[206] PRO, FO, 371/104159, CW 1663/17, Roberts to Strang, 30 Apr. 1953.
[207] Adenauer, *Memoirs*, 447.
[208] PRO, FO 1060/497, Roberts to Kirkpatrick, 13 Sept. 1952.

1952. His condition did not prevent him living until 1960, nor addressing a rally of service veterans immediately on his release. The ex-soldiers in question were members of the fanatically nationalist 'Green Devil' commando outfit, and at the event Kesselring recited the ritual call for the wholesale liberation of war criminals in Allied custody.[209]

Manstein's health was simply too good to be a reasonable pretext for remission. However, he was not far from the end of his sentence. With the initial reduction from eighteen to twelve years in 1950, a further remission of one-third of the revised term for good behaviour (a scheme which benefited almost every prisoner in British or American custody, regardless of their actual conduct in prison), and the Cabinet decision to deduct from the sentence time spent in custody prior to trial, he was due to be released formally on 7 May 1953. In fact, since his discharge from hospital in February 1953, Manstein had been taking a cure at a health resort in Allmendigen in the US zone—his home town.[210]

There is a final twist to this tale, springing from disagreement in the Cabinet about the official termination date of the sentence. Debate revolved around the question of whether he qualified for remission for 'good conduct' while on medical parole, as he had not been in prison. Were he to be denied this, his sentence would run approximately to September 1953, requiring further 'unsatisfactory' extensions of his convalescence period.[211] The solution to the quandary, constituting the final chapter in Britain's rather sordid relationship with Manstein, appeared as Anthony Eden was committed to hospital in April 1953 for a series of operations on his gall bladder and bile duct. In Eden's absence, Churchill took over the reins of the Foreign Office in addition to his normal duties, and predictably the Prime Minister was to share none of his colleague's concerns with legal stricture.[212] *Carte blanche* was effectively given to Selwyn Lloyd, Minister of State in the Foreign Office with responsibility for German Affairs, and one of Paget's contacts, to rid the government of the embarrassing burden of the former field marshals.

On 1 May 1953, Selwyn Lloyd proposed to the Prime Minister that the 'mean-minded' arguments against Manstein's formal release be disregarded.[213] This was perfectly acceptable to Churchill,[214] and it remained only for the two to apply the *coup de grâce*: the alteration of the Royal Warrant in collaboration with the War Office to enable clemency to be applied in the absence of the Foreign Secretary. Predictably, the War Office proved amenable.[215] And if Manstein

---

[209] LHCMA, Liddell Hart 9/24/69, 25 Oct. 1952; *Express* (25 May 1953).
[210] PRO, FO 371/104159, CW1663/13, Kirkpatrick to Eden, 23 Apr. 1953.   [211] Ibid.
[212] Robert Rhodes James, *Anthony Eden* (London: Weidenfeld and Nicolson, 1986), 364–5, for Churchill's departure from Eden's practices. Ivone Kirkpatrick recalled nostalgically 'the zest with which [Churchill] took charge of the Foreign Office in the absence . . . of the Foreign Secretary'. See his *The Inner Circle* (London: Macmillan, 1959), 261.
[213] BUA, FO 800/846, fo. 29, Selwyn-Lloyd to Churchill, 1 May 1953.
[214] PRO, FO 371/104159, CW1663/17, Selwyn-Lloyd to Churchill, 1 May 1953.
[215] BUA, FO 800/846, fo. 43, Selwyn-Lloyd to Churchill, 28 June 1953.

could now rest assured of his freedom, Selwyn Lloyd was making the most of Eden's hospitalization by further pursuing the confessed policy of 'clearing the decks. . . [as] regards the senior professional soldiers, *whose basic crime is that of having transmitted Hitler's orders*'.[216]

General Nicholas von Falkenhorst was now the highest-ranking German soldier still in British custody.[217] He had been condemned to death by a British military court in August 1946 for crimes committed while he was Commander-in-Chief of the German Armed Forces in Norway, being found guilty on seven charges of war crimes relating to the issuance of illegal orders and the handing over of prisoners to the SD, with all that that entailed. The sentence was subsequently and rather predictably commuted to life imprisonment.[218] Even Frank Roberts of the Foreign Office, who had opined that the BRD should have a say in the disposition of convicted war criminals, determined that clemency was not justifiable in this case.[219]

Falkenhorst's purported heart trouble duly became a salient issue. In a masterstroke of pure sophistry, Selwyn Lloyd reinforced the ill-health argument by compounding it with the contention that Falkenhorst's guilt was no greater than that of Kesselring, who had already been granted clemency.[220] Thus one act of political expediency was dressed up as precedent and moral justification for another, and with Falkenhorst's release the case of the most problematic class of war criminal was closed.

In Germany the releases were celebrated. Like the parallel situation in US foreign policy from 1951, if less openly facilitated, they had been initiated in large part to pander to the demands of nationalistic and militaristic elements in the Federal Republic, in an attempt to gain their allegiance in the era of German rearmament. Many of the German people appreciated this political motive; others took the moves as an admission of the injustice of trying in the first place.[221] Most had long since discounted the possibility that the soldiers had done anything reprehensible, perceiving them as functionaries—and heroic ones at that—of their fatherland. In 1956, a grim symmetry was established about the axis of Germany's defeat, when Manstein returned to the service of the western half of that fatherland in an advisory capacity to assist in the formation of an army for the BRD, the Bundeswehr.[222]

The outcome was the ultimate logic of semi-official British foreign policy. However, freeing Manstein and Kesselring was not just a matter of Cold War

[216] Ibid, fos. 41–2, Frank Roberts minute, 5 Feb. 1953. Emphasis added.

[217] For statistics on the remaining criminals in British custody, see BUA, FO 800/846, fos. 30–1, Selwyn-Lloyd to Churchill, 7 May 1953.

[218] On Falkenhorst's trial, see UNWCC, *Law Reports of Trials of War Criminals*, xi (London: HMSO, 1949).

[219] PRO, FO 1060/497, Roberts to Kirkpatrick, 13 Sept. 1952. On Robert's previous expressions of opinion, see Brochhagen, *Nach Nürnberg*.

[220] BUA, FO 800/846, fos. 32–4, Selwyn-Lloyd to Churchill, 18 May 1953.

[221] Reports 63, 70, 67 (respectively) in *The HiCog Surveys*, 106, 112, 110.

[222] Carver, 'Manstein', 244.

pragmatism. From Keightley in the military administration to Selwyn Lloyd in the Foreign Office to Churchill, there was a genuine belief that the soldiers had not really done wrong. These men had not been enduring and passionate opponents of all war crimes trials, but they shared some of the assumptions of such critics.

The international 'union of generals' identified by Bevin as the chief obstacle to the Manstein trial does indeed appear to have backed its own, and it was greatly supported by acolytes like Hankey and Liddell Hart. In August 1949, in opposition to the Manstein trial, Cyril Falls, then Chichele professor of military history at Oxford, sketched, unawares, the self-image of this collective: 'War is a rough business', he mused. 'Perhaps the world is revolting against the comradeship in arms which existed to some extent among enemies, and it may be that this was often to the disadvantage of the civilian. At the same time it did a great deal to mitigate the horrors of war.'[223]

The obvious questions in retrospect ask in what ways the horrors of the Barbarossa campaign were mitigated, and also what happened to the camaraderie between German and Soviet soldiers. Assessments of the nature of the German-Soviet conflict were critical not only in the seminal case of Manstein, but to the whole mythology of the Wehrmacht. As has been the case right up until the so-called 'historians' debate of the 1980s, and even more recently with Wehrmacht apologists in the army of the unified Germany, the widespread exculpation of German conduct in the post-war crucible featured distortion of the causes and effects of the Barbarossa campaign.[224]

4.8 THE REVISED RHETORIC OF THE WEHRMACHT'S WAR

The combative contentions of Reginald Paget in Manstein's defence were thoroughly congruent with the prevailing mood in Germany, and his efforts were well appreciated. One of the more extreme instances of this admiration figured on 4 January 1950. Leaflets were circulated by the newspaper *Das Neue Weltbild* to houses throughout the British zone, proclaiming the MP as the bearer of 'a new standard of justice', and advertising a forthcoming article, 'For the honour of the soldier', bearing information on the crimes committed by the Allies.[225] The *Frankfurter Allgemeine Zeitung* approached the issue in a far more sober way, yet still reflected the defence team's self-image as exemplars of British 'fair play', particularly in the light of repeated attacks on the lawyers from the East German and eastern European press.[226] Conversely, the Polish observer at the trial withdrew with the protest that the proceedings were 'developing into a trial of the millions of fighters against Nazi fascism' and a 'glorification of Nazism'.[227] The

[223] *Illustrated London News* (13 Aug. 1949).
[224] See Wette, 'Wehrmachtstradition und Bundeswehr', on the modern German army.
[225] 'Er hat sich zum Sprecher einer neuen Gerechtigkeit gemacht'.
[226] *Frankfurter Allgemeine Zeitung* (25 Nov. 1949).   [227] Bower, *Blind Eye to Murder*, 295.

latter contention was nearer the mark, as can be seen by two of his courtroom jousts, the tone of which was representative of the whole defence.[228]

As one of his innumerable attempts to discredit prosecution evidence, Paget queried a story about a Pole being shot and wounded on the grounds that such an incompetent piece of shooting—that is, in failing to kill the man—was unlikely from a German soldier. On another occasion, defence quibbled about the use of the word 'drowning' in the translation of a report by the secret military field police. To avoid further prolonging the matter, it was eventually agreed that the document should read 1,029 people 'caused to disappear by sinking them in the water'.[229]

More significant than his stereotyping of German military efficiency and blatant disregard of outright murder was Paget's general rhetoric of vicious anti-Communism. His closing address was described by *Le Monde* as providing a base for a revisionist German nationalism.[230] It brought together a number of the themes present in both German and Anglo-American opposition to trials, and amongst some of the Allied occupation policy-makers: attacking the attempt to prosecute Manstein for 'obeying orders' as 'positively totalitarian'; distinguishing clearly between the actions of the SS and those of the Wehrmacht; and suggesting that the unbridled criminality of the war in the 'east' was a consequence not of Nazi racism but of Russian barbarism and non-adherence to the laws of war.[231] As the Judge Advocate Collingwood declared in summing up the evidence for the bench, Paget seemed to be appealing to an audience beyond the courtroom.[232]

Manstein was convicted on nine of the seventeen counts facing him, but had not the Soviets withheld evidence in retaliation for the British failure to surrender Manstein, and had adequate weight been given to the Einsatzgruppen testimony,[233] he would likely have been convicted on rather more. (As we now know, relations between the Eleventh German Army and Einsatzgruppe D improved after Manstein became commander-in-chief on 17 September 1941, during the period when the killing of Jews expanded to include entire communities. Manstein was happy to let the killing squad get on with its prime task, rather than attempting to co-opt it for his own purposes as his predecessor had done.)[234]

---

[228] No detailed, objective account of Manstein's trial has been published. As far as it goes, Bower's *Blind Eye to Murder* gives a reliable flavour of the proceedings. The trial transcript is in PRO FO 1060, and in LHCMA.

[229] LHCMA, von Manstein 5/57, p. 3113; 5/58, p. 3201.   [230] *Le Monde* (21 Dec. 1949).

[231] LHCMA, von Manstein 5/51–2 for the closing address. See esp. 5/52, pp. 2858–60.

[232] *Keesing's Contemporary Archives*, 7 (1948–50), 10773–4.

[233] Ohlendorf, the head of the Einsatzgruppe D attached to Manstein's Eleventh Army, had recently been sentenced to death at Nuremberg. Defence claimed that he had only offered his evidence in exchange for some sort of consideration; this had the effect not only of discounting Ohlendorf's evidence, but of casting doubt upon the testimony of other Einsatzgruppen officers who corroborated his tale of a close relationship with the army. LHCMA, von Manstein 5/59, 3256–7.

[234] Andrej Angrick, 'Die Einsatzgruppe D', in Peter Klein (ed.), *Die Einsatzgruppen in der besetzten Sowjetunion 1941/42* (Berlin: Gedenk- und Bildungsstätte Haus der Wannsee-Konferenz, 1997), 88–110,

The only substantial accounts of Manstein's trial have been written by Paget and his German colleague, Paul Leverkühn. Both were as clearly partisan as was the courtroom defence, but whereas Leverkühn's tome was generally limited to matters legal, Paget sought to rewrite history.[235] His account faithfully recorded his courtroom exercises in minimizing Jewish losses under the Einsatzgruppen in an attempt concomitantly to minimize the complicity of his client. Working from the starting-point of Ohlendorf's estimate of 90,000 murdered in the area of the Crimea, by a series of spurious calculations based upon conjecture about the murderous capacity of any given subdivision of the killing squad, Paget concluded that at least one zero should be removed from the total of dead, and that in all probability there were only between 2,000 and 3,000 Jews murdered.

Just as the criticisms of the Manstein trial voiced by the 'anti-Nuremberg diner' and former Fascist British General J. F. C. Fuller found a favourable German audience, and as did Bishop Bell's and Victor Gollancz's rhetoric of conciliation,[236] and Churchill's condemnation of the Nuremberg Ministries trial and his contribution to Manstein's defence fund,[237] so did Paget's argumentation. Prior to the trial, Leverkühn had echoed Fuller's judgement that the trial was a function of Jewish vengeance—the 'Jehovah complex'. Further, he asked rhetorically if Manstein was to be 'an offering on the altar of the Soviet Union or Poland, reeking with the blood of millions of Germans'.[238] After the proceedings, the ostensibly liberal Hamburg newspaper *Die Welt* serialized Paget's book, which had been translated almost immediately into German, and advertised by the Stuttgart publishers Neuer Buchdienst alongside a straight biography of Rommel. The publicity material for the books made much play of both Hankey's and Montgomery's condemnations of the trials. The timing, in spring 1952, could not have been more telling, given what we know of the rearmament debate and the chronology of Manstein's prison term.[239] On the back of such revelations, how could the field marshal's release be seen as anything but the correction of a historical wrong, and the affirmation of what Manstein was perceived to have stood for?

The Manstein trial, or rather the way it has been presented for posterity, has provided ammunition for outright Holocaust deniers: Tom Bower has described how Paget's courtroom techniques strongly resembled those used in Richard Harwood's modern day neo-Nazi work, *Did Six Million Really Die?*[240] The

esp. 97–8; ibid. *passim*, for the collaboration between the army and the Einsatzgruppe. See Bloxham, 'Punishing German Soldiers during the Cold War', *passim*, for some of Manstein's specific orders.

[235] Leverkühn, *Verteidigung Manstein*; Paget, *Manstein*.

[236] On Adenauer's appreciation of Gollancz's stance, see Adenauer, *Memoirs*, 60.

[237] *Badische Zeitung* (23 Feb. 1950). In the same article, 'Der einstige Feind', attention is also drawn to the biography of Erwin Rommel by a British general, Desmond Young, which differentiates sharply between the actions of the army and those of the Waffen-SS.

[238] Bell papers, 38, pt I, fos. 246–8, Leverkühn to Basil Liddell Hart, 11 May 1949.

[239] See e.g. *Die Zeit* (25 Apr. 1952), citing the conduct of the Korean war, and asking 'What did Manstein do differently?' For the publicity flier for Paget's book, see Bell papers, 48, fos. 378–9.

[240] Bower, *Blind Eye to Murder*, 294.

influence of Paget's work in less extreme circles is, however, more widespread and more interesting. His contentions contributed to a revised edition of F. J. P. Veale's polemic, *Advance to Barbarism*. The subtitle of this book is, intriguingly, *How the Reversion to Barbarism in Warfare and War Trials Menaces our Future*. Broader in scope than Paget's writing, this 1953 publication effectively depicted the German attack on the Soviet Union as a pre-emptive strike aimed at defending the heart of civilized Europe from the Asiatic hordes. The war prior to the defeat of France, Veale opined, was purely a 'European civil war'. Thereafter, 'all Europeans' faced a dilemma: 'whether domination of Europe by the Soviet Union was too heavy a price to pay for the continuance of the civil war'. In other words, a parochial quarrel was overshadowed by the looming threat of the Red Army to both sides.[241]

Veale's 'European civil war', then, was of a slightly different nature to the *europäische Bürgerkrieg* of 1917–45, invented in a later decade by the conservative German historian, Ernst Nolte.[242] Also, unlike the latter, it did not trouble itself with explaining away the Holocaust, because Veale did not see the need to account for that as a significant episode. Nevertheless, *Advance to Barbarism* concretized the *Historikerstreit* arguments of Nolte and those of Veale's own contemporaries. He suggested that not only were Nazism and its crimes a reaction to Bolshevism and its record, but that events from 22 June 1941 were actually influenced by the extremity of Soviet behaviour. Reversing the true chronology, and again echoing Paget, and Keightley, and prefiguring Nolte's focus on the anti-partisan function of the SS, he attributed the murders of the Einsatzgruppen to a reaction to Communist atrocity. The 'SD', apparently, were called in to combat 'terror with terror'.[243]

We are also to infer that the Jews were not blameless: as Paget had argued, 'it would have surprised nobody if the SD when they got to a town screened the Jewish quarter first, because that was the quarter in which they were likely to find people who were most dangerous to the occupying power'.[244] Judaeo–Bolshevik or straightforward Soviet 'terror' was not simply held to be a function of an aggressive political system. Cultural chauvinism was at work, when Paget suggested that battlefield mutilation 'is a Russian and not a German habit'.[245] This was not far from the observation of Montgomery of Alamein—another trial critic—that 'the Russians, though a fine fighting race, were in fact barbarous Asiatics who had never enjoyed a civilisation comparable to that of the rest of Europe'.[246] Indeed, the line separating perceived political and cultural differences between west and east was always fine and frequently blurred.

---

[241] Veale, *Advance to Barbarism*, 116–25.

[242] Ernst Nolte, *Der europäische Bürgerkrieg: Nationalsozialismus und Bolschewismus* (Frankfurt am Main: Propyläen, 1987).

[243] Veale, *Advance to Barbarism*, 223.   [244] LHCMA, von Manstein 5/52, pp. 2847, 2852.

[245] Ibid. p. 2830.

[246] *The Memoirs of Field-Marshal the Viscount Montgomery of Alamein* (London: Collins, 1958), 356.

The CDU contrived to sell themselves to the Allies as representatives of the Christian tradition, opposed to the secularism which they considered had facilitated the rise of Nazism as well as that of the other totalitarian form, the inherently materialist Marxism. The occident—*Abendland*—was, they believed, the home and bastion of anti-materialist, Christian ideals.[247] The Allies were receptive to this notion, as is clear from the free hand that they allowed the German church in denazification, the promotion of men such as Niemöller and Kogon, and the resurrection of pre-war Christian anti-Communist imagery in their political debate.[248]

To draw on an example relevant to this book, we might consider the fact that a secret clause was inserted late in the 1940s in the terms of the British war criminals extradition legislation to be applied to eastern European nations.[249] This appears to have had cultural as well as political justifications. Thus when, in spite of British concerns over the quality of 'Communist' justice, Poland proved the equitable nature of its legal system, an explanation forwarded in Whitehall was that the Polish Catholic legacy was ensuring the survival of a 'strong sense of Christian justice'.[250] This did not mean, however, that the British were prepared to go so far as to transfer high-ranking soldiers to the Polish authorities.[251]

The contemporary absolution of Manstein and Kesselring was expedited at an auspicious moment by an influential British circle. In turn, Basil Liddell Hart's role in writing the history of the war made easy the perpetuation of the myth of Wehrmacht innocence for later military historians, who have frequently shied away from the criminal side of Barbarossa. Such historians have also elided the issue of Kesselring's murderous instructions by implying that the SS or SD were really responsible, and have cited in his defence the testimonies of Alexander and Churchill, who were thoroughly implicated in attempting to get the charges overturned. One has even gone so far as to say Kesselring was 'pardoned', with the implication that he deserved it.[252] It has also proved possible for war memoirs and histories alike to claim that Manstein had 'no involvement with war crimes', or to rely on the evidence of no less a personage than David Irving to illustrate that the field marshal was no Nazi.[253]

[247] Maria Mitchell, 'Materialism and Secularism: CDU Politicians and National Socialism, 1945–1949', *Journal of Modern History*, 67 (1995), 278–308.
[248] Philip Williamson, 'Christian Conservatives and the Totalitarian Challenge, 1933–40', *English Historical Review*, 115 (2000), 607–42, esp. 619–21.
[249] PRO, FO 371/85900, CG3382/17/184, Priss minute on discussion incl. Kirkpatrick, 21 Oct. 1950; Priss minute, 1 Nov. 1950.
[250] PRO, FO 371/70825 CG4646/34/184, Allied Liaison Branch report no. 10, June–July 1946.
[251] For an example other than Manstein, see chapter 5.2, below.
[252] Brett-Smith, *Hitler's Generals*, 242; Bidwell, 'Kesselring', 287.
[253] Mark Lynton, *Accidental Journey: A Cambridge Internee's Memoir of World War II* (Woodstock, NY: Overlook, 1995); Samuel W. Mitcham Jun., 'Kleist', in Correlli Barnett (ed.), *Hitler's Generals* (New York: Quill and Morrow), 249–63, esp. 259, 262; David Irving, *Hitler's War* (New York: Viking, 1977), 618.

One of the key underpinnings of this investigation is that one did not have to be a Nazi to be complicit in genocide. Hitler relied on thousands of 'ordinary men', policemen and soldiers alike, to do much of the killing in Poland and the Soviet Union. And though the Nazis infiltrated and co-opted the German élites, they still relied upon many of the traditional societal power-bases in running Germany, in preparing it for conquest, and in creating a discriminatory and finally genocidal state. Non-Nazis were co-responsible for the depth of Nazi criminality, and they were essential in giving that criminality its breadth.

The motive force behind the actions of the Wehrmacht in the USSR was not full-blown Nazi racism but a traditional, powerful anti-communism amongst the leadership corps, which also bought into the supposed connection between Bolshevism and Jewry.[254] And just as one did not need to be a Nazi to aid in imperialism and genocide, one did not need to be a Nazi to share in some of the conceptions the Nazis exploited (though the extremity of Veale's and Paget's positions has latterly been the preserve only of the political extreme).[255] The argument of the Soviet Union as original threat, for instance, present in Hitler's own rhetoric, was also used in defence at Nuremberg. Thereafter it was employed periodically in Germany and elsewhere, up to and beyond the *Historikerstreit*, often by mainstream historians and politicians concerned to recontextualize the Nazi experience.[256] But it had also been used, if in a very different context, in the British Conservative party in the 1930s, the period of general liberal-democratic theorizing about the twin totalitarian threat.[257] Certainly, seeing Communism as the paramount threat to world order and civilization had a good pedigree throughout the inter-war period.[258]

The Nazis themselves borrowed from pre-existing ideas about German expansion into eastern Europe, and the anti-Bolshevik 'crusade' was accompanied by a supposed superiority over the Slavic peoples that long predated the Third Reich, as well as an appropriation of Christian imagery for the conflict. (Who, indeed, was Barbarossa other than the crusader emperor?) This did not stop non-Nazi, if generally right-wing, politicians in the USA, Britain, and the CDU from using similarly Manichaean imagery during the Cold War. Nor did it stop men like Liddell Hart from playing Cold War politics while they were purportedly

[254] Streit, *Keine Kamaraden*; Manfred Messerschmidt, '"Harte Sühne am Judentum": Befehlswege und Wissen in der deutschen Wehrmacht', in Jörg Wollenberg (ed.), *'Niemand war dabei und keiner hat's gewusst': Die deutsche Öffentlichkeit und die Judenverfolgung 1933–1945* (Munich: Piper, 1989), 113–28. The order from which Messerschmidt's titular quote is culled, calling for the awareness of the German soldier for the 'harsh atonement of Jewry', the 'principal bearer of the Bolshevik terror', was actually issued by Manstein. See *Das Dritte Reich und seine Diener: Dokumente*, ed. Leon Poliakov and Josef Wulf (Berlin: Volk und Welt, 1975), 459–61.

[255] Peter Baldwin, 'The Historikerstreit in Context', in id. (ed.), *Reworking the Past: Hitler, the Holocaust, and the Historians' Debate* (Boston, Mass.: Beacon, 1990), 3–37, esp. 24.

[256] Ibid. 21–6.

[257] Williamson, 'Christian Conservatives', 636.

[258] Alastair Hamilton, *The Appeal of Fascism: A Study of Intellectuals and Fascism, 1919–1945* (London: Anthony Blond, 1971).

working in support of the apolitical figures, who happened to be the standard-bearers of the Vernichtungskrieg.

Inevitably, the opponents of trial would hail predominantly from the ranks of the cold warriors, whether they were so inclined by pragmatism or ideology. Yet it is hard to escape the conclusion that the Pagets, the Liddell Harts, and even the Bishop Bells and the Keightleys, who had some real idea of what had happened in eastern Europe, opposed the trial of soldiers because they were more comfortable with the genocidal assault on (Judaeo-)Bolshevism than they were with the 'concentration camps'. They contributed in no small way to keeping these related phenomena separate in the public sphere as well.

CONCLUSIONS

The release of the field marshals should contribute to a new perspective on the 'final solution of the war criminals question'. The tale embraces perhaps the one area of Allied war crimes policy in which the British input, while negative, was as significant as that of the United States. In fact, the American reviews did not tend to favour soldiers as a group above any others; perhaps, it is suggested, because McCloy did not wish to be seen to be bowing to the pressure exerted specifically on their behalf.[259] Nevertheless, at the end of the 1950–1 review, McCloy stressed what was by then *de rigueur*: 'these sentences reflect upon the individuals concerned, not upon the honor of the German military profession'.[260]

As for the wider social significance of soldiery in Germany, we see that the idea of untarnished military honour was embraced by a public which wished to vindicate the German war effort as, if misled by a criminal clique, nevertheless justified in the face of the Bolshevik threat.[261] The reputation of the Wehrmacht was preserved in Germany by the perpetuation of one myth of its 'unpoliticized' nature and of another of the German 'bulwark' against the Communist east. Encompassing both of these has been the image of the military as *the* defender of the integrity of Germany.[262]

The theory of Germany as bulwark against Communism—with the military and the nation indistinguishable, identified with and in terms of each other—was popularized not only in that country, but in the west also as the Cold War developed. The releases of the field marshals were facilitated to strengthen western Europe, and fed directly into the propaganda of the West German élites. And if the crucible of West German post-war identity was the Adenauer era, it is no surprise that the prevailing popular discourses of that period remained influential there for decades to come.

[259] Schwartz, *America's Germany*, 168.

[260] PRO LCO 2/4428, HiCoG Public Relations Division APO 757-A, p. 6.

[261] George Mosse, *Fallen Soldiers: Reshaping the Memory of the World Wars* (New York: Oxford University Press, 1990), 216–19; *Die Zeit* (8 Oct. 1953).

[262] Klaus Naumann, 'Wehrmacht und NS-Verbrechen: Wirklichkeiten und Wirkungen einer kollektiven Gewalterfahrung', *Mittelweg*, 36 (1992/1993), 130–6; esp. 132.

The disposition of Manstein and Kesselring was important in its own right, illustrating the peculiar circularity of our subject as political force imposed itself decisively over judicial authority and historical actuality. However, the episode is more significant in indicating what was acceptable rhetoric in the decade after the war. Opposition to the trials could stem from many roots; the opposition that was vocalized, however, was generally tied up with a specific raft of values.

For Germans, nationalism was the necessary factor and, often, also the sufficient one. In its various manifestations it could mean support for most of the things that Germany had done during the war, virulent anti-Communism, and opposition to anything the Allied occupiers imposed. Legalistic objections to trial were sometimes just that, but more often they masked these partisan concerns.

In the liberal democracies there were also complex issues involved. Senator Robert Taft in the USA and Victor Gollancz in Britain came close to exemplifying principled, reasoned objection to the trial ethic, but even they had corresponded with the chauvinist Montgomery Belgion. The vociferous anti-Communism of the American senators Langer, McCarthy, and Dondero dovetailed with the leanings of the British MP Richard Stokes and Reginald Paget. Some, like T. S. Eliot or General Fuller, combined right-wing views with outspoken antisemitism. The 'anti-Nuremberg diners' drew on each of these traditions. These people, with exceptions such as that of General Fuller, were not extremists by today's standards. At the time, Fuller included, they were considered to be respectable individuals; they were also opinion-formers, and the message that they were giving out was the opposite of that of Nuremberg.

If there was one idea that Jackson and Taylor tried to establish, it was the supremacy of the crime of aggressive war. Though failing to account for the pre-war atrocities committed within the Reich, there is considerable mileage in the idea that the pursuit of warfare not only provided new opportunities for the Nazi campaigns of racial hatred, but that it radicalized these into full-blown genocide. The trials of Manstein and the 'High Command' confronted the alliance of the regular armed forces with the specially designated agents of Nazi genocide, and these contributed to the scholarly view that the former emerged tainted by the crimes of the latter. The logic of the OCCPAC/OCCWC indictment was a far-reaching examination of German society, however, American trial policy failed to convince Germans that this was necessary;[263] the same is true of British policy.

While Frank Buscher ascribes this failure to the structure and execution of the trial programmes at the planning level, the document-centred courtroom practice of the IMT in particular contributed to making the legal medium a poor didactic tool. And beyond the courtroom, we should not just look to the primacy of Cold War politics and German nationalism. Even before the trials were

---

[263] Buscher, *The US War Crime Trial Program*, 159.

undermined by the general thrust of Allied and German rhetoric from 1947, the focus of the *Schuldfrage* was placed firmly on German society, not on Jews and not on Slavs, and the ground was prepared for a host of improbable apologia.

For much of the perpetrating society, defensive rejection of guilt, whether genuine or feigned, had become the order of the day since unconditional surrender had been imposed on Germany. The German élites decided that attack was the best form of defence, however, and questioned the bases of the trials, effectively accusing the Allies. Thus the only concerted national confrontation with guilt perverted the issue, bypassing German crimes—and once again their victims—in order to discredit the very idea of punishment. In this sophistry the Germans were not alone. But that the role of British and American citizens in rewriting history has not been deemed worthy of much attention is testament to the enduring belief that the murder of Jews and others was not 'our' problem anyway.

The Allied publics did not countenance wholesale distortion of the past, often opposing the premature liberation of convicted war criminals, particularly the well-known Alfried Krupp, and fearing a revival of German militarism. Indeed, though it was not a paramount concern, the Allied Governments remained sensitive to domestic public feeling on the war criminals issue throughout.[264] Without doubt, the uncovering of Buchenwald and Belsen left a deep imprint on the peoples of the liberal democracies, making concrete their pre-existing notions of German perfidy. Yet the general ignorance and lack of interest in the war in the east, and the tendency to exonerate soldiers from blame, allowed the perpetuation of misrepresentations of the war. The attitude towards the Wehrmacht also fed into a psychological need to believe that a fellow European culture had not been totally corrupted. (In this perhaps the collegiality shown at various levels by the British to the Germans was stronger than that exhibited by the USA.) There was no thought of the catastrophe of the war as an outcome of destructive forces inherent to that culture: the superior virtue of the 'occident' would be brought again to the fore by *Christian* restoration.

It has been observed that in occupied Germany there was an inherent 'tension between democracy on the one hand and memory and justice on the other'. The implication is that the vast number of Germans actively or passively complicit in the evils of Nazism would not, if given a say, allow an investigation of the past.[265] This dichotomy is not accurate. While democracy and justice may have been opposed, it is wrong simply to equate justice with memory. There was a genuine discrepancy between the law courts and the political consciousness, not just in Germany, but elsewhere also. And when military historians can ignore the

---

[264] *Gallup Polls, Great Britain, 1937–1975*, ed. Gallup, 238; PRO, PREM 8/1570, CP (51) 38, secret memo by Minister of State, 6 Feb. 1951; PRO, FO 1060/497, Hancock to Herchenroder, 3 Sept. 1952; PRO, FO 1060/497, Roberts to Kirkpatrick, 13 Sept. 1952; on the USA, see Schwarz, 'Die Begnadigung deutscher Kriegsverbrecher', 402.

[265] Herf, *Divided Memory*, 202–3.

criminal nature of Barbarossa—indeed, glorify it as a symbol of human heroism, as does at least one popular study—the danger of its marginalization in the history of twentieth-century genocide remains to this day.[266]

[266] Alan Clark, *Barbarossa* (London: Weidenfeld and Nicolson, 1995). The preface concludes with this poem: 'Two things have altered not, since first the World began, The beauty of the wild green earth and the bravery of man'.

Part III: The Trials and Posterity

CHAPTER FIVE

A Nuremberg Historiography of the Holocaust?

If the role of the Wehrmacht has recently been the subject of great popular debate, the scholarly scene of the last decade has also witnessed a flowering of specialist revelation on the crimes of the German police. Whether or not they were affiliated directly to the SS, it seems that almost every police grouping was involved at some level in the murder process, whether hunting Jews and others, guarding, them or shooting them. As the circle of complicity has grown, it has also incorporated the civilian administrations of the occupied and annexed eastern European territories. In the 'occupation climate',[1] these often corrupt agencies acted with colonial arrogance, and when required to conform to the murderous norm they did so, for the most part, with aplomb.

Unlike Wehrmacht criminality, little of this was established in the Allied courts with repercussions, it seems, for the history books: parallel absences in these media suggest the extent to which the historiography has been influenced by 'Nuremberg'. In part, the regular police and civilian functionaries benefited from the same public ignorance in the liberal democracies that served the Wehrmacht: the SS, and particularly the Gestapo, were seen as the sole malefactors.[2] In part also, only limited evidence was available to the prosecutors. However, the structure and priorities of the prosecution programmes and the particular uses of the Nazi documentation that was available also played a significant role in a process of inadvertent concealment. Two examples will be used in illustration: the first is the prosecution of the lesser-known elements of Himmler's SS and police empire, with particular reference to crimes against the Jews; the second is the treatment of crimes in the Reichskommissariat Ostland, the area incorporating the Baltic states, most of Belorussia, and parts of north-eastern Poland.

Succeeding these examinations, and mindful again of Hilberg's connection between detail and conceptual explanation, the chapter considers some of the explicit interpretative bequests of the trials. The number and diversity of people, and the complex of organizations involved in genocide raises fundamental questions of mass motivation on one hand, and, on the other, of the nature of decision-making and policy implementation. The 'Nuremberg legacy' will be assessed in two related areas. We shall first consider the homogenization of the

---

[1] Dieter Pohl, *Nationalsozialistische Judenverfolgung in Ostgalizien 1941–1944: Organisation und Durchführung eines staatlichen Massenverbrechens* (Munich: Oldenbourg, 1996).

[2] e.g. Smith, *The Road to Nuremberg*, 52–3.

motivations for Nazi genocide, and the simplification of the decision-making structure of the agencies of the Third Reich, which contributed to the misapprehensions of the 'intentionalist' school of Holocaust historiography and the elision of the dynamic relationships between different power strata in Nazi-occupied Europe. The shortcomings of the resulting Nuremberg model of the Holocaust are then drawn out with reference to the problematic concept of Jewish labour during the war, and to understandings of the term 'extermination through work'.

While the first two sections of the chapter are indicative of the priorities of the Allied prosecutors, which did not accommodate many investigations that might seem of great import to the historian of today, the second two are illustrative of what the trials produced 'in spite', as it were, of the relative diminution of the Jewish fate. Indeed, given the prevailing failure in the post-war courts to establish the proportional—let alone conceptual—importance of the Shoah, the achievements of the early Holocaust historians are still to be marvelled at as works of authority and insight. Raul Hilberg's work in particular has been vital in pointing the way to present-day research on the size and inclusivity of the 'machinery of destruction'.

5.1 LEGAL OMISSIONS (I): THE SS AND POLICE

The prosecution of the SS, and within that the Gestapo, was pivotal in OCC-PAC's and OCCWC's pursuit of the 'conspiracy-criminal organization' theory. It was an integral part of the first of the three pillars that Telford Taylor identified as Nazism, militarism, and economic imperialism. The IMT specifically declared criminal the Gestapo and SD, and the border police (Grenzpolizei), and the SS as a whole, including the Allgemeine-SS, the Waffen-SS, the SS-Totenkopfverbände, and 'any of the different police forces who were members'.[3] Telford Taylor's staff went on to examine in greater depth several of the facets of the SS and its affiliates, namely the WVHA, the Einsatzgruppen, the SS scientific and medical services, and, in the 'RuSHA' trial, a series of offices concerned with the reordering of Europe along 'racial' grounds.

Few would dispute the criminal nature of these groups. However, with the benefit of hindsight, a proportional representation of SS and police criminality would have demanded specific condemnations of other organizations and personnel. The higher SS and police leaders (Höheren SS- und Polizeiführer, or HSSPFs), the Reich detective police (Kriminalpolizei, or Kripo, office-group V of the RSHA), and the Order Police (Ordnungspolizei, or Orpo) are particularly striking omissions from the IMT judgement and the subsequent Nuremberg trials. Moreover, a substantial OCCWC investigation of the Waffen-SS, which had cursorily been declared criminal by the IMT, would have been desirable, not

---

[3] *IMT* i, 267–73. The IMT exonerated the SS Riding Corps, an organization that was actually implicated in mass murder.

least in the struggle against the dissemination of the myth of that institution's innocence in relation to the crimes of the SS as a whole.[4]

Telford Taylor has, however, recounted that it was essential when faced with the enormous collapsed Reich to draw certain '*a priori* conclusions about the *locus* of responsibility for crimes known to have been committed'.[5] It was axiomatic that some of these assumptions would be proved correct and others not. Thus, for instance, some of the organizations concerned in the RuSHA trial, their grand titles and unpleasant aspirations notwithstanding, were not as important in the implementation of Nazi racial policy as were others. As preconceptions about concentration camps were developed partially from impressions of the pre-war manifestations of Dachau and Buchenwald, so the depiction of the Gestapo was doubtless influenced by the 'totalitarian' model of an all-powerful secret police pervading the whole of German society throughout the Hitler era, in contrast to the undermanned, underfunded organization that it frequently was.[6] Similarly its pre-war reputation guaranteed that the SA was regularly used as a prime example of a criminal organization, though by wartime it had been marginalized.[7] Thus, even in 1947, Lucius Clay—a man who had a considerable interest in the progress of the trials—could confuse the SS with the 'stormtroopers' as the subject of an ongoing case.[8]

Many of these preoccupations were shared by those involved in the investigation of 'war crimes'. 'Gestapo' became almost a byword for the issue of criminal organizations before the IMT trial. Robert Jackson's conception of the trial of the major war criminals was represented by Hartley Shawcross as being against 'Göring and the Gestapo'.[9] This is not to imply that the Gestapo was over-investigated: the most insidious of that organization's organs, Eichmann's Judenreferat IVB4, was given scant direct attention in the immediate aftermath of the war, because of the circumscription of the investigation that developed into the Einsatzgruppen trial.[10] Rather, it is to suggest that the Allies believed they had located *the* criminal power-centres in Göring, the Gestapo, and, of course, the concentration camps and their authorities.

The more discerning authorities on the question realized that 'many crimes have been vaguely ascribed to the Gestapo by newspapermen or the man in the

---

[4] On this myth, see Charles W. Sydnor, 'The History of the SS Totenkopfdivision and the Postwar Mythology of the Waffen SS', *Central European History*, 6 (1973), 339–62. For a summary of the crimes of the Waffen-SS as a salutary reminder in the amnesiac times in which former members were being called to the service of the Bundeswehr, see B. Sagalowitz, 'Les Waffen-SS et la Nouvelle Armée Allemande', *Le Monde Juif*, nos. 75–6 (1956–7), 54–7.

[5] Taylor, *Final Report*, 76.

[6] Robert Gellately, *The Gestapo and German Society: Enforcing Racial Policy, 1933–1945* (Oxford: Clarendon Press, 1990).

[7] Smith, *The Road to Nuremberg*, 51–3.

[8] *Clay Papers*, ed. Smith, i, 420–1, Clay for Noce, 8 Sept. 1947.

[9] PRO, LCO 2/2980, minutes of meeting of committee on war crimes, 5 June 1945. See also u4628/29/73, 12 June 1945, on war criminals and the IMT.

[10] The RSHA was additionally all but ignored in the BRD: see below, Chapter 5.3.

street of the occupied countries but it is not impossible that some of them were
committed by other bodies such as the Sicherheitspolizei [*sic*], the Ordnungspolizei, or other branches of the SS'.[11] A handbook on concentration camps
drawn up by the political intelligence department of the Foreign Office in April
1945 identified several equally culpable bodies which deserved their 'share of the
blame which is associated in the public mind with the term Gestapo', yet the
authors deemed that to depart from the use of that catch-all term would be 'mere
pedantry'.[12]

With specific reference to the murder of the Jews, it was not until the discovery early in 1947 of the minutes of the infamous Wannsee conference that modi-
fications were made to the image of the SS as the sole fulcrum of the process.
However, the evidence had in-built limitations. The minutes, produced only in
time for the penultimate of the subsequent proceedings, precipitated investigations into the role of other culpable agencies of the Third Reich, such as the government ministries.[13] The conference was held in January 1942 in preparation
for the European-wide 'final solution' and contained little reference to the murders that had already occurred in Poland and the USSR, nor the many agencies
involved in those crimes. The elision of the immense complex of police, military
and civilian offices implicated in the annihilation of the Jews of the Pale of Settlement was exaggerated by the agenda of the conference convenor. As we have
seen, Reinhard Heydrich, head of the RSHA, wished to use the meeting to re-
affirm the authority of himself and his office in the developing 'final solution',
whilst securing the support of and implicating all the organizations he had invited.[14] Adolf Eichmann, Heydrich's subordinate, drew up the minutes to his
master's satisfaction.

In as much as the fate of the Jews was investigated at the IMT trial, the emphasis was predominantly on the killing centres. The very basic division between
murder by gas and by bullet was drawn, but the latter was the subject of surprisingly little attention, with the 'horror camps' holding sway. Little documentation was adduced on localized massacres because little had by then been found,
and much remained hidden for years afterwards, concealed in Soviet archives.
Indeed, it is doubtful that much evidence had been sought in the preparations for
the trial of the major war criminals, for the role of mobile killing squads was unclear in the investigators' minds. The major witness to these murders was the
aforementioned Otto Ohlendorf, erstwhile head of office-group 6 (one of the two
SD offices) of the RSHA, and of Einsatzgruppe D. The American prosecutor,
Whitney Harris, recalls how Ohlendorf was only sent to Nuremberg specula-
tively by his British captors, and that his new interrogators considered him only

[11] PRO, WO 219/3585, observations by Ecer, 10 Apr. 1945. Ecer was himself not altogether sure of the
differences between various perpetrating bodies—the Gestapo was in fact a component of the Sicherheitspolizei—nor of the unimportance during wartime of the SA, which he also included alongside the SS
at the end of this statement.

[12] PRO, LCO 2/2980, u3430/16/73, Political Intelligence Department to LCO, Apr. 1945, fo. 416.

[13] Kempner, *Ankläger eine Epoche*, 310–12.   [14] Longerich, *Die Wannsee-Konferenz*, 26.

to be a potential source of information on intelligence issues arising from his service in the former capacity. Ohlendorf then proved surprisingly willing to expand upon his murderous past. As Harris has said, he 'wrote the Einsatzgruppen case'.[15]

The discovery around the turn of 1946–7 of the Ereignismeldungen UdSSR (operational-situational reports) and the Meldungen aus den besetzten Ostgebieten (reports from the occupied eastern territories), which chronicled in great detail the activities of the Einsatzgruppen, spurred the plan to prosecute a number of their former leaders, with Ohlendorf to appear as chief defendant.[16] We know that these documents were highly esteemed by OCCWC, and that their seemingly uncomplicated and conclusive nature ultimately facilitated the Einsatzgruppen trial.[17] The simplicity of the case itself was, however, problematic in the establishment of the bigger picture, because the documents were not the faithful record the prosecutors assumed them to be.

It was an understandable and enduring characteristic of the post-war trials that prosecutors and judges alike found it hard to comprehend that perpetrators like Ohlendorf had taken a professional pride in their murderous work, even to the point of exaggerating the numbers of the dead; hence part of Jackson's reluctance to use these murderers as witnesses. Likewise, in the general belief in conspiracies to murder, little cognisance was taken of the fact that different agencies actually competed against each other for influence in the killing process.[18] The Einsatzgruppen reports were thus taken at face value, when in fact they concealed much about internecine rivalry.

The reports had originally been submitted to Heydrich after careful editing by Heinrich Müller, head of the Gestapo, and they were constructed to maximize the role of the Sicherheitspolizei (which formed most of the leadership corps of the Einsatzgruppen) in the exterminations in eastern Europe, to the detriment of the 'achievements' of other organizations. The contributions of the HSSPFs, of whom more later, were insufficiently acknowledged, as were those of auxiliary police forces (both German and local) and militias, and even those of the SD, the other main constituents of the RSHA.[19] Thus the main body of legal and historical evidence on itinerant killing organizations fed directly into the preconceptions of the Allied prosecutors and publics about the extent of Nazi criminality. Criminal proceedings in the BRD were the first to consider in any

---

[15] Whitney Harris, conference paper ('Nuremberg and Its Impact: Fifty Years Later'), US Library of Congress, 16 Nov. 1996; interview with Whitney Harris, in *Voices from the Holocaust*, ed. Harry James Cargas (Kentucky: University of Kentucky Press, 1993), 97–115, esp. 110–11. A roster of internees at the Nuremberg jail from 1 Dec. 1945 listed Ohlendorf only as 'Deputy to the Reich Minister of Economics'. See Dodd papers, box 320, file 'Prisoner lists 1945 Aug.–1946 Jan.'

[16] Kempner, *Ankläger eine Epoche*, 293; Ronald Headland, *Messages of Murder* (Cranbury, NJ: Associated University Presses, 1992), 14.

[17] See above, Chapter 2.

[18] For a case study of this phenomenon, see Christopher Browning, *The Final Solution and the German Foreign Office* (New York: Holmes and Meier, 1978).

[19] Headland, *Messages of Murder*, 188.

detail the role of police forces other than the stereotyped Gestapo and its RSHA affiliates.

Until very recently, and in some cases right down to the present day, the stereotypical composite picture of the 'final solution' handed down in general histories has been of Einsatzgruppen killings followed by camp killings. Surveys in English by Michael Marrus, Ronnie Landau, Dan Cohn-Sherbok, Lucy Dawidowicz, and Wolfgang Benz,[20] to give an incomplete list, have marginalized the other formations that massacred Jews in Soviet and Polish territory in 1941–2. To identify this phenomenon is not to exhibit the 'mere pedantry' suggested by the Foreign Office's Political Intelligence Department. First it is a straightforward matter of historical representation, for the importance of the Einsatzgruppen in the murder process varied greatly from area to area. Secondly, it opens up important questions of mass participation and individual motivation.

The Order Police was one of the largest contributors of personnel for shooting massacres in Poland from 1941 onwards and, to a lesser extent during 1941, the USSR. They provided around 19,000 men for the police presence in these countries, with the Einsatzgruppen contributing roughly 6,000 and Himmler's personal 'Kommandostab' 25,000.[21] While the latter two organizations and the Waffen-SS, which also provided thousands of killers functioning within and alongside them, can be considered generally to be strongly indoctrinated and to exhibit a high degree of identification with the aims of Nazism, this was not necessarily the case with the Order Police.

The Order Police may for our purposes be sub-divided into two groups: the career police and the reservists.[22] The latter were neither highly trained nor greatly indoctrinated, with comparatively low rates of membership of the Nazi party and the SS. Their tasks generally extended only to normal policing duties; indeed, many were considered unfit for military service. Yet entire battalions were directly co-opted to kill Jews and other 'undesirables' *in situ* in eastern Europe or to provide logistical support in the massacres; such units were also in whole or in part seconded as additional manpower to the Einsatzgruppen, in which capacity they served as did any members of those genocidal outfits.

[20] Michael Marrus, *The Holocaust in History* (Harmondsworth: Penguin, 1989); Ronnie Landau, *The Nazi Holocaust* (London: Tauris, 1992); id., *Studying the Holocaust* (London: Routledge, 1998); Dan Cohn-Sherbok, *Understanding the Holocaust* (London: Cassell, 1999); Lucy Dawidowicz, *The War Against the Jews, 1933–1945* (London: Penguin, 1987); Wolfgang Benz, *The Holocaust: A Short History* (London: Profile Books, 2000).

[21] On the Order Police: Christopher Browning, *Ordinary Men: Reserve Police Battalion 101 and the Final Solution in Poland* (New York: Harper, 1992); Daniel Jonah Goldhagen, *Hitler's Willing Executioners: Ordinary Germans and the Holocaust* (London: Abacus, 1997); more generally, in terms of organization and administration: Heiner Lichtenstein, *Himmler's grüne Helfer: Die Schutz- und Ordnungspolizei im 'Dritten Reich'* (Cologne: Bund, 1990). On the structures and deployment of some Order Police units, Hans-Joachim Neufeldt *et al.*, *Zur Geschichte der Ordnungspolizei 1936–1945* (Koblenz: Bundesarchiv, 1957). For the estimates advanced above, see Goldhagen, *Hitler's Willing Executioners*, 167.

[22] See Christopher Browning, *Nazi Policy, Jewish Workers, German Killers* (Cambridge: Cambridge University Press, 2000), 168–9, on the greater readiness to murder of the career policemen.

Why these 'ordinary men' were for the most part prepared to kill people for whom initially they had little demonstrable dislike became a central matter for historical debate in the 1990s. The obvious inference is that antisemitism itself was not always the incentive to murder. Nor, however, were these non-antisemites necessarily obliged to kill under the weight of senior orders: those who wished not to participate did not meet with draconian punishment, and on occasion the possibility to opt out was presented to them.

Unlike much current scholarship on Nazi policy in eastern Europe,[23] the rediscovery of the role of the Order Police is not a function of the post-Cold War opening of archives in the last decade. New documentation has enabled a more detailed empirical recreation of events in Poland and the USSR, but the existing historical and sociological analyses of the Order Police's actions are derived from trials conducted decades ago in the BRD. Even in 1945 the potential did exist to uncover something of the Order Police's role, but circumstances dictated that disclosures were not made, either in the courtroom or in the early history books.

The detailed information on the formations and roles of killing squads in eastern Europe compiled by the Bletchley Park code-breakers was, owing to its top secret classification, not made available at Nuremberg, and has only recently come to light in studies of Allied awareness of the murder of the Jews. However, contrary to what Richard Breitman has written, the absence of this intelligence was not the main obstacle to trial of the relevant SS leaders. Breitman suggests that the Nuremberg prosecutors did not target the head of the Order Police, SS-Obergruppenführer Kurt Daluege, because of a lack of available information.[24] This is not borne out by the facts. Daluege was certainly extradited to the Czechs for his actions as Protector of Bohemia and Moravia between mid-1942 and September 1943, and was consequently tried and executed in Prague in October 1946. Yet his connection with the Order Police had been emphasized previously, and there is no indication that the Allied authorities believed his claims of the organization's innocence.[25]

First there was some awareness before the end of the war that the Order Police as a whole had been extensively involved in criminal activities, and specifically that certain units had been actively complicit in 'security' policy and 'population control' in the occupied east.[26] Secondly, Daluege himself *was* a target of OCCPAC, with Jackson pressing for his inclusion in the IMT trial.[27] Anthony Eden had also listed him as one of the major enemy war criminals in June 1944 as

---

[23] e.g. the work of the contributors to Ulrich Herbert (ed.), *Nationalsozialistische Vernichtungspolitik: Neue Forschungen und Kontroversen* (Frankfurt am Main: Fischer, 1997).

[24] Breitman, *Official Secrets*, 221–2.

[25] A view expressed in e.g. *Telegraf* (14 Apr. 1946).

[26] PRO, WO 219/3585, Observations by Ecer, 10 Apr. 1945; WO 208/4448, Directorate of Military Intelligence personality file, incl. report of 29 May 1942; (subsequently) FO 371/57630, v2493/2493/73, 19 Feb. 1946.

[27] PRO, FO 1019/86, meeting of BWCE, 26 Sept. 1945 in which 'Delueger [*sic*]' was discussed; Jackson's pressure was recorded in a progress report, 3 Nov. 1945.

head of the Order Police as well as Protector of Bohemia and Moravia[28] and he had appeared on lists of possible defendants before the IMT.[29] It may well be that he did not appear alongside Göring simply because he was not a 'household name', though his influence was acknowledged, particularly amongst the BWCE and the Foreign Office officials connected with the case.[30] The number of defendants in the case may also have been a prime concern. Had his health allowed it, however,[31] there is a very strong possibility that Daluege would have been tried in part as a representative of the SS and police system.[32]

Yet there is a danger of being drawn into a circular argument in discussing the presence to hand or otherwise of appropriate evidence, for the *a priori* allocation of criminal responsibility by the hard-pressed Allied prosecution staffs meant that—as indeed in the preparations for the Doctors' trial—the hectic search for substantiation of charges might well begin after the decision to indict had been made.[33] Practical reasons, and the priorities of OCCWC, which did not include emphasizing the murder of the Jews, are the most probable reasons why Daluege was never tried in the 'west'.

In contrast to Daluege, Kaltenbrunner was tried as a major war criminal, and Pohl as chief defendant in the fourth subsequent Nuremberg trial. In addition, four other heads of SS-Hauptämter, along with several of their subordinates, were tried in the subsequent proceedings. The trials brought forth a vast corpus of accessible evidence on all facets of the organizations headed by these men. Daluege's trial concentrated on his involvement in regional-specific crimes, such as the destruction of Lidice and the deportation of Czech Jews. The marginalization of the functions of the Order Police as effected in the trial of its most senior member was not amended within the legal framework, for no other high-ranking members were tried after the war; and as we have seen, the main body of Nuremberg evidence that could most clearly have revealed its complicity—namely the Einsatzgruppen reports—did not.

The breadth of SS and police aberrance was personified in forty-seven individuals appointed by, and directly answerable to, Heinrich Himmler, the man at the head of the entire complex from 1936. The higher SS and police leaders were created in 1938 in each administrative district specifically to give Himmler a channel of authority over SS and police formations separate from those of the SS head offices. The HSSPFs were intended to have authority over the other police formations in joint actions of those organizations.

[28] PRO WO 32/10790, WP (44) 330, treatment of major enemy war criminals.

[29] PRO FO 371/57583, minute attached to Scott-Fox to German Dept. of FO, 7 June 1946.

[30] These facts were appreciated by the FO. See PRO, FO 371/57630, v2493/2493/73, profile of Daluege, 19 Feb. 1946. On 'household names', see FO 1019/86, BWCE meeting, 26 Sept. 1945.

[31] Whether or not Daluege did have congenital syphilis, a condition of which Breitman is sceptical, the British certainly thought that he did. See FO 1019/86, BWCE meeting, 26 Sept. 1945, and the related minutes by Beaumont and Passant.

[32] PRO, FO 1019/86, minutes of BWCE meeting, 26 Sept. 1945; WO 311/39, Maxwell-Fyfe to BWCE, 25 Jan. 1946; FO 371/57583, u1236, Maxwell-Fyfe's communique of 25 Nov. 1946.

[33] Weindling, 'Ärzte als Richter'.

Though the HSSPFs were frequently marginalized in the territories of the Reich, where the lines of power were better established, and where the competitiveness of Himmler's underlings and other agencies prohibited entry into an overcrowded market, in the occupied territories influence was 'up for grabs'.[34] Here, the HSSPFs had a genuine authority over all SS and police forces in their respective regions, and hence a large stake in genocide. Thus the conglomerate forces of Frederick Jeckeln, HSSPF for the southern Soviet Union (based in Kiev), amongst which were Order Policemen, murdered 44,125 Jews in August 1941 alone. It seems that he began to murder all Jews, irrespective of age or gender, even before the Einsatzgruppe C in the vicinity.[35] So influential was Jeckeln in the developing murder process that in October 1941 a subsection of Einsatzgruppe C, Einsatzkommando 4a, anxiously reported back to Berlin that it, too, had been involved in the killings, which were not the achievement of the HSSPF alone.[36] Dieter Pohl's study of the operations of Einsatzgruppe C in fact reveals that the squad 'had nowhere near the significance for the war of annihilation in the Ukraine that is often attributed to it': of the approximately 1.4 million Jews murdered there, the Einsatzgruppe claimed to have accounted for approximately 118,000, all except 45,000 of whom were killed in conjunction with the forces of the HSSPF.[37]

Jeckeln's counterpart in the central area of the occupied Soviet Union, HSSPF Erich von dem Bach-Zelewski, was equally important in the development of the 'final solution'. As with Jeckeln, when the murder of Soviet Jewry intensified in mid-July 1941, he was accorded regional authority over the vastly increased manpower of the SS brigades and police battalions now assigned to the USSR.[38] He both orchestrated a large proportion of the murders in the area and was personally present at some of the most significant massacres, acting to incite the shooters.[39]

Though there was obviously no trial of the HSSPFs, again we must take issue with Richard Breitman's claim that owing to the absence of German police decodes there was insufficient evidence to target individuals for prosecution. It seems that a number of HSSPFs *were* originally considered for trial either in a separate trial or alongside members of the RSHA. However, neither option was pursued because of manpower shortages within the OCCWC and the circumscribed nature of the Einsatzgruppen case.[40] In any event, we know that the

34 Hans Buchheim *et al.*, *Anatomie des SS-Staates*, 2 vols. (Olten and Freiburg im Breisgau: Walter Verlag, 1965), i, 133–4.

35 Heinz Höhne, *The Order of the Death's Head* (London: Pan, 1972), 333; Christopher Browning, *The Path to Genocide: Essays on Launching the Final Solution* (Cambridge: Cambridge University Press, 1992), 108–9.

36 Ruth Bettina Birn, *Die Höheren SS-und Polizeiführer: Himmlers Vertreter im Reich und in den besetzten Gebiete* (Düsseldorf: Droste, 1986), 171–2.

37 Pohl, 'Die Einsatzgruppe C'.   38 Browning, *Ordinary Men*, 10–11.

39 Ibid, 12–15, 24–5.

40 NARA, RG 238, OCCWC, Berlin branch, correspondence 1946, box 3, Walton to Taylor, 17 Mar. 1947; Walton to Sachs, 22 Mar. 1947.

investigation was of a low priority in the context of OCCWC's broader aims. None of the HSSPFs was tried for their crimes in that capacity by a British or an American court, and, despite their central importance in genocide, that class of criminal appears to have escaped almost as lightly in the historiography of the Third Reich, with only one serious monograph devoted to them.[41] Finally, and also in contrast to Breitman's insinuation that von dem Bach-Zelewski's preparedness to testify against other defendants kept him out of trouble with OCCWC, he was considered as a defendant in an abortive trial against the suppressers of the Warsaw uprising in 1944.[42]

The most notable HSSPF absentee from any Allied dock was Karl Wolff, and his fate is testament to the political factors that were simply beyond the control of any prosecutor. Wolff had previously been Himmler's adjutant, the SS liaison officer with Hitler's headquarters, and one of only three holders of the rank, Höchste SS- und Polizeiführer (Highest SS and Police Leader). He was implicated in crimes against humanity, and specifically against Jews, and as a result of his status was in any case suitable for indictment before the IMT—for which he was considered[43]—alongside Kaltenbrunner, who was inadequate as sole representative of the SS, the Gestapo, and the SD.[44] Wolff had figured highly on Allied lists of war criminals,[45] and an impression of his attitude towards the criminal practices of the SS can be gleaned from a notorious commendation to Himmler in 1942 in which he wrote of his 'besondere Freude'—his 'particular joy'—at the deportation of 5,000 Warsaw Jews per day to Treblinka.[46] The Americans did not try him, however, despite the fact that towards the end of the IMT trial he was on their daily interrogation list.[47]

The omission of Wolff was a result of services rendered by him in the closing days of the war in Europe. He had liaised with the OSS in order to effect a premature German surrender, ostensibly to prevent further unnecessary destruction and loss of life on the continent, but clearly also with a view to securing his future after the impending collapse of the Reich. The clandestine links established between SS intelligence and the OSS were the channel for a number of different bids for the role of peacemaker, with both Himmler and Kaltenbrunner

[41] See Birn, *Die Höheren SS- und Polizeiführer*, where only 168–85 focus upon the Holocaust; previously, the most detailed accounts were in: Hans Buchheim, 'Die Höheren SS und Polizeiführer', *VfZ*, 11 (1963), 362–91; Hans Buchheim et al., *Anatomie des SS Staates*, 2 vols. (Freiburg im Breisgau: Walter Verlag, 1965), i, 133–71.

[42] NARA, RG 153, Nürnberg administrative files, 1944–9, box 13, Taylor to Deputy Military Governor, 14 Mar. 1947, p. 10.

[43] PRO FO 1019/86, meeting of BWCE, 26 Sept. 1945.

[44] Robinson, 'The International Military Tribunal and the Holocaust', 608–20; Bradley F. Smith and Elena Agarossi, *Operation Sunrise: The Secret Surrender* (London: Andre Deutsch, 1979), 189. The other IMT defendants holding SS ranks did so in an honorary capacity.

[45] e.g. PRO, FO 1019/86, minutes of BWCE meeting, 26 Sept. 1945; minutes of meeting of Nuremberg chief prosecutors, 23 Aug. 1945.

[46] Nuremberg Document NO-2207.

[47] Dodd papers, box 321, file 'Documents concerning trial organisation and procedure', daily interrogation list Apr.–Aug. 1946.

vying to fill it at different times, both attempting to halt the ongoing murder of the Jews in the camps as their side of an imaginary bargain. However, the blatant guilt of the head of the SS and his plenipotentiary was such that neither were credible negotiators, and neither could cheat the ultimate reckoning, realization dawning upon Himmler rather sooner than Kaltenbrunner. Wolff's record was not so obviously black, and he was able to secure the trust variously of Allen Dulles of the OSS and the US Generals Airey and Lemnitzer, all of whom were prepared to testify on his behalf in the event of trial.[48] Indeed, it seems likely that he was given an informal assurance that he would not face legal proceedings.[49]

These 'diplomatic obstacles' to the trial of Wolff proved insurmountable for the OCCWC, as an official in the evidence division confided to the British liaison officer at Nuremberg.[50] The problem was transferred onto British shoulders in 1948 after an extradition order. It was then solved when Wolff was subjected to the tender mercies of a denazification tribunal that sentenced him to time already served.[51] The verdict was certainly influenced by his American patrons, who proved true to their word. Additionally, it is probable that the Governor of the British zone, General Robertson, exerted some pressure on behalf of the defendant.[52] A more comprehensive reckoning with Wolff's wartime activities had to wait until the 1960s, when in the aftermath of the Eichmann trial he was sentenced by a court of the BRD to fifteen years' forced labour for his 'complicity' (*Beihilfe*) in the murder of approximately 300,000 Jews.[53]

The horse-trading around Wolff's disposition was unfortunately all too common as the Second World War was supplanted by the Cold War.[54] It could be said that, just as during the Holocaust the aiding of the Jews by the Allies was subordinated to the effort to win the war, afterwards the will to punish those responsible for the genocide was often undermined by the determination to gain a decisive superiority over the USSR. On the level of 'minor' criminals, the role of the US in recruiting scientists and former Nazi intelligence agents with dubious wartime records has been well charted.[55]

It is counterfactual to consider whether wider perceptions of the Holocaust would have been altered by the trial of any of the aforementioned who escaped justice. Given the elementary popular understanding of its events and nature,

---

[48] Smith and Agarossi, *Operation Sunrise*, 188–91; NARA, RG 260, OMGUS, Adjutant-General files, box 325, Lemnitzer to Clay, Sept. 1948.

[49] Dodd papers, box 324, file 'Interrogation summaries 1945 Sep.–Nov.', report on interrogation of Wolff, 31 Aug. 1945.

[50] PRO, FO 1060/1392, N. G. Barr to Mercer, 21 Apr. 1948.

[51] 'Sie gehen mit fleckenlosem Kleid', *Aufbau* (1 July 1949); Wolff was thus not acquitted, contrary to what Smith and Agarossi, and Black, respectively, maintain.

[52] NARA, RG 260, OMGUS, Adjutant-General files, Clay to Army Dept., Aug. 1948.

[53] Michel Mazor, 'Le procès de Karl Wolff', *Le Monde Juif*, no. 45 (1967), 23–8.

[54] For details of lesser criminals receiving 'consideration' by the Allies, see Donald Bloxham 'The Holocaust on Trial', Ph.D. thesis (Southampton, 1998), ch. 5, section i (a).

[55] See e.g. Christopher Simpson, *Blowback: The First Full Account of America's Recruitment of Nazis, and Its Disastrous Effect on Our Domestic and Foreign Policy* (New York: Collier, 1989); Tom Bower, *The Paperclip Conspiracy* (London: Grafton, 1988).

the addition of extra defendants or supplementary trials at Nuremberg would likely have little changed the general construction of what Lord Russell of Liverpool called 'the scourge of the swastika'. On the level of historiography, and specifically that concerning the SS and police, the considerations are rather different, and the potential value of thoroughly documented trials of Daluege, Wolff, and their underlings is great. The same applies to Gruppenführer Artur Nebe, former head of the Kriminalpolizei and of Einsatzgruppe B, who died before capture and his planned trial; and to any of the plethora of heads of SS offices and their subsections who were considered for trial, like Adolf Eichmann in the first instance, or like the (probably) deceased Heinrich 'Gestapo' Müller and Richard Glücks,[56] former Inspector of Concentration Camps, and Wilhelm Burger and Gerhardt Maurer of WVHA Amtsgruppe D, who were apprehended too late for arraignment in the Pohl case;[57] and to all the HSSPFs and to the Waffen-SS leadership. Bearing in mind that the SS was at the centre of Allied perceptions of Nazi criminality, there was greater potential still for misplaced emphasis in fields of less concern.

It has been observed that the total geographical scope of the Holocaust was not accounted for by the IMT.[58] This was true also of the subsequent Nuremberg tribunals and exaggeratedly so in the Royal Warrant series. In examining one particular area, the lands comprising Alfred Rosenberg's eastern empire, we shall see how Anglo-American trial policy prevented full consideration of the Jewish catastrophe in one of the most blood-soaked regions of all Europe.

5.2 LEGAL OMISSIONS (II): THE 'OSTLAND' CRIMINALS

On 17 July 1941 Hitler appointed Rosenberg Minister for the Occupied Eastern Territories, a post with responsibility for the civil government of the Ukraine, parts of Belorussia, and north-eastern Poland, Latvia, Lithuania, and Estonia. The final five of these regions, when lumped together, formed that area known in Nazi-German parlance as the 'Reichskommissariat Ostland'. The murder of the Jews in these territories of the former Soviet Union has been somewhat marginalized in the western historiography of the Shoah, chiefly because most of the relevant documentation fell into Soviet hands at the end of the war,[59] but also because the evidence produced by the local war crimes commissions was rather distrusted in the west, though it is now used, if carefully, by some of the most discerning scholars of the regional development of the Holocaust.

---

[56] PRO, FO 1019/86, progress report no. 1, 3 Nov. 1945; Maxwell-Fyfe's list of possible defendants in a second IMT trial, 11 Mar. 1946.

[57] NARA, RG 260, OCCWC, witnesses and defendants of Special Projects Division, box 2, file 'Program—war crimes trials', Taylor to Chief of Staff, OMGUS, 20 May 1947.

[58] Robinson, 'The International Military Tribunal and the Holocaust'.

[59] Margers Vestermanis, 'Der "Holocaust" in Lettland: Zur "postkommunistischen" Aufarbeitung des Themas in Osteuropa', in Arno Herzig and Ina Lorenz (eds.), *Verdrängung und Vernichtung der Juden unter den Nationalsozialismus* (Hamburg: Hans Christians Verlag, 1992), 101–30, esp. 107.

The activities of Einsatzgruppe A, the most notorious organization to operate in the area, and the most murderous of the Einsatzgruppen, were documented in the operational-situational reports, and representatives of the squad were tried in the subsequent Nuremberg proceedings. Beyond the police groupings, there were two other German concerns that, during 1941 at least, had considerable influence over the disposition of Jews. Unfortunately, the records of both the civil administration and the military authority remained inaccessible until the fall of Communism. Moreover, a third group that influenced the conduct of mass murder but avoided the public record until recently were the local collaborators.

Prime representatives of each of these echelons were actually in Allied custody, but none was exposed because of the quirks of trial policy. First, we have Victor Arajs and his confederates, members of the Latvian auxiliary unit that massacred thousands in the Riga ghetto and throughout the country, at the instigation of the Einsatzgruppe leader, Walther Stahlecker.[60] Their deeds were originally brought to British attention in the second quarter of 1948, but the trial of the suspects was postponed, despite protests from Jewish groups.[61] By the time the authorities came to consider the matter at the end of the year, there was no longer a court with competent jurisdiction. German courts had not yet been authorized to consider cases in which Allied nationals were the victims, and the requisites of British foreign policy had determined that no more cases of crimes against humanity could be tried in control commission courts after October 1948.[62]

This situation was consistent with the prevailing trend in British trial policy, and with the political climate in an era when the Labour government, like its American counterpart, had actively discouraged Jewish 'displaced persons' from entering the country. Simultaneously, they were encouraging the immigration of Baltic and Ukrainian workers, some of whom were suspected of collaboration with the Nazis in genocide.[63] It is no less remarkable that Arajs managed to find work early in 1949 as a driver for a military unit in the British zone of Germany after his release from custody following a writ of *habeas corpus*. His record was unknown to his new employers, as was the fact that subsequently the German authorities were seeking him for trial.[64] The case had been handed over to the provincial court (Landgericht) in Hamburg, where twenty years later it was still

[60] Ibid. 107.

[61] For the initial registration of the case, PRO, WO 267/602, report for the quarter ended 30 June 1948. See also FO 371/77060, CG 3545/15/184, Foreign Office to Lübbecke, 29 Nov. 1949, concerning representations made by the committee for the Investigation of Nazi Crimes in the Baltic Countries. Cf. CG 496/15/184, Elwyn-Jones to Bevin, 9 Feb. 1949.

[62] PRO, FO 1060/267, minute by Deputy Legal Advisor (Political), 16 Feb. 1950.

[63] Cesarani, *Justice Delayed*; Allan Ryan, *Quiet Neighbours: Prosecuting Nazi War Criminals in America* (New York: Harcourt Brace Jovanovich, 1984).

[64] PRO, FO 371/77060, CG 3545/15/184, FO to Lübbecke, 29 Nov. 1949; CG 3709/15/184, Starke to Maxwell-Fyfe, 30 Nov. 1949.

being pursued with a considerable lack of enthusiasm.[65] Arajs was only brought to trial there in 1979, whereupon he was sentenced to life imprisonment.[66]

Next is Hinrich Lohse, former Reichskommissar of the Ostland. As holder of the office of Gauleiter (district chief) Lohse was also a high-ranking Nazi party official. Like many of the leaders of the civil administration in the 'Occupied Eastern Territories', he had played as significant a role as any representative of an organization involved in anti-Jewish policies. Specifically, Lohse had had a hand in the policy both to ghettoize and exploit Jews within his jurisdiction. Yet Lohse was not to face trial by his American captors: the reason, it seems, being that a criminal of his profile could not be accommodated in the prosecution programme.

The category of the Nazi leadership corps of which Lohse was a member was to receive surprisingly light treatment at Nuremberg, with only three of its number facing trial. And of these three—Sauckel, Streicher, and Ernst Wilhelm Bohle—none was tried primarily for his activities as Gauleiter. The reason that they could not be tried as a collective was that the surviving district leaders were predominantly veterans of the German Gaue, whose worst crimes, Taylor considered, predated the war and were against German nationals.[67] We know that the subsequent Nuremberg tribunals did not look sympathetically upon attempts to class these acts as criminal under CCL10, and exceptions within the group did not fit easily into any of OCCWC's categories. Lohse's irregularity therefore contributed to his salvation.

At the beginning of 1948, the Central Committee of Liberated Jews, based in Munich, wrote to the OCCWC, noting that Lohse was shortly to be tried by a British denazification court, and fearing that, 'as is customary in the British zone, Lohse will get off with a small fine'.[68] In any case, the maximum sentence such a body could impose was ten years imprisonment. Despite American assurances that Lohse would be tried 'by the proper authorities', in keeping with British trial priorities, he duly appeared before a denazification board and received ten years—but was subsequently released in 1951 on the familiar grounds of ill health.[69]

The selection policy of the OCCWC meant that no exception could be made with the Lohse case, and consequently a major criminal escaped with only the

---

[65] Robert M. W. Kempner, 'Vingt-cinq ans après Nuremberg', *Le Monde Juif*, no. 60 (1961), 6–15, esp. 14.

[66] He died in jail in 1988. See Vestermanis, 'Der "Holocaust" in Lettland', 121; *The Independent*, 4 Jan. 2000.

[67] Taylor, *Final Report*, 83–4.

[68] NARA, RG 260, OCCWC, defendants and witnesses, box 102, file 'Correspondence incoming', memo from Paul Gantt, 8 Jan. 1948.

[69] NARA, RG 260, OCCWC, defendants and witnesses, box 103, file 'Correspondence outgoing', Lang to Central Committee of Liberated Jews, 5 Jan. 1948. On Lohse's treatment: Hilberg, *Destruction*, 710. The British authorities in Germany believed Lohse to be innocent of complicity in the organized brutality in the Baltic states: see PRO, FO 1060/267, CCG Lübbecke to FO German Section, 12 Apr. 1949.

mildest of punishments and no investigation of his crimes. Similar circumstances safeguarded the future of Georg Leibbrandt. It will be recalled that Leibbrandt was one of the representatives at the Wannsee conference who, despite Jewish petitioning, was not tried in the Ministries case on the grounds of inadequate time and courtroom space. He had attended the conference in his capacity as state secretary and head of the Political Department in Rosenberg's Ostministerium. However, despite Taylor's promise that Leibbrandt would not escape justice, the criminal proceedings that were turned over to the Nürnberg–Fürth district court for prosecution by the Germans were discontinued in 1952, in common with many such investigations in the Federal Republic.[70] Leibbrandt's deputy, Otto Bräutigam, met with the same treatment.[71]

Finally, we have the case of Lieutenant General Walter Braemer. As Wehrmacht Befehlshaber Ost, he was the supreme military authority in the Ostland after the instalment of the civil government, and was heavily implicated in the radicalization of the 'anti-partisan' conflict in that area to include mass murders of Jews.[72] He was another beneficiary of the lobbying power of the 'trades union of generals' and the closure of the British trial programme. The British appear to have known about some at least of Braemer's criminal past, but nothing had been done about bringing him to trial until, as with Manstein, foreign intervention drew attention to his case.

Again Poland was a plaintiff. On 30 August 1948 the Polish government requested his extradition for the murder of twenty hostages and several hundred civilians in that country in 1939 and, by the admission of a Foreign Office official, the facts were not disputed, not 'even by Braemer himself'. The date of the application is significant—two days before the institution of the limitation on extraditions to those cases in which a prima-facie case of murder under the German penal code was established.[73] The British authorities in Wahnerheide not only treated the request as if it had been submitted after 1 September, they applied the 'secret' clause in the terms of reference of the extradition tribunal, which, it will be recalled, was expressly designed to hinder the surrender of prisoners to eastern bloc nations.[74] A British preliminary tribunal played its hand to the full and, while purportedly assessing whether the Poles did have a strong prima-facie case, it effectively tried the case for the Poles. It concluded that, since the judgement in the Nuremberg Balkan generals' trial had decreed that under certain circumstances the shooting of hostages *might* be justified, Braemer

---

[70] See below, Chapter 5.3.

[71] NARA, RG 260, witness and defence files, box 100, file 'General Staff and High Command lists', Gantt to Taylor, 15 Mar. 1948. For Bräutigam's treatment in the BRD: Hilberg, *Destruction*, 705.

[72] Hannes Heer, 'Killing Fields: Die Wehrmacht und der Holocaust', in Hannes Heer and Klaus Naumann (eds.), *Vernichtungskrieg: Verbrechen der Wehrmacht 1941 bis 1944* (Hamburg: HIS, 1995), 57–77, esp. 65–73.

[73] PRO, FO 371/85900, CG3034/17/184, ML Priss minute, 22 Sept. 1950. On the implications of this stipulation, see below, Chapter 5.3.

[74] Ibid. CG3382/17/184, Priss minute on discussion incl. Ivone Kirkpatrick, 21 Oct. 1950; Priss minute, 1 Nov. 1950.

deserved the benefit of the doubt.[75] Thus, after much prevarication, late in 1950 the extradition request was refused.[76]

It would be well nigh impossible to draw up an exhaustive list of the many criminals who, by death, escape, extradition, clandestine agreement, or simply by being overlooked, evaded the British and American courts to the detriment of justice or the historical record or both. At Nuremberg such omissions were relevant beyond the immediate interests of justice because the trials were an attempt to create a representative image of Nazism. The profile of the accused had a significant effect not only on the crimes accounted for, but on the interpretation of causation imposed on those crimes.

5.3 THE NUREMBERG LEGACY (I): MOTIVATION FROM THE NAZI ÉLITE TO
     THE EXECUTIONERS

The benefit of the 'top-down' approach employed at Nuremberg lay in the investigation of the mechanisms of power in the Third Reich. Alongside the Nazi vanguard it implicated those organs which were equally adept at facilitating the smooth, non-criminal running of parallel, 'ordinary' societies. It was only a start, but the examination of, say, parts of the military, the SS, the civil service, and the medical profession shed the first light on the scope and varieties of German malfeasance, and contributed to Raul Hilberg's conceptualization of the 'machinery of destruction', 'structurally no different from organized German society as a whole'.[77]

The Medical trial in particular has made an impact on the post-war world. Aside from a substantial historiography that has relied heavily upon its findings, there is some sign of the very sort of introspection that Jackson and Taylor hoped would arise from the Nuremberg venture, though the initial reaction from Germany was distinctly frosty.[78] Within the medical profession this has taken the form of an ethical code based upon the principles outlined in, and named after, the Nuremberg judgement. The Helsinki Declaration and the Tokyo Convention also expressed a similar reaction to professional abuses.[79] The fiftieth anniversary of the trial witnessed a sprouting of historical and medical conferences and publications worldwide, as testament not only to the Nazis' deeds, but to their punishment.[80]

---

[75] PRO, FO 371/ 85900, CG3034/17/184, Chancery, Wahnerheide to FO, 4 Sept. 1950.

[76] Ibid. CG2481/17/184, Chancery, Wahnerheide to FO, 6 July 1950; CG3034/17/184, Priss minute, 22 Sept. 1950.

[77] Hilberg, *Destruction*, 640.   [78] Mitscherlich and Mielke, *Medizin ohne Menschlichkeit*, 15.

[79] George Annas and Michael Grodin, *The Nazi Doctors and the Nuremberg Code: Human Rights in Human Experimentation* (Oxford: Oxford University Press, 1992), considers many of the legacies of the trial. On the links between the prosecution of German medical war crimes and the post-war development of eugenics, see Paul Weindling, 'Eugenics and Medical War Crimes after 1945', *Tartu University History Museum Annual Report 1998* (Tartu: Tartu University Press, 1999), 86–99.

[80] A random assortment includes 1997 conferences at the United States Holocaust Memorial Museum and Oxford University, as well as special editions of both the *British Medical Journal* (7 Dec. 1996) and *Le Monde Juif* (7–8 Dec. 1986).

Of the subsequent proceedings, the trial of German jurists perhaps comes closest to the Medical trial in terms of its professional legacy. But we are concerned here more with the strict historiographical record than with what may broadly be termed the 'lessons' of the trials. The Nuremberg prosecutions compare favourably with the record of the BRD, which made no attempt to trace the orchestration of genocide in either the upper or the intermediate layers of Reich command or bureaucracy.

Two connected obstacles hindered more extensive prosecutions in Germany. The first relates to the general suppression of Nazi crimes. The integration of Nazi élites into the Bundesrepublik was facilitated by the actions of a civil service itself heavily implicated in discrimination and genocide. As the German legal system was entrusted with continuing the purge begun by the Allies, its many members who had been compromised prior to 1945 were in the ideal position to see that not only they, but other societal élites equally complicit, avoided the law courts. Thus the potentials for personal embarrassment and punishment were removed, and the national metamorphosis to the post-war period was rendered less painful.[81] This process was aided by a very compliant statutory system.

In as much as the BRD has concerned itself with investigating the genocides of its predecessor regime, the emphasis has remained very much upon the direct perpetrators of atrocities, and in particular those who displayed excessive cruelty in the task of murder. Einsatzgruppen members, Order Policemen, and camp guards have all faced trial, but those who have been able to prove that they did not go beyond the bounds of their orders in making their victims suffer have met largely with mind-boggling leniency. As Jörg Friedrich noted, they were given the sort of punishments doled out to 'second rate cheque forgers'.[82] This forbearance is a function of the German legal requirement to establish the 'base motive' of a killer in order that his action be declared outright murder. Obedience to orders, tellingly, has generally not been considered a motive within this category, establishing the killer as an accomplice to murder rather than a perpetrator *per se*, even though he or she may actually have fired the fateful bullet. In terms of the structures within which these murders were permitted, this is a vital consideration, for it has rendered problematic the establishment of cases against the swathe of criminals between the extremes of the killing ground artisans and the ruling ideologues. (It should be remembered that the loophole provided by the definition of murder under German law was exploited by the British authorities, too, as in the case of Braemer.)

How to discern the driving force behind the preparation, signing, or stamping of a document by an official of the Reichsbahn,[83] or even of the RSHA itself, so

---

[81] Ralph Giordano, *Die zweite Schuld oder von der Last ein Deutscher zu sein* (Hamburg: Rasch and Röhrig, 1987), 19; Friedrich, *Die kalte Amnestie, passim*; Broszat, 'Siegerjustiz oder strafrechtliche Selbstreinigung?'.

[82] Friedrich, *Die kalte Amnestie*, 337.   [83] The Nazi railways authority.

remote in Berlin from the killing fields, when those actions in and of themselves had no immanent moral value? In such cases the defence of simply 'doing the job' was in itself flawless.[84] In post-war Germany, the upper limit of this middle category of imponderables was frequently pushed right up to just below Hitler and his immediate deputies. For our purposes, the vast majority of perpetrators of the Holocaust were thus cast as mere accomplices, and though this was no obstacle to trial on its own, the fact that outright murder was the only Nazi crime which escaped the BRD's statute of limitations most certainly was.[85]

The Eichmann trial was the major post-war trial of a 'desk-murderer', and he was far from typical of this group of mid-ranking, pen-pushing perpetrators. His dedication to work and his improvisation outstripped the call of duty, and his importance was greater than his SS rank of Obersturmbannführer (Lieutenant-Colonel) implied. The minority of desk-murderers who reached trial in Germany shared in the Nuremberg legacy. Christopher Browning's pioneering monograph, *The Final Solution and the German Foreign Office*, studied a group of middle-level German governmental bureaucrats involved in the 'final solution'.[86] The book was based in part on Nuremberg documentation, from the IMT and the Ministries trial, and substantially on the trials of a group of officials from within department D III of the Foreign Office. The evidence on these men was initially gathered and forwarded to the German authorities by the special projects division of OCCWC, for they were considered too junior to be tried at Nuremberg.[87]

This episode suggests that if the focus of the Nuremberg trials on the role of 'dominant men' in history[88] was their strength, it was also their weakness. OCCPAC and OCCWC were indifferent to the deeds of those below the arbitrarily defined level of 'major war criminal of the second rank', and the interpretative peculiarities ensuing from this approach will be dealt with shortly. The victims, of course, were excluded from any function but that of limited illustration—the 'color', as Jackson put it. We have seen that the objectivity and accuracy of their testimony was questioned, and they were not thought to be able to contribute anything to the study of the German crime. The approach was mirrored in the early historiography of the Shoah.

Poliakov, Reitlinger, and Hilberg all refrained from using substantial Jewish testimony. The first two explicitly discounted it on grounds of putative subjectivity: Reitlinger with his warning about the rhetoric of the 'East European Jew'; Poliakov with his wish 'to forestall objections' by citing the murderers instead of

---

[84] This is exactly the sort of 'division of labour' to which Zygmunt Bauman has pointed in his *Modernity and the Holocaust* (New York: Cornell University Press, 1992), as enabling widespread participation in genocide.

[85] De Mildt, *In the Name of the People*, 34–5. The salient change in the legal code occurred in 1968.

[86] Browning, *The Final Solution and the German Foreign Office*.

[87] NARA, RG 260, witness and defence files, box 103, 'Chronological file', Lang to Gantt, 12 Mar. 1948.

[88] Kushner, *The Holocaust and the Liberal Imagination*, 3–4, on Reitlinger's *The Final Solution*.

the Jews. Hilberg's justification was less judgmental: his study was 'concerned with the storm that caused the wreckage', so the little that he wrote of the victims and their institutions was 'primarily through the eyes of the Germans'.[89]

In this methodology lay the seeds of one of the great historiographical debates about the murder of the Jews: the question of their own role in their extermination. In that little space which he devoted to it, Hilberg famously denounced what he saw as almost complete Jewish passivity, even acquiescence, in the destruction process. His opinion was echoed by Hannah Arendt in her commentary on the Eichmann trial,[90] and together they have comprised a foil for those showing that study of the Jewish communities themselves revealed a variety of responses.

The most ardent advocate of the latter approach was Isaiah Trunk, whose 1972 tome, *Judenrat*, set about comparing the actions of the Jewish councils in the ghettos.[91] It illustrated the agonizing choices confronting these unfortunates, depicted acts of bravery alongside simple compliance and, most importantly, rendered generalization on Jewish behaviour impossible. However, the kernel of Hilberg's problem was discerned as soon as his book appeared. A contemporary reviewer reasoned that it was impossible to study the Shoah without recourse to the victims.[92] It does not take a great leap of the imagination to see the link between the greater part of Hilberg's source material and his conclusions. It was unavoidable that trials would in large measure be perpetrator-centric; it is equally apparent now that the views of the accused on the victims were not more 'objective' versions of those available from the Jews themselves.

On the German policy-making side the effects of Nuremberg's élite focus are even more evident, and the links with the historiography are causal as well as conceptual. The Nuremberg trials were as much about exposing Nazism-militarism-economic imperialism as condemning their chief exponents. This 'orgy of revelation', as Telford Taylor called it, was directed chiefly at clarifying the complicity of the 'unholy trinity'. Relatively little emphasis was put on exploring motivation. The simple reason for this was that it was assumed the ruling principles of each interconnecting strand were self-evident.

The pejorative terms 'militarism' and 'economic imperialism' carry with them implications of inherent atavism, a self-propelling urge for conquest of one sort or another. In the 'conspiracy-criminal organization' plan, Nazism was held to unite these with a third quality: malignant ideology. For our purposes the relevant part of that ideology was racist hatred, and particularly murderous anti-semitism.

---

[89] Reitlinger, *The Final Solution*, 531; Poliakov, *Harvest of Hate*, p. xiv; Hilberg, *Destruction*, p. v.

[90] Hannah Arendt, *Eichmann in Jerusalem: A Report on the Banality of Evil* (New York: Viking, 1963).

[91] Isaiah Trunk, *Judenrat: The Jewish Councils in Eastern Europe under Nazi Occupation* (New York: Macmillan, 1972).

[92] *The Jewish Observer and Middle East Review* (16 Mar. 1962), 26–7. The critic, Reuben Ainsztein, later crystallized his views in *Jewish Resistance in Nazi-Occupied Eastern Europe* (New York: Elek, 1974).

Though in Jackson's mind the impetus to the Shoah was subordinate to the plan for aggressive war, he never denied its motivating power, describing it variously as 'an end in itself, as a measure of preparation for war, and as a discipline of conquered people'. 'Determination to destroy the Jews', he maintained, 'was a binding force which at all times cemented the elements of [the criminal] conspiracy'.[93] Only one of these was accurate—destruction as an end in itself. Having worked that out, the IMT was happy to conclude the obvious, by adjudging that 'the Nazi anti-Semitic program did not originate from any . . . extraneous purpose, but rather from a blind, unreasoning hatred of Jews which came from Hitler's own disordered mind'.[94]

Ostensibly, the murder of the Jews was a product purely and inevitably of antisemitism, with Hitler, then his 'true believers', inciting a nation to genocide out of hatred alone. Erich von dem Bach-Zelewski justified this interpretation from the witness-stand: 'if one preaches for years, for decades, that the Slavonic race is an inferior race, and that the Jews are not human beings at all, then it must come to such an outburst'.[95] The evidence for simple cause and effect appeared conclusive, from the oft-cited *Mein Kampf* to the deployment of the Einsatzgruppen alongside the armies invading the USSR; and a glance at the judgement of the IMT shows that it was accepted completely. This interpretation ramified in the long-running debate over the timing and context of the decision to murder the European Jews.

As has variously been stated, the influential interpretation of the 'final solution' known as 'intentionalism' was 'born' at Nuremberg.[96] And though the debate amongst a small circle of scholars has now moved to a level of sophistication where pure 'intentionalism' is maintained by few, it was for a long time a position that had to be addressed by historians, and in many a classroom is still touted as one side of an informed hermeneutical discussion.

Ian Kershaw has provided an oft-quoted analysis of the instinctive attractiveness of this intentionalist position—'deducing the development of the Third Reich from Hitler's ideological intentions'—and of its flaws:

Seldom has a politician stuck with such fanatical consistency to an ideological fixation as Hitler appears to have done in the period extending from his entry into politics to his suicide in the bunker. That the quest for *Lebensraum* and the extermination of the Jews . . . became horrific reality and were implemented as government policy by a regime led by Hitler, seems to point conclusively to the validity of the 'intentionalist' argument. [However, as the historian Tim Mason has argued,] a concentration on Hitler's intentions short-circuits all fundamental questions of social, economic, and political agencies of change. Underlying the approach is the dubious assumption that historical development can be explained by recourse to intuitive understanding of the motives and intentions of

---

[93] *IMT*, ii, 127.   [94] Biddle papers, box 6, 'Notes on evidence', vol. 11, p. 82.
[95] Cited in De Mildt, *In the Name of the People*, 5.
[96] Marrus, *The Holocaust in History*, 36; Michael Biddiss, *The Nuremberg Trial and the Third Reich* (London: ETHOS, 1993), 128–63.

leading actors in the drama. Subsequent events are then rationalized in necessary teleo-logical fashion by their relation to such intentions.[97]

There is little substantive difference between the 'conspiracy-criminal organization' plan and the intentionalist interpretation. The emphasis is altered in the latter approach, depicting aggressive warfare as a predetermined camouflage for genocide, rather than in itself as the prime directive of Nazism, but both are predicated on the principles of long-term planning and unwavering dedication to a goal, and uniformity of purpose amongst the implementers.

Presupposition of intent was particularly important in the trial of the Einsatz-gruppen leaders. The trial provided the arena for the first substantive evidence on the timing of a putative order to kill all Soviet Jews, irrespective of gender, age, or status. The existence of this instruction as such, which has come to be known as the 'Führer Order', and that it was delivered before the invasion of the Soviet Union has been accepted as a matter of course by intentionalist historians believing the Barbarossa campaign to be a facilitation of long-held plans. Indeed, they consider that the intention of the Germans was to use the invasion as a cover for their plans to murder all Jews everywhere.[98]

'Functionalist' historians, on the other hand, have challenged both the nature of the directive and the assumption that it was delivered at all. They prefer to see the genocide as a strategy developed within the context of the war as a result less of Hitler's direct input than of mid-level officials suggesting ever more radical 'solutions to the Jewish question' in accordance with the prevailing antisemitic climate and the brutal quasi-racial conflict with the USSR.[99] Though with slightly different explanations of motive and causation, this is also the position of those scholars who, since the end of the Cold War, have conducted detailed localized studies of the Nazi occupation of Poland and the USSR.[100]

Contrary to popular perception, the 'disagreement' between 'intentionalists' and the various shades of 'functionalist' has not been over the role of

---

[97] Ian Kershaw, *The Nazi Dictatorship: Problems and Perspectives of Interpretation* (London: Arnold, 1989), 69.

[98] Dawidowicz, *The War against the Jews*, is a classic statement of this view. Marrus, *The Holocaust in History*, surveys the arguments of Dawidowicz and the other chief 'intentionalists' and juxtaposes them with those of the 'functionalists'.

[99] Martin Broszat, 'Hitler und die Genesis der "Endlösung": Aus Anlass der Thesen von David Irving', *VfZ*, 25 (1977), 737–75; Hans Mommsen, 'The Realisation of the Unthinkable: The "Final Solution of the Jewish Question" in the Third Reich', in Gerhard Hirschfeld (ed.), *The Policies of Genocide* (London: German Historical Institute, 1986), 93–144.

[100] Thomas Sandkühler, *"Endlösung" in Galizien: Der Judenmord in Ostpolen und die Rettungsinitiativen von Berthold Beitz 1941–1944* (Bonn: Dietz, 1996); Pohl, *Nationalsozialistische Judenverfolgung*; id., *Von der 'Judenpolitik' zum Judenmord: Der Distrikt Lublin des Generalgouvernements 1939–1944* (Frankfurt am Main: Lang, 1993); Christian Gerlach, *Krieg, Ernährung, Völkermord: Forschungen zur deutschen Vernichtungspolitik* (Hamburg: Hamburger Edition, 1998); Herbert (ed.), *Nationalsozialistische Vernichtungspolitik*; Ian Kershaw, 'Improvised Genocide? The Emergence of the Final Solution in the Warthegau', *Transactions of the Royal Historical Society*, 6, vol. 2 (1992), 51–78. See also Peter Longerich's massive study *Politik der Vernichtung: Eine Gesamtdarstellung der nationalsozialistischen Judenverfolgung* (Munich: Piper, 1998).

antisemitism. 'Functionalists' accept its pivotal influence in the Third Reich, but they share Mason's awareness of the complexity of historical development in modern society. The most recent research suggests that genocide emerged out of a sort of mutual goal-orientation or consensus politics between the power-centre in Berlin and their provincial satraps: the former sent out periodical radicalizing messages and the latter implemented these and spent the interim periods pursuing their own, often equally murderous, initiatives.

In all likelihood there was no pre-existing order to kill all Soviet Jews.[101] The killing programme clearly developed over the first months of the war as the circle of victims expanded from males of arms-bearing age to include female Jews and children, and then entire communities; the move to kill *en masse* Jews from elsewhere in Europe was later still, and total, continent-wide murder was still developing as a policy until spring 1942.[102]

We have already seen that the Einsatzgruppen proceeded at different rates, and it seems that their leaders had 'considerable latitude' in the interpretation of those instructions they were given.[103] Most of the leaders maintained at Nuremberg that they had been given unequivocal directives at training camps established prior to the invasion. The murderous nature of these incitements is undoubted and, as Ohlendorf's counsel put it in his opening address, 'the leaders of the Einsatzgruppen and Kommandos were executive officers with instructions'. This was true enough, but defence went on to contend that the authority of the leaders 'as to decisions started only with the actual execution of their orders'.[104] This, of course, begs the question of the substance of the orders, and thus whether or not there was 'latitude' built into their implementation. It was this matter which remained unaddressed at Nuremberg.

It is instructive to contextualize the defence arguments for Ohlendorf. The admission of the Führer order was preceded by a dissertation on the legal defence of obedience to senior orders, and by the misleading contention that the Einsatzgruppen were completely subordinate to the army. It was also accompanied by another strand of argumentation: that of *Putativnotwehr*. That was the now-familiar contention that the invasion of the Soviet Union and the accompanying 'security measures' were pre-emptive strikes against an enemy—Judaeo-Bolshevism—which was held to be marshalling its anti-German forces.[105]

There was no evading the documentation in the possession of the OCCWC, so some form of justification of their revelations was required to save the skins of the defendants. In this surreal picture, the genocides were not only necessary owing to the 'eastern' threat, they were unavoidable. The weight of the senior orders imperative from Berlin allegedly specified the exact nature of the task to

---

[101] Browning, *Nazi Policy*, 30.   [102] Longerich, *Politik der Vernichtung*.
[103] Browning, *Fateful Months*, 19–20.
[104] *TWC*, iv, 70; for the full text of the opening address for Ohlendorf, see NMT, Case 9, pp. 257–97.
[105] *TWC*, iv, 55, 64–5.

be performed, while the presence of military superiors in the field enforced the implementation of these orders.

That all of this was presented in the context of an opening address for the defence suggests that it was an adopted strategy, and a subsequent admission by Aschenauer adds weight to this contention.[106] It was not only the vagaries of German law which protected subordinates acting according to predetermined instructions; CCL10, we know, also declared that the imposition of senior orders might be held in mitigation. There was less chance of mitigation if the Einsatz-gruppen leaders could be shown to have exploited the 'latitude' of coded instruc-tions, and none whatsoever if they had gone beyond the bounds of the initial orders.

In the event, in the courtroom, these points were relegated to academic status. In order to gain convictions, and in order for the tribunal to inflict the severest penalty on some of the defendants, it was not necessary to establish the existence or otherwise of the Führer order, but merely to show that the Einsatzgruppen leaders were fully aware of the inherent criminality of their task. The extremity of the crimes did the rest. The defence gambit had failed, and the nature and tim-ing of the Führer order was not considered at Nuremberg.

When the judges were forced to declare upon points of interpretation they did so with conviction, disdaining the 'monstrous' defence of *Putativnotwehr*. Yet not only did the judges not need to account for the Führer order, they seemed convinced by its existence. The prosecution had contended that the European-wide genocidal plans had formed in 1939, and consequently that the Einsatz-gruppen were given full instructions in advance of Barbarossa.[107] No-one at the trial except the defendants doubted this, so the opportunity was missed to arrive at a closer approximation to the 'truth' about the chronology of killing. The court had arrived at its conclusion not by analysing the propositions of the men on trial—some of whom would soon be dead, and therefore unable to contribute further—but rather by working from a preconception about the nature of Naz-ism. In this spirit, the putative existence of a Führer order as depicted by the de-fendants has long sustained the 'intentionalists'.

In an extended analogy created to explain the simultaneous irrationality and consistency of Nazi antisemitism, the tribunal depicted a fictitious national Ger-man campaign against grey-eyed people. The arbitrary selection of the 'other' notwithstanding, it was held, the persecution and eventual murder of the grey-eyed was explicable in the light of a concerted, long-term marshalling of propa-ganda and judicial decree against them.[108] It was thus adjudged that in the Einsatzgruppen reports as a whole, 'the reference to individual categories of

---

[106] *Rassenpolitik und Kriegführung: Sicherheitspolizei und Wehrmacht in Polen und in die Sowjetunion 1939–1942*, ed. Hans-Heinrich Wilhelm (Passau: Richard Rothe, 1991); Alfred Streim, 'The Tasks of the SS Einsatzgruppen', *Simon Wiesenthal Center Annual*, 4 (1987), 309–28.

[107] *TWC*, iv, 30–6; more fully, NMT, Case 9, pp. 30–60.   [108] *TWC*, iv, 474–6.

Jews is only macabre window dressing because . . . *all* Jews were killed regardless of antecedents'.[109]

As earlier discussion of the Pohl trial has shown, there was the potential at the subsequent proceedings to discern subtle disparities in purpose between Nazi organizations. However, in that instance such differentiation—establishing the WVHA as uninstrumental in the *organized* mass murder in the camps—was vital to the outcome of the case. In the Einsatzgruppen trial it was not, for the defendants had clearly been at the coal-face of genocide, and so a key historical question remained unanswered because it was not relevant judicially, and the 'intentionalist' cause had been aided by default.

The problems inherent in the conspiracy-intentionalist interpretation of the 'final solution' are all brought to the fore in the consideration of a related practice: that of using Jews for labour purposes during the war. In a way that has yet to be fully dissected, Nuremberg bequeathed an image of this phenomenon that ignored disparities over time and between different interests at different levels of the power structure, by promoting the idea of 'extermination through work' as a coherent Nazi policy.[110] By means of a more detailed reconstruction and analysis than hitherto, this particular Nuremberg legacy will serve as a case study to illuminate, on one hand, the reductionism of the Nuremberg prosecutors and some subsequent historians and, on the other, the reality of Nazi Jewish policy which, within its ideological guidelines, was not always internally consistent and which left space for individual initiative on the geographical periphery, and not infrequently for dissonance between authorities over the immediate disposition of some Jews.

5.4 THE NUREMBERG LEGACY (II): 'EXTERMINATION THROUGH WORK'

We know that the Americans were struggling well into the subsequent proceedings with the idea that the SS could embody conflicting aims. The presence within the WVHA of office-group D, the inspectorate of concentration camps (Inspektion der Konzentrationslager: IKL) from March 1942[111] was ostensibly an indication to OCCPAC that the conspiracy idea was worthwhile, that even a body with a title pertaining to economics was really angled towards genocide. Thus an OCCPAC prosecutor discerned that the IKL was responsible for the 'entire internal management of the camps, including the use of prisoners [and] the determination of their very right to live'. But he also attributed a plan of extermination to the WVHA.[112] This misapprehension has been shared much

---

[109] *TWC*, iv, 420. Emphasis in original.

[110] For a more in-depth analysis of the issues, see Bloxham, ' "Extermination through Work"'; id.; 'Jewish Slave Labour and Its Relationship to the "Final Solution" ', in *Remembering for the Future 2000: The Holocaust in an Age of Genocide*, (London: Macmillan, forthcoming).

[111] Hermann Kaienburg, 'KZ-Haft und Wirtschaftsinteresse', in id. (ed.), *Konzentrationslager und deutsche Wirtschaft 1939–1945* (Opladen: Leske and Budrich, 1996), 29–60.

[112] *IMT*, iv, 191–2.

more recently by Zygmunt Bauman, whose stimulating analysis, *Modernity and the Holocaust*, has represented the catastrophe as the outcome of a modern-industrial society in which a goal, once established, is rationally pursued to its logical outcome, however extreme, in accordance with the ideal of societal perfectibility. In this interpretation, once Jews were defined as 'other', their extirpation was enacted according to the same principles of rational administration, organization, and economy as any other far-reaching societal project. Not only does this not allow for differing agendas within the circle of law-givers, it requires that an organization entitled 'business—administration head office' be intimately involved in the pursuit of genocide.[113]

Something closer to reality was achieved as the American prosecutor observed that 'the shift of control [of the camps] to the WVHA ... coincided with a change in the basic purposes of the concentration camps. Political and security reasons, which previously had been the ground for confinement, were abandoned; and the camps were ... made to serve the slave-labor program.'[114] However, OCCPAC was still missing the point; the shift in power did not coincide with the change in policy, it was a clear 'expression of the [partial] change in the role of the camps'.[115] The WVHA, under Himmler's chief economist Oswald Pohl, had been assigned administrative control of the camps by the Reichsführer-SS in order to realize the latter's long-held intentions to make the SS a genuinely economic as well as a political-ideological force.[116]

The advantage the SS leaders had over private industry and the official government economic agencies was a vast reservoir of free labour, and the aim now was to exploit that more fully than previously. This policy would only achieve a limited success in the ensuing years, however, and chiefly during the long Nazi retreat on all fronts and its consequent diminution of the foreign forced labour available. Moreover, the ideological imperatives that had traditionally governed the treatment of concentration camp inmates frequently dictated that their working capacity would be exploited to only a fraction of its true potential, before being reduced to zero by death.[117]

Where though, it may be asked, did the Jews fit into all of this? Their deployment was not equivalent to that of the other concentration camp inmates, for they occupied an even more despised place in the Nazi world-view,[118] and for

[113] Bauman, *Modernity and the Holocaust*, 14.   [114] *IMT*, iv, 200.
[115] Buchheim *et al.*, *Anatomie des SS-Staates*, ii, 132.
[116] Enno Georg, *Die wirtschaftlichen Unternehmungen der SS* (Stuttgart: Deutsche Verlags-Anstalt, 1963), 72; Hermann Kaienburg, *'Vernichtung durch Arbeit': Der Fall Neuengamme: Die Wirtschaftsbestrebung der SS und ihre Auswirkungen auf die Existenzbedingungen der KZ-Gefangenen* (Bonn: J.H.W. Dietz, 1990), 452–3.
[117] Kaienburg, *'Vernichtung durch Arbeit'*, 466–8; id., 'KZ-Haft und Wirtschaftsinteresse', 52–3, 56–7.
[118] Ulrich Herbert, 'Arbeit und Vernichtung', in Dan Diner (ed.), *Ist der Nationalsozialismus Geschichte?* (Frankfurt am Main: Fischer, 1987), 198–237. On the 'racial' hierarchy: Michael Zimmermann, 'Arbeit in den Konzentrationslagern: Kommentierende Bemerkungen', in Ulrich Herbert, Karin Orth, and Christoph Dieckmann (eds.), *Die nationalsozialistischen Konzentrationslager: Entwicklung und Struktur*, 2 vols. (Göttingen: Wallstein, 1998), 730–51, esp. 747.

most of the war comparatively few were under the control of the IKL/WVHA. However, the presumptions of the conspiracy plan, when combined with the limited OCCPAC perception of the camp system, determined that the differing treatment of Jews and non-Jews would not be brought into relief. Conversely, the genuine importance that many Nazis attached to Jewish labour as a productive force at certain times was significantly underplayed. Seeking to accommodate what was perceived to be a broad, general policy of extermination with another of labour, the Americans hit upon a notion provided for in some now infamous Nazi correspondence. They simply merged the two trends into a third of 'extermination through work'.

In this scheme, the Nazis allegedly 'placed all Allied nationals [*sic*] in concentration camps and forced them, along with the other inmates of the concentration camps, to work under conditions which were set actually to exterminate them'.[119] The idea was derived from an agreement between Himmler and the Reich Justice Minister, Thierack. In September 1942 the decision was made to transfer 'asocial' elements from prison to the Reichsführer-SS for extermination through work—'Vernichtung durch Arbeit'. Included amongst these elements were 'without exception . . . persons under protective arrest, Jews, Gypsies, Russians and Ukrainians, Poles with more than 3-year sentences, Czechs, and Germans with more than 8-year sentences, according to the decision of the Reich Minister for Justice'.[120]

This particular group, treated under the broad category of 'asocials', was unusual in being slated for total destruction. The prisoners were turned over for incarceration and murder at Mauthausen, which retained its established character as one of the very worst of the penal punishment centres, and was thus scarcely representative of developments in the camp system as a whole. (There were 12,658 people involved and 5,935 of them had died by 1 April 1943.)[121] However, by extrapolating too broadly from the document, OCCPAC elided the fundamental difference between broader collectives earmarked for annihilation and those for brutal oppression.

The document not only appears to have convinced the IMT judges, who focused on the catchy phrase at the end of the passage quoted in court, and then the prosecutors both at the subsequent proceedings and the Eichmann trial;[122] but as a result of its prominence at Nuremberg it was seized upon by the British as of universal importance. It would apparently be 'invaluable' at future

---

[119] *IMT*, iii, 460.

[120] *IMT*, iii, 462–4; iv, 200; Nuremberg document PS-654. The French also found the concept of extermination through work appropriate: *IMT*, vi, 379; xix, 547; Nuremberg document PS-682.

[121] Buchheim *et al.*, *Anatomie des SS-Staates*; Evelyn Le Chene, *Mauthausen: The History of a Death Camp* (London: Methuen, 1971), 64–6; more generally on the treatment of such groups, Nikolaus Wachsmann, ' "Annihilation through Labour": The Killing of State Prisoners in the Third Reich', *Journal of Modern History*, 71 (1999), 624–59.

[122] On the Eichmann trial, Gideon Hausner, *Justice in Jerusalem: The Trial of Adolf Eichmann* (London: Nelson, 1967), 161–2; on the reception by the IMT, Biddle papers, box 3, vols. 1–3, p. 156.

concentration camp trials under the Royal Warrant, none of which concerned Mauthausen.[123] Such a case was the proceedings against the personnel of the Neuengamme camp. Major Stephen Stewart of the JAG's staff was to marshal the 1946 trial of fourteen former guards, and as a principal tool in illustrating the premeditated nature of their regime, he selected the Himmler-Thierack agreement.[124]

This document has spawned broad generalizations in both the public and the academic spheres, and has been used freely by some scholars of Nazi labour policy to corroborate their theories.[125] Most uncritical in this regard is an influential early overview of the use of Jewish slaves by the Nuremberg prosecutor, Benjamin Ferencz. A convinced intentionalist, Ferencz has uncritically employed the Himmler-Thierack agreement in his untenable contention that 'a compromise' was reached between extermination and employment. Not least of Ferencz's inaccuracies is his failure to differentiate properly between Jewish and non-Jewish labour.[126]

Ferencz's work has been superseded; indeed, even the subsequent Nuremberg proceedings went on to study in some depth the use of Auschwitz inmate labour by the Krupp concern and by IG Farben.[127] However, there remain significant gaps in our knowledge of the treatment of slave labour, and particularly Jewish slave labour, and the enduring allure of the simplistic interpretation is illustrated in Daniel Goldhagen's *Hitler's Willing Executioners*. His sections devoted to work camps are dismissive of the thought that Jews in any way played a useful economic role after 1941. And though Goldhagen is quite right to stress that, by the time of the most widespread deployment of racial and political enemies of Nazism, the murder machinery had engulfed the majority of its Jewish victims,[128] this is no revelation. His chapters on the 'work' camps imply more about high-political conflict over the immediate disposition of the Jews than they tell us of the 'ordinary' guards of the work camps and the instructions under which the latter operated.[129]

---

[123] PRO, WO 311/39, Somerhough to Wade, 1 Mar. 1946.

[124] *The Times* 16 May 1995. Neuengamme has become the subject of one of the major case studies of the applicability of the term 'extermination through work' in the concentration camps: Kaienburg, '*Vernichtung durch Arbeit*'.

[125] e.g. Falk Pingel, *Häftlinge unter NS-Herrschaft: Widerstand, Selbstbehauptung und Vernichtung in Konzentrationslager* (Hamburg: Hoffmann and Campe, 1978); Gerd Wysocki, 'Häftlingsarbeit in der Rüstungsproduktion', in *Dachauer Hefte, 2. Sklavenarbeit im KZ*, (Munich: Deutscher Taschenbuch Verlag, 1986), 35–67, esp. 37; Benjamin Ferencz, *Less than Slaves: Jewish Forced Labor and the Quest for Compensation* (Cambridge, Mass.: Harvard University Press, 1979).

[126] Ferencz, *Less than Slaves*, 18–23.

[127] Pankowicz, 'Das KL Auschwitz in den Nürnberger Prozessen', 283–364.

[128] Goldhagen, *Hitler's Willing Executioners*, 283–323.

[129] Wolfgang Sofsky, *Die Ordnung des Terrors: Das Konzentrationslager* (Frankfurt am Main: Fischer, 1993), goes further even than Goldhagen, in stating without empirical substantiation that labour within the camps as a whole functioned only as another manifestation of terror, and ultimately annihilation.

A brief consideration of Jewish slave labour from 1941, when the 'final solution' began to unfold, shows that the idea of productive Jewish labour was not always a phantom or a camouflage for murder, though it was always conducted in the shadow of genocide. In the first instance, the most important location is Poland,[130] where the native Jews were killed over an extended period, and where Jews from elsewhere in Europe were deported.

After Poland had been overrun, the ideological and economic interests of the SS could be pursued more aggressively than ever. This they were, but not in the first instance chiefly through the medium of the SS economic and administrative offices or the IKL, for, as we have seen in consideration of the SS and police system, the 'east' represented an area where power was there to be fought for. In the territory of the Generalgouvernement there was only one main camp administered by the IKL: Majdanek.[131] SS power elsewhere in the Generalgouvernement was exercised primarily through the offices of Himmler's HSSPFs and their local agents. In this connection a mass of 'camps' emerges about which little is known.[132]

Forced labour camps for Jews (Zwangsarbeitslager für Juden: ZALs) were dotted in their hundreds all over the landscape of Poland. In June 1943, surrounded by the murderous mayhem of Aktion Reinhard, these camps contained around 120,000 Polish Jews who had been seized in the first instance from their homes or later from ghettos.[133] Authority in the ZALs varied from the civil governments to the military to industry to the SS. Some of them were equivalent in size to the largest of the German camps, and featured mortality rates which were often much higher.[134] For the purposes of this study, the ZALs must not be examined in isolation, but rather in their relationship to Nazi jurisdictional conflicts and the development of the 'final solution'.

Labour camps had first been conceived around February 1940, and by the middle of that year, in the Lublin district alone there were between 50,000 and 70,000 Jews working in the decentralized ZAL system, and a large number likewise outside. This trend was not reversed after the invasion of the Soviet Union. Rather, as non-Jewish Poles were then taken to work in the Reich in large numbers, some Generalgouvernement Jews were required to take their place in the

[130] On the essentially persecutory nature of Jewish labour in the Reich, see Wolf Grüner, *Der geschlossene Arbeitseinsatz deutscher Juden: Zur Zwangsarbeit als Element der Verfolgung 1938–1943* (Berlin: Metropol, 1997); Garbe, 'Absonderung', 182–3. The following conclusions on Jewish labour in Poland find broad substantiation in Browning, *Nazi Policy*.

[131] Cf. Kranz, 'Das KL Lublin', 363–89.

[132] Gudrun Schwarz, *Die nationalsozialistischen Lager* (Frankfurt am Main: Campus, 1990), 61, 73–6.

[133] Dieter Pohl, 'Die grossen Zwangsarbeitslager der SS- und Polizeiführer für Juden im Generalgouvernement 1942–1945', in Ulrich Herbert, Karin Orth and Christoph Dieckmann (eds.), *Die nationalsozialistischen Konzentrationslager: Entwicklung und Struktur*, 2 vols. (Göttingen: Wallstein, 1998), 415–38, esp. 415.

[134] See e.g. Felicja Karay, *Death Comes in Yellow: Skarzysko-Kamienna Slave Labor Camp* (Amsterdam: Harwood Academic Publishers, 1996), 51.

Polish economy.[135] Exigency of a different sort dictated that Jews be put to work in the ghettos.

The Polish ghettos were not established uniformly or as long-term entities, but as holding-centres prior to the proposed deportation 'eastwards' of the Jews. However, for military reasons—the failure of the Wehrmacht to conquer the USSR up to the Urals—the deportations did not take place. The ghettos, mostly created and sealed in the course of 1940, were thus faced after 22 June 1941 with an impossible task: provision, without any economic links with the outside world, for hundreds of thousands of starving inhabitants. The often bitter debate that consequently emerged between German (civil) ghetto managers has been characterized as one between 'attritionists' and 'productionists': that is, between those who reasoned that the death rates of the ghettos were desirably congruent with Nazi intentions for the Jews, and those who considered that the best practical course was to make the ghettos economically viable.[136]

For a while, and over varying time-scales the 'productionists' gained a partial ascendancy in the largest ghettos, but despite their limited successes in making the ghettos more economically viable, they still had to contend with the intractable problem that feeding the Jews was the lowest of all Reich priorities. Death rates did diminish with increased productivity, yet remained horrific.[137] The most important context, however, was the development of the 'final solution' as a project explicitly of murder. From October onwards, sporadic massacres of Jews were enacted by the SS and police. Commissioned by Himmler to find both a more efficient and secretive method of murder, SS and Police Leader (SSPF) Odilo Globocnik offered the expertise of the former 'euthanasia' gassing specialists, and began the development of the extermination camp of Belzec.[138]

This development did not symbolize the total murder of Polish Jewry. Until spring 1942 there was space for some male Jews to be used for labour as one of a series of policy-streams aimed at the gradual diminishment of the Jewish communities in eastern Europe.[139] Indeed, while Aktion Reinhard was in full swing the sliver of Polish Jewry remaining at work became an object of some debate amongst the different German agencies of power.

The minority of Generalgouvernement Jews who avoided deportation to the Aktion Reinhard camps in 1942 and 1943 were either in hiding or working as slave labourers. The latter were in turn only a small residue of the workers who had been employed chiefly in textile and woodwork in the Cracow district, and in

---

[135] Alfred Konieczny, 'Die Zwangsarbeit der Juden in Schlesien im Rahmen der "Organisation Schmeldt"', in Götz Aly and Suzanne Heim (eds.), *Sozialpolitik und Judenvernichtung: Gibt es eine Ökonomie der Endlösung?* (Beiträge zur NS-Gesundheits- und Sozialpolitik 5; Berlin: Rotbuch, 1987), 91–110, esp. 95; Labour Department circular (Lublin), 18 Mar. 1942, in *Faschismus—Getto—Massenmord*, ed. Berenstein *et al.*, 233; Pohl, '*Judenpolitik*', 81–5.

[136] Browning, *The Path to Genocide*, 28–56.

[137] Ibid. 52.   [138] Pohl, '*Judenpolitik*'; id., *Nationalsozialistische Judenverfolgung*.

[139] Longerich, *Politik der Vernichtung*.

armaments production in Radom.[140] Most of the ZALs and ghettos from which these Jews worked were 'dissolved' from the summer of 1943 onwards. At the beginning of November 1943, the final large massacre of Jews in the General-gouvernement ('Aktion Erntefest'; 'harvest festival') occurred; 42,000 were killed in Lublin in the space of five days. This murder spree included many who had previously been categorized as important for the war economy (*kriegs-wichtig*). It was centrally ordered by Himmler in response to the 'threat' posed by the recent Jewish uprisings in Sobibor and Treblinka.[141] Of around 50,000 survivors of the massacre, 20,000 were in Plaszow near Cracow and 25,000 in Radom, mostly in ZALs run by private companies for Speer's armaments ministry.

'Erntefest' was the final act of Aktion Reinhard. From early on in that campaign Himmler had ordered the concentration of the scattered remnants of Polish Jewry into 'collection centres' under SS authority. His intention had been to concentrate the remainder of the Generalgouvernement's Jews into a closed, WVHA-run concentration camp economy that would take on the responsibility of delivering military orders. He planned gradually to replace the Jewish work force with Poles, and murder the then-redundant Jews.[142]

Himmler's policy had resulted in an incomplete transition. Many small ZALs were closed, some existing ones enlarged, and a few large ones founded (Plaszow, for instance). These survived because of their particular importance for the war effort.[143] Meanwhile, in an altered form some ghettos remained as ersatz camps or, in the Nazi parlance, Julags—Judenlager.[144] On the other hand, though deriving most of their labour power from the Reich concentration camps as well as Auschwitz and Majdanek, the WVHA's industrial concerns were not restricted to those camps run by the IKL. In the Generalgouvernement the entrenched strength of the equally brutal civil powers, and particularly the local SSPFs, made it necessary for the WVHA to co-operate with the existing system of labour usage.

One expression of the compromises that had to be made was in the running of the SS business enterprise, Eastern Industries Co. Ltd. It was established in March 1943 as the first SS company specifically concerned with the exploitation of Jewish labour, as well as with the expropriation of any Jewish capital.[145] Globocnik was appointed to the board of directors alongside WVHA men. As

[140] Dieter Pohl, 'Die Ermordung der Juden im Generalgouvernement', in Ulrich Herbert (ed.), *Nationalsozialistischen Vernichtungspolitik: Neue Forschungen und Kontroversen* (Frankfurt am Main: Fischer, 1997), 98–121, esp. 106.

[141] Thomas Sandkühler, 'Das Zwangsarbeitslager Lemberg-Janowska 1941–1944', in Ulrich Herbert, Karin Orth and Christoph Dieckmann (eds.), *Die nationalsozialistischen Konzentrationslager: Entwicklung und Struktur*, 2 vols. (Göttingen: Wallstein, 1998), 606–35, on the Erntefest massacres as a logical conclusion of developments in the Generalgouvernement.

[142] Himmler order, 9 Oct. 1942, in *Faschismus—Getto—Massenmord*, ed. Berenstein *et al.*, 446–7.

[143] e.g. Karay, *Skarzysko-Kamienna*.

[144] Pohl, 'Die grossen Zwangsarbeitslager', 418–19; Georg, *wirtschaftlichen Unternehmungen*, 91–2.

[145] Georg, *Die wirtschaftlichen Unternehmungen*, 92–3.

part of the arrangement, the remaining ten Jewish ZALs in the Lublin district were finally transferred to the control of the WVHA (and thus the Eastern Industries board) in September 1943. These camps were to become sub-camps of Majdanek. However, by the time of 'Erntefest', the process was by no means complete.[146] Subsequent to the November massacres, all the remaining SSPF-controlled ZALs in the Generalgouvernement, with their tiny Jewish remnant, were transferred to the total control of the WVHA.[147]

'Erntefest' cut short the Eastern Industries enterprise, and it is clear that the entire 'final solution' itself after mid-1942 was fundamentally incompatible with economic considerations, and illustrates Christopher Browning's and Ulrich Herbert's notion of the 'primacy of ideology', at least among the major decision-makers.[148] It seems that whatever the contribution made by local initiatives to the development of the 'final solution', the seminal decisions of Aktion Reinhard were Himmler's, as he travelled around inciting ever-wider destruction.[149] However, the problems caused to the Polish economy by the massacre of Polish Jewry were commented upon repeatedly by the military and civil labour authorities of the Generalgouvernement, who asked for special dispensations for Jews who were prominent in some trades vital to the war effort.[150] Even HSSPF Friedrich Wilhelm Krüger expressed concern midway through 1943.[151] Moreover, it seems that the SSPFs had betrayed their original function of reinforcing Himmler's authority by pursuing a tendency to empire-building, sometimes on the back of Jewish labour.[152]

It was only on the level of the supreme policy-makers that the tendency to total murder could be altered decisively in the short term, and after 'Erntefest' such a shift did occur, affecting a substantial number of Jews from outside the Generalgouvernement. Chiefly these Jews were from western and central Europe, but also included several thousand from the incorporated parts of Poland that had not been touched by the November massacres, particularly the Upper Silesia region.[153] Alongside hundreds of thousands of non-Jewish concentration camp inmates, these were assigned to a more centralized system of labour for German public and private companies.

---

[146] Nuremberg document NO-599; Pohl, *'Judenpolitik'*, 163; Georg, *Die wirtschaflichen Unternehmungen*, 96, 98.

[147] Nuremberg document NO-1036, Baier to chief, office WVHA W IV, 19 Jan. 1944.

[148] Jan Erik Schulte, 'Rüstungsunternehmen oder Handwerksbetrieb? Das KZ-Häftlinge ausbeutende SS-Unternehmen "Deutsche Ausrüstungswerke GmbH" ', in Ulrich Herbert, Karin Orth and Christoph Dieckmann (eds.), *Die nationalsozialistische Konzentrationslager: Entwicklung und Struktur*, 2 vols. (Göttingen: Wallstein, 1998), 558–83.

[149] Pohl, *'Judenpolitik'*, 179; implicit in Sandkühler, 'Lemberg-Janowska', 627–8.

[150] See e.g., Frauendorfer note, 22 June 1942, and Hänecke to the High Command of the Wehrmacht, 18 Sept. 1942, in *Faschismus—Getto—Massenmord*, ed. Berenstein et al., 438–9, 444–6, respectively.

[151] Meeting of the Generalgouvernement government, 31 May 1943: ibid. 450–1.

[152] Pohl, *'Judenpolitik'*, 162–3; Sandkühler, 'Lemberg-Janowska', 627.

[153] Konieczny, ' "Organisation Schmeldt" ', 106–7.

The availability of labour from the concentration camps developed real significance for the war economy only after Stalingrad and the accompanying conscription campaigns. The shortage of workers was worsened by Hitler's refusal to deploy women labourers in sufficiently large numbers. Simultaneously, the pressure was increasing for use of the available camp labour from armaments minister, Albert Speer.[154] 'Rationalizing' impulses also hailed from some members of the WVHA with whom Speer had developed a good relationship.[155]

The moves for camp inmate deployment in the armament industry ultimately also affected some Jews. In the WVHA work schemes that were partially realized from 1942 onwards, non-Jews and later Jews over whom it had authority (mainly those who were sent to Auschwitz), were hired out for exploitation by private and state industry;[156] many were also distributed within the SS for its own purposes. From late in 1943 this arrangement was expanded. The most concerted use of Jewish labour followed on from the deportation of the largest Jewish community remaining in Europe, the Hungarian Jews, from May 1944. Of the 458,000 deported, at least 108,000 were put at the disposal of the German war economy, compounding the several thousand Jews of other nationalities under the control of the WVHA.[157]

The murder process, of course, continued. The strength of the murderous impulses emanating from Berlin reflected years of 'cumulative radicalization', and Adolf Eichmann's determination to murder all of the Hungarian Jews as quickly as possible matched the WVHA's inclination to exploit their labour in the short term.[158] As Rudolf Höss recalled, there were times when he was lambasted by Oswald Pohl for his failure to divert sufficient Jews to labour projects and chastised by the Gestapo for failing to execute more.[159] While some Hungarian Jews were being exploited for their labour, hundreds of thousands more were being murdered in the Birkenau gas chambers during the busiest period in that camp's history. As throughout the period, with some exceptions,[160] labour did not replace gassing as a defined means of murdering Jews at Auschwitz. Gassing

---

[154] Ulrich Herbert, 'Von Auschwitz nach Essen: Die Geschichte des KZ-Aussenlagers Humboltstrasse', in *Dachauer Hefte, 2. Sklavenarbeit in KZ* (Munich: Deutscher Taschenbuch Verlag, 1986), 13–34, esp. 18–19.

[155] Michael Thad Allen, 'Engineers and Modern Managers in the SS', Ph.D. thesis (Pennsylvania, 1995).

[156] See Franciszek Piper, *Arbeitseinsatz der Häftlinge aus dem KL Auschwitz* (Auschwitz: Auschwitz State Museum, 1995), 81, 291, for figures.

[157] Figures cited in Birgit Weitz, 'Der Einsatz von KZ-Häftlingen und jüdischen Zwangsarbeitern bei der Daimler-Benz AG (1941–1945)', in Hermann Kaienburg (ed.), *Konzentrationslager und deutsche Wirtschaft 1939–1945* (Opladen: Leske and Budrich, 1996), 169–95, esp. 175. This number may well be too low: 39,000 Jews, mostly Hungarians, were used in 1944–5 in the Dachau Aussenlager of Kaufering and Mühldorf alone: Raim, *Die Dachauer KZ-Aussenkommandos Kaufering und Mühldorf*, 176–8.

[158] Garbe, 'Absonderung, Strafkommandos und spezifischer Terror', in Arno Herzig and Ina Lorenz (eds.), *Verdrängung und Vernichtung der Juden unter dem Nationalsozialismus* (Hamburg: Hans Christians, 1992), 173–204, p. 195.

[159] Nuremberg interrogation of Höss, 2 Apr. 1946, 13–15, printed in *The Holocaust: Selected Documents in Eighteen Volumes*, ed. John Mendelsohn (New York: Garland, 1982), xii, 56–127.

[160] Bloxham, ' "Extermination through Work" ', 25–6.

continued alongside the labour process, and exhausted workers were gassed, but so were many who were eminently capable of work.

Generalizations are also possible about those put to work. Direct employment by the SS and the civil authorities in the east was almost certain to end in murder. Here the formula 'extermination through work' acted more as a justification for keeping 'productive' Jews alive in the short term for economic reasons. Under German industry, too, the majority of the slaves were worked murderously hard, and death rates were concomitantly staggering. However, while it is apparent that transfer to private industry in many cases meant no alleviation in the severity of the workload and no improvement in working conditions,[161] it is also evident that it did imply a certain discretion on behalf of the management concerned.[162] That this leeway (*Handlungsspielraum*) was often not exploited for the betterment of inmate care is not, however, to be attributed to a total identification with the Nazis' genocidal goals, but rather to more prosaic factors.

From the purely utilitarian point of view taken by many industrialists, there were strong arguments for the use of slave labourers. Many firms were unwilling to make substantial capital investments in 1943–4 in anticipation of Germany losing the war. Expensive military production lines would soon be rendered redundant, they reasoned; thus it was far better to make production labour intensive, particularly when that labour and its upkeep were cheap. The existence of large labour forces would give the impression of high-tempo production and prevent the dissolution of companies during the war, thus preserving them in the long term.[163]

The callous attitude of such firms to their imprisoned workforces should be attributed to economic considerations calculated in an environment of moral tunnel vision created over years of collusion with Nazism and acted upon within the parameters of the racial hierarchy established by the regime. Profit, efficiency, self-preservation, and long-term survival planning were conceived in terms of instrumental rationality—that is, irrespective of the human cost. Firms expected to get some economic benefit from using slaves,[164] and to maximize that benefit they wished to provide the bare minimum in terms of outlay for these people. Besides, they reasoned, there would always be replacements for the dead. Many leading industrialists were nazified, but all were interested in what

---

[161] Herbert Obenaus, 'Die Aussenkommandos des Konzentrationslagers Neuengamme in Hannover', in Hermann Kaienburg (ed.), *Konzentrationslager und deutsche Wirtschaft 1939–1945* (Opladen: Leske and Budrich, 1996), 211–26, esp. 219–21.

[162] Thomas Sandkühler, 'Zwangsarbeit und Judenmord im Distrikt Galizien des Generalgouvernements', in Hermann Kaienburg (ed.), *Konzentrationslager und deutsche Wirtschaft 1939–1945* (Opladen: Leske and Budrich, 1996), 239–62, esp. 261; implicit in Neil Gregor, *Daimler-Benz in the Third Reich* (New Haven, Conn.: Yale University Press, 1998), 216–17; Manchester, *The Arms of Krupp*, 535–66.

[163] Ludolf Herbst, *Der Totale Krieg und die Ordnung der Wirtschaft* (Stuttgart: Deutsche Verlags-Anstalt, 1982). Mark Spoerer, 'Profitierten Unternehmen von KZ-Arbeit?', *Historische Zeitschrift*, 268 (1999), 61–95, esp. 72–3, 89; Gregor, *Daimler-Benz*; id., 'The Normalisation of Barbarism: Daimler-Benz in the "Third Reich" ', *Journal of Holocaust Education*, 6, no. 3 (1997), 1–20, esp. 15.

[164] Spoerer, 'Profitierten', 87–90.

capitalists are interested in—the success of their ventures. There are some notable cases in which leeway was used: the well-known case of Oskar Schindler and the less-renowned deeds of the Karpathen-Öl employee Berthold Beitz, for instance.[165] The benevolent actions of these men were, however, only possible because of structural factors: their operations had been declared *kriegswichtig*.

This is not merely an exercise in semantics: it shows that the interaction of practicality and ideological determinacy is not to be explained by the compromise formula of 'extermination through work', but by a combination of high-political shifts, mid-level initiatives, and 'shop-floor' callousness. The employment of Jews was only a temporary concession to the dictates of the war economy, and, in terms of the numbers of people forced to work by the Third Reich, Jewish labour was not very important. However, it is certain that *some* Jews were *always* being used for work. Further, at the moment in which Jewish labour did achieve a real quantitative importance, in 1944, the exterminatory impulse was tempered in some spheres: Jews were even allowed back into the Reich in that year on the instruction of Hitler himself, a notable concession given the prior success in rendering the territory 'free of Jews'.[166] Such developments inadvertently made a very real difference to the life-chances of some Jews,[167] but the chief relevance of the investigation lies more in comprehending the Nazi system of persecution. Contrary to the 'Nuremberg' line, that system was neither monolithic nor (indeed) entirely ideologically driven.

5.5 CONCLUSIONS

A glimpse at the footnotes of any history of the Holocaust indicates the extent to which the Nuremberg interrogations and documentary base have 'factually' informed thinking up to and including the present day. Providence, and 'the bureaucratic mania of Nazi officials' in preserving a 'documentary abundance'[168] contributed greatly to this bounty of evidence, but this should not detract from the significant input of the war crimes investigators and OCCPAC and OCCWC staff in locating and organizing the material. A significant elementary bequest was the number of Jewish dead, the first such estimate forwarded by a non-Jewish body. The 6 million figure has become totemic for the morally outraged and a target for deniers. On this symbolic level the importance of a judicial pronouncement on the murder of the Jews is self-evident. By the most recent estimates the total may actually be on the low side.[169]

Nuremberg could only be a beginning, however, and it is unfortunate that the gauntlet cast down there was not seriously taken up by the courts of the Bundesrepublik. Rather like the British Royal Warrant series, if with different emphases, the German prosecutors retreated to investigation of the direct

---

[165] Sandkühler, *'Endlösung' in Galizien*, 421.   [166] Herbert, 'Von Auschwitz nach Essen'.
[167] Ibid.   [168] Smith, *The Road to Nuremberg*, 239.
[169] Sandkühler, 'Die Täter des Holocaust', 46, suggests approx. 6.2 million.

implementers of atrocity. They ignored the formulators of policy and those vast swathes in between who 'made the trains run on time' but who had also to decide when the trains ran, where to, and who was put in them.

The Nuremberg prosecutors wished to establish the responsibility of the individual under international law even in a totalitarian state. However, the liberal-democratic understanding of 'totalitarian' Nazism stereotyped it as a system. Therein, ran the assumption, lesser participants were simply faced with the choice of whether or not to obey orders. The idea of the bit-part players on the geographical periphery actually establishing a dialectic relationship with the power-centre was not admitted by the conspiracy theory and was probably never conceived of by prosecutors whose imaginations were always one step behind the terrible reality of the Third Reich. In any case, the primary prosecutorial task was to gain convictions of the senior Germans who stood in the dock, which meant emphasizing their influence: once again, the privileging of the perpetrator's person over the perpetrated event. The locus of the criminal responsibility of most of the 'lesser' perpetrators in eastern Europe added another layer of confusion and distance from the reality of the crime, as the abbreviated investigation of Aktion Reinhard showed.

On the 'new' historiographical revelations of the 'consensus politics' characterizing the development of the 'final solution' in eastern Europe, and the mass participation in the crime, we are once again drawn back to the unique but oft-ignored insight of the victim as represented by the Israeli ambassador at the opening of the Vernichtungskrieg Exhibition in Aachen. 'The survivors of the Holocaust', he said, have never made a distinction between the German police, the . . . Einsatzgruppen, SS or Wehrmacht'.[170] Grasping the full extent of complicity in the 'final solution' may well have been beyond the legal imagination between 1945 and 1949, but once again, the evidence of it was available.

As the case study of 'extermination through work' shows, a focused examination of Hilberg's minutiae reveals the complex, multi-faceted nature of Nazi-German Jewish policy. When taken alongside detailed motivational studies such as Christopher Browning's portrait of the 'ordinary men' of the Reserve Order Police—absent again from 'Nuremberg', for reasons explored above—with its conclusion that the routes to killing were also diverse, it becomes clear that general models explaining the 'final solution' are by nature imprecise. However, given Daniel Goldhagen's recent restatement of what is effectively an intentionalist-conspiracy interpretation, if depicting a conspiracy which is as broad as the German population of the Hitler era,[171] the temptation will seemingly always be there for some to reduce the Shoah completely to its concrete core of antisemitism. In this vision, ordinary men become zealots and ZALs and Aussenlager become extermination centres, which at times they were, *de facto* if

---

[170] 'Ansprache des Botschafters des Staates Israel', ed. Wisser, 2.
[171] Goldhagen, *Hitler's Willing Executioners.*

not *de jure*, but at other times they were clearly not; and the generalistic concept of the 'camp' bequeathed by the post-war trials again rears its head.

Yet while some contemporary historians may be held culpable for clinging to undiluted reductionist interpretations of the 'final solution' and Nazi Germany, the same is not true of the Allied prosecutors and jurists. To try to map from first principles the genesis and operation of the genocidal state would have taken more time and historical perspective than they had, or than the impatient, amnesiac peoples of their contemporary world would allow. Motivation—the ultimate 'why' of the Holocaust—was a matter of assumption rather than investigation. OCCPAC, OCCWC, the British and American JAGs, and the multitude of judges garnered from the military and civilian ranks of either country were frequently and understandably off the mark. Students of history today can do little that is more important than revising and concluding their work.

Conclusions

Writing the histories of the myriad Nazi shooting massacres in eastern Europe is not always a precise process owing to the nature of the evidence. Many such killings have only been disclosed through German legal proceedings against the perpetrators, and the death tolls given in the courtrooms are by necessity minimums. We might attribute this phenomenon to the 'structural' parameters of the trial process: it is a reduction of the past based upon the need to establish the provable rather than the probable, and encapsulates the difference between legal and historical evidence. In the same category of obstructions to historical representation come restrictions on the cumulative use of evidence, such that it is not essential to show that 'X' killed 1,000 people if he will be convicted on the proof of 100 murders. Relatedly, as with the judgement on Viktor Brack in the Nuremberg Medical trial, defendants may be damned on one crime without need of recourse to other episodes.

A different kind of parameter is imposed by the notion of 'judicial notice', whether formally or informally applied. The idea of taking for granted matters of 'common knowledge' backfired when, as in the case of Konrad Morgan's and Kurt Gerstein's evidence on the Reinhard killing centres, evidence contradicted what was held to be 'true' of the extreme nature of the western concentration camps, and seemed fantastic. Common knowledge and common sense are not the constants that they at first appear, particularly when dealing with extreme acts.

A mixture of structural limitation and judicial assumption characterized the judgement on the Einsatzgruppen leaders and the 'Nuremberg' depiction of the Nazi state as a whole. The evidence pointed to a staggering number of deaths and broad complicity. Some of the guilty men stood in the dock, clearly linked to mass murder by the documentation to hand. The racist motivation seemed obvious, and as Nazism had been an authoritarian/totalitarian system, it was also assumed that, as some of the defendants pleaded, superior orders were the be-all and end-all of policy implementation. The legal process did not demand that anyone read between the lines of the documents to discern that complicity was even broader than it appeared, and stemmed from many different roots. Nor did it require that the defences of the accused be broken down to find that not every murder had been ordered from Berlin, and that alongside broad genocidal directives killing policy could develop incrementally and locally, and sometimes inconsistently.

As so much evidence on the murder of the Jews has emerged from the legal milieu, understanding that context is an important step in understanding the genocide, and in breaking down the generalizations used to construct all-encompassing concepts like 'the Holocaust'. Slave labour, for instance, was an integral aspect of the fate of many Jews during the war, and as such requires closer examination; it also represents one of the frayed edges of the Holocaust meta-narrative that was bequeathed to us from the post-war trials. The seemingly self-explanatory 'extermination through work' was a red herring left in the documentation so valued by OCCPAC, and was seized upon unquestioningly because it fitted a prosecution strategy. For the historian of the present day, discerning such complexities within Nazi Jewish policy is as important a task as was that in previous decades of pinpointing the Shoah as a particular entity amongst many 'crimes against humanity'.

Much has been written in this book about the absence of the victims' voices at crucial points during the formation of perceptions of Nazi genocide. That situation has happily been remedied in recent years as the Holocaust has assumed huge proportions in the historical consciousness of the 'west', and survivors have become important conduits for its contemplation. Paradoxically, the call now should be for scholars to regain interpretative ground. The dimensions and form of the Holocaust are approximately known—Belzec, Sobibor, and Treblinka are no longer so well hidden—and the vast suffering has been given a human face. The time is upon us for sensitive yet informed assessments of the period. Nevertheless, the weight of public and academic discourse obscures the fact that the incremental expansions and refinements of our knowledge which are the contributions first of the archival researcher are being made by comparatively few. In the best of all worlds, a genuine synthesis of the perspectives of eyewitness and document would replace the process of alternating dominance that has characterized examination of the Holocaust since Nuremberg.

Assessing the historiographical legacy of the trials is not the ahistorical exercise that it may at first seem. The Nuremberg prosecutors effectively established themselves as historical authorities. In the extent of their concern with historical and moral 'lessons' they arguably went beyond the traditional remit of their profession. In the methods that they used to illustrate their case, they certainly exceeded the boundaries of legal precedent, and thereby created something of a hostage to fortune.

Around the courtroom itself, however, the interpretative problems were of a different nature. The difficulties which Allied officials and jurists had in comprehending the deeds of a fellow occidental, Christian culture must not be underestimated. The very term 'genocide' was introduced into popular parlance in the crucible of the post-war years to accommodate the German extermination policies, and if the concept of eradicating a people was not in itself new, the manner in which the Nazis carried it out certainly was. Thus with hindsight, removing the trials for a moment from the circumstances in which they were conducted, the chief criticism of Allied war crimes policy does not concern the peculiarities of the procedure, but rather the failure to try more perpetrators on more counts.

What we may say of the trials, particularly the thirteen Nuremberg cases, is that they were the greatest, most enduring attempts to investigate Nazism and its effects in something approaching a detached way. Trials long outlived 're-education' policy as it was initially conceived, and eventually they stood as the only official conduit for the examination of the Nazi past. Though the legal machinery was eroded swiftly in the late 1940s, and crumbled completely in the 1950s, the trial records remained, indelible. And though the Nuremberg authors trod on unsure legal ground, they also instituted an invaluable precedent for the future punishment of state crimes. Judging 'Nuremberg' purely in terms of the achievements and legacy of OCCPAC and OCCWC, it seems justified to extend Michael Biddiss's assessment of the IMT trial, and award the whole venture if not three cheers then very decidedly two.[1]

But the trials did not occur in a vacuum. If 'Nuremberg' as a concept is seen, in Telford Taylor's words, not simply as what transpired there in the post-war years but as 'what was said and done about it, there and subsequently',[2] then it is inevitable that judgements will go hard on it. The trials have served in Germany as a totemic but dual-faceted reminder both of guilt and of the imposition of punishment by alien powers. The latent presence of each of these competing demons was made manifest during the Vietnam War, as evidence of American atrocities and the suspicion of imperialist ends elicited criticism of American hypocrisy in the conduct of international affairs and a comparison of American guilt with that of German youth's own fathers. Manifestly symbolic also was the inauguration by the German Green Party of a 'war crimes' tribunal in Nuremberg at the height of the arms race, designed to draw attention to American nuclear strategy.[3]

What of the immediate milieu of the trials? All-too-many historians of the trial of the major war criminals in particular have lifted it out of its surroundings, with two major consequences. In one direction, the approach has allowed historians to overlook the fact that many of the participants of that trial viewed it as the beginning of a greater purge, and that many other trials were in distinct relationships with the IMT case. In some instances that relationship was purely negative, in the attempts of, say, the British to dissociate themselves from the American venture. In other cases, and those handled by the OCCWC are the most obvious examples, the legal-theoretical legacy is clear. Whichever course other British and American proceedings took, it was impossible to move entirely beyond the shadow cast by the IMT trial, so as well as being a seminal event in its own right the trial was also part of a process.

[1] Biddiss, 'The Nuremberg Trial: Two Exercises in Judgement'.
[2] Telford Taylor, *Nuremberg and Vietnam: An American Tragedy* (New York: Bantam, 1971), 4.
[3] Dan Diner, *Verkehrte Welten: Antiamerikanismus in Deutschland: Ein historischer Essay* (Frankfurt am Main: Eichborn, 1993), 141–2, 147–8; Jochmann, *Gesellschaftskrise und Judenfeindschaft*, 337.

Moreover, despite the narrowness of the Royal Warrant, the absence of written opinions in judgements under that legislation, and the prevailing suspicion of the principles of 'Nuremberg', the British players were drawn inexorably into the broader exercise of re-education. The context of the occupation, with its pronouncements on aggression, complicity, and depravity ensured this. German eyes remained on the occupiers and the Allied treatment of suspected war criminals—if not their crimes—became very significant. This brings us to the second problem of studying the IMT trial in isolation.

Michael Marrus's examination of the trial of the major war criminals, along with that of Jürgen Wilke, ignores the way that the revelations of that case fitted into other available representations and narratives of Nazi genocide. For while the IMT case was the dominant legal form, it was only one of a number of influences on perceptions of Nazi criminality. The prevalent concentration camp imagery of 1945–6, with its attendant complexities, was of enduring international importance, as in a different way in Germany was the guilt literature of the period. What emerges from this study is the complex interrelation between the German political and psychological situation and British and American domestic, foreign, occupation, and trial policies, which in turn fed off cultural assumptions about Nazism and totalitarianism, and also about Jews and anti-semitism.

It is a staple of deconstructionism that the writing of history is influenced by the socio-cultural predispositions of the writer. Not every proto-historian of the post-war era had such extreme partisan interests as Reginald Paget, but each none the less prejudged to some degree. By the same token the Royal Warrant may signify what we might term, by today's tenets, an 'inappropriate' approach to German criminality. The British zonal trial programme never came to terms with Nazi genocide, and nor was it designed to do so. Yet in 1945 the Royal Warrant was undeniably the product of a particular 'common sense'—a liberal, Anglo-Saxon, legalistic 'common sense'. Notwithstanding the conspiracy-criminal organization plan and the other legal innovations of the period, OCCPAC and OCCWC were not able to escape completely from the experiences and value system that spawned them: OCCPAC's treatment of the camp system is sufficient testimony to that.

If we look to the determinants of American policy that impinged on representations of the Shoah, we encounter matters both strategic and ideological. The disproportionately document-led approach, with its debt to technical anti-trust suits, set the tone for the IMT trial and beyond. It bored observers and simultaneously obscured some of the more extreme crimes of which documentary evidence had been destroyed or successfully concealed. Although the strategy was understandable and was predicated in part on practicality, it also slotted into a tradition of suspicion in Anglo-American officialdom of the evidence of victims, particularly Jews and particularly eastern Europeans. Furthermore, it was a means of marshalling identifiable strands of the recent past, some of which were ethnic-specific, for a liberal, universalist goal for the future: the juridical condemnation of aggressive war.

'Antisemitism' is far too crude and perjorative a term to be of use in analysing the Allied reaction to the murder of the Jews. It is even less useful when discussing trial policy, where legal considerations were thrown into the political mixture. What we may say with surety is that British legalism was not prepared to embrace the precarious idea of 'crimes against humanity', and British liberalism did not permit the murder of the Jews to be given any specific consideration even within those legal constraints. Somewhat differently, the Nuremberg strategists were disposed to make allowance for crimes committed outside the context of military engagement, yet they could not let the centrality of antisemitism in the Third Reich displace their own analysis of Nazism. Not only would a more accurate representation of the Nazi system have detracted from the prioritizing of aggressive war in the OCCPAC-OCCWC plan, it would have contravened the unwritten rule of the liberal democracies that the Jewish fate—and, by definition, Jews—should not be allowed to steal the show.

The conspiracy-criminal organization theory and its effects have been central to much of this book. If the concept brought into court persecutions that would otherwise have remained inadmissible, it also deflected attention from the persecutions themselves towards an abstract set of structures and putative causes. In this way the Nuremberg trials exaggerated the essential characteristic of the judicial process: its focus on the perpetrator, defined broadly as Nazism and narrowly as the defendants in the dock. In this way also the trials were something of a microcosm of the whole 're-education' process, which sponsored a peculiarly narrow and victim-free analysis of the Nazi years.

As a didactic model, though hardly as one of legal propriety, the Americans might perversely have taken a lead from the Soviet purge trials.[4] As propaganda tools, these were much more effective in focusing, often in agonizing detail, upon the deeds of the accused in order to stimulate revulsion. It is presumably no accident that, while formulating the IMT's judgement, one of the Soviet judges asked for a greater examination of the Nazi crimes—including a detailed account of the gas chamber operations—alongside the theoretical exposition of law.[5] The paradox of the use of due process to illustrate both the evils of Nazism and the benefits of democratic justice was that it invited, and duly received, scrutiny of the legal mechanisms and of the Allied treatment of the defendants. A common thread links the shock waves caused by the reported ill-treatment of the Malmédy murderers to the revulsion at trying the 'half-blind' Manstein: the perpetrators were now the objects, themselves prisms through which to view the conduct of the occupiers.

In the short term, in the polities on either side of the trial divide, the opponents of the trials exploited all of their shortcomings: the early collaboration with

---

4 I thank Lisa Kirschenbaum for this observation.
5 Biddle papers, box 14, file 'Notes on judgment: meetings of tribunal to discuss judgment', 31.

the Soviets; the creation of a legal mechanism specifically for the trial of the defeated by the victors; the use of *ex post facto* law; and the absence of appellate procedure. On the broader public level, the switch of focus from that which had been intended, between Germany and its past, to that between occupied and occupier, marginalized the substance of the trials. This was no more evident than in the case of Manstein in particular and the Wehrmacht in general.

Despite Jackson's and Taylor's best efforts, the twin phenomena of 'camp' and soldierly criminality remained distinct in the perceptions of most observers in Germany and to the west. That state of affairs has only been modified recently, and primarily in Germany, to the credit of that country's historical profession. The camps, it was perceived after the initial anti-German outpourings of 1945, remained the preserve of the 'beastly' SS men, and women: Josef Kramer of Belsen and Ilse Koch of Buchenwald to the fore. The genuine extermination camps in Poland were accorded little attention. The Vernichtungskrieg, in as much as it was acknowledged at all beyond eastern Europe, remained a function of a different tradition altogether—a Prussian 'militarism' which, if undesirable, was still in some way 'western' and thus 'civilized', and was in any case more a matter of virile aggression than depravity. If genocide was not simply written out of the conflict by the military interest, it remained an abstract crime committed at a distance. German and 'Allied' rationalization of the Wehrmacht's role in the USSR was made progressively easier as the latter was re-elevated to the status of enemy of the occident.

Meanwhile, the homicidal gas chamber may well have entered western consciousness in 1945, but it did not signify the apparatus of total murder of a particular, racially defined victim group. Rather, and in no small measure as a result of the early trials, it remained bound up with ill-defined notions of 'concentration camps' that could symbolize anything from the suffering of Jews to that of German political prisoners to the threat posed by the Soviet Union. Obviously, neither of the latter two images was conducive to pressure for a thorough-going reform of German society in the post-war context, and it bears restating that the first was not promoted by occupation regimes which remained distinctly ambivalent about prioritizing Jewish suffering.

It would be a historical misrepresentation to attribute the course of West German *Vergangenheitspolitik* to the occupation and trial policies of the Allies. The way that the BRD dealt with its past developed predominantly from within a society characterized on one hand by the trauma of collapse and the requisites of regeneration, and on the other by continuities from the Nazi period. What is apparent though is that, regardless of intent, little the Allies did ran in practical terms counter to the German process of 'mastering the past', much that they did easily accommodated it, and some of their measures actually fortified it.

Elsewhere, the role of trials in the memory process was also a function of the surrounding social and political milieux. Official readings of the past in the Communist bloc were layered thickly on top of judicial findings, and though some of the post-war scholarship pursued behind the Iron Curtain was not as precon-ditioned as is often thought, the popularized version does not stand up to histor-ical scrutiny, especially as regards the Holocaust. In the matter of the murder of the Jews, the eastern European nations also had their own competing narratives of communal suffering under Nazism which were in themselves legitimate, even if they also acted as convenient tools in the official sculpting of post-war identity. Indeed, most of continental Europe, whether 'Communist' or not, had records of suffering and 'martyrdom' to promote, and records of collaboration or acquiescence—again, particularly in the Holocaust—to downplay.

The IMT trial, with its huge remit, allowed most vested interests to pick what they wanted from the proceedings, as the French did with Marie-Claude Vail-lant-Couturier and her story of resistance. But to understand the French refrac-tion of their own occupation is impossible without recourse to *l'épuration*, the political purge at the end of the war and its psychological effects. The French case, like those of the eastern bloc nations, must also be assessed in terms of the pre-war history of those countries, marked as they were by complex and often unfriendly relations between Jews and non-Jews.

Britain and the USA are ostensibly more straightforward cases, as they had re-mained unoccupied, and in their self-images were less ideologically doctrinaire. Nevertheless, there were still powerful national meta-narratives to pursue in the liberal democracies. There, the war had been a dichotomized battle of good against evil, freedom against bondage, but at no time had it been fought specific-ally to end the greatest evil: Hitler's programmes of genocide. When the concen-tration camps were liberated, they were held up as *ex post facto* justifications of what 'we' had been fighting against; this had never been made specific in the rhetoric of what 'we' had been fighting *for*.[6] And when Holocaust survivors arrived on 'our' shores, they were provided with homes and means of living, but not with an ear for their experiences, because these were increasingly seen as dis-tasteful reminders of the war amongst populations anxious to get on with the peace.

It is impossible to predict what the effect would have been of a radically different occupation policy, though it is reasonable enough to suppose that in the absence of the Cold War more criminals would have been tried and the early releases of the 1950s would have been more controversial, had they happened at all. Jeffrey Herf has suggested that not too much should be made of the international situ-ation as a factor in the process, because the democratic development of the BRD meant that the German population would not tolerate much public 'memory' of their crimes. Notwithstanding the fact that repression of memory was not a regi-mented phenomenon, the subtle differences between Allied 'justice' and genu-ine 'memory' of the Holocaust have already been highlighted. Moreover, the

---

[6] Reilly, *Belsen*; Kushner, *The Holocaust and the Liberal Imagination*.

Allied publics, and indeed the whole of Europe,[7] grew tired of hearing about war crimes and trials in a similar time-frame to the west Germans. Conversely, the actions of the South African Truth and Reconciliation Committee, albeit in a different historical context, have suggested that it is possible to combine democratic development with some consciousness of the crimes of apartheid but with less 'justice' in the commonly held sense of the term.[8] The South African analogy seems to indicate that the mode of instruction *is* important; this book has attempted to show in what ways that may be the case.

[7] Deak's introduction to Deak, Gross, and Judt (eds.), *The Politics of Retribution in Europe*, 12.
[8] Robert I. Rotberg and Dennis Thompson (eds.), *Truth v. Justice: The Morality of Truth Commissions* (Princeton, NJ: Princeton University Press, 2000).

Appendices

The Tribunal established . . . for the trial and punishment of the major war criminals of the European Axis countries shall have the power to try and punish persons who, acting in the interests of the European countries, whether as individuals or as members of organizations, committed any of the following crimes.

The following acts, or any of them, are crimes coming within the jurisdiction of the Tribunal for which there shall be individual responsibility:

(a) Crimes against Peace: namely, planning, preparation, initiation or waging of a war of aggression, or a war in violation of international treaties, agreements or assurances, or participation in a Common Plan or Conspiracy for the accomplishment of any of the foregoing;

(b) War Crimes: namely violations of the laws or customs of war. Such violations shall include, but not be limited to, murder, ill-treatment or deportation to slave labor or for any other purpose of civilian populations of or in occupied territory, murder or ill-treatment of prisoners of war or persons on the seas, killing of hostages, plunder of public or private property, wanton destruction of cities, towns or villages, or devastation not justified by military necessity;

(c) Crimes against Humanity: namely, murder, extermination, enslavement, deportation, and other inhumane acts committed against any civilian population, before or during the war, or persecutions on political, racial, or religious grounds in execution of or in connection with any crime within the jurisdiction of the Tribunal, whether or not in violation of domestic law of the country where perpetrated.

Leaders, organizers, instigators, and accomplices participating in the formulation or execution of a Common Plan or Conspiracy to commit any of the foregoing crimes are responsible for all acts performed by any persons in execution of such a plan.

The individual defendants each faced permutations of the four counts into which the three criminal classes outlined in Appendix A were divided, viz:

1. the common plan or conspiracy;
2. crimes against peace;
3. war crimes;
4. crimes against humanity.

Defendants

Göring, Hermann: Reichsmarschall and Commander in Chief of the Airforce.
Indicted on all four counts, convicted on all four.

Hess, Rudolf: the Führer's Deputy for Party Affairs until 1941.
Indicted on all four counts, convicted on all four.

Ribbentrop, Joachim von: Foreign Minister.
Indicted on all four counts, convicted on all four.

Rosenberg, Alfred: Reichsleiter for Ideology and Foreign Policy and Minister for the Occupied Eastern Territories.
Indicted on all four counts, convicted on all four.

Frank, Hans: Governor-General of the Generalgouvernement region of Poland.
Indicted on counts 1, 3, and 4, convicted on 3 and 4.

Kaltenbrunner, Ernst: Head of the RSHA from 1942.
Indicted on counts 1, 3, and 4, convicted on 3 and 4.

Frick, Wilhelm: former Reich Minister of the Interior and Protector of Bohemia and Moravia.
Indicted on all four counts, convicted on 2, 3, and 4.

Streicher, Julius: antisemitic propagandist and Gauleiter of Franconia until 1940.
Indicted on counts 1 and 4, convicted on 4.

Keitel, Wilhelm: Field Marshal and Chief of the High Command of the Armed Forces.
Indicted on all four counts, convicted on all four.

Funk, Walther: President of the Reichsbank from 1939.
Indicted on all four counts, convicted on 2, 3, and 4.

Schacht, Hjalmar: Minister of Economics, 1934–7 and President of the Reichsbank until 1939.
Indicted on counts 1 and 2, acquitted on both.

Dönitz, Karl: Commander-in-Chief of the Navy and Chancellor, May 1945.
Indicted on counts 1, 2, and 3, convicted on 2 and 3.

Schirach, Baldur von: Leader of the Hitler Youth and Gauleiter of Vienna.
Indicted on counts 1 and 4, convicted on 4.

Sauckel, Fritz: Plenipotentiary-General for Labour Allocation and Gauleiter of Thuringia.
Indicted on all four counts, convicted on 3 and 4.

Speer, Albert: Minister for Armaments and War Production.
Indicted on all four counts, convicted on 3 and 4.

Papen, Franz von: former Vice-Chancellor and Special Envoy to Vienna.
Indicted on counts 1 and 2, acquitted on both.

Jodl, Alfred: Chief of Operations Staff of the High Command of the Armed Forces.
Indicted on all four counts, convicted on all four.

Neurath, Constantin von: Foreign Minister, 1932–8 and former Protector of Bohemia and Moravia.
Indicted on all four counts, convicted on all four.

Seyss-Inquart, Artur: Reich Commissioner for the Netherlands.
Indicted on all four counts, convicted on 2, 3, and 4.

Raeder, Erich: Commander-in-Chief of the Navy, 1928–43.
Indicted on counts 1, 2, and 3, convicted on all three.

Fritzsche, Hans: Head of the Broadcasting Division in the Propaganda Ministry.
Indicted on counts 1, 3, and 4, acquitted on all three.
Bormann, Martin (*in absentia*): Head of the Party Chancellery.
Indicted on counts 1, 3, and 4, convicted on counts 3 and 4.

Organizations

The indicted organizations were adjudged simply upon whether or not they were 'criminal'.
The Reich cabinet: declared not to be criminal.
The leadership corps of the Nazi Party: declared to be criminal.
The SS: declared to be criminal.
The Gestapo and SD: declared to be criminal.
The SA: declared not to be criminal.
The General Staff and High Command of the Armed Forces: declared not to be criminal.

APPENDIX C: THE SUBSEQUENT NUREMBERG PROCEEDINGS

Case no. 1: USA versus Karl Brandt *et al.* ('the Medical trial'): involving senior doctors and scientists implicated in experiments on concentration camp inmates and in the 'euthanasia' programme.
Case no. 2: USA versus Erhard Milch ('the Milch trial'): concerning his involvement in the slave labour programme and medical experiments on Dachau inmates.
Case no. 3: USA versus Josef Altstötter *et al.* ('the Justice trial'): involving high-ranking jurists charged with perverting the course of justice during the Nazi years.
Case no. 4: USA versus Oswald Pohl *et al.* ('the Concentration camp/WVHA trial'): involving the staff of the SS Business Administration Head Office responsible for the administration of concentration camps and related economic enterprises.
Case no. 5: USA versus Friedrick Flick *et al.* ('the Flick trial'): involving representatives of an industrial concern implicated in slave labour, spoliation, and the 'aryanization' of Jewish capital.
Case no. 6: USA versus Karl Krauch *et al.* ('the Farben trial'): involving representatives of a chemical conglomerate charged with aiding and abetting the Nazi plans for aggressive war, and for the use of slave labour.
Case no. 7: USA versus Wilhelm List *et al.* ('the Balkan generals/hostages trial'): involving high-ranking military personnel charged with various war crimes, including reprisal murders and the illegal killing of hostages.
Case no. 8: USA versus Ulrich Greifelt *et al.* ('the RuSHA trial'): involving representatives of various SS offices concerned in the forced evacuation and 'Germanization' of occupied countries, and with other Nazi plans of 'racial re-organization'.
Case no. 9: USA versus Otto Ohlendorf *et al.* ('the Einsatzgruppen trial'): involving leading members of SS and police units responsible for racially and politically motivated mass murders.
Case no. 10: USA versus Alfried Krupp *et al.* ('the Krupp trial'): involving the eponymous industrialist and his associates charged with aiding and abetting the Nazi plans for aggressive war, and with the use of slave labour.

Case no. 11: USA versus Ernst von Weizsäcker *et al.* ('the Ministries trial'): involving a range of defendants, including government officials, SS leaders, economists, and propagandists, on charges ranging from crimes against peace to crimes against humanity.

Case no. 12: USA versus Wilhelm von Leeb *et al.* ('the High Command trial'): involving high-ranking military personnel charged with planning for aggressive war and with war crimes and crimes against humanity.

Bibliography

PRIMARY SOURCES (I): UNPUBLISHED MATERIALS

Records from the following collections and classes:

Germany
Institut für Zeitgeschichte, Munich:
    FG 16, report of the deputy judge advocate

The Netherlands
International Court of Justice, the Hague:
    Minutes of the closed sessions of the International Military Tribunal

United Kingdom
Bodleian Library, Oxford:
    Goodhart papers
Churchill College archives, Cambridge:
    Hankey papers
    Kilmuir papers
Durham Records Office:
    Cuthbert Headlam diaries
House of Lords Records Office, London:
    Beaverbrook papers
    Stow-Hill papers
Imperial War Museum library, London:
    Official film of the trial of the major war criminals
    Welt im Film
Lambeth Palace library, London:
    Bell papers
Liddell Hart Centre for Military Archives, King's College, London:
    Bishop papers
    Hakewill-Smith papers
    Liddell Hart papers
    Von Manstein trial transcripts
National Library of Wales, Aberystwyth:
    Elwyn Jones papers
Public Record Office, Kew:
    Cabinet papers, CAB 65, 66, 128, 129, 130
    Foreign Office papers, FO 371, 937, 945, 1019, 1032, 1049, 1060
    Lord Chancellor's Office papers, LCO 2
    Prime Minister's papers, PREM 4, 8
    Treasury Solicitor's papers, TS 26
    War Office papers, WO 32, 204, 208, 219, 235

Shropshire County Record Office, Shrewsbury:
  Bridgeman papers
University of Birmingham Archive:
  Avon papers
University of Southampton Archive:
  Jewish Chronicle Archive
  Papers of the International Military Tribunal
  Papers of the subsequent Nuremberg military tribunals
  Nuremberg interrogation summaries
  Papers of the Institute of Jewish Affairs
University of Sussex Archive:
  Mass-Observation Archive:
    Diaries (1945–50)
    File reports (1945–50)
    Directives (1945–50)
    Topic collections (1945–50)
University of Warwick, modern records centre:
  Gollancz papers
Wiener Library, London:
  Nuremberg documents collection

United States of America
John F. Kennedy library, Boston:
  Sprecher papers
Library of Congress, Washington, DC:
  Jackson papers
  Leventhal papers
  Stimson papers
  Taft papers
National Archives and Record Administration, College Park, Maryland:
  Assistant Secretary of War papers, RG 107
  Combined Chiefs of Staff, RG 218
  Microfilms T-175 (Nuremberg interrogations)
  Microfilms 00049103–8, USA *versus* Martin Gottfried Weiss *et al*
  OCCPAC papers, RG 238
  Secretary of War papers, RG 107
  State Department papers, RG 59
  War Department papers, G-1, RG 165
  War Department papers, JAG, RG 153
  War Department papers, OMGUS, RG 260
Syracuse University Archive:
  Francis Biddle papers
United States Holocaust Memorial Museum archives, Washington, DC:
  Ferencz papers
University of Connecticut archives:
  Dodd papers

PRIMARY SOURCES (II): CORRESPONDENCE WITH EYEWITNESSES

Morris Anspacher
Peter Calvocoressi
Theodor Fenstermacher
Benjamin Ferencz

PRIMARY SOURCES (III): FILMS AND NEWSREEL

British Paramount News, 1945 (UK)
Die Mörder sind unter uns (East Germany, 1946)
Frieda (UK, 1947)
Gaumont British News, 1945 (UK)
Nürnberg und seine Lehren (West Germany, 1947)
Shoah (Claude Lanzmann, 1985)
Todesmühlen (West Germany, 1946)
Welt im Film, 1945–1946 (West Germany)
Your Job in Germany (USA, 1944)

PRIMARY SOURCES (IV): PUBLISHED MATERIALS

Antworten: Politik im Kratfeld der öffentlichen Meinung, ed. Elisabeth Noelle and Erich Peter Neumann (Allensbach: Verlag für Demoskopie, 1954).

Archives of the Holocaust: An International Collection of Selected Documents, xvi United Nations Archives, New York: United Nations War Crimes Commission, ed. George J. Lankevich (New York: Garland, 1990–3).

Befreier und Befreite: Krieg, Vergewaltigungen, Kinder, ed. Helke Sander and Barbara Johr (Munich: Verlag Antje Kunstmann, 1992).

Das Dritte Reich und seine Diener: Dokumente, ed. Leon Poliakov and Josef Wulf (East Berlin: Verlag Volk und Welt, 1975).

Das Jahr '45: Dichtung, Bericht, Protokoll deutscher Autoren, ed. Hans Rauschning (Munich: Wilhelm Heyne Verlag, 1985).

Der Krieg ist aus—und nun? Sommer '45 Berichte, Erfahrungen, Bekenntnisse, ed. Sybil Schönfeldt (Munich: Deutscher Taschenbuch Verlag, 1985).

Documents of Destruction: Germany and Jewry, 1933–1945, ed. Raul Hilberg (Chicago: Quadrangle, 1971).

Documents on British Policy Overseas, Ser. 1, Germany and Western Europe, 11 Aug.–31 Dec. 1945, ed. Her Majesty's Stationery Office (London: HMSO, 1990).

Documents on the Holocaust, ed. Yitzhak Arad *et al.* (Oxford: Pergamon Press, 1981).

Deutschland im Jahre 1. Reportagen aus der Nachkriegszeit, ed. Josef Müller-Marein (Munich: Deutscher Taschenbuch Verlag, 1986).

Eyewitnesses at Nuremberg, ed. Hilary Gaskin (London: Arms and Armour, 1990).

Faschismus—Ghetto—Massenmord: Dokumentation über Ausrottung und Widerstand der Juden in Polen während des zweiten Weltkrieges, ed. Tatiana Berenstein *et al.* (East Berlin: Rütten and Loening, 1960).

German Crimes in Poland, ed. Central Commission for Investigation of German Crimes in Poland, 2 vols. in 1 (New York: Fertig, 1982).

International Military Tribunal, *Trial of the Major War Criminals before the International Military Tribunal*, 42 vols. (Nuremberg: IMT, 1947–9).

Jahrbuch der öffentlichen Meinung 1947–1955, ed. Elisabeth Noelle and Erich Peter Neumann (Allensbach: Verlag für Demoskopie, 1956).

Mann, Thomas, *Deutsche Hörer! Radiosendungen nach Deutschland aus den Jahren 1940–1945* (Frankfurt am Main: Fischer, 1987).

Nazism, 1919–1945: A Documentary Reader, iii, ed. Jeremy Noakes and Geoffrey Pridham (Exeter: University of Exeter Press, 1988).

Nuremberg Military Tribunals, *Trials of War Criminals before the Nuremberg Military Tribunals under Control Council Law No. 10*, 15 vols. (Washington, DC: USGPO, 1949–53).

OCCPAC, *Nazi Conspiracy and Aggression*, 8 vols. (Washington, DC: USGPO, 1946).

Public Opinion in Occupied Germany: the OMGUS Surveys, 1945–1949, ed. Anna J. Merritt and Richard L. Merritt (Chicago: University of Illinois Press, 1970).

Public Opinion in Semisovereign Germany: The HICOG Surveys, 1949–1955, ed. Anna J. Merritt and Richard L. Merritt (Chicago, Ill.: University of Illinois Press, 1980).

Rassenpolitik und Kriegführung: Sicherheitspolizei und Wehrmacht in Polen und in der Sowjetunion 1939–1942, ed. Hans-Heinrich Wilhelm (Passau: Richard Rothe, 1991).

The Death Camp Treblinka: A Documentary, ed. Alexander Donat (New York: Holocaust Library, 1979).

The Gallup International Public Opinion Polls: Great Britain, 1937–1975, i: *1937–1964*, ed. George Gallup (New York: Random House, 1976).

The Gallup Poll: Public Opinion, 1935–1971, i: *1935–1948*, ed. George Gallup (New York: Random House, 1972).

The Germans: Public Opinion Polls, 1947–1966, ed. Elisabeth Noelle and Erich Peter Neumann (Westport, Conn.: Greenwood Press, 1981).

The Holocaust: Selected Documents in Eighteen Volumes, ed. John Mendelsohn (New York: Garland, 1982).

The Papers of General Lucius D. Clay: Germany, 1945–1949, ed. Jean Edward Smith, 2 vols. (Bloomington, Ind: University of Indiana Press, 1974).

The Trial of Josef Kramer and Forty-Four Others, ed. Raymond Phillips (London: William Hodge, 1949).

The Trial of Wolfgang Zeuss et al, ed. A. M. Webb (London: William Hodge, 1949).

United Nations War Crimes Commission, *Law Reports of Trials of War Criminals, Selected and Prepared by the United Nations War Crimes Commission*, 15 vols. (London: HMSO, 1947–9).

Voices from the Holocaust, ed. Harry James Cargas (Kentucky: University of Kentucky Press, 1993).

What Do the Americans Know about the Holocaust?, ed. Jennifer Golub and Renae Cohen (New York: American Jewish Committee, 1993).

What Do the British Know about the Holocaust?, ed. Jennifer Golub and Renae Cohen (New York: American Jewish Committee, 1993).

What Do the French Know about the Holocaust?, ed. Jennifer Golub and Renae Cohen (New York: American Jewish Committee, 1994).

Hansard: House of Commons debates, 1942–1953
Hansard: House of Lords debates, 1945–1953
Jackson, Robert H., 'Report of Justice Robert H. Jackson, Chief-of-Counsel for the United States in the Prosecution of Axis War Criminals, June 7, 1945', *American Journal of International Law*, suppl., 39, no. 3 (1945), 178–90.
Taylor, Telford, *Final Report to the Secretary of the Army on the Nuernberg War Crimes Trials under Control Council Law No. 10* (Washington, DC: USGPO, 1949).

American
New York Times, Public Opinion Quarterly, Stars and Stripes, Times Herald, Washington Post, Nation, Washington Star
British
Express, Illustrated London News, Keesing's Contemporary Archives, Manchester Guardian, News Chronicle, Sunday Times, The Independent, The Times
French
Le Monde, Le Monde Juif
German
Aufbau, Badische Zeitung, Christlicher Nachrichtendienst, Frankfurter Hefte, Frankfurter Rundschau, Frankfurter Zeitung / Allgemeine Zeitung, Hamburger Nachrichtenblatt der Militärregierung, Neue Illustrierte Presse, Neue Zeitung, Telegraf, Merkur, Der Tagesspiegel, Die Zeit
Jewish
The Jewish Chronicle, Jewish Gazette, The Jewish Monthly, Jewish Telegraphic Agency Bulletins, Polish-Jewish Observer, Zionist Review
Miscellaneous
Polish Fortnightly Review

Abzug, Robert H., *Inside the Vicious Heart: Americans and the Liberation of Nazi Concentration Camps* (Oxford: Oxford University Press, 1985).
Adam, Uwe Dietrich, 'The Gas Chambers', in Michael R. Marrus (ed.), *The Nazi Holocaust*, 9 pts. (London: Meckler, 1989), pt 6, ii, 1057–84.
Adenauer, Konrad, *Memoirs, 1945–1953* (London: Weidenfeld and Nicolson, 1966).
Ainsztein, Reuben, 'Review of Hilberg's *Destruction of the European Jews*', in *The Jewish Observer and Middle East Review*, 16 Mar. 1962, 26–7.
—— *Jewish Resistance in Nazi-Occupied Eastern Europe* (London: Elek, 1974).
Allen, Michael Thad, 'Engineers and Modern Managers in the SS', Ph.D. thesis (Pennsylvania, 1995).

Aly, Götz, and Heim, Suzanne (eds.), *Sozialpolitik und Judenvernichtung: Gibt es eine Ökonomie der Endlösung?* (Beiträge zur NS-Gesundheits- und Sozialpolitik, 5; West Berlin: Rotbuch, 1987).

—— and —— 'Die Ökonomie der "Endlösung": Menschenvernichtung und wirtschaftliche Neuordnung', in Götz Aly and Suzanne Heim (eds.), *Gibt es eine Ökonomie der Endlösung?*, 7–90.

—— and —— 'The Economics of the Final Solution: A Case Study from the General Government', *Simon Wiesenthal Center Annual*, 5 (1988), 3–48.

—— and —— *Vordenker der Vernichtung: Auschwitz und die deutschen Pläne für eine neue europäische Ordnung* (Frankfurt am Main: Fischer, 1993).

—— Peter Chroust and Christian Pross (eds.), *Cleansing the Fatherland: Nazi Medicine and Racial Hygiene* (Baltimore, MD: Johns Hopkins University Press, 1994).

—— *'Final Solution': Nazi Population Policy and the Murder of the European Jews* (London: Arnold, 1999).

Anatoli, A., *Babi Yar* (London: Sphere, 1978).

Angrick, Andrej, 'Die Einsatzgruppe D', in Peter Klein (ed.), *Die Einsatzgruppen in der besetzten Sowjetunion 1941/42*, (Berlin: Gedenk- und Bildungsstätte Haus der Wannsee-Konferenz, 1997), 88–110.

Annas, George, and Grodin, Michael, *The Nazi Doctors and the Nuremberg Code: Human Rights in Human Experimentation* (Oxford: Oxford University Press, 1992).

'Ansprache des Botschafters des Staates Israel, A. Primor anlässlich der Eröffnung der Ausstellung "Vernichtungskrieg, Verbrechen der Wehrmacht von 1941 bis 1944" am 17 Apr. 1998 in Aachen', ed. Ulrich Wisser (World Wide Web: www Verlag Ulrich Wisser, 1998).

Apenszlak, Jacob (ed.), *The Black Book of Polish Jewry: An Account of the Martyrdom of Polish Jewry under the Nazi Occupation* (New York: Roy, 1943).

Arad, Yitzhak, *Belzec, Sobibor, Treblinka: The Operation Reinhard Death Camps* (Bloomington, Ind: University of Indiana Press, 1987).

Arendt, Hannah, *The Origins of Totalitarianism* (London: George Allen and Unwin, 1958).

—— *Eichmann in Jerusalem: A Report on the Banality of Evil* (New York: Viking, 1963).

Aronson, Shlomo, 'Preparations for the Nuremberg Trial: The OSS, Charles Dwork, and the Holocaust', *Holocaust and Genocide Studies*, 12 (1998), 257–81.

Backer, John, 'From Morgenthau Plan to Marshall Plan', in Robert Wolfe (ed.) *Americans as Proconsuls: United States Military Government in Germany and Japan, 1944–1952* (Carbondale, Ill.: Southern Illinois University Press, 1984), 155–65.

Baeyer, Wanda von, 'Das Publikum im Film "Nürnberg und sein Lehren" ', *Frankfurter Hefte*, 4 (Apr., 1949), 360–1.

Baldwin, Peter (ed.), *Reworking the Past: Hitler, the Holocaust, and the Historians' Debate* (Boston, Mass.: Beacon, 1990).

Baldwin, Peter, 'The Historikerstreit in Context', in Peter Baldwin (ed.), *Reworking the Past: Hitler, the Holocaust and the Historians' Debate* (Boston, Mass.: Beacon, 1990), 3–37.

Bance, Alan (ed.), *The Cultural Legacy of the British Occupation in Germany* (Stuttgart: Hans-Dieter Heinz Akademischer Verlag, 1997).

Barnett, Correlli (ed.), *Hitler's Generals* (New York: Quill and Morrow, 1989).

Bartoszewski, W.T., *The Convent at Auschwitz* (London: Bowerdean, 1990).

Bartov, Omer, *The Eastern Front, 1941–1945: German Troops and the Barbarization of Warfare* (New York: St. Martin's Press, 1985).

—— *Hitler's Army: Soldiers, Nazis and War in the Third Reich* (Oxford: Oxford University Press, 1992).

Bauer, Yehuda, 'When Did They Know?', *Midstream*, 14 (1968), 51–8.

—— *Jews for Sale?* (New Haven, Conn.: Yale University Press, 1994).

—— 'The Holocaust in Hungary: Was Rescue Possible?', in David Cesarani (ed.), *Genocide and Rescue: The Holocaust in Hungary, 1944* (Oxford: Berg, 1997), 193–210.

Bauman, Zygmunt, *Modernity and the Holocaust* (New York: Cornell University Press, 1992).

Belgion, Montgomery, *Epitaph on Nuremberg* (London: Falcon Press, 1946).

Bell, George, *Humanity and the Refugees* (London: Woburn Press, 1939).

Bender, Hans, *Die Hostie*, (Munich: Carl Haenser, n.d.).

Benton, W. E., and Grimm, Georg, *Nuremberg: German Views of the War Trials* (Dallas, Tex: Southern Methodist University Press, 1955).

Benz, Wolfgang, *Von der Besatzungsherrschaft zur Bundesrepublik: Stationen einer Staatsgründung, 1946–1949* (Frankfurt am Main: Fischer Taschenbuch Verlag, 1985).

—— 'Auschwitz und die Deutschen: Die Erinnerung an den Völkermord', in Arno Herzig and Ina Lorenz (eds.), *Verdrängung und Vernichtung der Juden unter dem Nationalsozialismus* (Hamburg: Hans Christians Verlag, 1992), 333–47.

—— 'The Persecution and Extermination of the Jews in the German consciousness', in John Milfull (ed.), *Why Germany? National Socialist Anti-Semitism and the European Context* (Providence: Berg, 1993), 91–104.

—— *The Holocaust: A Short History* (London: Profile Books, 2000).

Bergen, Doris, *Twisted Cross: The German Christian Movement in the Third Reich* (Chapel Hill, NC: University of North Carolina Press, 1996).

Berghahn, Volker R., *Der Stahlhelm: Bund der Frontsoldaten 1918–1935* (Düsseldorf: Droste, 1966).

Bergmann, Werner, 'Die Reaktion auf den Holocaust in Westdeutschland von 1945 bis 1989', *Geschichte in Wissenschaft und Unterricht*, 43 (1992), 327–50.

Bernstein, Victor, *Final Judgment: The Story of Nuremberg* (New York: Boni and Gaer, 1947).

Best, Geoffrey, 'Nuremberg and After', *The Stenton Lecture* (Reading: University of Reading, 1984).

Biddiss, Michael, 'The Nuremburg Trial: Two Exercises in Judgement', *Journal of Contemporary History*, 16 (1981), 597–615.

—— *The Nuremberg Trial and the Third Reich* (London: ETHOS, 1993).

Biddle, Francis, *In Brief Authority* (New York: Doubleday, 1962).

Birn, Ruth Bettina, *Die Höheren SS- und Polizeiführer: Himmlers Vertreter im Reich und in den besetzten Gebieten* (Düsseldorf: Droste Verlag, 1986).

Black, Peter R., *Ernst Kaltenbrunner: Ideological Soldier of the Third Reich* (Princeton, NJ: Princeton University Press, 1984).

—— 'Rehearsal for "Reinhard"? Odilo Globocnik and the Lublin *Selbstschutz*', *Central European History*, 25 (1992), 204–26.

Bloxham, Donald, 'The Holocaust on Trial: The War Crimes Trials in the Formation of History and Memory', Ph.D. thesis (Southampton, 1998).

Bloxham, Donald, 'Punishing German Soldiers during the Cold War: The Case of Erich von Manstein', *Patterns of Prejudice*, 33, no. 4 (1999), 25–45.

—— ' "Extermination through Work": Jewish Slave Labour under the Third Reich', *Holocaust Educational Trust Research Papers*, 1, no. 1 (1999–2000).

—— 'Jewish Slave Labour and Its Relationship to the "Final Solution"', in *Remembering for the Future, 2000: The Holocaust in an Age of Genocide* (London: Macmillan, forthcoming).

Boll, Bernd, 'Wehrmacht vor Gericht: Kriegsverbrecherprozesse der Vier Mächte nach 1945', *Geschichte und Gesellschaft*, 24 (1998), 570–94.

Böll, Heinrich, *Frankfurter Vorlesungen* (Cologne: Verlag Kiepenheuer and Witsch, 1966).

—— *Wo warst du Adam?* (Munich: Deutscher Taschenbuch Verlag, 1972).

—— *Heinrich Böll: Werke. Essayistische Schriften und Reden*, i, ed. Bernd Balzer (Cologne: Gertrand Middelhauve Verlag, n.d. [1978]).

—— *Heinrich Böll: Werke. Romane und Erzählungen*, i. 1947–1951 ed. Bernd Balzer (Cologne: Gertrand Middelhauve Verlag, n.d. [1977]).

Bond, Brian, 'Brauchitsch', in Correlli Barnett (ed.), *Hitler's Generals* (New York: Quill and Morrow, 1989), 75–101.

Borkin, Joseph, *The Crime and Punishment of I. G. Farben* (New York: Free Press, 1978).

Bosch, William J., *Judgment on Nuremberg: American Attitudes toward the Major German War-Crime Trials* (Chapel Hill, NC: University of North Carolina Press, 1970).

Bosworth, R. J. B., *Explaining Auschwitz and Hiroshima: History Writing and the Second World War, 1945–1990* (London: Routledge, 1991).

Boveri, Margret, *Der Diplomat vor Gericht* (Berlin: Minerva, 1948).

Bower, Tom, *Blind Eye to Murder: Britain, America and the Purging of Nazi Germany— A Pledge Betrayed* (London: Warner, 1997).

—— *The Paperclip Conspiracy* (London: Grafton, 1988).

Braham, Randolph, *The Politics of Genocide: The Holocaust in Hungary*, ii (New York: Columbia University Press, 1981).

—— and Vago, Bela (eds.), *The Holocaust in Hungary Forty Years Later* (New York: Columbia University Press, 1985).

Brand, James T., 'Crimes against Humanity and the Nuernberg Trials', *Oregon Law Review*, 28 (1949), 93–119.

Breitman, Richard, 'Nazi Jewish Policy in 1944', in David Cesarani (ed.), *Genocide and Rescue: The Holocaust in Hungary, 1944* (Oxford: Berg, 1997), 77–92.

—— *Official Secrets: What the Nazis Planned, What the British and Americans Knew* (London: Allen Lane, 1999).

Brett-Smith, Richard (ed.), *Hitler's Generals* (San Rafael, Calif.: Presidio, 1977).

Bridgman, John, *The End of the Holocaust: The Liberation of the Camps* (London: Batsford, 1990).

Brochhagen, Ulrich, 'Vergangene Vergangenheitsbewältigung: Zum Umgang mit der NS-Vergangenheit während der fünfziger und frühen sechziger Jahre', *Mittelweg*, 36 (1992), 145–54.

—— *Nach Nürnberg: Vergangenheitsbewältigung und Westintegration in der Ära Adenauer* (Hamburg: Junius, 1994).

Broder, Henryk M., *Volk und Wahn* (Hamburg: Spiegel Buchverlag, 1996).

Broszat, Martin (ed.), *Rudolf Höss: Kommandant in Auschwitz: Autobiographische Aufzeichnungen* (Munich: Deutscher Taschenbuch Verlag, 1963).

—— *Nationalsozialistische Polenpolitik* (Frankfurt am Main: Fischer, 1965).

—— 'Hitler und die Genesis der "Endlösung": Aus Anlass der Thesen von David Irving', *Vierteljahreshefte für Zeitgeschichte*, 25 (1977), 737–75.

—— 'Siegerjustiz oder strafrechtliche Selbstreinigung: Aspekte der Vergangenheitsbewältigung der deutschen Justiz während der Besatzungszeit', *Vierteljahreshefte für Zeitgeschichte*, 29 (1981), 477–544.

Brown, Anthony Cave, *The Last Hero: Wild Bill Donovan* (New York: Vintage, 1982).

Browning, Christopher, *The Final Solution and the German Foreign Office* (New York: Holmes and Meier, 1978).

—— *Fateful Months: Essays on the Emergence of the Final Solution* (New York: Holmes and Meier, 1991).

—— *The Path to Genocide: Essays on Launching the Final Solution* (Cambridge: Cambridge University Press, 1992).

—— *Ordinary Men: Reserve Police Batallion 101 and the Final Solution in Poland* (New York: Harper, 1992).

—— *Nazi Policy, Jewish Workers, German Killers* (Cambridge: Cambridge University Press, 2000).

Buchheim, Hans, 'Die Höheren SS und Polizeiführer', *Vierteljahreshefte für Zeitgeschichte*, 11 (1963), 362–91.

—— *et al.*, *Anatomie des SS-Staates*, 2 vols. (Olten und Freiburg im Bresgau: Walter Verlag, 1965).

Büchler, Yehoshua, 'Kommandostab Reichsführer-SS: Himmler's Personal Murder Brigades in 1941', *Holocaust and Genocide Studies*, 1 (1986), 11–25.

Burleigh, Michael, *Death and Deliverance: 'Euthanasia' in Germany, 1900–1945* (Cambridge: Cambridge University Press, 1994).

Buruma, Ian, *Wages of Guilt: Memories of War in Germany and Japan* (London: Jonathan Cape, 1994).

Buscher, Frank, *The US War Crimes Trial Program in Germany, 1946–1955* (Westport, Conn.: Greenwood Press, 1989).

—— 'Kurt Schumacher, German Social Democracy and the Punishment of Nazi Crimes', *Holocaust and Genocide Studies*, 5 (1990), 261–73.

Bush, Jonathan, Conference paper ('Nuremberg and Its Impact: Fifty Years Later'; United States Holocaust Memorial Museum, 17 Nov. 1996).

Bussmann, Walter, 'Zur Enstehung und Überlieferung der "Hossbach-Niederschrift"', *Vierteljahreshefte für Zeitgeschichte*, 16 (1968), 373–84.

Calvocoressi, Peter, *Nuremberg: The Facts, the Law and the Consequences* (London, Chatto and Windus, 1948).

Carver, Field-Marshal Lord, 'Manstein', in Correlli Barnett (ed.), *Hitler's Generals* (New York: Quill and Morrow, 1989), 221–48.

Cesarani, David, *Justice Delayed* (London: Mandarin, 1992).

—— *The Jewish Chronicle and Anglo-Jewry, 1841–1991* (Cambridge: Cambridge University Press, 1994).

—— (ed.), *The Final Solution: Origins and Implementation* (London: Routledge, 1994).

—— ' "Le crime contre l'Occident": les réactions brittaniques à la libération des camps de concentration nazis en 1945', in Marie-Anne Matard-Bonucci and Edouard Lynch (eds.), *La libération des camps et le Retour des déportés: l'histoire en souffrance* (Brussels: Éditions Complexe, 1995), 238–49.

Cesarani, David, *Genocide and Rescue: The Holocaust in Hungary, 1944* (Oxford: Berg, 1997).

—— 'Britain and the Holocaust, 1945–90' (unpublished typescript).

Chamberlin, Brewster S., 'Todesmühlen: Ein früher Versuch zur Massen "Umerziehung" in besetzten Deutschland 1945–1946', *Vierteljahreshefte für Zeitgeschichte*, 29 (1981), 420–36.

Charlesworth, Andrew, 'Contesting Places of Memory: The Case of Auschwitz', *Environment and Planning D: Society and Space*, 12 (1994), 579–93.

Clark, Alan, *Barbarossa* (London: Weidenfeld and Nicolson, 1995).

Clay, Lucius D., *Decision in Germany* (Westport, Conn.: Westview, 1950).

Cohn-Sherbok, Dan, *Understanding the Holocaust* (London: Cassell, 1999).

Conot, Robert E., *Justice at Nuremberg* (New York: Harper and Row, 1983).

Cooper, R. W., *The Nuremberg Trial* (Harmondsworth: Penguin, 1947).

Cowles, William B., 'Trials of War Criminals (Non-Nuremberg)', *American Journal of International Law*, 42 (1948), 299–319.

Craig, Gordon A., *The Politics of the Prussian Army, 1640–1945* (New York: Oxford University Press, 1964).

Culbert, David, 'American Film Policy in the Re-Education of Germany after 1945', in Nicholas Pronay and Keith Wilson (eds.), *The Political Re-Education of Germany and Her Allies after World War II* (London: Croom Helm, 1985), 173–202.

Cyprian, Tadeusz, and Sawicki, Jerzy, *Nuremberg in Retrospect: People and Issues of the Trial* (Warsaw: Western Press Agency, 1967).

Dale Jones, Priscilla, 'British Policy towards German Crimes against German Jews, 1939–1945', *Leo Baeck Institute Year Book*, 36 (1991), 339–66.

—— 'Nazi Atrocities against Allied Airmen: Stalag Luft III and the End of British War Crimes Trials', *Historical Journal*, 41 (1998), 543–65.

Dallin, Alexander, *German Rule in Russia, 1941–1945* (London: Macmillan, 1957).

Davidson, Eugene, *The Trial of the Germans: An Account of the 22 Defendants before the International Military Tribunal at Nuremberg* (New York: Macmillan, 1966).

Davies, A. J., *To Build a New Jerusalem* (London: Abacus, 1996).

Dawidowicz, Lucy, *The War against the Jews, 1933–1945* (London: Penguin, 1987).

Deak, Istvan, Gross, Jan T., and Judt, Tony (eds.), *The Politics of Retribution in Europe: World War II and Its Aftermath* (Princeton, NJ: Princeton University Press, 2000).

Deighton, Anne, *The Impossible Peace: Britain, the Division of Germany and the Origins of the Cold War* (Oxford: Oxford University Press, 1990).

De Martini, Emil, *4 Millionen Tote klagen an! Erlebnisse im Todeslager Auschwitz* (Munich: von Weber, 1948).

De Mildt, Dick, *In the Name of the People: Perpetrators of Genocide in the Reflection of Their Post-War Prosecution in West Germany: The 'Euthanasia' and 'Aktion Reinhard' Trial Cases* (The Hague: Martinus Nijhoff, 1996).

Dieckmann, Christoph, 'Der Krieg und die Ermordung der litauischen Juden', in Ulrich Herbert (ed.), *Nationalsozialistische Vernichtungspolitik: Neue Forschungen und Kontroversen* (Frankfurt am Main: Fischer, 1997), 292–329.

Diner, Dan (ed.), *Ist der Nationalsozialismus Geschichte?* (Frankfurt am Main: Fischer, 1987).

—— *Verkehrte Welten: Antiamerikanismus in Deutschland: Ein historischer Essay* (Frankfurt am Main: Eichborn, 1993).

—— 'Massenverbrechen in 20. Jahrhundert: Über Nationalsozialismus und Stalinismus', in Rolf Steininger (ed.), *Der Umgang mit dem Holocaust: Europa—USA—Israel* (Cologne: Böhlau Verlag, 1994), 468–81.

Dirks, Walter, 'Der Weg zur Freiheit: Ein Beitrag zur deutschen Selbsterkenntnis', *Frankfurter Hefte*, 1 (July 1946), 50–60.

—— 'Partei und Staat', *Frankfurter Hefte*, 1 (Dec. 1946), 820–32.

—— 'Die Freiheit der Presse', *Frankfurter Hefte*, 2 (Jan. 1947), 12–13.

Doman, Nicholas, 'Political Consequences of the Nuremberg Trial', *American Academy of Political and Social Sciences, Annals*, no. 246 (1946), 81–90.

Doosry, Yasmin (ed.), *Representations of Auschwitz* (Auschwitz: Auschwitz State Museum, 1995).

Douglas, Lawrence, 'Film as Witness: Screening *Nazi Concentration Camps* before the Nuremberg Tribunal', *Yale Law Journal*, 105 (1995), 449–81.

—— 'The Shrunken Head of Buchenwald: Icons of Atrocity at Nuremberg', *Representations*, no. 63 (1998), 39–64.

Dulles, Allen, *Germany's Underground* (New York: Macmillan, 1947).

DuBois, Josiah, *The Devil's Chemists: 24 Conspirators of the International Farben Cartel who Manufacture Wars* (Boston, Mass.: Beacon, 1952).

Dwork, Deborah, and Pelt, Robert Jan van, *Auschwitz: 1270 to the Present* (New York: W. W. Norton, 1996).

East London Auschwitz Committee, *Auschwitz: An Exhibition* (London: Graphi Press, 1983).

Eberan, Barbro, *Luther? Friedrich 'der Große'? Wagner? Nietzsche? . . . ? . . . ? Wer war an Hitler schuld? Die Debatte um die Schuldfrage 1945–1949* (Munich: Minerva, 1983).

Ehard, Hans, 'Der Nürnberger Prozess gegen der Hauptkriegsverbrecher', *Süddeutsche Juristen-Zeitung*, 3 (1948), cols. 353–68.

Ellwood, David W., *Rebuilding Europe: Western Europe, America and Postwar Reconstruction* (London: Longman, 1992).

Elwyn Jones, Frederick, *In My Time: An Autobiography* (London: Futura, 1983).

Engel, David, *In the Shadow of Auschwitz: The Polish Government-in-Exile and the Jews, 1939–1942* (Chapel Hill, NC: University of North Carolina Press, 1987).

Enssle, Manfred J., 'Five Theses on German Everyday Life after World War II', *Central European History*, 26 (1993), 1–19.

Ermarth, Michael (ed.), *America and the Shaping of German Society, 1945–1955* (Providence: Berg, 1993).

Eschebach, Insa, 'NS-Prozesse in der sowjetischen Besatzungszone und der DDR: Einige Überlegungen zu den Strafverfahrensakten ehemaliger SS-Aufseherinnen des Frauenkonzentrationslagers Ravensbrück', in KZ-Gedenkstätte Neuengamme (ed.), *Die frühen Nachkriegsprozesse: Beiträge zur Geschichte der nationalsozialistischen Verfolgung in Norddeutschland*, iii, (Bremen: Edition Temnen, 1997), 65–74.

Ezergailis, Andrew, *The Holocaust in Latvia: The Missing Centre* (Riga: Historical Institute of Latvia, 1996).

Fabreguet, Michel, 'Frankreichs Historiker und der Völkermord an den Juden 1945–1993', in Rolf Steininger (ed.), *Der Umgang mit dem Holocaust: Europa—USA—Israel* (Cologne: Böhlau Verlag), 317–28.

Ferencz, Benjamin, *Less than Slaves: Jewish Forced Labor and the Quest for Compensation*, (Cambridge, Mass.: Harvard University Press, 1979).

Finch, George A., 'The Nuremberg Trial and International Law', *American Journal of International Law*, 41 (1947), 20–37.

Fishman, Jack, *Long Knives and Short Memories: The Spandau Prison Story* (London: Souvenir, 1986).

Fitzgibbon, Constantine, *Denazification* (London: Michael Joseph, 1969).

Fleming, Gerald, *Hitler and the Final Solution* (Oxford: Oxford University Press, 1986).

Forbes, Gordon W., 'Some Legal Aspects of the Nuremberg Trial', *Canadian Bar Review*, 24 (1946), 584–99.

Förster, Jürgen, 'The Relation between Barbarossa as an Ideological War of Extermination and the Final Solution', in David Cesarani (ed.), *The Final Solution: Origins and Implementation* (London: Routledge, 1994), 85–102.

Foschepath, Josef, 'German Reaction to Defeat and Occupation', in Robert Moeller (ed.), *West Germany under Construction* (Ann Arbor, Mich.: University of Michigan Press, 1997), 73–89.

Fox, John P., 'The Jewish Factor in British War Crimes Policy in 1942', *English Historical Review*, 92 (1977), 82–106.

Fratcher, William F., 'American Organization for Prosecution of German War Criminals', *Missouri Law Review*, 13 (1948), 45–75.

Frei, Norbert, ' "Wir waren blind, ungläubig und langsam": Buchenwald, Dachau und die amerikanischen Medien im Frühjahr 1945', *Vierteljahreshefte für Zeitgeschichte*, 35 (1987), 385–401.

—— ' "Vergangenheitsbewältigung" or "Renazification"? The American Perspective on Germany's Confrontation of the Nazi Past in the Early Years of the Adenauer Era', in Michael Ermarth (ed.), *America and the Shaping of German Society, 1945–1955* (Providence: Berg, 1993), 47–59.

—— 'Das Problem der NS-Vergangenheit in der Ära Adenauer', in Bernd Weisbrod (ed.), *Rechtradikalismus in der politischen Kultur der Nachkriegszeit: Die verzögerte Normalisierung in Niedersachsen* (Hanover: Hahnsche Buchhandlung, 1995), 19–31.

—— *Vergangenheitspolitik: Die Anfänge der Bundesrepublik und die NS-Vergangenheit* (Munich: Verlag C. H. Beck, 1996).

Frey, Herbert, 'The German Guilt Question after the Second World War: An Overview', Ph.D. thesis (Washington, 1979).

Friedländer, Saul, *Counterfeit Nazi: The Ambiguity of Good* (London: Weidenfeld and Nicolson, 1969).

—— *Nazi Germany and the Jews: The Years of Persecution, 1933–39* (London: Weidenfeld and Nicolson, 1997).

Friedrich, C. J., and Brzezinski, Z. K., *Totalitarian Dictatorship and Autocracy* (Cambridge, Mass.: Harvard University Press, 1965).

Friedrich, Jörg, *Die kälte Amnestie: NS-Täter in der Bundesrepublik* (Frankfurt am Main: Fischer, 1984).

Fulbrook, Mary, *German National Identity after the Holocaust* (Cambridge: Polity Press, 1999).

Fuller, J. F. C., *Armament and History* (London: Eyre and Spottiswoode, 1946).

Gallus, Gallieri, *Nuremberg and After* (Newtown: Montgomeryshire Printing and Stationery Co., 1946).

Garbe, Detlev, 'Absonderung, Strafkommandos und spezifischer Terror: Jüdische Gefangene in nationalsozialistischen Konzentrationslagern 1933 bis 1945', in Arno Herzig and Ina Lorenz (eds.), *Verdrängung und Vernichtung der Juden unter dem Nationalsozialismus* (Hamburg: Hans Christians Verlag, 1992), 173–204.

Gatze, Hans W., *Germany and the United States: A 'Special Relationship'?* (Cambridge, Mass.: Harvard University Press, 1980).

Gellately, Robert, *The Gestapo and German Society: Enforcing Racial Policy, 1933–1945* (Oxford: Clarendon Press, 1990).

Georg, Enno, *Die wirtschaftlichen Unternehmungen der SS* (Stuttgart: Deutsche Verlags-Anstalt, 1963).

Gericke, Hans Otto, 'Die Presseberichterstattung über den Nürnberger Prozess und die Überwindung des faschistischen Geschichtsbildes', *Zeitschrift für Geschichtswissenschaft*, 33 (1985), 916–24.

Gerlach, Christian, 'Die Einsatzgruppe B', in Peter Klein (ed.), *Die Einsatzgruppen in der besetzten Sowjetunion 1941/42* (Berlin: Gedenk- und Bildungsstätte Haus der Wannsee-Konferenz, 1997), 52–70.

—— 'Deutsche Wirtschaftsinteressen, Besatzungspolitik und die Mord an der Juden in Weissrussland 1941–1943', in Ulrich Herbert (ed.), *Nationalsozialistische Vernichtungspolitik: Neue Forschungen und Kontroversen* (Frankfurt am Main: Fischer, 1997) 263–91.

—— *Krieg, Ernährung, Völkermord: Forschungen zur deutschen Vernichtungspolitik im Zweiten Weltkrieg* (Hamburg: Hamburger Edition, 1998).

—— 'Verbrechen deutscher Fronttruppen in Weissrussland 1941–1944: Eine Annäherung', in Karl Heinrich Pohl (ed.), *Wehrmacht und Vernichtungspolitik: Militär in nationalsozialistischen System* (Göttingen: Vandenhoeck and Ruprecht, 1999), 89–114.

Gilbert, G. M., *Nuremburg Diary* (New York: Farrar and Strauss, 1947).

Gilbert, Martin, *Auschwitz and the Allies* (London: Michael Joseph, 1981).

—— *Winston S. Churchill*, viii (London: Heinemann, 1988).

Gimbel, John, 'Cold War Historians and the Occupation of Germany', in Hans Schmitt (ed.), *US Occupation in Europe after World War II* (Kansas: Kansas University Press, 1978), 86–102.

Ginsburgs, George, and Kudriavtsev, V. N. (eds.), *The Nuremburg Trial and International Law* (Dordrecht: Martinus Nijhoff, 1990).

Giordano, Ralph, *Die Zweite Schuld oder von der Last ein Deutscher zu sein* (Hamburg: Rasch and Röhrig, 1987).

Gisevius, Hans Bernd, *Bis zum bitteren Ende*, i. *Vom Reichstagsbrand zur Fritschkrise*, ii. *Vom Münchener Abkommen zum 20 Juli 1944* (Darmstadt: Claasen, 1947–8).

Glees, Anthony, 'The Making of British Policy on War Crimes: History as Politics in the UK', *Contemporary European History*, 1, no. 2 (1992), 171–97.

Glover, Edward, *War, Sadism and Pacifism* (London: George Allen and Unwin, 1947).

Goldhagen, Daniel Jonah, *Hitler's Willing Executioners: Ordinary Germans and the Holocaust* (London: Abacus, 1997).

Goldhagen, Erich, 'Der Holocaust in der Sowjetischen Propaganda und Geschichtsschreibung', *Vierteljahreshefte für Zeitgeschichte*, 28 (1980), 502–7.

Gollancz, Victor, *Let My People Go* (London: Gollancz, 1942).

—— *What Buchenwald Really Means* (London: Gollancz, 1945).

—— *In Darkest Germany* (London: Gollancz, 1947).

Gordon, Sarah, *Hitler, Germans and the 'Jewish Question'* (Princeton, NJ: Princeton University Press, 1984).

Goschler, Constantin, 'The Attitude towards Jews in Bavaria after the Second World War', in Robert Moeller (ed.), *West Germany under Construction* (Ann Arbor, Mich.: University of Michigan Press, 1997), 231–50.

Govier, Robert Allen, 'Heinrich Böll as a Critic of Contemporary German Society', Ph.D. thesis (Iowa, 1967).

Gräbitz, Helge, 'Die Verfolgung von NS-Verbrechen in der Bundesrepublik Deutschland, der DDR und Österreich', in Rolf Steininger (ed.), *Der Umgang mit dem Holocaust: Europa—USA—Israel* (Cologne: Böhlau Verlag, 1994), 468–81.

Gregor, Neil, 'The Normalisation of Barbarism: Daimler-Benz in the "Third Reich" ', *Journal of Holocaust Education*, 6, no. 3 (1997), 1–20.

—— *Daimler-Benz in the Third Reich* (New Haven, Conn.: Yale University Press, 1998).

Grosser, Alfred, *Germany in Our Time* (New York: Praeger, 1971).

Grossmann, Kurt, 'What Were the Jewish Losses?', *Congress Weekly*, 20, no. 26 (1953), 9–11.

Grothmann, Wilhelm H., 'Das Menschenbild bei Heinrich Böll', Ph.D. thesis (Kansas, 1968).

Gruchmann, Lothar, 'Das Urteil von Nürnberg nach 22 Jahren', *Vierteljahreshefte für Zeitgeschichte*, 16 (1968), 385–9.

Grüner, Wolf, *Der geschlossene Arbeitseinsatz deutscher Juden: Zur Zwangsarbeit als Element der Verfolgung 1938–1943* (Berlin: Metropol, 1997).

Gutman, Yisrael, and Berenbaum, Michael (eds.), *Anatomy of the Auschwitz Death Camp* (Bloomington, Indianapolis: University of Indiana Press, 1994).

Habicht, Hubert (ed.), *Eugen Kogon—ein politischer Publizist in Hessen: Essays, Aufsätze, Reden zwischen 1946 und 1982* (Frankfurt am Main: Insel, 1982).

Haensel, Carl, 'Nürnberger Probleme', *Deutsche Rechts-Zeitschrift*, 1 (1946), 67–9.

—— 'Der Ausklang von Nürnberg', *Neue Juristische Wochenschrift* (May 1949), 367–70.

—— *Das Gericht vertagt sich: Aus dem Tagebuch eines Verteidigers bei den Nürnberger Prozessen* (Hamburg: Classen, 1950).

Halbritter, Maria, *Schulreformpolitik in der britischen Zone von 1945 bis 1949* (Weinheim: Beltz Verlag, 1979).

Hale, Winfield B., 'Nuernberg War Crimes Tribunals', *Tennessee Law Review*, 21 (1949), 8–19.

Hamilton, Alastair, *The Appeal of Fascism: A Study of Intellectuals and Fascism, 1919–1945* (London: Anthony Blond, 1971).

Hankey, Lord, *Politics, Trials and Errors* (Oxford: Pen-in-Hand, 1950).

Harris, Whitney, *Tyranny on Trial: The Evidence at Nuremberg* (Dallas, Tex: Southern Methodist University Press, 1954).

—— Conference paper ('Nuremberg and Its Impact: Fifty Years Later'; US Library of Congress, 16 Nov. 1996).

Harwood, Richard, *Did Six Million Really Die? The Truth at Last* (Ladbroke: Historical Review Press, 1977).

—— *Nuremberg and Other War Crimes Trials* (Ladbroke: Historical Review Press, 1978).

Hausner, Gideon, *Justice in Jerusalem: The Trial of Adolf Eichmann* (London: Nelson, 1967).

Hayek, F., 'Die Fronten', *Frankfurter Hefte*, 1 (Nov. 1946), 689–91.

Headland, Ronald, *Messages of Murder* (Cranbury, NJ: Associated University Presses, 1992).

Heer, Hannes, 'Killing Fields: Die Wehrmacht und der Holocaust', in Hannes Heer and Klaus Naumann (eds.), *Vernichtungskrieg: Verbrechen der Wehrmacht 1941 bis 1944* (Hamburg: HIS, 1995), 57–77.

—— and Naumman, Klaus (eds.), *Vernichtungskrieg: Verbrechen der Wehrmacht 1941 bis 1944* (Hamburg: HIS, 1995).

Henke, Klaus-Dietmar, *Die amerikanische Besetzung Deutschlands* (Munich: Oldenbourg, 1995).

Hennessy, Peter, *Never Again: Britain, 1945–51* (London: Jonathan Cape, 1992).

Herbert, Ulrich, 'Von Auschwitz nach Essen: Die Geschichte des KZ-Aussenlagers Humboltstrasse', in *Dachauer Hefte, 2. Sklavenarbeit im KZ* (Munich: Deutscher Taschenbuch Verlag, 1986), 13–34.

—— 'Arbeit und Vernichtung', in Dan Diner (ed.), *Ist der Nationalsozialismus Geschichte?* (Frankfurt am Main: Fischer, 1987), 198–237, trans. as 'Labour and Extermination: Economic Interest and the Primacy of *Weltanschauung* in National Socialism', *Past and Present*, no. 138 (1993), 144–95.

—— *Hitler's Foreign Workers: Enforced Foreign Labour in Germany under the Third Reich* (Cambridge: Cambridge University Press, 1997).

—— *Nationalsozialistische Vernichtungspolitik: Neue Forschungen und Kontroversen* (Frankfurt am Main: Fischer, 1997).

—— Orth Karin, and Dieckmann, Christoph (eds.), *Die nationalsozialistischen Konzentrationslager: Entwicklung und Struktur*, 2 vols. (Göttingen: Wallstein, 1998).

Herbst, Ludolf, *Der Totale Krieg und die Ordnung der Wirtschaft* (Stuttgart: Deutsche Verlags-Anstalt, 1982).

Herf, Jeffrey, *Divided Memory: The Nazi Past in the Two Germanys* (Cambridge, Mass.: Harvard University Press, 1997).

Herzig, Arno, and Lorenz, Ina (eds.), *Verdrängung und Vernichtung der Juden unter dem Nationalsozialismus* (Hamburg: Hans Christians Verlag, 1992).

Heydecker, Joe, and Leeb, Johannes, *Der Nürnberger Prozess: Bilanz der Tausend Jahre* (Cologne: Kiepenheuer and Witsch, 1959).

Hilberg, Raul, *The Destruction of the European Jews* (New York: Harper, 1961).

Hillgruber, Andreas, 'Die ideologisch-dogmatische Grundlagen der nationalsozialistischen Politik der Ausrottung der Juden in den besetzten Gebieten der Sowjetunion und ihre Durchführung 1941–1944', *German Studies Review*, 2 (1979), 293–6.

Hilton, Norman, *Alexander of Tunis: A Biographical Portrait* (London: W. H. Allen, 1952).

Hirschfeld, Gerhard (ed.), *The Policies of Genocide* (London: German Historical Institute, 1986).

Hoffmann, Christa, *Stunden Null? Vergangenheitsbewältigung in Deutschland 1945 und 1989* (Bonn: Bouvier, 1992).

Hoffmann, J. H., 'German Field Marshals as War Criminals? A British Embarrassment', *Journal of Contemporary History*, 23 (1988), 17–36.

Höhn, Maria, 'Frau im Haus und Girl im *Spiegel*: Discourse on Women in the Interregnum Period of 1945–1949 and the Question of German Identity', *Central European History*, 26 (1993), 57–90.

Höhne, Heinz, *The Order of the Death's Head: The Story of Hitler's SS* (London: Pan, 1972).

Holocaust Remembrance Group, *Holocaust: The Facts about the Destruction of European Jewry by the Nazis. In Question and Answer Form* (London: Holocaust Remembrance Group, 1978).

Honig, Frederick, 'Kriegsverbrecher vor englischen Militärgerichten', *Schweizerische Zeitschrift für Strafrecht*, 62 (1947), 20–33.

Horne, Alastair, *Back into Power* (London: Max Parrish, 1955).

Horowitz, Gordon J., *In the Shadow of Death: Living outside the Gates of Mauthausen* (London: Tauris, 1991).

Hyde, H. Montgomery, *Norman Birkett* (London: Hamish Hamilton, 1964).

Institute of Jewish Affairs, *The Prosecution of War Criminals since the End of the War: A Brief Survey* (New York: Institute of Jewish Affairs, 1961).

Irry, Itzhak, 'The Conspiracy of Silence Surrounding the Holocaust', *Jewish Frontier*, 43, no. 1 (1976), 12–14.

Irving, David, *Hitler's War* (New York: Viking, 1977).

Jäckel, Eberhard, *Hitler's World View: A Blueprint for Power* (Cambridge, Mass.: Harvard University Press, 1981).

—— 'On the Purpose of the Wannsee Conference', in James S. Pacy and Alan P. Wertheimer (eds.), *Perspectives on the Holocaust: Essays in Honor of Raul Hilberg* (Oxford: Westview, 1995), 39–49.

James, Robert Rhodes, *Anthony Eden* (London: Weidenfeld and Nicolson, 1986).

Janowitz, Morris, 'German Reactions to Nazi Atrocities', *American Journal of Sociology*, 52 (1946), 141–6.

Jasper, R. C. D., *George Bell—Bishop of Chichester* (London: Oxford University Press, 1967).

Jaspers, Karl, *Die Schuldfrage: Von der Politischen Haftung Deutschlands* (Munich: Piper, 1965).

Jochmann, Werner, *Gesellschaftskrise und Judenfeindschaft in Deutschland 1870–1945* (Hamburg: Hans Christians Verlag, 1988).

Joffroy, Pierre, *A Spy for God: The Ordeal of Kurt Gerstein* (London: Collins, 1971).

Johe, Werner, *Neuengamme: Zur Geschichte der Konzentrationslager in Hamburg* (Hamburg: Landeszentrale für politische Bildung, 1986).

Jones, Jill, 'Eradicating Nazism from the British Zone of Germany: Early Policy and Practice', *German History*, 8 (1990), 145–62.

Judt, Tony, 'The Past is Another Country: Myth and Memory in Postwar Europe', in Istvan Deak, Jan T. Gross and Tony Judt (eds.), *The Politics of Retribution in Europe: World War II and Its Aftermath* (Princeton, NJ: Princeton University Press, 2000), 293–323.

Kaienburg, Hermann, *'Vernichtung durch Arbeit': Der Fall Neuengamme: Die Wirtschaftsbestrebungen der SS und ihre Auswirkungen auf die Existenzbedingungen der KZ-Gefangenen* (Bonn: J. H. W. Dietz, 1990).

—— 'KZ-Haft und Wirtschaftsinteresse: Das Wirtschaftsverwaltungshauptamt der SS als Leitungszentrale der Konzentrationslager und der SS-Wirtschaft', in H. Kaienburg (ed.), *Konzentrationslager und deutsche Wirtschaft 1939–1945* (Opladen: Leske and Budrich, 1996), 29–60.

—— (ed.), *Konzentrationslager und deutsche Wirtschaft 1939–1945* (Opladen: Leske and Budrich, 1996).

—— 'Die britischen Militärgerichtsprozesse zu den Verbechen im Konzentrationslager Neuengamme', in KZ-Gedenkstätte Neuengamme (ed.), *Die frühen Nachkriegsprozesse: Beiträge zur Geschichte der nationalsozialistischen Verfolgung in Norddeutschland*, iii (Bremen: Edition Temmen, 1997), 56–64.

Karay, Felicja, *Death Comes in Yellow: Skarzysko-Kamienna Slave Labor Camp* (Amsterdam: Harwood Academic Publishers, 1996).

Kempner, Robert, 'The Nuremberg Trials as Sources of Recent German Political and Historical Materials', *American Political Science Review*, 44 (1950), 447–59.

—— 'Vingt-cinq ans après Nuremberg', *Le Monde Juif*, no. 60 (1961), 6–15.

—— *Ankläger einer Epoche: Lebenserinnerungen* (Frankfurt am Main: Fischer, 1983).

Kennan, George, *American Diplomacy, 1900–1950* (Chicago, Ill.: Chicago University Press, 1953).

Kershaw, Ian, *The Nazi Dictatorship: Problems and Perspectives of Interpretation* (London: Arnold, 1989).

—— 'Improvised Genocide? The Emergence of the Final Solution in the Warthegau', *Transactions of the Royal Historical Society*, 6, vol. 2 (1990), 51–78.

Kiersch, Gerhard, and Kleszcz-Wagner, Annette, 'Frankreichs verfehlte Vergangenheitsbewältigung', in Jürgen Weber and Peter Steinbach (eds.), *Vergangenheitsbewältigung durch Strafverfahren? NS-Prozesse in der Bundesrepublik Deutschland* (Munich: Olzog, 1984), 164–76.

Kirkpatrick, Ivone, *The Inner Circle* (London: Macmillan, 1959).

Kleefisch, T., 'Gedanken über Inhalt und Wirkung des Nürnberger Urteils', *Juristische Rundschau* (Aug. 1947), 45–9.

Klein, Peter (ed.), *Die Einsatzgruppen in der bestezten Sowjetunion 1941/42* (Berlin: Gedenk- und Bildungsstätte Haus der Wannsee-Konferenz, 1997).

Klein-Zolty, Muriel, 'Perception du génocide juif dans les "DNA" et dans Le Monde de 1944 à 1946', *Le Monde Juif*, no. 150 (1994), 109–20.

Klotz, Johannes (ed.), *Vorbild Wehrmacht: Wehrmachtsverbrechen, Rechtsextremismus und Bundeswehr* (Cologne: Papy Rossa, 1998).

Knieriem, Aug. von, *Nürnberg: Rechtliche und Menschliche Probleme* (Stuttgart: Ernst Klett, 1953).

Knilli, Friedrich, and Zielinski, Siegfried (eds.), *Betrifft 'Holocaust': Zuschauer schreiben an der WDR* (Berlin: Verlag Volker Spiess, 1983).

Kochavi, Arieh J., 'Anglo-Soviet Differences over a Policy towards War Criminals, 1942–1943', *Slavonic and Eastern European Review*, 69 (1991), 458–77.

—— 'The Moscow Declaration, the Kharkov Trial and the Question of a Policy on Major War Criminals in the Second World War', *History*, 76 (1991), 401–17.

—— 'The British Foreign Office versus the United Nations War Crimes Commission during the Second World War', *Holocaust and Genocide Studies*, 8 (1994), 28–49.

—— *Prelude to Nuremberg* (Chapel Hill, NC: University of North Carolina Press, 1998).

Koebner, Thomas (ed.), *Idole des deutschen Films* (Munich: Edition Text und Kritik, 1997).

Koessler, Maximilian, 'American War Crimes Trials in Europe', *The Georgetown Law Journal*, 39 (1950), 18–112.

Kogon, Eugen, and Dirks, Walter, 'Nürnberg und die Geschichte', *Frankfurter Hefte*, 1 (Apr., 1946), 3–5.

—— 'Ärtzte als Knechte des Todes', *Frankfurter Hefte*, 2 (Feb. 1947), 123–4.

—— 'Gericht und Gewissen', *Frankfurter Hefte*, 1 (Apr. 1946), 25–37.

—— *Der SS-Staat: Das System der Deutschen Konzentrationslager* (Frankfurt am Main: Europäische Verlagsanstalt, 1961); Verlag der Frankfurter Hefte, 1946; 3rd edn., 1948, trans. as *The Theory and Practice of Hell* (Secker and Warburg: London, 1950).

Kogon, Michael (ed.), *Eugen Kogon: Ideologie und Praxis der Unmenschlichkeit: Erfahrungen mit dem Nationalsozialismus* (Berlin: Quadriga, 1995).

Kolinsky, Martin, and Kolinsky, Eva, 'The Treatment of the Holocaust in West German Textbooks', *Yad Vashem Studies*, 10 (1974), 149–216.

Konieczny, Alfred, 'Die Zwangsarbeit der Juden in Schlesien im Rahmen der "Organisation Schmeldt"', in Götz Aly and Suzanne Heim (eds.), *Sozialpolitik und Judenvernichtung: Gibt es eine Ökonomie der Endlösung?* (Beiträge zur NS-Gesundheits- und Sozialpolitik, 5; West Berlin: Rotbuch, 1987), 91–110.

Korman, Gerd, 'The Holocaust in American Historical Writing', *Societas*, 2 (1972), 251–70.

Kosthorst, Erich, *Die Geburt der Tragödie aus dem Geist des Gehorsams: Deutschlands Generäle und Hitler—Erfahrung und Reflexionen eines Frontoffiziers* (Bonn: Bouvier Verlag, 1998).

Kosyk, Kurt, *Pressepolitik für Deutsche 1945–49. Geschichte der deutschen Presse*, pt 4 (Berlin: Colloquium, 1986).

Krakowski, Shmuel, 'Documents on the Holocaust in Archives of the Former Soviet Union', in David Cesarani (ed.), *The Final Solution: Origins and Implementation* (London: Routledge, 1994), 291–9.

Kranz, Tomasz, 'Das KL Lublin—zwischen Planung und Realisierung', in Ulrich Herbert, Karin Orth, and Christoph Dieckmann (eds.), *Die nationalsozialistischen Konzentrationslager: Entwicklung und Struktur*, 2 vols. (Göttingen: Wallstein, 1998), 363–89.

Kraus, Ota, and Kulka, Erich, *Massenmord und Profit: Die faschistische Ausrottungpolitik und ihre ökonomischen Hintergründe* (Berlin: Dietz, 1963).

—— and Wilhelm, Hans-Heinrich, *Die Truppe des Weltanschauungskrieges: Die Einsatzgruppen der Sicherheitspolizei und des SD 1938–1942* (Stuttgart: Deutsche Verlags-Anstalt, 1981).

Kushner, Tony, 'Anti-Semitism and Austerity: The August 1947 Riots in Britain', in Panikos Panayi (ed.), *Racial Violence in Britain, 1840–1950* (Leicester: Leicester University Press, 1993), 149–68.

—— *The Holocaust and the Liberal Imagination: A Social and Cultural History* (Oxford: Blackwell, 1994).

—— 'Different Worlds: British Perceptions of the Final Solution during the Second World War', in David Cesarani (ed.), *The Final Solution: Origins and Implementation* (London: Routledge, 1994), 246–67.

KZ-Gedenkstätte Neuengamme (ed.), *Die frühen Nachkriegsprozesse: Beiträge zur Geschichte der nationalsozialistischen Verfolgung in Norddeutschland*, iii (Bremen: Edition Temmen, 1997).

Landau, Ronnie, *The Nazi Holocaust* (London: Tauris, 1992).

—— *Studying the Holocaust* (London: Routledge, 1998).

Langbein, Hermann, *et al* (eds.), *Nationalsozialistischen Massentötungen durch Giftgas: Eine Dokumentation* (Frankfurt am Main: Fischer, 1983).

—— 'Arbeit in KZ-System', in *Dachauer Hefte, 2. Sklavenarbeit im KZ* (Munich: Deutscher Taschenbuch Verlag, 1986), 3–12.

Laqueur, Walter, *The Terrible Secret* (London: Weidenfeld and Nicolson, 1980).

Large, David Clay, ' "A Beacon in the German Darkness": The Anti-Nazi Resistance Legacy in West German Politics', *Journal of Modern History*, 64, suppl. (1992), 173–86.

—— *Germans to the Front: West German Rearmament in the Adenauer Era* (Chapel Hill, NC: University of North Carolina Press, 1996).

Lawrence, Lord Justice, 'The Nuremberg Trial', *International Affairs*, 23 (1947), 151–9.

Lawson, Thomas, ' "The Splendid Image of a Christian Conscience Unbowed": The Development and Implications of the Myth of Martin Niemöller', section of Ph.D. thesis in preparation (Southampton).

Le Chene, Evelyn, *Mauthausen: The History of a Death Camp* (London: Methuen, 1971).

Le Monde Juif (ed.), 'Pillages: "L'action Reinhardt" ', *Le Monde Juif*, no. 17 (1949), 17–18.

Lenz, Johann Maria, *Christus in Dachau: Ein Kirchengeschichtliches Zeugnis* (Mödling nr. Vienna: Missionsdruckerei St Gabriel [private press], 1960).

Leventhal, Harold *et al.*, 'The Nuernberg Verdict', *Harvard Law Review*, 60 (1947), 857–907.

Leverkühn, Paul, *Verteidigung Manstein* (Hamburg: Nölke, 1950).

Levin, Nora, *The Jews in the Soviet Union since 1917*, 2 vols. (London: Tauris, 1988).

Lichtenstein, Heiner, *Himmler's grüne Helfer: Die Schutz- und Ordnungspolizei im 'Dritten Reich'* (Cologne: Bund, 1990).

—— 'NS-Prozesse', in Andreas Nachama and Julius Schoeps (eds.), *Aufbau nach dem Untergang: Deutsche-Judische Geschichte nach 1945* (Berlin: Argon Verlag, 1992), 141–9.

Lippman, Mathew, 'The Other Nuremberg: American Prosecutions of Nazi War Criminals in Occupied Germany', *Indiana International and Comparative Law Review*, 3 (1992), 1–100.

London, Louise, *Whitehall and the Jews* (Cambridge: Cambridge University Press, 2000).

Longerich, Peter, *Politik der Vernichtung: Eine Gesamtdarstellung der nationalsozialistischen Judenverfolgung* (Munich: Piper, 1998).

—— *Die Wannsee-Konferenz vom 20 Januar 1942: Planung und Beginn des Genozids an den europäischen Juden* (Berlin: Gedenk- und Bildungsstätte Haus der Wannsee-Konferenz, 1998).

Lorenz, Dagmar, *Verfolgung bis zum Massenmord: Holocaust-Diskurse in deutscher Sprache aus der Sicht der Verfolgten* (Vienna: Lang, 1992).

Lottman, Herbert R., *The People's Anger: Justice and Revenge in Post-Liberation France* (London: Hutchinson, 1986).

Lozowick, Yaacov, '*Rollbahn Mord*: The Early Activities of Einsatgruppe C', *Holocaust and Genocide Studies*, 2 (1987), 221–41.

Lüdtke, Alf, ' "Coming to Terms with the Past": Illusions of Remembering, Ways of Forgetting Nazism in West Germany', *Journal of Modern History*, 65 (1993), 542–72.

Lynton, Mark, *Accidental Journey: A Cambridge Internee's Memoir of World War II* (Woodstock, NY: Overlook, 1995).

Manchester, William, *The Arms of Krupp, 1587–1968* (New York: Bantam, 1970).

Manoschek, Walter, 'Verbrecherische Befehle—Verbrecherische Taten: Sie gehörten zum Kriegsalltag der Wehrmacht', *Mittelweg*, 36 (1992), 137–44.

Manstein, Erich von, *Verlorene Siege* (Bonn: Athenäum, 1955).

Mant, A. Keith, 'The Medical Services in the Concentration Camp of Ravensbrück', *The Medico-Legal Journal*, 17 (1949), 99–118.

Marrus, Michael R., and Paxton, Robert O., *Vichy France and the Jews* (New York: Basic Books, 1981).

—— *The Holocaust in History* (London: Penguin, 1988).

—— (ed.), *The Nazi Holocaust*, 9 pts (London: Meckler, 1989).

—— 'The Holocaust at Nuremberg', *Yad Vashem Studies*, 26 (1998), 5–41.

Maser, Werner, *Nürnberg: Tribunal der Sieger* (Düsseldorf: Econ Verlag, 1977).

Matard-Bonucci, Marie-Anne, and Lynch, Edouard (eds.), *La Libération des camps et le Retour des déportés: L'histoire en souffrance* (Brussels: Éditions Complexe, 1995).

Maugham, Viscount, *U.N.O. and War Crimes Trials* (London: John Murray, 1951).

Mayring, Eva A., 'The Impact of British Occupation on Political Culture in Germany after 1945', in Alan Bance (ed.), *The Cultural Legacy of the British Occupation in Germany* (Stuttgart: Hans-Dieter Heinz Akademischer Verlag, 1997), 189–204.

Mazor, Michel, 'Le procès de Karl Wolff', *Le Monde Juif*, no. 45, (1967), 23–8.

Messerschmidt, Manfred, ' "Harte Sühne am Judentum": Befehlswege und Wissen in der deutschen Wehrmacht', in Jörg Wollenberg (ed.), *'Niemand war dabei und keiner hat's gewusst': Die deutsche Öffentlichkeit und die Judenverfolgung, 1933–1945* (Munich: Piper, 1989), 113–28.

—— 'Vorwärtsverteidigung: Die "Denkschrift der Generäle" für den Nürnberger Gerichtshof', in Hannes Heer and Klaus Naumann (eds.), *Vernichtungskrieg: Verbrechen der Wehrmacht 1941 bis 1944* (Hamburg: HIS, 1995), 531–50.

Milfull, John (ed.), *Why Germany? National Socialist Anti-Semitism and the European Context* (Providence: Berg, 1993).

Mitcham, Samuel Jun., 'Kleist', in Correlli Barnett (ed.), *Hitler's Generals* (New York: Quill and Morrow), 249–63.

Mitchell, Maria, 'Materialism and Secularism: CDU Politicans and National Socialism, 1945–1949', *Journal of Modern History*, 67 (1995), 278–308.

Mitscherlich, Alexander, and Mielke, Fred, *Medizin ohne Menschlichkeit: Dokumente des Nürnberger Ärzteprozesse* (Frankfurt am Main: Fischer, 1960).

—— and Mitscherlich, Margarete, *Die Unfähigkeit zu trauern: Grundlagen kollektiven Verhaltens* (Munich: Piper, 1967).

Moeller, Robert, 'War Stories: The Search for a Usable Past in the Federal Republic of Germany', *American Historical Review*, 101 (1996), 1008–48.

—— 'Writing the History of West Germany', in Robert Moeller (ed.), *West Germany under Construction* (Ann Arbor, Mich.: University of Michigan Press, 1997), 1–30.

Mommsen, Hans, 'The Realization of the Unthinkable: The "Final Solution of the Jewish Question" in the Third Reich', in Gerhard Hirschfeld (ed.), *The Policies of Genocide* (London: German Historical Institute, 1986), 97–144.

Montgomery of Alamein, *Memoirs* (London: Collins), 1958.

Morgan, J. H., *The Great Assize* (London: John Murray, 1948).

Morgan, Robert, *The United States and West Germany, 1945–73: A Study in Alliance Politics* (London: Oxford University Press, 1974).

Morse, Arthur, *While Six Million Died* (New York: Random House, 1968).

Mosse, George, *Fallen Soldiers: Reshaping the Memory of the World Wars* (New York: Oxford University Press, 1990).

Musial, Bogdan, 'Bilder einer Ausstellung: Kritische Anmerkungen zur Wanderausstellung "Vernichtungskrieg: Verbrechen der Wehrmacht 1941 bis 1944"', *Vierteljahreshefte für Zeitgeschichte*, 47 (1999), 563–91.

Nachama, Andreas, and Schoeps, Julius (eds.), *Aufbau nach dem Untergang: Deutsche-Jüdische Geschichte nach 1945* (Berlin: Argon Verlag, 1992).

Naumann, Klaus, 'Wehrmacht und NS-Verbrechen: Wirklichkeiten und Wirkungen einer kollektiven Gewalterfahrung', *Mittelweg*, 36 (1992), 130–6.

Neave, Airey, *Nuremberg: A Personal Record of the Trial of the Major War Criminals* (London: Hodder and Stoughton, 1978).

Nelte, Otto, *Die Generale: Das Nürnberger Urteil und die Schuld der Generale* (Hanover: Verlag des anderen Deutschlands, 1947).

Neufeldt, Hans-Joachim *et al.*, *Zur Geschichte der Ordnungspolizei 1936–1945* (Koblenz: Bundesarchiv, 1957).

Niedhart, Gottfried, and Riesenburger, Dieter (eds.), *Lernen aus den Krieg? Deutsche Nachkriegszeiten 1918 und 1945* (Munich: C. H. Beck, 1992).

Niethammer, Lutz, *Entnazifizierung in Bayern: Säuberung und Rehabilitierung unter amerikanische Besatzung* (Frankfurt am Main: Fischer, 1972).

Nolte, Ernst, *Der europäische Bürgerkrieg: Nationalsozialismus und Bolschewismus* (Frankfurt am Main: Propyläen, 1987).

Novick, Peter, *The Holocaust in American Life* (New York: Houghton Mifflin, 1999).

Obenaus, Herbert, ' "Man spielt so gern mit dem Begriff Opfer": Wiedergutmachung und Annahme der NS-Vergangenheit in Niedersachsen bis zum Anfang der fünfziger Jahre', in Bernd Weisbrod (ed.), *Rechtradikalismus in der politischen Kultur der Nachkriegszeit: Die verzögerte Normalisierung in Niedersachsen* (Hanover: Hahnsche Buchhandlung, 1995), 33–64.

—— 'Die Aussenkommandos des Konzentrationslagers Neuengamme in Hannover', in Hermann Kaienburg (ed.), *Konzentrationslager und deutsche Wirtschaft 1939–1945* (Opladen: Leske and Budrich, 1996), 211–26.

Osiel, Mark, *Mass Atrocity, Collective Memory and the Law* (New Brunswick, NJ: Transaction, 1997).

Otto, Reinhard, *Wehrmacht, Gestapo und sowjetische Kriegsgefangene im deutschen Reichsgebiet 1941/42* (Munich: Oldenbourg, 1998).

Overesch, Manfred, *Deutschland 1945–1949: Vorgeschichte und Gründung der Bundesrepublik* (Düsseldorf: Athenäum and Droste, 1979).

—— *Buchenwald und die DDR; oder, Die Suche nach Selbstlegitimation* (Göttingen: Vandenhoeck and Ruprecht, 1995).

Pacy, James S., and Wertheimer, Alan (eds.), *Perspectives on the Holocaust: Essays in Honor of Raul Hilberg* (Oxford: Westview, 1995).

Paget, Reginald T., *Manstein: His Campaigns and His Trial* (London: William Collins, 1951).

Pankowicz, Andrzej, 'Das KL Auschwitz in den Nürnberger Prozessen', *Hefte von Auschwitz*, 18 (1990), 247–367.

Peitsch, Helmut, '*Deutsche Gedächtnis an seine dunkelste Zeit*': *Zur Funktion der Auto-biographik in den Westzonen Deutschlands und den Westsektoren von Berlin 1945 bis 1949* (Berlin: Sigma, 1990).

Pendaries, Yveline, *Les procès de Rastatt (1946–1954): Le jugement des crimes de guerre en zone française d'occupation en Allemagne* (Berne: Lang, 1995).

Perels, Joachim, 'Verpasste Chancen: Zur Bedeutung der Nürnberger Nachfolge-prozesse vor dem Hintergrund der ungenügenden Strafverfolgung von NS-Tätern in der BRD', in KZ-Gedenkstätte Neuengamme (ed.), *Die frühen Nachkriegsprozesse: Beiträge zur Geschichte der nationalsozialistischen Verfolgung in Norddeutschland*, iii, (Bremen: Edition Temmen, 1997), 30–7.

Perkins, Dexter, *America's Quest for Peace* (Bloomington, Indianapolis: University of Indiana Press, 1962).

Perz, Bertrand, and Sandkühler, Thomas, 'Auschwitz und die "Aktion Reinhard" 1942–45. Judenmord und Raubpraxis in neuer Sicht', *Zeitgeschichte*, 26 (1999), 283–316.

Peterson, Edward N., *The American Occupation of Germany* (Detroit: Wayne State University Press, 1977).

Pingel, Falk, *Häftlinge unter SS-Herrschaft: Widerstand, Selbstbehauptung und Vernich-tung in Konzentrationslager* (Hamburg: Hoffmann and Campe, 1978).

—— 'Nationalsozialismus und Holocaust in westdeutschen Schülbuchern', in Rolf Steininger (ed.), *Der Umgang mit dem Holocaust: Europa—USA—Israel* (Cologne: Böhlan Verlag, 1994), 221–32.

Pinter, Istvan, and Szabo, Laszlo (eds.), *Criminals at Large* (Budapest: Pannonia, 1961).

Piper, Franciszek, *Die Zahl der Opfer von Auschwitz* (Auschwitz: Verlag Staatlichen Museums, 1993).

—— *Arbeitseinsatz der Häftlinge aus dem KL Auschwitz* (Auschwitz: Auschwitz State Museum, 1995).

Pohl, Dieter, *Von der 'Judenpolitik' zum Judenmord: Der Distrikt Lublin des Generalgou-vernements 1939–1944* (Frankfurt am Main: Lang, 1993).

—— *Nationalsozialistische Judenverfolgung in Ostgalizien 1941–1944: Organisation und Durchführung eines staatlichen Massenverbrechens* (Munich: Oldenbourg, 1996).

—— 'Die Einsatzgruppe C', in Peter Klein (ed.), *Die Einsatzgruppen in der besetzten Sowjetunion 1941/2* (Berlin: Gedenk- und Bildungsstätte Hans der Wannsee Kon-ferenz, 1997), 71–87.

—— 'Die Ermordung der Juden im Generalgouvernement', in Ulrich Herbert (ed.), *Nationalsozialistische Vernichtungspolitik: Neue Forschungen und Kontroversen* (Frank-furt am Main: Fischer, 1997), 98–121.

—— 'Die grossen Zwangsarbeitslager der SS- und Polizeiführer für Juden im General-gouvernement 1942–1945', in Ulrich Herbert, Karin Orth, and Christoph Dieck-mann (eds.), *Die nationalsozialistischen Konzentrationslager: Entwicklung und Struktur*, 2 vols. (Göttingen: Wallstein, 1998), 415–38.

Pohl, Karl Heinrich, ' "Vernichtungskrieg. Verbrechen der Wehrmacht 1941–1944." Ueberlegungen zu einer Ausstellung aus didaktischer Perspektive', in K. H. Pohl (ed.), *Wehrmacht und Vernichtungspolitik: Militär in nationalsozialistischen System* (Göttingen: Vandenhoeck and Ruprecht, 1999), 141–63.

—— (ed.), *Wehrmacht und Vernichtungspolitik: Militär in nationalsozialistischen System* (Göttingen: Vandenhoeck and Ruprecht, 1999).

Polevoi, Boris *The Final Reckoning: Nuremberg Diaries* (Moscow: Progress Publishers, 1978).

Poliakov, Leon, *Harvest of Hate* (London: Elek, 1956).

—— 'Le Dossier Kurt Gerstein', *Le Monde Juif*, no. 36 (1964), 4–20.

—— 'Nouveaux documents sur Kurt Gerstein', *Le Monde Juif*, no 37 (1964), 4–16.

Polonsky, Antony (ed.), *My Brother's Keeper? Recent Polish Debates on the Holocaust* (London: Routledge, 1990).

Pronay, Nicholas, and Wilson, Keith (eds.), *The Political Re-Education of Germany and Her Allies after World War II* (London: Croom Helm, 1985).

Prümm, Karl, *Walter Dirks und Eugen Kogon als Katholische Publizisten der Weimarer Republik* (Heidelberg: Karl Winter, 1984).

Racja, C., and Wisniewska, A., *Majdanek: Nazilager in Lublin* (Lublin: State Museum, 1986).

Raim, Edith, *Die Dachauer KZ-Aussenkommandos Kaufering und Mühldorf: Rüstungs-bauten und Zwangsarbeit im letzten Kriegsjahr 1944/5* (Landsberg am Lech: Landsberger Verlagsanstalt Martin Neumeyer, 1992).

Reichel, Peter, *Politik mit der Erinnerung: Gedächtnisorte im Streit um die national-sozialistische Vergangenheit* (Munich: Hanser, 1995).

Reid, J. H., *Heinrich Böll: A German for His Time* (New York: Berg, 1988).

Reilly, Joanne, *Belsen: The Liberation of a Concentration Camp* (London: Routledge, 1998).

Reitlinger, Gerald, *The Final Solution* (London: Vallentine, Mitchell and Co., 1953).

—— *The SS: Alibi of a Nation* (London: Arms and Armour, 1981).

Rengstorf, K. H., 'Crime and Atonement', *Wiener Library Bulletin*, 3 (May–July 1949), 20.

Richman, Frank N., 'Highlights of the Nuernberg Trials', *Federal Rules Decisions*, 7 (1948), 581–4.

Robinson, Jacob, 'The International Military Tribunal and the Holocaust: Some Legal Reflections', in Michael R. Marrus (ed.), *The Nazi Holocaust*, 9 pts (London: Meckler, 1989), pt 9, 608–20.

—— and Sachs, Henry (eds.), *The Holocaust: The Nuremburg Evidence, pt 1: Documents, Digest, Index and Chronological Tables* (Jerusalem: Yad Vashem, 1976).

Rollyson, Carl, *Rebecca West: A Saga of the Century* (London: Hodder and Stoughton, 1995).

Rosenberg, Tina, 'From Nuremberg to Bosnia', *The Nation* (15 May 1995), 688–92.

Rossino, Alexander, 'Destructive Impulses: German Soldiers and the Conquest of Pol-and', *Holocaust and Genocide Studies*, 11 (1997), 351–65.

Rotberg, Robert I., and Thompson, Dennis (eds.), *Truth v. Justice: The Morality of Truth Commissions* (Princeton, NJ: Princeton University Press, 2000).

Rothfels, Hans, and Eschenburg, Theodor (eds.), 'Augenzeugenbericht zu den Massen-vergasung', *Vierteljahreshefte für Zeitgeschichte*, 1 (1953), 177–94.

Rousso, Henry, *The Vichy Syndrome: History and Memory in France since 1944* (Cambridge, Mass.: Harvard University Press, 1991).

Rozanski, Zenon, *Mützen ab . . . Eine Reportage aus der Strafkompanie des KZ Auschwitz* (Hanover: Verlag des anderen Deutschland, 1948).

Rückerl, Adalbert (ed.), *NS-Vernichtungslager im Spiegel deutscher Strafprozesse: Belzec, Sobibor, Treblinka, Chelmno* (Munich: Deutscher Taschenbuch Verlag, 1977).

Rückerl, Adalbert (ed.), *NS-Verbrechen vor Gericht: Versuch einer Vergangenheitsbewälti-gung* (Heidelberg: C. F. Müller, 1982).

Russell, Bertrand, and Sartre, Jean-Paul (eds.), *Das Vietnam Tribunal; oder, Amerika vor Gericht* (Hamburg: Rowohlt, 1970).

Russell of Liverpool, Lord, *The Scourge of the Swastika* (London: Cassell, 1954).

Ryan, Allan, *Quiet Neighbors: Prosecuting Nazi War Criminals in America* (New York: Harcourt Brace Jovanovich, 1984).

Sagalowitz, B., 'Les Waffen-SS et la Nouvelle Armée Allemande', *Le Monde Juif*, nos. 75–6, (1956–7), 54–7.

Sander, Helke, and Johr, Barbara (eds.), *Befreier und Befreite: Krieg, Vergewaltigungen, Kinder* (Munich: Verlag Antje Kunstmann, 1992).

Sandkühler, Thomas, *'Endlösung' in Galizien: Der Judenmord in Ostpolen und die Ret-tungsinitiativen von Berthold Beitz 1941–1944* (Bonn: J. H. W. Dietz, 1996).

—— 'Zwangsarbeit und Judenmord im Distrikt Galizien des Generalgouvernements', in Hermann Kaienburg (ed.), *Konzentrationslager und deutsche Wirtschaft 1939–1945* (Opladen: Leske and Budrich, 1996), 239–62.

—— 'Das Zwangsarbeitslager Lemberg-Janowska 1941–1944', in Ulrich Herbert, Karin Orth, and Christoph Dieckmann (eds.), *Die nationalsozialistischen Kon-zentrationslager: Entwicklung und Struktur*, 2 vols. (Göttingen: Wallstein, 1998), 606–35.

—— 'Die Täter des Holocaust: Neuere Überlegungen und Kontroversen', in Karl Heinrich Pohl (ed.), *Wehrmacht und Vernichtungspolitik: Militär in nationalsozialist-ischen system* (Göttingen: Vandenhoeck and Ruprecht, 1999), 39–66.

Schachter, Hans, *The Holocaust: A Brief Survey* (Jerusalem: World Zionist Organisation Information Division, 1975).

Schäffer, Rudolf, 'Soldaten und Militaristen', *Frankfurter Hefte*, 1 (Sept. 1946), 8–9.

—— 'Die Polizei', *Frankfurter Hefte*, 1 (Oct. 1946), 590–2.

Schaller, Michael, *The American Occupation of Japan: The Origins of the Cold War in Asia* (Oxford: Oxford University Press, 1985).

Scheffler, Wolfgang, 'Die Einsatzgruppe A', in Peter Klein (ed.), *Die Einsatzgruppen in der besetzten Sowjetunion 1941/42* (Berlin: Gedenk- und Bildungsstätte Haus der Wannsee-Konferenz, 1997), 29–51.

Schildt, Axel, 'Solidarisch mit der Schuld des Volkes: Die öffentliche Schulddebatte und das Integrationsgebot der Kirchen in Niedersachsen nach dem Zweiten Weltkrieg', in Bernd Weisbrod (ed.), *Rechtsradikalismus in der politischen Kultur der Nachkriegszeit: Die verzögerte Normalisierung in Niedersachen* (Hanover: Hahnsche Buchhandlung, 1995), 269–95.

Schmitt, Hans (ed.), *US Occupation in Europe after World War II* (Kansas: Kansas University Press, 1978).

Schneider, Christian, 'Denkmal Manstein: Psychogramm eines Befehlshabers', in Hannes Heer and Klaus Naumann (eds.), *Vernichtungskrieg: Verbrechen der Wehrmacht 1941 bis 1944* (Hamburg: HIS, 1995), 402–17.

Schneider, Christof, *Nationalsozialismus als Thema im Programm des Nordwestdeutshen Rundfunks (1945–1958)* (Potsdam: Verlag für Berlin-Brandenburg, 1999).

Scholz, Heinrich, 'Zur deutschen Kollektiv-Verantwortlichkeit', *Frankfurter Hefte*, 2 (Apr. 1947), 357–73.

Schulte, Jan Erik, 'Rüstungsunternehmen oder Handwerksbetrieb? Das KZ-Häftlinge ausbeutende SS-Unternehmunen "Deutsche Ausrüstungswerke GmbH" ', in Ulrich Herbert, Karin Orth, and Christoph Dieckmann (eds.), *Die nationalsozialistischen Konzentrationslager: Entwicklung und Struktur*, 2 vols. (Göttingen: Wallstein, 1998), 558–83.

Schulze, Rainer, 'A Difficult Interlude: Relations between British Military Government and the German Population and Their Effects for the Constitution of a Democratic Society', in Alan Bance (ed.), *The Cultural Legacy of the British Occupation in Germany* (Stuttgart: Hans-Dieter Heinz Akademischer Verlag, 1997), 67–109.

Schwartz, Thomas Alan, 'Die Begnadigung deutscher Kriegsverbrecher: John J. McCloy und die Häftlinge von Landsberg', *Vierteljahreshefte für Zeitgeschichte*, 38 (1990), 375–414.

—— *America's Germany: John J. McCloy and the Federal Republic of Germany* (Cambridge, Mass.: Harvard University Press, 1991).

Schwarz, Gudrun, *Die nationalsozialistischen Lager* (Frankfurt am Main: Campus, 1990).

Seckendorf, Martin, 'Ein williges und fügsames Instrument: Die Wehrmacht in Italien—1943 bis 1945', in Johannes Klotz (ed.), *Vorbild Wehrmacht: Wehrmachtsverbrechen, Rechtsextremismus und Bundeswehr* (Cologne: Papy Rossa, 1998), 66–95.

Segev, Tom, *The Seventh Million: The Israelis and the Holocaust* (New York: Hill and Wang, 1993).

Seidl, Claudius, *Der deutsche Film der fünfziger Jahre* (Munich: Wilhelm Heyne, 1987).

Seltzer, William, 'Population Statistics, the Holocaust, and the Nuremberg Trials', *Population and Development Review*, 24 (1998), 511–52.

Shawcross, Hartley, *Life Sentence: The Memoirs of Lord Shawcross* (London: Constable, 1995).

Sigel, Robert, *Im Interesse der Gerechtigkeit: Die Dachauer Kriegsverbrecherprozesse 1945–48* (Frankfurt am Main: Campus Verlag, 1992).

Simpson, Christopher, *Blowback: The First Full Account of America's Recruitment of Nazis, and Its Disastrous Effect on Our Domestic and Foreign Policy* (New York: Collier Books, 1989).

—— *The Splendid Blond Beast: Money, Law and Genocide in the Twentieth Century* (Monroe, ME: Common Courage Press, 1995).

Sington, Derek, *Belsen Uncovered* (London: Duckworth, 1946).

Smith, Bradley F., *Reaching Judgment at Nuremberg* (New York: Basic Books 1977).

—— and Agarossi, Elena, *Operation Sunrise: The Secret Surrender* (London: André Deutsch, 1979).

—— *The Road to Nuremberg* (London: André Deutsch, 1982).

—— 'Die Überlieferung der Hossbach-Niederschrift im Lichte neuer Quellen', *Vierteljahreshefte für Zeitgeschichte*, 38 (1990), 329–36.

Smith, H. A., *The Crisis in the Law of Nations* (London: Stevens and Sons Ltd., 1947).

Smolen, Kazimierz, *Auschwitz 1940–1945* (Auschwitz: Auschwitz State Museum, 1961).

Sofsky, Wolfgang, *Die Ordnung des Terrors: Das Konzentrationslager* (Frankfurt am Main: Fischer, 1993).

Speier, Hans, *From the Ashes of Disgrace: A Journal from Germany, 1945–1955* (Amherst, Mass.: University of Massachusetts Press, 1981).

Spender, Stephen, *European Witness* (London: Hamish Hamilton, 1946).

Spoerer, Mark, 'Profierten Unternehmen von KZ-Arbeit?', *Historische Zeitschrift*, 268 (1999), 61–95.

Stallbaumer, L.M., 'Big Business and the Persecution of the Jews: The Flick Concern and the "Aryanization" of Jewish Property before the War', *Holocaust and Genocide Studies*, 13 (1999), 1–27.

Steinbach, Peter, 'Nationalsozialistische Gewaltverbrechen in der deutschen Öffentlichkeit nach 1945', in Jürgen Weber and Peter Steinbach (eds.), *Vergangenheitsbewältigung durch Strafverfahren? NS-Prozesse in der Bundesrepublik Deutschland* (Munich: Olzog, 1984), 13–39.

—— 'Krieg, Verbrechen, Widerstand: Die deutsche Wehrmacht im NS-Staat zwischen Kooperation und Konfrontation', in Karl Heinrich Pohl (ed.), *Wehrmacht und Vernichtungspolitik: Militär in nationalsozialistischen System* (Göttingen: Vandenhoeck and Ruprecht, 1999), 11–38.

Steininger, Rolf (ed.), *Der Umgang mit dem Holocaust: Europa—USA—Israel* (Cologne: Böhlau Verlag, 1994).

—— *Deutsche Geschichte seit 1945: Darstellung und Dokumente in vier Bänden*, i. *1945–1947* (Frankfurt am Main: Fischer, 1996).

Stern, Frank, *The Whitewashing of the Yellow Badge: Antisemitism and Philosemitism in Postwar Germany* (Oxford: Pergamon Press, 1992).

—— 'The Historic Triangle', in Robert Moeller (ed.), *West Germany under Construction* (Ann Arbor, Mich.: University of Michigan Press, 1997), 199–230.

Sternberger, Dolf, and Rengstorf, K. H., 'Crime and Atonement', *Wiener Library Bulletin*, 3 (May–July 1949), 20.

Streim, Alfred, 'The Tasks of the SS Einsatzgruppen', *Simon Wiesenthal Center Annual*, 4 (1987), 309–28.

—— 'Saubere Wehrmacht?', in Hannes Heer and Klaus Naumann (eds.), *Vernichtungskrieg: Verbrechen der Wehrmacht 1941 bis 1944* (Hamburg: HIS, 1995), 569–97.

Streit, Christian, *Keine Kameraden: Die Wehrmacht und die sowjetischen Kriegsgefangenen 1941–1945* (Stuttgart: Deutsche Verlags-Anstalt, 1981).

Sydnor, Charles W., 'The History of the SS Totenkopfdivision and the Postwar Mythology of the Waffen SS', *Central European History*, 6 (1973), 339–62.

—— *Soldiers of Destruction: The SS Death's Head Division, 1933–1945* (London: Guild Publishing, 1989).

Tartu University (ed.), *Tartu University History Museum Annual Report, 1998* (Tartu: Tartu University Press, 1999).

Taylor, Telford, *Nuremberg and Vietnam: An American Tragedy* (New York: Bantam, 1971).

—— *The Anatomy of the Nuremburg Trials: A Personal Memoir* (London: Bloomsbury, 1993).

Tenenbaum, Joseph, *Race and Reich: The Story of an Epoch* (Westport, Conn.: Greenwood Press, 1956).

Tent, James F., *Mission on the Rhine: Reeducation and Denazification in American-Occupied Germany* (Chicago, Ill.: University of Chicago Press, 1982).

Thomas, Michael, *Deutschland, England über alles: Rückkehr als Besatzungsoffizier* (Berlin: Siedler Verlag, 1984).

Trevor-Roper, H. R., *The Last Days of Hitler* (London: Macmillan, 1947).

Trunk, Isaiah, *Judenrat: The Jewish Councils in Eastern Europe under Nazi Occupation* (New York: Macmillan, 1972).

Tusa, Ann, and Tusa, John, *The Nuremburg Trial* (London: Atheneum, 1983).

United Nations War Crimes Commission, *History of the United Nations War Crimes Commission and the Development of the Laws of War* (London: HMSO, 1948).

Veale, F. J. P., *Advance to Barbarism: How the Reversion to Barbarism in Warfare and War Crimes Trials Threatens our Future* (Appleton, Wis.: Nelson, 1953).

Vestermanis, Margers, 'Der "Holocaust" in Lettland: Zur "postkommunistischen" Aufarbeitung des Themas in Osteuropa', in Arno Herzig and Ina Lorenz (eds.), *Verdrängung und Vernichtung der Juden unter dem Nationalsozialismus* (Hamburg: Hans Christians Verlag, 1992), 101–30.

Vidal-Naquet, Pierre, *Assassins of Memory* (New York: Columbia University Press, 1992).

Wachsmann, Nikolaus, ' "Annihilation through Labour": The Killing of State Prisoners in the Third Reich', *Journal of Modern History*, 71 (1999), 624–59.

Wasserstein, Bernard, *Britain and the Jews of Europe, 1939–1945* (Oxford: Clarendon Press, 1979).

Walsh, Edmund A., *Total Power: A Footnote to History* (New York: Doubleday, 1948).

Weber, Jürgen, and Steinbach, Peter (eds.), *Vergangenheitsbewältigung durch Strafverfahren? NS-Prozesse in der Bundesrepublik Deutschland* (Munich: Olzog, 1984).

Wechsler, Herbert, 'The Issues of the Nuremberg Trial', *Political Science Quarterly*, 52 (1947), 11–26.

Weindling, Paul, 'Ärzte als Richter', in C. Wieseman and A. Frewer (eds.), *Medizin und Ethik im Zeichen von Auschwitz* (Erlangen: Palm and Enke, 1996), 31–44.

—— 'The Anatomy of the Nuremberg Medical Trial', presented at the 'Nuremberg Medical Trial Symposium', Linacre College, Oxford, 14 Mar. 1997 (unpublished).

—— 'Eugenics and Medical War Crimes after 1945', *Tartu University History Museum Annual Report*, 1998, 86–99.

—— 'From International to Zonal Trials: The Origins of the Nuremberg Medical Trial', *Holocaust and Genocide Studies*, 14 (forthcoming).

Weingartner, James, *Crossroads of Death: The Story of the Malmédy Massacre and Trial* (Berkeley, Calif.: University of California Press, 1979).

Weinstock, Rudolf, *Das Wahre Gesicht Hitler-Deutschlands': Häftling Nr. 59000 erzählt von dem Schicksal der 10000 Juden aus Baden, aus der Pfalz und aus dem Saargebiet in den Höllen von Dachau, Gurs-Drancy, Auschwitz, Jawischowitz, Buchenwald* (Singen: Volksverlag, 1948).

Weisbrod, Bernd (ed.), *Rechtradikalismus in der politischen Kultur der Nachkriegszeit: Die verzögerte Normalisierung in Niedersachsen* (Hanover: Hahnsche Buchhandlung, 1995).

Weiss, Hermann, 'Dachau und die internationale Öffentlichkeit', *Dachauer Hefte, 1. Die Befreiung* (Munich: Deutscher Taschenbuch Verlag, 1993), 12–38.

Weitz, Birgit, 'Der Einsatz von KZ-Häftlingen und jüdischen Zwangsarbeitern bei der Daimler-Benz AG (1941–1945)', in Hermann Kaienburg (ed.), *Konzentrationslager und deutsche Wirtschaft 1939–1945* (Opladen: Leske and Budrich, 1996), 169–95.

Wellers, Georges, 'Les chambres à gaz et le témoignage Gerstein', *Le Monde Juif*, no. 86 (1976–7), 46–62.

—— 'Encore sur le "Témoignage Gerstein" ', *Le Monde Juif*, no. 97 (1980–1), 23–34.

—— 'A propos d'une thèse de doctorat "explosive" sur le "Rapport Gerstein" ', *Le Monde Juif*, no. 121 (1986), 1–17.

Wendehorst, Stephan, 'British Jewry, Zionism and the Jewish State, 1936–1956', D.Phil. thesis (Oxford, 1997).

West, Rebecca, *A Train of Powder* (New York: Viking, 1953).

Westermann, Bärbel, *Nationale Identität im Spielfilm der fünfziger Jahre* (Frankfurt am Main: Lang, 1990).

Wette, Wolfram, 'Wehrmachtstraditionen und Bundeswehr', in Johannes Klotz (ed.) *Vorbild Wehrmacht: Wehrmachtsverbrechen, Rechtsextremismus und Bundeswehr* (Cologne: Papy Rossa, 1998), 126–54.

Wheeler, George S., *Die amerikanische Politik in Deutschland* (Berlin: Kongress, 1958).

Wieseman, C., and A. Frewer (eds.), *Medizin und Ethik im Zeichen von Auschwitz* (Erlangen: Palm and Enke, 1996).

Wiesenthal, Simon, *Justice Not Vengeance* (London: Mandarin, 1990).

Wieviorka, Annette, 'La construction de la mémoire du génocide en France', *Le Monde Juif*, no. 149 (1993), 23–37.

—— 'Jewish Identity in the First Accounts by Extermination Camp Survivors from France', *Yale French Studies*, no. 85 (1994), 135–51.

Wilke, Jürgen, 'Ein früher Beginn der "Vergangenheitsbewältigung": Der Nürnberger Prozess und wie darüber berichtet wurde', *Frankfurter Allgemeine Zeitung* (15 Nov. 1995).

—— *et al.*, *Holocaust und NS-Prozesse* (Cologne: Böhlau, 1995).

Williams, Rhys, ' "The Selections of the Committee Are not in Accord with the Requirements of Germany": Contemporary English Literature and the Selected Book Scheme in the British Zone of Germany (1945–1950)', in Alan Bance (ed.), *The Cultural Legacy of the British Occupation in Germany* (Stuttgart: Hans-Dieter Heinz Akademischer Verlag, 1997), 110–38.

Williamson, Philip, 'Christian Conservatives and the Totalitarian Challenge, 1933–40', *English Historical Review*, 115 (2000), 607–42.

Wilmovsky, Tilo von, *Warum wurde Krupp verurteilt? Legende und Justizirrtum* (Stuttgart: Friedrich Vorwerk, 1950).

Woetzel, Robert K., *The Nuremberg Trials in International Law* (London: Stevens, 1960).

Wolfe, Robert (ed.), *Americans as Proconsuls: United States Military Government in Germany and Japan, 1944–1952* (Carbondale, Ill.: Southern Illinois University Press, 1984).

Wollaston, Isabel, 'Auschwitz and the Politics of Commemoration: The Christianisation of the Holocaust', *Holocaust Educational Trust Research Papers*, 1, no. 5 (1999–2000).

Wollenberg, Jörg (ed.), *'Niemand war dabei und keiner hat's gewusst': Die deutsche Öffentlichkeit und die Judenverfolgung 1933–1945* (Munich: Piper, 1989).

Wrocklage, Ute, 'Majdanek und Auschwitz in der internationalen Bildpresse 1945', in Yasmin Doosry (ed.), *Representations of Auschwitz* (Auschwitz: Auschwitz State Museum, 1995), 35–44.

Wyman, David S., *The Abandonment of the Jews* (New York: Pantheon, 1984).

Wysocki, Gerd, 'Häftlingsarbeit in der Rüstungsproduktion: Das Konzentrationslager Drütte bei den Hermann-Göring-Werken in Watenstedt-Salzgitter', in *Dachauer Hefte, 2: Sklavenarbeit im KZ* (Munich: Deutscher Taschenbuch Verlag, 1986), 35–67.

Zeck, William Allen, 'Nuremberg: Proceedings Subsequent to Goering et al.', *North Carolina Law Review*, 26 (1948), 350–89.

Ziemke, Earl F., 'Rundstedt', in Correlli Barnett (ed.), *Hitler's Generals* (New York: Quill and Morrow, 1989), 175–208.

Zimmermann, Michael, 'Arbeit in den Konzentrationslagern: Kommentierende Bemerkungen', in Ulrich Herbert, Karin Orth, and Christoph Dieckmann (eds.), *Die nationalsozialistischen Konzentrationslager: Entwicklung und Struktur*, 2 vols. (Göttingen: Wallstein, 1998), 730–51.

Index

Printed in the United States
101736LV00001B/122/A